RUSSIA

NEW NATIONS RISING

The Fall of the Soviets
and the Challenge
of Independence

**NADIA DIUK &
ADRIAN KARATNYCKY**

JOHN WILEY & SONS, INC.
New York · Chichester · Brisbane · Toronto · Singapore

Copyright © 1993 by Nadia Diuk and Adrian Karatnycky
Published by John Wiley & Sons, Inc.

Library of Congress Cataloging-in-Publication Data:

Diuk, Nadia.
New nations rising : the fall of the Soviets
and the challenge of independence
/ Nadia Diuk and Adrian Karatnycky.
p. cm.   Includes bibliographical references and index.
ISBN 0-471-58263-8 (pbk.)
1. Former Soviet republics—Politics and government.
2. Nationalism—Former Soviet republics.
I. Karatnycky, Adrian. II. Title.
DK293.D58   1993 ГЧР
323.1'47—dc20   92-40195

Printed in the United States of America

10 9 8 7 6 5 4 3 2 1

CONTENTS

PREFACE

This book was to have been an updated paperback edition of our study of the rise of national movements in the USSR, *The Hidden Nations*, published by William Morrow. In that book, we outlined the ethnic and national sources of the USSR's instability that foreshadowed the collapse of the Soviet state. Yet when we came to the task of updating the text, we realized that although we had pointed to the explosive force of rising nationalism in the USSR, the events that led to the fall of the Soviet empire required of us a fundamentally new book.

The result, *New Nations Rising*, is something of a hybrid. The structure of the book derives much from *The Hidden Nations*. Indeed, readers of *The Hidden Nations* will find that we lightly revised those sections that dealt with issues of history, culture, economics, and demographics. Nevertheless, the body of this book, well over two-thirds of its content, consists of entirely new material. *New Nations Rising* takes the story of the unraveling of the USSR and the rise of separatist movements through to the collapse of the USSR and on to the emergence of fifteen new states in Eastern Europe and Central Asia. It seeks to place the processes that led to the fall of the Soviets in historical context, describes the complex and divergent process of nation-building and nascent statehood in the newly independent states, offers an assessment of the changed geopolitical context that has emerged as a result of the unraveling of the USSR, and attempts to project trends in interstate relations among these new players on the European, Asian, and world scene.

This book, we believe, is the first book on the Soviet collapse, the emergence and almost simultaneous unraveling of the Commonwealth of Independent States, and the process of nation- and state-building that commenced after the failed coup of August 1991.

New Nations Rising benefited from the suggestions, encouragement, and attention of our editors at John Wiley & Sons. We would like to thank Roger Scholl, then of Wiley, and now of Doubleday, who worked with us on this book in its early stages and helped us develop the structure. We are grateful as well to Emily Loose, our editor at Wiley, who made helpful suggestions and who skillfully picked up where Roger Scholl left off. We are also grateful to Jude Patterson, a diligent and careful copyeditor, who faced the daunting task of finding the new standard spellings for place names as each newly independent state emerged and changed the names of its streets and towns.

In gathering material for this book, the authors benefited from visits to Estonia, Latvia, Lithuania, Armenia, Georgia, Azerbaijan, Ukraine, Belarus, Russia, Uzbekistan, and Kazakhstan.

We would like to acknowledge the many people who have contributed to the work by discussing their ideas, providing information, and by encouraging our endeavor.

We would like to thank Lane Kirkland, President of the AFL-CIO, who has been a steady source of encouragement to both authors, one of whom is in his employ. His committment and understanding of the democratic struggle in Eastern Europe, has enabled the authors to glean many insights about social processes and politics in the region.

We would also like to thank Carl Gershman, President of the National Endowment for Democracy, who has been no less a tireless tribune for the voices of democracy. He understood sooner than most, the contradictions and tensions within the Soviet Union and the implications for democracy. His kind support and personal interest in this project has been much appreciated by the authors.

We are grateful as well to many friends, colleagues, and acquantances who assisted us in bringing this project to fruition. We would like to thank Ludmilla Alexeyeva, Bill Bodie, Patricia Carley, Devon Gaffney Cross, Paul Goble, Barbara Haig, Mykola Haliw, Paul Henze, Ojars Kalnins, Marta Kolomayets, Nadia and Robert McConnell, Rick Messick, Viktor Nakas, Martha Brill Olcott, Vyacheslav Pikhovsek, Arch Puddington, Mari-Ann Rikken, Ivan Sierant, Sonya Sluzar, Jan Strucker, S. Enders Wimbush, and George Zarycky.

We also benefited from the ideas of a number of democratic activists in the republics. We thank Serhii Holovaty, Vyacheslav Chornovil, Najaf Najafov, Ghia Nodia, Gleb Pavlovsky, Galina Starovoytova, Lev Ponomaryov, among many others.

Some of the materials and many of the ideas in this book are based on writings undertaken during the project. We are grateful to Michael Mandelbaum of the Aspen Institute, to William Hyland, then editor of Foreign Affairs, and Wladyslaw Pleszczynski, of the American Spectator, who commissioned work from us and so helped us shape our views on aspects of post-Soviet states.

Above all we give thanks to Barbara Lowenstein, our agent, who has always been a source of support and who has guided our endeavor from its inception. She encouraged the first version of this book and maintained her belief in the importance of the subject through to the conclusion of this volume.

In the end, however, all the imprecisions and obfuscations remain our own. It is always difficult to capture the essence of a revolution while it is in progress. But we hope that this volume will have helped to illuminate the movements, the people, and the events that have reshaped the face of Europe and Asia.

Nadia Diuk and Adrian Karatnycky

Washington D.C.

Chapter One

Nationalism and the Fall of the Soviets

And empires gleam, like wrecks of a dissolving dream.

SHELLEY

The fall of the Soviet Union is the most momentous event of the second half of the twentieth century, rivaled only by the defeat of fascism in World War II. Nevertheless, the end of the Soviets was not forseen by the vast majority of Soviet affairs experts. Just a decade ago, the Soviet state and the Communist system were judged impregnable, stable, and durable by the overwhelming majority of Sovietologists.

At the center of the collapse of the Soviet Union was the dramatic rise of nationalism. Nationalism and the desire for independence broke the "eternal union of fraternal peoples" into fifteen discrete states. And while there can be no question that many factors contributed to the fall of communism, it was nationalism and its capacity to mobilize broad masses of citizens in behalf of independence that proved the decisive force in the unraveling of totalitarianism.

Nationalism—not in its xenophobic form, but in its patriotic and democratic aspects—was the force that in large measure helped defeat the August 1991 coup. In Russia, as in Ukraine, Armenia, and the Baltic States, it was national democratic movements that led the opposition to the illegal actions of the coup plotters. And it was the loyalty of many in the military and in the military-industrial complex to newly elected leaders of their republics—including the democratically elected president of Russia, Boris Yeltsin—that fostered deep internal divisions, confused the lines of authority, and contributed to the failure of the coup.

With the collapse of totalitarian communism came the collapse of a highly centralized Soviet empire that was heir to a centuries-old czarist imperial tradition. Remarkably, the collapse of the Soviet Union and of its totalitarian system came without a major war or massive violence. And although in the year after the dissolution of the USSR a number of dangerous conflicts simmered on the periphery of the old Soviet empire, many were the legacy of decades, if not centuries, of colonial rule. They were also the consequence of a Soviet rule that had brutalized and lumpenized broad segments of society. Amid an economic crisis, the post-Soviet future was fertile ground for dictators and demagogues. However, there was also strong ground for optimism, for the liberal democratic movements that led the assault on communism and the empire had won substantial mass support and respect. Together with the many new institutions of a normal democratic civil society, these democratic movements were in a strong position to influence events in a majority of the new states that emerged out of the Soviet empire.

The first signs of the mass discontent that would contribute to the Soviet empire's collapse could be discerned as early as 1986, especially in the non-Russian republics, where nearly half the population of the Soviet Union lived.

From December 1986 until Mikhail Gorbachev's surrender of office five years later, millions upon millions of Soviet citizens—Ukrainians, Georgians, Lithuanians, Belarusians, Crimean Tatars, Estonians, Tajiks, Azerbaijanis, Uzbeks, Armenians, Latvians, and Moldavians—took to the streets in an outpouring of popular discontent. Millions more took part in general strikes to protest the ethnic, economic, and political policies of the Soviet state. These mass protests shook the very foundations of the USSR and altered Western conceptions about the stability of the "indissolvable union of socialist states."

Hundreds died, thousands were injured, and hundreds of thousands were driven from their homes in fierce interethnic conflicts that were largely the consequence of the denial of sovereignty and of appalling economic misery. Hundreds, too, perished as a consequence of Red Army and Soviet police actions in Azerbaijan, Armenia, Georgia, and Kazakhstan.

Yet for several years, the events that were the growing signs of the momentous unraveling of the Soviet superpower were not reported as such. Throughout the 1980s, news dispatches on the USSR's non-Russian peoples seemed to lurch from crisis to crisis. In Armenia and Azerbaijan, territorial disputes were said to be behind the political ferment and mass protest. In Uzbekistan and Kyrgyzstan, interethnic hatreds were reported as the cause of violence. In Moldova, deep-seated resentments over native language rights were blamed for inspiring unrest. In Ukraine, the mass protests were said to be fueled by unhappiness with local Brezhnev-style bosses. Yet all these tensions derived from a common source: the imperial nature of the Soviet Union. The unprecedented unrest grew out of the impatience and urgency of the USSR's non-Russian subjects, who increasingly felt that the political relaxation that characterized the Gorbachev years made the time ripe for change, and for freedom.

The Security State

For some seventy years, the totalitarian Soviet system single-mindedly crushed all efforts toward independent organization. In the post-Stalin years, under Khrushchev, Brezhnev, Andropov, and Chernenko, non-Russians made up the vast majority of political prisoners—even before national dissent blossomed into mass movements in the 1980s. From the 1920s to the mid-1980s, individual dissenters were trapped in a web of repression spun by the internal espionage network of the KGB and its string of informants and by the Ministry of Internal Affairs, with its uniformed militia and dreaded Sixth Detachment, armed with rubber truncheons and ferocious attack dogs. An extremely regimented system of controls made it well-nigh impossible for most independent organizations to rent a meeting place, much less photocopy a statement or print a leaflet, without official approval. For decades the absence of a free press contributed to the weakness of independent life and the resultant atomization of the Soviet public.

For nearly three-quarters of a century, the USSR's citizens kept their most deeply held views to themselves. Their outward passivity even led many Western experts to conclude that the traditions, values, and bonds of the past had been irretrievably lost and sundered—that a new type of docile citizen had been shaped by totalitarianism and mass repression.

Even prominent Soviet dissidents joined in this pessimistic chorus. The brilliant Russian writer and philosopher Aleksandr Zinoviev characterized national issues in the USSR in his deeply cynical book *The Reality of Communism*, published in 1983: "The Communist regime deals successfully with national problems, as Soviet experience has shown. In particular it has been extremely effective in raising the educational, cultural and living standards of the more backward peoples and groups of the population to a comparatively high level. These peoples become a bulwark of the new society." According to Zinoviev, the Communist system had a strong capacity to destroy national barriers and eliminate ethnic differences. Communism created a new, bland, homogenized community of people who, Zinoviev argued, were "beyond nationality." Those features of the Soviet system led the writer to wrongly conclude that "any expectation that conflicts between nationalities will cause the ruin of the Soviet Empire derives from a total misconception."

These words were written by one of the most acute analysts of Soviet life, an insightful man who spent more than half a century living under Soviet communism. Today, his assessment has been disproved by the remarkable national rebirth that has helped bring about the collapse of the USSR. Yet Zinoviev had good reason for skepticism and cynicism based on the status quo of the Soviet Union in the 1970s and early 1980s. Much of the national spirit and energy of the USSR's peoples endured beneath the surface, repressed by the police state and hidden under the superficial and glib assertions of the self-confident totalitarian media.

The rapid rise of widespread and wide-ranging national movements marked an astounding shift in the consciousness of the peoples that made up the Soviet Union. After the accession of Mikhail Gorbachev to the pinnacle of power and the emergence of the policies of *glasnost* (openness) and *perestroika* (socioeconomic restructuring), the institutions and instruments of repression and control were forced to work under new constraints and rules. Regulations governing the use of force were promulgated; most of the best-known political prisoners were released; the psychiatric prison system underwent reform; and overzealous security *apparatchiki* were chastised and, on occasion, even brought to trial and punished. More important, the array of the Soviet state's mechanisms of social control became the subject of limited but often very real and honest scrutiny in the increasingly independent official press.

Such press scrutiny and shifts in regulations were all part of the upheaval that accompanied the reforms required by perestroika and glasnost, as well as by the highly ballyhooed Gorbachev campaign for the "humanization of the KGB." Under President Mikhail Gorbachev, military actions against protesters, as in Soviet Georgia, often resulted in unwanted parliamentary commissions of inquiry and embarrassing, highly public denunciations of military and security personnel. Illegal interceptions of mail sometimes resulted in the loss of livelihood for a KGB or Ministry of Internal Affairs functionary and occasionally led to criminal sanctions. Press exposés of security excesses occasionally appeared on the front pages of widely circulated newspapers and magazines. The openness of debates in the newly formed USSR's Congress of People's Deputies and, to a lesser extent, in the

USSR's more tightly controlled full-time parliament, the Supreme Soviet, also provided a lively, new forum for the airing of abuses.

Scrutiny and criticism of the state's most secret instruments of oppression and control did not prevent these institutions from monitoring such prominent elected leaders as Boris Yeltsin and, in late 1991, even Mikhail Gorbachev and his family. But they did bring a measure of instability and uncertainty to the Soviet security apparatus: It was no longer clear what was sanctioned and what was forbidden. This uncertainty, in turn, created an opening for political activism and independent organizing.

To be sure, under Gorbachev, KGB and MVD surveillance was not curtailed, nor was there an independent judiciary to protect civil liberties. Most national rights advocates assumed that files on their emerging movements were growing thicker by the day. We found in our travels throughout the USSR in 1989, 1990, and 1991 that, although groups of independent activists were being closely monitored, there was an obvious absence of fear. Gorbachev's exhortations to "democratize" the system and to increase popular participation in political life also helped raise expectations in the long-quiescent republics.

When he came to power as general secretary in March 1985, Mikhail Gorbachev could not have anticipated that he was ushering in an unprecedented era of national ferment. Few Western analysts could have predicted the important liberalizations that glasnost would bring to culture and politics in the USSR. Gorbachev's maiden speech revealed little sign of a major policy shift. In it and other early addresses there are timeworn references to "combatting shortcomings," "strengthening discipline," and "inculcating patriotism and internationalism."

There was little evidence of innovation in Gorbachev's pronouncements on ethnic and national issues. Speaking on the occasion of the fortieth anniversary of the "victory of the Soviet people" in World War II, Gorbachev was keen to praise the "mass heroism" of Soviet citizens, "united and inspired by the Great Russian people, whose bravery, endurance, and unbending character were an inspiring example of an unconquerable will to victory." "The blossoming of nations and nationalities," Gorbachev went on, "is organically linked to their wideranging drawing together [*sblizheniye*]." A shift in policy could be found only in Gorbachev's use of the term *sblizheniye* "drawing together," which appeared to be a step away from the Brezhnev doctrine of *sliyaniye*, the "merger" of nations. Perhaps this was an early indication of the Soviet leader's more relaxed approach to non-Russians.

By 1986, the tone of Gorbachev's speeches had undergone a remarkable alteration. The USSR's economy was in a state of crisis, he insisted, and there was a need for "radical restructuring." The terms *glasnost* and *perestroika* had made their famous, if only temporary, entry into the modern political lexicon. But the Soviet leader was notably reticent about offering any sense of a major change in the area of national relations.

Within the republics, 1986 saw the usual denunciations by local Party leaders of "bourgeois nationalists" and exhortations for a "struggle against nationalist and chauvinist sentiments." The first storm clouds of national ferment appeared at the Congress of the USSR Writers' Union, where the Georgian writers' delegation stormed out over the issue of "Great Russian nationalism," the idea that it is Russia's destiny to rule over a great empire. And the Ukrainian poet Boris Oliynik (a loyal Communist, who later became the deputy chairman of the Soviet of Nationalities in the USSR's parliament) castigated "great power chauvinists." Radicalized by the nuclear accident in Chernobyl, he denounced his fellow countrymen who were servile to Brezhnev-style political orthodoxy. In Oliynik's view, self-serving Party officials from his republic had been given pieces of political turf in "their own native land in exchange for speaking broken Russian" to satisfy their Russian masters in the Kremlin.

Moved to action by the Chernobyl catastrophe, grass-roots ecological movements began to emerge in late 1986 in Ukraine, Belarus (then still known as Byelorussia), Armenia, and Lithuania. The pollution of native lands was increasingly becoming a catalyst for the political mobilization of forces eager to break free of the domination of the central authorities. Protests calling for the closing of nuclear power plants in Ukraine and Lithuania, and the curbing of industrial pollution in Armenia, drew people away from state-controlled organizations and led to the emergence of small, highly effective independent groups.

In December of 1986, amid growing ferment on ecological and language issues, Gorbachev got his first taste of the incendiary power of national upheaval. The event that signaled the first salvo of an ensuing wave of unrest occurred not near Moscow, but in the distant capital of Kazakhstan, Alma Ata. There on December 17 and 18, students and young workers gathered by the thousands in what was then still known as Brezhnev Square to protest the removal of an ethnic Kazakh from the republic's top Party position and his replacement by a Russian. They carried signs with the slogan Kazakhstan for the Kazakhs and sang patriotic songs. In the evening, some in the crowd dispersed, but thousands remained to stage a sit-down strike in front of the Central Committee building.

Finally, according to eyewitness accounts, the authorities moved—first with water cannon, then with trucks. In the melee, a young girl was crushed by one of the vehicles and a struggle broke out. The police and soldiers moved in and beat students mercilessly with truncheons and sticks. Even after the demonstration at the square had been suppressed, the authorities went after the students and workers at their university and schools. One Kazakh eyewitness claims that soldiers tore into residence halls and threw resisting students out of dormitory windows. In all, several thousand protesters were said to have been arrested. Estimates of the death toll range from a couple of dozen to nearly three hundred. Hundreds were wounded, and hundreds were later expelled from the university and polytechnic institute. Although the Soviet authorities long thwarted an open and thorough inquiry and insisted that only two died in the demonstrations, the event signaled the reemergence of ethnic unrest as a major factor in Soviet politics.

In 1987, movements for national rights were given a further stimulus when Gorbachev released hundreds of political prisoners—the bulk of them nationalist activists from the non-Russian republics—from the Soviet prisons and forced-labor camps. Many of them returned to their homes and began to rebuild the national rights organizations sundered by the repression of the Brezhnev era. At the same time, even as ecological issues were creating a new opportunity for independent public organization, non-Russian intellectuals were once again raising the issue of granting Ukrainian, Belarusian, and other non-Russian languages the status of state language in their republics.

By the summer of 1987, mass demonstrations had begun to break out around the USSR. Five thousand Latvians gathered in Riga to commemorate the forced deportation of thousands of their countrymen in 1941. In July, around one thousand Crimean Tatars came to Moscow to protest the forced deportation of their entire nation by Stalin. A similar protest near Tashkent by five thousand Crimean Tatars was broken up by the authorities. In October, several thousand protesters demonstrated in Armenia and several hundred nationally minded Belarusian youth marched in Minsk.

The year 1987 was a landmark in Soviet history. It marked the rise of independent organizations, dubbed in the Soviet press as the *nyeformaly* (informals), the vast majority of which originated in the non-Russian republics. The year also saw the rapid emergence of a lively underground press. Although the new periodicals were generally copied on carbon paper and distributed by hand, they provided a new outlet for nationalist and separatist ideas.

In the atmosphere of greater press openness and with the release of most political prisoners, the climate of fear that had characterized the Brezhnev era was rapidly diminishing. And by early 1988, the USSR witnessed the eruption of mass protests in a number of non-Russian republics. In early 1988, independent activism reached a new benchmark with a demonstration in Yerevan on February 23, when approximately 1 million Armenians called for the transfer of the predominantly Armenian region of Nagorny Karabakh to their republic. By the summer, 40,000 protesters led by the National Self-Determination Association were pressing for outright Armenian independence.

On June 21, 1988, on the eve of the Nineteenth All-Union Conference of the Communist Party of the Soviet Union, more than 50,000 Ukrainians took to the streets of Lviv in unsanctioned protests for national rights, while Azerbaijanis organized mass protests in Baku that erupted in violent ethnic conflict between their countrymen and Armenians. By September 1988, a rapidly growing national movement in the Baltic republics had brought out as many as 300,000 protesters into the streets of Tallinn, Estonia. When October arrived, it was Belarus's turn, as 10,000 nationalists marched for cultural and political autonomy. Demonstrations by as many as 100,000 protesters took place in Tbilisi, Georgia, on November 12 under banners proclaiming Long Live Independent Georgia, and An End to Russification!

By the early autumn, a new phase in the protests by non-Russians had been reached with the creation of popular fronts. Initially, these were self-styled citizens' initiatives to "support perestroika." Some Western experts felt that they were initiated by liberal Communist Party activists eager to bolster Gorbachev in his struggle to purge old-line, Brezhnev-style conservatives. But very early on, it became clear that for the non-Russians who flocked to the popular fronts, reform of the Soviet Union meant national sovereignty, if not outright independence.

The Estonian popular front (Rahvarinne), the Popular Front of Latvia, and the Lithuanian Reform Movement (Sajudis) were the first organizations to hold founding congresses and soon became powerful organizations around which hundreds of thousands of Baltic citizens united. Simultaneously, popular fronts emerged among the Belarusians, Ukrainians, Georgians, Azerbaijanis, Uzbeks, Moldavians, Tajiks, and Turkmenians. A similar national organization was active also in Armenia.

In 1989, the USSR saw even more remarkable ferment and heightened political pressure for national self-determination. A major breakthrough for the movements for national sovereignty was achieved on March 26, 1989, with the defeat of many Communist Party candidates in elections to the USSR's Congress of People's Deputies. In the Baltic States, the popular fronts swept the elections, and similar groups were elected in Ukraine and Armenia. Many town and city councils were taken over by newly elected candidates from democratic and proindependence groups.

The year also saw the emergence of independent trade unions in Latvia and Lithuania and of militant strike committees in the coal-mining regions of Ukraine, Russia, and Kazakhstan. General strikes motivated by a rising tide of nationalism became a regular feature on the Soviet landscape in Georgia, western Ukraine, Azerbaijan, and Armenia. Violence and tragedy were also part of the ferment. In Georgia, Soviet troops killed peaceful demonstrators. Armed conflict erupted between Meshkhetian Turks and Uzbeks, Abkhazians and Georgians, and in Kazakhstan, and the death toll mounted in tragic territorial disputes between Armenians and Azerbaijanis.

In 1990, the bloodletting continued unabatedly. January saw an explosion of violence in Baku, Azerbaijan, where thirty died in anti-Armenian pogroms before the violence was stopped through the intercession of Azerbaijani democratic activists, who had helped spirit Armenians, Russians, and Jews out of the city. But days after the violence had ceased, Soviet troops entered Baku and proceeded to impose a brutal military rule in which nearly 150 civilians were killed. In the days that followed, the Soviet military moved to repress the popular front and other independent groups. In February, more than twenty were killed and five hundred injured in antigovernment riots in Dushanbe, the capital of Tajikistan. In May, blood was shed in Armenia, where dozens were mowed down by the Soviet army in what dissidents said was an attempt to provoke unrest as a pretext for crushing proindependence forces. In June 1990, violence in Kyrgyzstan pitted impoverished Uzbeks against Kyrgyz in a struggle over land rights.

The Gorbachev Effect

In April 1989, Aleksandr Yakovlev, a Politburo member and perhaps Gorbachev's closest confidant and ally, admitted candidly to a Georgian member of the Congress of People's Deputies, the filmmaker Eldar Shengelaya: "We just never expected national feelings to arise as they have." Such an honest admission reveals a great deal about the thinking of Mikhail Gorbachev and the team of insiders he assembled to help restructure the increasingly moribund Soviet state and economy. Many of the members of the Gorbachev team were respected academics and competent technical experts; in short, pragmatically oriented technocrats. With a technocratically, rather than an ideologically, oriented team around him, Gorbachev was ill equipped to understand the depth of feeling attached to such ideas as nationalism and cultural heritage. His experience of ethnic aspirations was exceedingly limited. Gorbachev was the first Soviet leader since Lenin who had not served in a multinational setting: Before he moved to Moscow, he spent his formative political years in Stavropol, where Russians make up about 90 percent of the local population.

Unlike Gorbachev, previous Communist Party general secretaries, including Stalin, Khrushchev, and Brezhnev, cut their political teeth on the knotty national question. Stalin served as the commissar for national affairs, and, as an ethnic Georgian, he was quite familiar with the depth of nationalist sentiments in his native land. Khrushchev served as first secretary in Ukraine before being called up to Moscow. He was well skilled in taming the nationalism of the Ukrainians, having presided over the brutal suppression of broad-based resistance to western Ukraine's incorporation into the USSR in 1939. There, a substantial guerrilla movement waged a fierce war until 1949 against the Soviets and across the border against the Kremlin's Polish Communist allies. Brezhnev, too, emerged out of the Ukrainian crucible, albeit in the less nationally conscious city of Dnipropetrovsk. Even the short-lived leaders Yury Andropov and Konstantin Chernenko had important experience in national issues. Andropov, as head of the KGB, had supervised the suppression of nationalist dissent throughout the USSR, and Chernenko had been posted in Moldova.

Gorbachev's inexperience in ethnic and national issues revealed itself in a series of blunders early on in his tenure. While on a highly publicized visit to Ukraine in June of 1986, in the midst of an impromptu street conversation in the Ukrainian capital, Kiev, and before an audience of millions of Soviet television viewers, Gorbachev confused Russia with the Soviet Union and offended Ukrainian sensibilities: "Listen, we coped after the Imperialist war, after the civil war, when the country was in ruins. . . . Nothing was left after that. But we coped. We coped. They predicted Russia would never rise again after the war. But we rose again. . . . For all the people who are striving for good, Russia—er, the Soviet Union, I mean—that is what we call it now, and what it is in fact—for them it is a bulwark."

He compounded this blunder with an early policy mistake as 1986 drew to a close. In replacing a corrupt, longtime leader of the Kazakhstan Party apparatus, the Kazakh Dinmukhamed Kunaev, Gorbachev opted for a clever, efficient ethnic Russian, with little experience in Kazakhstan—Gennady Kolbin. The appointment of the technocratic outsider outraged the Kazakh populace and led to the mass student-led demonstrations in front of Party headquarters in Alma Ata. This was Gorbachev's baptism by fire. Three years passed before the Soviet leader grudgingly conceded his tactical error: He elevated Kolbin to a top post in Moscow and replaced him with Nursultan Nazarbaev, a native Kazakh.

Despite the Gorbachev team's initial surprise at the rise of national sentiments, with time they became well aware that the mass protests in the republics were not isolated or random manifestations of pent-up discontent, but part of a profound national awakening that challenged the imperial basis of the Soviet centralized state. They understood that this national rebirth was accompanied in all of the USSR's republics by an upsurge in independent cultural activity, by an intensely spiritual rediscovery of national tradition, by a profound revival of religious faith, and by a substantial independent press published outside the purview of the authorities.

This renaissance of nationalism brought with it the emergence of popular democratic movements that successfully challenged the monopoly enjoyed by the Communist Party. Those movements openly and successfully sought power by engaging in electoral politics. The March 1989 election results would have been even more impressive had local officials not resorted to vote rigging or antidemocratic manipulation of the nomination process.

Between January and March 1990, proindependence movements flexed their political muscles once again in Supreme Soviet elections. In the Baltic republics, where popular fronts had their own newspapers and access to state-run television, proindependence forces scored overwhelming victories. In Latvia, they captured over two-thirds of all seats. In Estonia, the popular front won 49 of the 105 seats in the Supreme Soviet, while the slate backed by the Estonian Communist Party, which had emphasized its independence from the Communist Party of the Soviet Union (CPSU), captured 29 seats. In Lithuania, Sajudis-backed candidates won approximately 70 percent of the seats to the republic's legislature, paving the way to their declaration of independence from the USSR.

In other republics, such as Ukraine and Belarus, proindependence forces made impressive gains despite having been denied access to the mass media and subjected to relentless smear campaigns. In Ukraine, 60 percent of the 191 candidates of the Rukh-supported Democratic bloc won, holding a quarter of the seats in the republic's parliament. Ukrainian nationalists also captured the majority of seats in the regional councils of Lviv, Ivano-Frankivsk, and Ternopil, as well as in the city council of the capital city, Kiev. In Belarus, the popular front, Adradzhenne, came close to capturing control of Minsk, but lost badly in rural areas and in smaller towns. And in the huge Russian republic, proreform forces running on a platform of Russian sovereignty did well in the March 1990 elections, capturing overwhelming control of the Moscow and Saint Petersburg (then Leningrad) legislatures and temporarily establishing a slim proreform majority in the republic's legislature, which elected Boris Yeltsin as its chairman on a plank promising to build Russian statehood.

The upsurge in popular assertiveness among the USSR's many nations reflected a trend unprecedented since the consolidation of Soviet power. A confluence of factors had led to something exciting and exhilarating—a massive outpouring of popular activism, most of it unofficial and informal, on the part of diverse political, cultural, and social interest groups. As 1990 began, most of that activism, however, was not yet to be found in the heart of the Soviet empire—in Russia proper—but on its peripheries, where nearly half the Soviet Union's citizens—its hidden nations—lived.

What's in a Name?

The rise of national movements that pressed for statehood and independence sprang from something far more deeply rooted than the mere lifting of the most onerous restrictions of the totalitarian state. The call of the people was for something far more profound than simply the necessary amelioration of economic injustices. They had suffered through decades of discontentment, struggling against a complex state structure that had many of its origins deep in the history of the Russian empire.

For decades, the West's misconceptions about the Soviet Union were best demonstrated by the interchangeable use of the terms "USSR" and "Russia." Soviet citizens were frequently called Russians in a fashionable shorthand. In the 1960s and 1970s, even the *New York Times* consistently employed this imprecision. Such conventions persisted in many respected American and British periodicals until the very collapse of the USSR.

For the nearly 50 percent of the Soviet population that was not Russian, this practice had relegated them to a netherworld, making the non-Russian peoples, in essence, hidden nations. This imprecision in nomenclature masked an insensitivity to the cultural richness, history, and ethnic variety of the Soviet population. It also made it easier to ignore the decline of the languages and traditions of distinctive peoples with ancient histories and independent identities. Few voices were raised when individual nations withered, or, as was the case with several dozen small ethnic groups, virtually disappeared as a result of forced assimilation, deportation of entire peoples, and, in earlier decades, genocide.

The profound spiritual crisis of identity among non-Russian peoples was only dimly understood by the rest of the world. In part, this state of affairs, this hidden reality, was reinforced by the extensive restrictions placed on Western correspondents based in the USSR. For decades, their dispatches were Moscow-centered. So cumbersome and fruitless were most efforts to secure permission to travel that few correspondents tried. Those who were more adventurous, including Andrew Nagorski of *Newsweek* and David Satter of the *Financial Times*, were punished with expulsion in the mid-1980s for their enterprising reportage.

Although travel became far easier under Mikhail Gorbachev, Moscow-based reporters typically visited the non-Russian regions for only two or three days at a time, often to cover some mass protest or breaking political crisis, thus having little chance to immerse themselves more deeply in what are immensely rich cultures, traditions, and political movements. Even now in the context of the disintegration of the USSR, not a single full-time American correspondent is posted anywhere besides Moscow. Although non-Russians had been the topic of numerous specialized academic studies, as of mid-1992 they were rarely the subjects of books of reportage, and were relegated at best to a cursory chapter or two in books on the USSR.

Such inadequacies helped shape Western consciousness. In turn, the attitudes of Western reporters on ethnic politics were shaped by the conceptions of experts and policymakers back home. And in the 1970s and 1980s, Soviet affairs experts were exceedingly skeptical about the potential for mass unrest among the non-Russian peoples. Although a few Western experts— most notably Hélène Carrere D'Encausse, Zbigniew Brzezinski, and Richard Pipes—pointed to the potential of the non-Russian factor, the majority of the academic community was convinced in the mid-1980s that the force of nationalism in the USSR had been successfully suppressed by state control.

For decades, the West sidestepped the issue of ethnic relations in the Soviet Union. Americans, in particular, tended to assume that the Soviet Union, while a multinational state, was becoming a great melting pot of nations, merging through intermarriage, a common Russian language, a common Soviet culture, and mass migration. In part, Americans projected their own domestic arrangements onto a Soviet setting, believing that the Soviet republics were something more or less akin to the states of their own union. Typical of such misperceptions were the views of Robert Strauss, the American ambassador to the unraveling USSR, who, in the fall of 1991, commented that the republics seeking independence from the USSR were like "teenage children" who had run away from home. Soon they would come back, the ambassador argued condescendingly.

In its waning years the Soviet Union remained, in large measure, what it had been at its inception: an agglomeration of national republics with a dominant indigenous national group, bound to the center by a complex network of economic links and to political associations revolving around the centralized structure of the Communist Party. The formation of the Soviet Union had been accomplished with the conquest of a number of non-Communist independent states in the aftermath of World War I. The collapse of czarist Russia in 1917 had meant that new, democratic states proclaimed their independence in Ukraine, Lithuania, Latvia, Estonia, Georgia, Armenia, and Azerbaijan. And in Central Asia, a powerful insurgency, the Basmachi, valiantly challenged Sovietization between 1918 and 1923. To achieve unification among most of these independent regions required not only the military power of the Red Army, but tactical alliances between the Bolsheviks and some strata of the regions' indigenous patriotic groups. As a result, the early years of Soviet power were characterized by policies of "indigenization" designed to develop loyal local non-Russian Communist elites, and thereby allay local fears about Russian domination. Yet even through its early years, the Party never tolerated the independence of the Communist parties of the constituent republics. Buffeted by rising industrial unrest, wearied by a long war, and in large measure driven by the necessity to build support in the struggle against the monarchist White Russians, Lenin and the Bolsheviks had paid more than lip service to the national aspirations of the native non-Russian populations.

The Soviet state formed in 1923 was far from the Marxist-Leninist ideal and carried within it some of the seeds of its eventual destruction. The product of a collision between Marxism-Leninism and local demands for autonomy, the Soviet state has been described by Harvard historian Richard Pipes as "a compromise between doctrine and reality: an attempt to reconcile the Bolshevik striving for absolute unity and centralization of all power in the hands of the party, with the recognition that the empirical fact of nationalism did survive the old order. It was viewed as a temporary solution only, as a transitional stage to a completely centralized and supra-national world-wide Soviet state."

Pipes notes that although the Bolsheviks destroyed all rival parties, centralized power, and eliminated independent institutions, they also granted non-Russians two important concessions: "constitutional recognition of the multinational structure of the Soviet population" and the establishment of the "national-territorial principle as the base of the state's political administration." In the light of this very narrow interpretation of federalism, some may be surprised that until the day the Soviet flag was taken down in the

Kremlin, the Soviet constitution reflected the notion of a formally voluntary union: Article 70 of the Soviet constitution (ratified in 1977) asserted the "free self-determination of nations and the voluntary association of equal Soviet Socialist Republics," and Article 72 stated that "each Union Republic shall retain the right freely to secede from the USSR."

While the Soviet constitution itself, since 1924, guaranteed the right of secession from the Union, in practice the right was suppressed. The few bold souls who dared try to exercise that right were subjected to brutal repression. One case in point was the Ukrainian dissident leader Levko Lukyanenko. A lawyer by training, Lukyanenko was a thirty-three-year-old firebrand who decided to test his rights under the law by creating in 1960 the Ukrainian Peasant and Worker Party, which included in its platform a call for a referendum on the secession of Ukraine from the USSR. The call, made at the height of the Khrushchev era, brought a swift and vicious response. Lukyanenko was sentenced to death by shooting "for treason," a sentence that was later commuted to a fifteen-year term of imprisonment.

Lukyanenko, who in mid-1992 was a free Ukraine's ambassador to Canada, spent twenty-six years in prison, forced labor, and exile—as punishment for invoking a constitutionally protected right. Only on April 3, 1990, under pressure of growing nationalist ferment, did the USSR's Supreme Soviet adopt an extremely onerous and drawn-out procedure for the secession of constituent republics from the USSR.

Although the roots of a centralized Soviet Union were in place in the 1920s, there was some relaxation in the cultural sphere. Millions of formerly illiterate non-Russians were educated in their native languages, and some economic prerogatives remained with the republics, particularly during the period of Lenin's New Economic Policy. The process of *korenizatsiya* (indigenization) was introduced in 1923 to win the hearts and minds of the non-Russian citizens of the new state and to build a loyal non-Russian Communist cadre. As the years passed, and as a consequence of Stalin's relentless drive toward the fulfillment of the Bolshevik imperative of centralization and concentration of power, the rights of non-Russians were slowly eroded. By the 1930s, the privileged role of Russians was openly asserted and celebrated, while a brutal purge of non-Russian elites was conducted. Though ethnically a Georgian, Stalin revealed himself to be an extreme Russian chauvinist in his policies. For example, he toasted the Nazi surrender: "I drink firstly to the health of the Russian nation because it is the leading nation of all nations belonging to the Soviet Union . . . it earned in this war general recognition as the guiding force of the Soviet Union among all the peoples of our country."

After Stalin died in 1953 and his security chief, Lavrenty Beria, was purged, the Soviet government's daily newspaper, *Izvestiya*, proclaimed a continuity in this chauvinistic celebration of the Russians when it declared: "The Russian people rightfully merited recognition as the most outstanding, the directing nation of the USSR." Under Leonid Brezhnev, the ambitious aim of creating a monolithic "Soviet people" reached a modern-day apogee. The Soviet leader raised the Russian ante further when he claimed that "the revolutionary energy, the selflessness, diligence and profound international-ism of the Great Russian people have rightfully won them the sincere respect of all the peoples of our socialist homeland." It was, "above all, the Great Russian people," Brezhnev said, who strengthened and developed the "mighty union of equal peoples."

Mikhail Gorbachev's putative mentor Yury Andropov was also a propo-nent of this line. In his first major speech as the new Soviet leader in 1983, the former KGB chief offered his "gratitude to the Russian people [without whom] in none of the republics would the present achievements have been conceivable."

Other articles in the Communist press of the 1980s extolled the Rus-sians as "first among equals" and a nation with a "special role" in the development of Soviet society. The Gorbachev years echoed similar tones. In September 1989, the Communist Party unflinchingly pronounced "Russia . . . the consolidating principle of our nation" and told non-Russians that Russia "made a decisive contribution to the elimination of the backwardness of the outlying national districts."

Decades of such paeans had a clear effect on the national consciousness of non-Russians. The resentment such glorification fostered revealed itself with full force in the late 1980s and early 1990s and helped explain why the exalted Russians were among the last national groups to rise up and chal-lenge the Soviet system.

For seven decades, the Soviets masked the true state of ethnic relations in their domain by projecting two simultaneously false images: one, of their own polity as a voluntary agglomeration of peoples linked by the promise and success of "real, existing socialism," and the other, of the Soviet Union as the foremost ally of national liberation movements opposed to "Western imperialism." Both of these images today appear distant and archaic, yet throughout the 1960s and 1970s they proved remarkably attractive instru-ments in Soviet expansionist foreign policy.

The outward complexity of the Soviet Union's ethnic mix long masked the underlying basis of national relations in the empire. While outwardly the USSR appeared as an intricate latticework of more than one hundred separate nations, ethnic relations in the USSR were not hopelessly tangled and inapproachable. The USSR was dominated by a handful of larger nations; ten ethnic groups made up more than 90 percent of the Soviet population. And the pattern was even simpler, for out of 287 million Soviet citizens, 147 million were Russians, 43 million were Ukrainians, and around 55 million were ethnic Turks. These three groups alone accounted for nearly 85 percent of the Soviet population.

According to the 1989 census, Russians represented a little more than half (50.8 percent) of all Soviet citizens. Of those, the vast majority (81.3 percent) lived in the territory of the Russian Soviet Federative Socialist Republic, then one of the fifteen constituent republics. Similarly, these republics held, in the majority, their own peoples. In each of the fifteen republics, with the exception of Kazakhstan, the indigenous population constituted the majority; and in an overwhelming number of republics, more than two-thirds of the population. According to the 1989 census figures, these proportions were increasing.

For these diverse peoples, Soviet rule meant a constant, wide-ranging attack on the integrity of national cultures. Some distortions arose because of the widespread Communist politicization of culture, affecting Russians and non-Russians alike. But non-Russians bore the heaviest burden of the USSR's policies. The central government fostered the Russian language as a kind of all-encompassing cultural cement to hold the Union together, and glorified aspects of Russian tradition, particularly its imperial past.

The introduction of such policies led to decades of profound cultural degradation. Native cultures and traditions faded and were replaced by a superficially Russian culture drained of its spirituality and rendered empty and vapid by totalitarianism. By the late 1980s, however, national pride was reasserting itself, and these once hidden nations became the center of a storm of protest and political mobilization that provoked the collapse of the Soviet Union.

The Soviet Man

Much of the discontent of the peoples of the former Soviet Union remained hidden in the 1970s, the widely reviled period of Leonid Brezhnev's rule. It was then that a new twist on the idea of nationality was added—the concept of the "Soviet man." Communist "theoreticians" and ideologists argued that as the "socialist" Soviet society moved inexorably toward communism, a new type of human being was emerging—internationalist in outlook,

Communist in ideals, severed forever from the old order's parochialisms, patriotisms, and nationalisms, which Soviet rule had supplanted.

The affirmation of the inevitable, natural movement toward the Communist man created both disturbing and dismaying formulations. Stalin, for example, had laid the groundwork for the Brezhnevite "Soviet man" when he proclaimed an astonishing revolutionary faith in his exotic work *Marxism and Linguistics*:

> After the victory of socialism on a world scale we will have . . . hundreds of national languages from which at first the most enriched single zonal languages will emerge as a result of lengthy economic, political, and cultural cooperation of nations, and subsequently the zonal languages will fuse into one common international language . . . neither German, nor Russian, nor English, but a new language which has absorbed the best elements of the national and zonal languages.

This concept, carrying within it the optimistic aim of creating a new society and a new type of citizen, was given further, more elaborate theoretical impetus in the 1970s, long after Stalin's passing, by the Communist Party's hard-line ideological czar, Mikhail Suslov. According to Ukrainian Party chief Petro Shelest, Suslov's colleague on the Politburo until his purge in 1972, the Kremlin's chief ideologist provided the theoretical underpinnings for the notion of sliyaniye, the 'merger' of nations. In practical terms, a merger was not remotely natural, but was instead conducted with a high degree of coercion and, oftentimes, outright repression. At the center of this approach to "nationalities" was the policy of Russification—the compulsory learning of Russian and the use of the Russian language by the institutions of Party and state authority in the non-Russian republics.

Russification was particularly advanced in Ukraine and Belarus, whose languages, while differing from Russian more than Spanish differs from Portuguese, and somewhat less than Spanish from Italian, were the ideal locus of Russificatory efforts. It was Suslov's personal belief and the Kremlin's apparent conclusion that Russian dominance of an increasingly non-Russian USSR would be assured if the Russian bloc were to be joined by the other two Slavic-speaking nations in the empire. Russification, according to this approach, was to be used as an instrument for stability: the creation of a Russian-speaking Slavic majority.

Interestingly, although Russification had also been a mainstay of the Soviet state under Stalin and Khrushchev, Brezhnev and Suslov revived it in the 1970s with an almost missionary zeal. The policy, however, was not a novel construct of Communist totalitarianism, but, like many features of statecraft in the Soviet Union, it had antecedents in the prerevolutionary czarist empire. As the eminent British historian of nationalism, the late Hugh Seton-Watson, has written in his *History of the Nation State*, the leaders of the powerful Russian nation "considered it their task, and indeed their moral duty to impose their nationality on all their subjects—of whatever religion, language or culture. As they saw it, by drawing these people upwards into their own superior culture, they were conferring benefits upon them; while at the same time they were strengthening their state by creating within it a single homogeneous nation."

Such policies came into vogue in the middle of the nineteenth century and were given ideological shape and coherence in the doctrine of official nationality formulated under Czar Nicholas I. The doctrine became the ideology of the conservative Alexander III and was carried out as well by his reactionary successor, Nicholas II. The policy included the introduction of czarist decrees—ukases—that banned the use of non-Russian languages in publishing and education.

While the Soviet totalitarian state did not go quite so far as to rigidly restrict non-Russian publishing and education, it created various career incentives for those who were Russian speakers, and a "voluntary" policy of Russification was introduced as the counterpart of political centralism. Today, even among some liberal Russians, one still encounters the notion that the introduction of the Russian language and culture had a civilizing effect on the more backward nations, particularly those of the east.

For the canny ideologue Suslov and his superior, Brezhnev, the non-Russian nations were not only a source of potential instability and an impediment to the exercise of total central control, they were a potential obstacle to scientific progress and economic growth. The single economic network needed a single language for the wheels of commerce to turn easily and efficiently. Unless effectively Russified, the non-Russians could prove unreliable members of the Red Army. Such Russification made eminent sense for the powerful Soviet military and its requirements for coordinated command and control.

Under Mikhail Gorbachev, the Soviet authorities slowly attempted to edge away from some of these discredited tenets. Leading Party figures began to acknowledge that the USSR was a gigantic muscle-bound, inefficient system of economic, social, cultural, and political institutions, a system that had, in turn, led to a growing economic crisis. It was equally apparent that the leaders of the Communist Party and Gorbachev would not orchestrate the dissolution of their superpower state into a series of smaller, weaker geopolitical entities.

President Gorbachev's views on this matter were made explicit in a series of statements in the summer and fall of 1989. Gorbachev left no doubt that the USSR, as then constituted, was indivisible. Moreover, he believed that the ruling Communist Party itself must remain a unitary multinational entity, implicitly dominated by the majority Russian population—the bedrock of a strong union. From 1989 to his resignation on Christmas Day, 1991, Gorbachev consistently lashed out at "separatists," warning that their formulas were incendiary and exceedingly dangerous. He and the Party he led rejected and in the end unsuccessfully resisted efforts to pry loose the Communist parties from the control of the center. He and his immediate circle failed as well to stem the tide of proindependence sentiment in the republics. By contrast, what Gorbachev was willing to hold out was the prospect of significant economic and cultural autonomy, yet such cultural and economic concessions when put into practice only further fueled the great awakening of peoples that was occurring throughout the Soviet Union.

According to Soviet doctrine, the USSR's many nations and "nationalities" were amicable partners in a voluntary union—a union in which there was social justice, ethnic equality, and fraternity among peoples. But the reality proved radically different. Resentments among national groups were sometimes deep-seated. In the 1960s and 1970s, there were sporadic eruptions of interethnic conflicts, often in the form of violent street fights and soccer riots.

Ethnic resentments were also reflected in a broad lexicon of ethnic slurs that demonstrated underlying attitudes that are certain to persist in the post-Soviet era. Among Russians, the pejorative for Armenians is *Armyashka* (little Armenian); Central Asians and the darker-skinned Caucasian peoples (Georgians, Armenians, and Azerbaijanis) are called *Chernozhopy* (black asses); Ukrainians are called *Khokhly*, a slur that connotes stupidity and stubbornness. In turn, Ukrainians and Lithuanians call Russians *Katsapy*, a pejorative of unknown etymology and meaning. Central Asians and the feared and hated Chinese are called *Kosoglazy* (slant eyes) or *Ploskomordy* (flat snouts) and even *Zhopomordy* (ass faces). Ukrainians, many of whom have pursued military careers as noncommissioned officers, are called *Makarnonniki* (macaronis) for their corporal or sergeant stripes. In Russian, the widely used slur *Zhid* means "yid" or "kike."

Such phrases, heard quite frequently in ethnically homogeneous settings, were widespread in the Soviet army, where young men from different ethnic groups were thrown into an ethnically diverse setting for the first time in their lives. Between 1988 and 1991, as national self-assertion grew in most of the Soviet republics, many non-Russians claimed that their young men were being killed while on military service, as a result of growing interethnic tensions and Russian resentment.

Insensitivity to other peoples revealed itself in many ways in Soviet society, yet it was only recently that ethnic minorities began to raise their voices against manifestations of such rudeness. In 1989, one prominent Uzbek writer was justifiably outraged at a new Russian handbook on dog breeding that offered Uzbek and other Turkic names as suggestions for the names of canine pets. Among those suggested by the handbook's author as appropriate were Rafik, Alisher, Akbar, Anwar, and Mukhtar. The article reminded its readers that "friendship begins with respect."

Clearly, respect was in short supply in the sphere of intergroup relations. Even the widely used *natsmen*, an acronym meaning "national minority," is a latter-day pejorative. Connoting "colonial" or "wog," it is applied indiscriminately to non-Russians even now in everyday conversation, reflecting a culture in which many national tensions are far from resolved, and are percolating very near the surface. Ever-mindful of the power of words to alter perceptions, Soviet doctrine coined a special term for the peoples of the USSR—"nationalities"—a formulation that suggested a new category less fully authentic than that represented by the term "nation." It helped to conveniently hide the fact that the USSR was composed of a series of full-fledged nation states and, as Zbigniew Brzezinski reminded us, contributed to the obfuscation of Soviet reality.

The Last Great Empire

Just as with culture, governance, and politics, the demographics and geography of national and ethnic life in the USSR may have appeared hopelessly confusing or intricate. But, despite this outward complexity, there were, broadly speaking, national winners and losers in the USSR. Decades after the decolonization of Africa, the British retreat from India, the French defeat in the Battle of Algiers, and the withdrawal of Portugal from Mozambique and Angola, the Soviet Union was at last forced to confront a challenge to its very nature as the last great empire.

Some pundits and policy experts, both in the Soviet Union and in the West, argued that Gorbachev had made a terrible miscalculation when he consented even to a modest relaxation of central control in the area of national relations. Yet those critics not only failed to appreciate the depths of national discontent and the resultant popular mobilization, but also underestimated the intended focus of Gorbachev's economic reforms. The principal aim of the Soviet leader's program was the release of the creative economic powers that he believed were latent in the Soviet population. For non-Russians, such an aim could not have been attained without the transfer of power from the center to the peripheries; thus, the many ills that confronted the Soviet Union could not be solved unless the Soviet Union's national question was openly discussed and forthrightly resolved.

The question was whether the USSR could survive the resolution of that issue. Gorbachev and his team believed that it could. But the intensity of the political revival of the nations of the former USSR grew with each passing day.

In his last years in office Gorbachev acknowledged that no question was more decisive to the success or failure of reform, no issue more critical to the Soviet Union's future, than that of growing nationalism. In his last two years in office, most of Gorbachev's energy was spent trying to stem the tide of rising separatism, in trying to hold the USSR together.

For Western policymakers, nationalism in the USSR was hardly likely to be a priority in the years of the nuclear balance of terror. Western experts focused primarily on Soviet global conduct or on the inner workings of the all-powerful Party and state. As a result of that focus, the West knew comparatively little about these exceedingly diverse nations' desires, their level of political culture, their agenda, or their national self-image. This lack of familiarity meant that non-Russians were frequently misperceived as backward-looking, opposed to modernization and reform. At worst, their republics were suspected of antidemocratic tendencies—xenophobic, violent dictatorships in the making.

A few pioneering writers and political specialists in the West warned that the multinational Soviet society was an unnatural and unstable entity that might one day begin to unravel. The USSR was, they maintained, certain to be a source of lasting political instability. Yet theirs was long a minority view, ignored in the rush for cordial relations. Attention to this issue was more evident during the early years of the Cold War in the 1950s and 1960s. It was in that period that first Radio Liberation and later Radio Liberty were created by the United States to broadcast uncensored information in the languages of the non-Russian peoples. Yet even then, in the West's approach, the idea of the Soviet Union as a colonial empire was subordinated to the dominant, anti-Communist critique.

By the time of the Nixon-era detente, such concepts as the defense of the national rights of non-Russian nations came to be regarded as retrograde, a holdover of the Cold War, an obstacle to the necessary East-West rapprochement—in short, an unwelcome intrusion into the United States–Soviet relationship. During the Nixon-Ford years, the prerogatives of detente banished the non-Russians to the back burner of policy concerns. And under President Jimmy Carter, even the annual commemoration of Captive Nations Day was forgotten.

Carter's advocacy of global human rights linked American government interventions almost exclusively to the personal fate of individual dissidents, and not to the fate of nations. During the early years of the Reagan administration, a turnaround occurred in United States policy, most notably at the United Nations, where, under Ambassador Jeane J. Kirkpatrick and her counselor, Carl Gershman, the United States began articulating a coherent view of the rights of nations, including the USSR's national minorities, by counterposing the Wilsonian view of national sovereignty with that offered by Leninism. Emphasis, too, was placed on the Baltic States, whose forced incorporation into the USSR was not recognized by the United States government.

With President Bush, the pendulum once again swung in the direction of business as usual, as Bush relegated the rights of the increasingly independent republics to the back burner. He was exceedingly cautious in asserting American support for Baltic independence, refusing to recognize their 1991 referenda on state independence. And in July of 1991, he traveled to Kiev to lecture Ukrainian proindependence democrats about the dangers of "suicidal nationalism," implicitly backing Gorbachev's goal of preserving the USSR.

Years of Western silence and shortsightedness notwithstanding, the contradictions that issued from national inequity would not go away. And in the republics of the Soviet Union, the late 1980s and early 1990s were a new spring of nations, akin to two periods in modern history—the Europe of 1848 and the Russian empire of 1905.

In 1848, after a protracted cultural flowering, European nations rose to make a quick dash for freedom. The idea of nationalism and the struggle for independence from empire had been celebrated a generation earlier in the poetry of Byron and Shelley. Greece's struggle for independence from Ottoman rule became a byword for liberal democratic values of the generation of the 1820s, who embraced the famous failed Greek rising against the Turks at Missalonghi as the first cry of that century's "hidden nations." Then came Shelley's revolutionary lament for the internal contradiction of empire: "And empires gleam, like wrecks of a dissolving dream."

In 1848 the names of revolutionary nationalists like Italy's Mazzini and

Garibaldi and Hungary's Petofi and Kossuth were inextricably linked with representative governance and democracy. The struggle was waged in an atmosphere of infectious international solidarity. When a Polish rising was crushed by the Prussians in May of that fateful year, thousands of workmen and students gathered in Paris's Place de la Concorde to shout, "*Vive la Pologne.*" After Kossuth was driven into exile and his revolution crushed, tens of thousands of New Yorkers poured out to greet him in a massive, enthusiastic show of support. He was lionized by American editorialists and hailed by the houses of Congress.

While 1848 was, as Lewis B. Namier wrote, "the revolt of the intellectuals," that spring of nations also had its decidedly anti-intellectual aspects. Not all writings then were scrupulously democratic. Nevertheless, the intelligentsia of that age felt, rightly or wrongly, the inexorable pull of the people and a seamless kinship with the nation. The once rarefied issues of language and the recovery of a vanished past occupied the thoughts of many more than the schooled elites. In a brief essay for the *Times Literary Supplement*, written in 1923, Namier characterized the state of affairs in the last century:

> About 1848 the nationalities inside the Habsburg Monarchy formed two marked strata: there were the historic nations—the Germans, Magyars, Italians and Poles—with well-developed upper classes, and therefore with cultural continuity and an articulate political life; and the peasant races— the Czechs, Slovaks, Yugo-Slavs, Ukrainians and Roumanians—who, having in previous centuries lost their upper classes, had practically no historic experience. But with the rise of a new middle-class intelligentsia and the entry of the working classes into political life, the subject races recovered conscious national individuality and entered upon a bitter struggle against the master nations.

While the Europe of 1848 resonated in the events of the unraveling USSR, the experience of 1905 more precisely resembled the struggles of the nations of the USSR. In 1905, the Russian empire was dealt a severe setback through its defeat in the Russo-Japanese War. The failure of the Russian army created a crisis of confidence in the ruling czarist elite and encouraged revolutionary agitation and unrest. Still, the year-long revolution of 1905 was, above all, a rising of the Russian empire's peripheries—populated mainly by non-Russians. Its eventual failure resulted from a lack of cohesiveness among the dissatisfied middle classes, discontented workers, and impoverished peasants.

The condition of Europe from 1848 to 1914 resembled the processes surrounding the recent movement of the peoples that brought about the fall of the Soviets. Today among the peoples of the former USSR there exist the same strata described by Namier. Among the historic nations are the peoples of the Baltic seacoast—the Lithuanians, Estonians, and Latvians—and the Georgians and Armenians of the Caucasus. Each of those nations preserved a great measure of cultural continuity and a sense of national political tradition, despite the traumas of Communist repression. There was a middle, transitional stratum—consisting of the Ukrainians, the Belarusians, and the Azerbaijanis. The former two are Slavic nations, whose ruling classes had been Russified, cultural elites marginalized, and cultural continuity disrupted by the carnage of Stalinism. In the Gorbachev years, these peoples made significant progress in rebuilding their sundered national, cultural, and political institutions. Similarly, the Turkic Azerbaijanis, led by the intelligentsia and workers of Baku, have succeeded in building a sophisticated national movement. These three peoples clearly had reached the point where a "new middle-class intelligentsia" and the working class massively entered political life.

The remaining large non-Russian nations—the Turkic-speaking Uzbeks and Kazakhs—were further behind. The processes of political mobilization had occurred, but their educated middle classes and their working classes were far less extensive than those of other mobilized non-Russian peoples. While an atomized peasantry is still the dominant class in terms of population, they are clearly embarking on the process of political mobilization, and their newfound state independence is likely to accelerate the process.

Occupying an as yet ambiguous place in this scheme is the predominant nation of the new Commonwealth of Independent States—the Russians—who have a clearly defined ruling elite, but who are seeking to define their own national identity in a post-Soviet and postimperial age. Russian history was long lionized in the Soviet state-controlled media and in the education system, but even as it was glorified, it was also altered and fundamentally distorted. Before the recent emergence of Boris Yeltsin, Russians never articulated a sense of the limits of their own ethnos; they lived instead with only a vague notion of where their state and people begin and end.

If nationalism in the nineteenth century was heroic and democratic, nationalism in the twentieth century took a far different turn, a detour. National socialism and fascism severed the link between nationalism and democracy. Today, many in the West, particularly Americans, regard nationalism as an ideology of extremism and backwardness. For them, the images of nationalism include Mussolini's jackboot and Hitler's gas chamber, and represent an atavism commingled with irrational paganism in the metaphors of blood and soil.

Contemporary perceptions of nationalism, too, were shaped by the national liberation struggles conducted against Western European colonies in Asia and Africa and against American geopolitical interests in the rice paddies of Southeast Asia. In this latter variant, nationalism was linked in Western consciousness to economic backwardness and marginality. It was a manifestation of the rage of the permanently disadvantaged, often erupting into the mass murder represented by Pol Pot's killing fields. The experience of fascism, decolonization, Vietnam, and Kampuchea became part of a mythology that hindered Americans and Europeans in understanding and endorsing the national awakening in the Soviet Union. As the essayist William Pfaff noted, America's historic failure has been its inability to factor the power and persistence of nationalism around the world into its foreign policy.

Yet ideas of democracy found strength precisely in the new redoubts of nationalism around the unraveling Soviet empire. Poland's Solidarity movement was, after all, driven as much by the logic of Polish patriotism and wounded dignity as by trade union solidarity. In Hungary, Czechoslovakia, and Bulgaria, the recent democratic upsurge sprang not only from a desire to restore cultures debased by Marxism-Leninism but also from opposition to the chilling presence of Soviet troops. Protesters in the streets of Prague, Warsaw, Budapest, and Sofia were driven by anger at the violation of their national sovereignty as well as by a generalized unhappiness at the failure of the Russian-imposed Communist economic and social model.

The non-Russian peoples of the Soviet Union felt similarly. They were brutalized and dehumanized by almost three-quarters of a century of totalitarianism. For non-Russians, Marxism-Leninism was an alien ideology. In most of the non-Russian republics, the Soviet system had been imposed by a foreign Red Army, often aided and abetted by a segment of the Russian-dominated urban population. The idea that there were authentic Communist revolutions in the non-Russian nations was a fiction given reality only by the instruments of Soviet propaganda. The violence that erupted in several republics has fueled the notion that the leaders of the national movements of the non-Russian peoples are voices of atavistic tribal instincts. Yet this popular view verges on a new form of racism, stemming from a near total unfamiliarity with the cultural, religious, and political traditions of the non-Russian nations, and reflecting a belief that a single, albeit immensely powerful, USSR was for all its faults inherently stable. The collapse of the USSR, many in the West believed, would bring about the Balkanization of a vast Eurasian landmass riddled with unstable border disputes.

But most Democrats in the USSR did not share those fears. The late Dr. Andrey Sakharov in his last months became a strong defender of the national movements in the Baltic States, Armenia, and Ukraine. This towering moral figure clearly did not give credence to the theory that the growing proindependence movements might help unsettle the process of democratization.

In the last years of Soviet rule, with centralized power under increasing pressure, the Soviet authorities desperately sought to paint a picture of a country dangerously close to a bloody abyss. On July 1, 1989, Mikhail Gorbachev took over the Soviet airwaves to deliver a widely publicized major address on the theme of relations among the nationalities. The twenty-minute address came after a tumultuous month of mounting inter-ethnic turmoil and death in Uzbekistan, Kazakhstan, and Georgia. Speaking in measured, somber, even angry tones, Gorbachev warned of a "tremendous danger" arising from interethnic conflicts. He resolutely denounced those who were sowing interethnic hatred and fanning the flames of separatism and nationalism. He warned that he would take "the most resolute measures, in accordance with the requirements of law and the people's vital interests, against those who provoke interethnic clashes and call for borders to be redrawn and for the expulsion of national minorities."

Gorbachev made an impassioned appeal to the intelligentsia, urging it to behave responsibly, and in rather demagogic fashion exhorted the Soviet working class to exercise its internationalist obligations:

> We must not take the road of destroying . . . and abandoning what the federation has already yielded, which can be magnified within its framework. Therefore, calls for economic autarky and spiritual isolation must be deemed profoundly alien to the vital interests of any people and of the entire society. Their implementation would throw us all a long, long way back and bring immense material and moral losses to each nation and every person.

In September 1989, just days before a critical Communist Party plenum to examine the question of interethnic relations, Gorbachev delivered yet another somber-toned address to the nation, in which he retreated from his cataclysmic scenarios of ethnic strife and concentrated on excoriating those alarmists who were opposed to his program of perestroika. Downplaying the idea that the rise of ethnic movements was tearing the USSR apart, Gorbachev told Soviet citizens, "It is a fact that some people would like to create . . . an atmosphere of alarm, a feeling that there is no way out, a feeling of uncertainty." Instead of retrenching, however, the Soviet leader promised to "continue along the road of planned change."

In 1990, Gorbachev alternated between intimidation and negotiation as he grappled with the movements for independence. After Lithuania's declaration of independence on March 11, 1990, the Soviet president responded with an economic blockade. By June, however, Gorbachev had moved away from confrontation, indicating that he was ready to negotiate with the Baltic States and with all the USSR's constituent republics about independence or sovereignty within a radically decentralized USSR.

Gorbachev was never consistent in his dealings with the restive republics of his unraveling Union. As 1989 drew to a close, a sequence of events became a case in point. Although the Party he headed and the deputy prime minister he had put in place—the moderate Leonid Abalkin—had offered a decidedly conservative plan for restructuring relations between the Kremlin and the republics, the Supreme Soviet dealt a rebuff to the proposal to reassert the prerogative of the central state. But on November 20, 1989, the Supreme Soviet rejected by a vote of 211 to 149 a proposal that would restrict the rights of the USSR's constituent republics, doing so because the proposed legislation did not go far enough in providing independence from Moscow's central control.

The effort, led by nationalist-minded legislators from the Baltic republics, could not have succeeded without the tacit support of Gorbachev, as no more than 20 percent of the membership of the Supreme Soviet was in the hands of democratic reformers. Growing ferment throughout the Soviet bloc contributed to the change of thinking within the Soviet legislative hierarchy. While Gorbachev clearly hoped that some limited concessions toward home rule would dampen the trend toward independence that was gaining momentum on the peripheries of the USSR, the maneuver failed.

Just days before the vote on national sovereignty was taken, the then Communist-led legislature of Soviet Georgia unanimously reaffirmed the "holy and inviolable right" to secede from the USSR and asserted its view that Georgia had been annexed to the USSR as a result of "military intervention and occupation." In so voting, the Georgians affirmed the sovereign rights of their republic following action taken by the legislatures of Azerbaijan, Estonia, Latvia, and Lithuania that had proclaimed the right to veto any legislation passed by the central USSR legislature. In January 1990 the Communist Party of Lithuania likewise rebuffed Gorbachev's entreaties and voted for complete independence from the CPSU. Only days later, as Soviet troops moved into Azerbaijan to quell separatist opposition under cover of stopping ethnic rioting, the legislature there warned that it would proclaim the republic's secession from the USSR unless all Soviet occupational forces were removed from its territory.

In the face of secessionist threats in Azerbaijan, the Soviet authorities were forced to acknowledge that a dialogue with the leaders of the popular fronts was inevitable. And as the Baltic States of Lithuania and Estonia moved toward independence in March and April of 1990, the Kremlin's response was one of saber-rattling military maneuvers and the seizure of key buildings, not of outright repression. Still, the unwillingness or inability of Soviet authorities to introduce full-scale police state repression was more an indicator of the power of the independent movements among the non-Russians than evidence of Gorbachev's good will.

This meant that as the 1990s began, the USSR was headed for a protracted period of ideological battle and skillful use of the mass media. When necessary, the Kremlin signaled a desire for compromise to avoid resorting to martial law. Such widespread repression, Gorbachev realized, would have put an end to what he believed were the crucial reforms of glasnost and perestroika.

Critical events in 1990 showed that the struggle over the very future of the Soviet Union was advancing to another stage. By the spring of that year, a series of elections in many republics had swept democratic nationalists into power in Latvia, Lithuania, Estonia, and Armenia. In Ukraine, the Democratic bloc, supported by the Rukh, captured a quarter of the seats in the Ukrainian Supreme Soviet. Just as significantly, city councils and regional legislatures, primarily in western Ukraine, including Lviv, Ivano-Frankivsk, and Ternopil, were now led by proindependence forces. Democrats also controlled 50 percent of the capital city, Kiev's council, and an association of Democratic councils and Democratic blocs was established to coordinate activities.

By the fall of 1990, the signs of an empire in retreat, a system in decline, were evident throughout the vast expanses of the Soviet Union. At the empire's center, in the once great cities of Moscow and Saint Petersburg, residents were endlessly queuing for bread, cigarettes, and gasoline. Despite a bumper crop, the USSR's deteriorating system of harvesting, storage, and distribution ensured that the Soviet harvest was down per capita from the year before, in part a consequence of the catastrophic state of farm equipment: Some 120,000 harvesters stood as idle victims of a lack of spare parts. By the first half of 1990, economic production had fallen by 2 percent and worker productivity was down by 1.5 percent. Strikes had increased by 300 percent to an annual rate of 20 million lost work days.

In an August 29, 1990, article in the USSR government daily, *Izvestiya*,

Sergey Alekseev, head of the USSR legislature's Constitutional Oversight Committee, admitted that the legislative body's work had "found itself temporarily paralyzed" in the face of proclamations of national sovereignty or outright independence by most republics. "The real events of political life have brought [the USSR] to a point beyond which general paralysis, general incapacity, and the withering and collapse of the Union and all its institutions and subdivisions begin."

The power exercised through city, territorial, and republican councils (soviets), rapidly eroded the prerogatives and authority of the Soviet center. In Moscow and Saint Petersburg, the Baltic States, and large parts of Ukraine (including Kiev and Lviv) nationalists and Democrats controlled education, public works, and large segments of the mass media. In several republics the patriotic Democratic movements grabbed for power from an increasingly indecisive Soviet president who more and more was coming to resemble another leader who presided over a Russian empire in disintegration: Aleksandr Kerensky. At a hearing on Capitol Hill, Zbigniew Brzezinski rather matter-of-factly asserted: "The Soviet Union is doomed; it will not endure and will probably cease to exist as we know it in a few years."

A mood of crisis had infected the upper rungs of the Soviet establishment. *Pravda* editor Ivan Frolov, a Politburo member whose aquaintance with Gorbachev stems from college days, when his wife and Raisa Gorbachev were roommates, told the Italian daily *La Repubblica* in mid-July 1990: "I am beginning to fear the upheavals that could result from this revolution [perestroika]. I fear bloodshed; I fear civil war." Such fears of violence were overdrawn, part of the center's last desperate argument against the forces of democratic nationalism. In point of fact, ethnic violence had been limited to the Soviet south and was the by-product of intense poverty occasioned by malign neglect by the center. Yet even in these harsh settings, it was the national democratic movements and not the presence of the Red Army or the USSR's militia that injected into political life a climate of peaceful discourse and stability.

As 1990 drew to a close, political forces favoring national sovereignty either held a parliamentary majority or commanded the majority support of public opinion in most Soviet republics. Even the parliaments of republics with a Communist majority desperately sought to preempt proindependence forces by declaring support for "national sovereignty" and "the primacy of local laws."

In the Russian republic, where more than half the USSR's citizens lived, Boris Yeltsin pressed for a sovereign Russian state within the context of a "comity" or "confederation" of nations, in which the central state is responsible only for the coordination of defense and the maintenance of a unitary currency.

In an August 8, 1990, interview with the *Komsomolskaya Pravda*, Yeltsin was outspoken in his criticism of the Soviet empire. He called for "normal relations, not slave relations" betweeen countries and denounced the Gorbachev policy of blockading republics making a dash for independence. "With regard to Lithuania, it is a major political mistake," Yeltsin declared, "for there was no such blockade against Hungary, Czechoslovakia, or the GDR. And this is right. If a people strives for independence, you cannot restrain them by force. And the more pressure the authorities exert, the stronger the people's resistance will be." Public opinion soundings left no doubt that Yeltsin had emerged as the USSR's single-most popular politician—popular in his home base of Russia and in the non-Russian republics that saw him as a proponent of a voluntary union and so of their independence.

The Communist Party itself was rent by growing disunity. It had weathered Yeltsin's defection and those of the popular mayors of Moscow and Saint Petersburg. Yet even before their public defections, the Party suffered a net loss of about 10 percent of its total membership in 1990. As one leading Party official admitted, "A certain concern is caused by the fact that there are very few young people among the new Party members." Ivan Polozkov, the reactionary leader of the Communist Party of Russia, revealed that as a result of declining membership and collapsing revenues, the Russian Party was forced to lay off at least half of its 120,000 full-time workers despite a subsidy of 285 million rubles from the central CPSU.

The Party was also breaking up into factions, such as the Marxist platform, which espoused a backward-looking orthodoxy, and the Democratic platform, which led an exodus of disgruntled reformers to form a new rival political organization. In each of the republics, once-loyalist parties came under the pressure of nationalism, thus distancing themselves from the Soviet center. The Communist parties in Latvia, Lithuania, and Estonia had left Moscow's orbit, while those in Georgia and Armenia had been taken up by nationalist passions. Aware of the reality of a resurgent Ukrainian patriotism and driven by the revival of national communism, the Communist chairman of the Ukrainian parliament (and now president), Leonid Kravchuk, asserted on September 8, 1990: "We do not intend to create a unitarian state, but a commonwealth of free, sovereign, socialist states."

Even the Soviet military was no longer the reliable instrument for quelling nationalist unrest and protest. Disunity had infected the Soviet military, where non-Russians now represented the majority of recruits. In 1989, sixty-five hundred young men failed to appear for military duty, the lion's share of them from the Baltic States, where proindependence forces encouraged resistance to service in the "army of occupation." In the summer 1990 military call-up, massive levels of draft dodging in some republics served as a barometer of growing national discontent: In Armenia only 7.5 percent of the expected recruits turned up; in Georgia, 27.5 percent; in Lithuania, 33 percent; in Estonia, 40 percent; and in Latvia, only 54 percent of the expected draftees reported.

Soviet draftees, particularly non-Russians, were swept up in the national reawakening of their republics. Many had been active participants in patriotic demonstrations, general strikes, and informal youth organizations. This politicization created growing conflicts with ethnic Russian recruits that have led to the mistreatment and even murder of soldiers from Latvia, Estonia, Lithuania, Georgia, Azerbaijan, and Central Asia. According to Georgetown's Murray Feshbach, of 3,900 noncombat-related deaths, nearly 3,000 were linked to ethnic-related hazing, bullying, and male rape.

Economic decline and growing signs of the collapse of the Soviet state forced Kremlin authorities into action. Throughout the fall and into the winter of 1990, the Soviet press began to feature articles arguing for a return of the iron hand. As part of the counterattack on proindependence forces, hard-line Communist Party activists in the republics began to play on ethnic Russian fears in an attempt to build opposition to new governments in the republics. It was in this period that the interfronts and intermovements began to mobilize demonstrations in the Baltics while local Communists proclaimed an independent Dniester republic in Moldova. In a bid to cause difficulties for Boris Yeltsin's increasingly independent-minded course, and to insulate themselves against democratic reforms, local hard-line Communist authorities pressed for regional sovereignty within the Russian Federation. All these movements and difficulties have persisted into the post-Soviet period.

At the end of 1990, Gorbachev began to turn to the right. In mid-October, the Soviet president rejected economist Stanislav Shatalin's republic-favoring 500-days plan that would have ceded significant economic and political power to the republics. Instead, the USSR Supreme Soviet voted to give Gorbachev sweeping powers to issue decrees with the force of law. The legislature also adopted a document titled "Basic Directions for the Stabilization of the National Economy and Transition to a Market Economy" that, despite its high-minded title, strengthened the powers of the central USSR government at the expense of the republics.

In the weeks that followed, Gorbachev threw in his lot with the very forces that just months later would later conspire to stage a coup d'état. With 1990 drawing to a close, Gorbachev began perfervidly to denounce nationalist and democratic forces in the republics. On December 17, in a speech to the Congress of People's Deputies, Gorbachev denounced separatist tendencies in the republics, blaming them for bringing the USSR to a state of "chaos." On December 19, Soviet Chief of the General Staff Mikhail Moiseev, Russian Orthodox patriarch Aleksey II, and writer Yury Bondarev called for the imposition of a "state of emergency." Appearing to oblige, Gorbachev declared that he was considering the imposition of a "state of emergency or presidential rule" in major conflict zones. On December 20, amid this mounting hard-line rhetoric, Gorbachev's close colleague, Foreign Minister Eduard Shevardnadze, resigned and warned that "dictatorship was coming. If you create a dictatorship," Shevardnadze said, "no one can say who will become the dictator."

In a New Year's message to the people, President Gorbachev emphasized that "no cause [was] more sacred" than the preservation of the USSR. It soon became clear by what means he intended to preserve that union. On January 2, 1991, special forces of the USSR Ministry of Internal Affairs seized the main publishing plant in Riga, Latvia. In the days that followed, the Police Special Duties Detachment (OMON) took control of Communist Party buildings and offices in the three Baltic States. On January 13, Soviet troops initiated a bloody takeover of the Vilnius television broadcasting tower, and the wave of repression in Lithuania took at least fifteen lives. Similar military actions claimed additional victims in Estonia and Latvia. As the events in the Baltics unfolded, censorship of the USSR's press and television was tightened. Popular independent television programs were banned and the brutal suppression in the Baltics was distorted before millions of Soviet television viewers.

A combination of Western condemnation and wide-ranging protests in Russia led to a halt in the violent repression and to a retreat from the hard line. In retrospect, it is probable that the crackdown was less an attempt to reimpose a full-scale dictatorship than an effort to weaken democratic nationalist movements in the weeks leading up to Gorbachev's referendum on the future of the USSR. That referendum, held on March 17, 1991, asked an ambiguous if not contradictory question: "Do you consider necessary the preservation of the Union of Soviet Socialist Republics as a renewed federation of equal sovereign republics in which the rights and freedoms of an individual of any nationality will be fully guaranteed?" The question thus linked the ideas of federation, basic rights and freedoms, and sovereignty in a bid to maximize support for the USSR.

Throughout the USSR, amid a voter turnout of 80 percent, about 76 percent of the voters endorsed the Union. Yet considering the overwhelming barrage of pro-Union propaganda, the results could not have been entirely reassuring to the Soviet leadership. The governments of Georgia, Armenia, Lithuania, Latvia, Estonia, and Moldova did not consent to the referendum. In Azerbaijan, Communist authorities decided to go ahead with the poll at the last minute, claiming that 75 percent of voters turned out and 92 percent supported the referendum question. But leaders of the Popular Front of Azerbaijan, which called for a boycott, claimed that the real turnout had been closer to 15 percent. In Belarus, the "yes" vote was 83 percent amid a voter turnout of 83 percent, and similar results were yielded in Central Asia. In Ukraine, amid an 80 percent turnout, 70 percent supported the Union, while 80 percent endorsed a second question that affirmed Ukraine's sovereignty. Opposition to the USSR was overwhelming in western Ukraine and in the capital, Kiev.

While Boris Yeltsin did not explicitly oppose the referendum, he warned that a "yes" vote would mean support for a policy "aimed at preserving the imperial, unitary structure of the Union." For this reason, he was prevented from addressing the Russian people on the eve of the vote, yet there was widespread opposition to the Union in major Russian urban centers. Overall, in Russia the "yes" vote was 71 percent, with 70 percent voting in favor of a second question that established the elected office of president for the republic, while in the politically active central cities of Moscow and Saint Petersburg, nearly half of all voters opposed the Union. And in Yeltsin's hometown of Ekaterinburg, only 34 percent did so. In all these areas, the Democratic Russia movement was well organized.

If Gorbachev had hoped that the referendum would stem the tide of separatism, he was quickly disappointed. Nevertheless, the referendum's results did make it possible for Gorbachev to convince his Politburo and Kremlin colleagues that it would be possible to reach an agreement with the leaders of most republics. The momentum to quickly conclude an agreement with Yeltsin and other republic leaders was given added impetus by a widening wave of strikes. Begun in March 1991 by coal miners in Vorkuta and the Kuznetsk coal basin of Russia, the Donbass and Lviv regions of Ukraine, and in Karaganda in Kazakhstan, industrial unrest soon spread to Belarus, which had long been regarded as one of the most economically prosperous and quiescent republics. The worker protests, which demanded new elections, the banning of the Communist Party, and the resignation of the Soviet government, frightened the central authorities. Gorbachev and his Kremlin colleagues moved quickly to try to reach an accommodation.

That accommodation, known as the nine-plus-one agreement, was reached in Novo-Ogaryevo, a dacha on the outskirts of Moscow. Gorbachev expected the Novo-Ogaryevo pact to lead to the quick ratification of a new Union treaty. Yet on June 27, 1991, the Ukrainian parliament, under strong pressure from its nationalist movement, decided to postpone a discussion of the draft treaty until mid-September. Another factor weakened the Soviet president's hand: By June, Yeltsin had won the election as president of the RFSFR with 57.5 percent of the vote. Gorbachev's preferred candidate—his former prime minister, Nikolay Ryzhkov—came in a poor second with 17.5 percent of the vote in a six-way race.

With his new mandate, Yeltsin proceeded to blaze a trail for Russia's state independence. He declared that after Russia signed the Union treaty, the central authorities would relinquish to the republics all power with the exception of defense, border control, railway transportation, and communication. All political and economic decisions would be the province of republics.

Russia, Kazakhstan, and Uzbekistan were to sign the Union treaty on August 20, 1991, with the Central Asian republics and Belarus quickly to follow. But at 6:00 A.M. on August 19, Soviet television reported that a temporary Committee for the State of Emergency had taken power. The announcement said that in view of President Gorbachev's poor health, his vice president, Gennady Yanaev, was carrying out the president's functions.

The leaders of the coup, united in a body that was soon calling itself the State Committtee for the State of Emergency, made it clear that they were acting to help preserve the Soviet Union. One year after the putsch, Gorbachev's traitorous vice president Yanaev explicitly asserted that the main reason for the coup was to defend the unity of the USSR against centrifugal forces in the republics and against the Union treaty. In an August 1992 interview on Soviet television Yanaev, who served as the state committee's formal head, stated: "A great country was in the process of being destroyed. My colleagues and I wanted to make one last effort to try to save it." Similar motives were echoed in comments by Vladimir Kryuchkov, who, as head of the KGB, had been in charge of much of the planning of the fatally flawed gambit: "History will hold responsible for the fate of the Soviet Union not those who made an attempt to save it, but those who ruined our powerful and united motherland." But the coup leaders, detached from public opinion after their many years at the pinnacle of power, could not appreciate the power that the ideas of sovereignty and national independence had acquired, and failed to understand the bond that now existed between citizens and their democratically elected leaders.

The true story of the August 1991 coup and President Gorbachev's role in it remains to be written. It is clear that the Soviet president was present at Politburo meetings in 1990 at which violent provocations were planned in the Baltic States, so it is not out of the question that, as the prominent Russian dissident Vladimir Bukovsky speculated, Gorbachev agreed to the idea of introducing a state of emergency at an appropriate moment. Yet the timing of the coup went against everything Gorbachev wanted. He believed he had struck a compromise with Boris Yeltsin and other republic leaders that would preserve a unified, if circumscribed, central state.

There are many theories about why the coup didn't succeed, but the least plausible is the one most readily offered: that the bungling and incompetence of the coup plotters led to failure. The putsch was initiated by the top figures in the Communist Party, the military, and the KGB, who would not have stepped into action without a clear and decisive course of action.

The coup failed because of the growing power of republican sovereignty. The lasting image of the famous days of August 1991 is that of the white-blue-red Russian tricolor. It was no accident that the flag that represented a sovereign Russian state was used to rally the people in the struggle against the Soviet state's last desperate effort at self-preservation. Hundreds of thousands of Russian soldiers had voted for Yeltsin just weeks before, just as hundreds of thousands of soldiers had voted for their leaders in Ukraine, the Baltic States, Georgia, and Armenia. This duality of power contributed to the erosion of loyalty to the central state and made it possible for new centers of power to organize resistance. In this sense, patriotism played a central role in the collapse of the coup.

The coup also failed because of a profound split at the heart of the military-industrial complex. One instrument for that split was the USSR Scientific and Industrial Union (now the Russian Union of Industrialists and Entrepreneurs), a then-little-known association headed by a former aide to Yury Andropov, Arkady Volsky. Volsky's organization became the instrument that sharpened the division of the progressive, reform-oriented captains of Soviet industry from their more backward counterparts. Volsky's union also played an essential role in linking the huge industrial molochs, the grandchildren of Stalinist economics, including much of the military-industrial complex, to the reformist entrepreneurs, cooperative movement activists, and leaseholders, who now are said to constitute as much as 15 percent of the Soviet work force. And while Volsky himself may have tried to hedge his bets before the final outcome, many of his colleagues were forthright in their support of Boris Yeltsin.

The failure of the coup accelerated the process of imperial disintegration. The tumultuous events of August 19–21 destroyed the cohesiveness of the three pillars of the Soviet state: the Communist Party, the KGB, and the military. The banned Party collapsed or had been driven underground. With its offices shut down and its bank accounts frozen, the news media in Russia and Ukraine began revealing sensational details of illegal and wasteful Communist financial doings. The KGB, which formerly had a force of 488,000 workers, in large measure was broken up along republic lines, and part of its personnel laid off or transferred to other jurisdictions. The army and military also began to fragment and certainly were in no mood to intervene directly to preserve the old order.

If the Soviet Union in 1990 could be described as a society undergoing disintegration and collapse, the post-Soviet setting could be described as one of fast-paced nation-building and democratic reconstruction. The collapse of central authority in its military, governmental, and ideological dimensions was matched by an invigorating process of consolidation among democratic nationalists, particularly in Russia and Ukraine. In this setting, Boris Yeltsin and other leaders of the new nation states that emerged from the ashes of the Soviet Union had reason to celebrate. They had peacefully secured independence for their nations and unraveled the world's last empire with a minimum of upheaval and almost no bloodshed. At the heart of President Yeltsin's statecraft was his embrace of an anticolonial program aimed at the dissolution of the USSR, a political program that was a product of the thinking of the *mladoturki*, the "Young Turks" in the Russian president's entourage. They included longtime Yeltsin cohort Gennady Burbulis, the able foreign minister Andrey Kozyrev, and economics minister (and later, Acting Prime Minister) Yegor Gaidar.

For months after the August 1991 coup, it was not entirely clear how quickly the Soviet Union would unravel. And if it is true that President Yeltsin vacillated in the first weeks after the coup, Gorbachev's unwillingness to promote decentralization forced Yeltsin's hand and strengthened the arguments of the "Young Turks," who were eager to get on with reform and nation-building within Russia.

In the weeks after the putsch, Gorbachev's irrelevance became more and more apparent with each passing day. The country he claimed to rule was no more. Gorbachev's central state was taking a daily beating in the increasingly independent republics. In Azerbaijan all USSR government offices were ordered closed as of October 19, 1991. By late November, Yeltsin had taken control of the economic levers of central state power, when he announced that Russia would cease payments to support the work of more than seventy central ministries. In all, some 100,000 bureaucrats from Gorbachev's apparatus appeared to be headed for the unemployment line. Even when this dismissal was revoked, it was clear that President Yeltsin and not President Gorbachev controlled the purse strings and was paying the salaries of the central state's apparatus. When conflicts arose among the republics, it was Yeltsin and Nursultan Nazarbaev who plunged into action, as when they brokered a temporary respite to the Armenian-Azerbaijani conflict in early October. When contentious economic issues such as dividing the Soviet debt were at issue, it was Kiev—not Moscow—that was the venue and Ukrainian leader Leonid Kravchuk—not Gorbachev—who hosted the deliberations. Gorbachev was also deliberately excluded when ministers and presidents of the republics gathered in Alma Ata, Kazakhstan, to initiate the basis of a post-Soviet economic community. And it was Minsk, the former USSR's westernmost capital, that became the venue of the empire's Iron Curtain call.

December 8, 1991, marked the end of the USSR, buried by the democratically elected presidents of Ukraine and Russia, with the concurrence of Belarus's parliamentary chairman, Stanislav Shushkevich. Together they signed the obituary of the last empire: "The Union of Soviet Socialist Republics," they asserted, "as a subject of international law, and a geopolitical reality, is ceasing its existence." Their declaration was a call upon the world community to withdraw diplomatic recognition from the Soviet Union and to confer recognition upon the newly independent republics turned full-fledged states.

In dispensing with Gorbachev's USSR, the legitimate leaders of Europe's new nation states were not opting for anarchy and civil war, but rather creating a loose new structure: the Commonwealth of Independent States. Though their action was driven by urgency and necessity, it was hardly the irrational act of three careless men. As events later showed, Yelstin, Kravchuk, and Shushkevich would not have acted without at least some assurance from the Soviet military that it would back their gambit.

The urgency of their undertaking was made clear by a worsening economic crisis, paralysis of the institutions of a now feckless, if not willfully destructive, central state, and military uncertainty about whom to serve. The new Commonwealth of Independent States was further proof that democratic nationalism and the desire for statehood were the main political engine in the collapse of communism and the unraveling of the empire. As early as October 1991, the USSR had been replaced by a loose economic community. After the coup, less than half of the former USSR's fifteen republics—Russia, Belarus, Kazakhstan, Uzbekistan, Kyrgyzstan, Turkmenistan, and Tajikistan—participated in the reorganized Supreme Soviet. Yet even this parliamentary structure, which underwent a facelift following the August coup, could not survive. It was too closely linked to the discredited Soviet central state. By December 11, the Supreme Soviet of the USSR, with Russia and Belarus no longer participating, could no longer even muster a quorum. Its only significant legislative initiative came on November 19: a law guaranteeing deputies six months' severance pay in the event of the dissolution of the parliament.

In a news conference given just two weeks before his Christmas Day resignation, Mikhail Gorbachev lashed out at the Yeltsin camp's antiimperial designs:

> I could sense that there were secret schemes afoot and certain premises behind this. . . . It is Burbulis's blueprint. At some stage he wrote a memorandum. I have it. It made the rounds. . . . It was marked Strictly Confidential. What, briefly, is the gist of the memorandum? It is that Russia already had lost half of what it had gained in the August putsch. Cunning Gorbachev is weaving nets, seeking to restore the old center in the eyes of the world. Republics unfavorably disposed to Russia will back him. The process has to be stopped. The Yavlinsky [economic] plan involved a strong center, and so on. Our plan is as follows: independent republics, or rather states, and a soft union for the divorce proceedings—not in order to cooperate, but to strengthen independence.

Even if we allow for a certain measure of hyperbole in the thenembattled Soviet president's remarks, Gorbachev was clearly suggesting that the Yeltsin camp knowingly orchestrated the collapse of the Soviet Union and was using the Commonwealth of Independent States as a structure through which to move away from the empire.

Although, like Mikhail Gorbachev, Boris Yeltsin may not have fully anticipated the powerful sentiment for statehood in the non-Russian states, he had long made it clear that he would not be party to the use of force to hold the USSR together. Yeltsin's Democratic Russia bloc had taken the first steps toward defining a specifically Russian national interest as early as March 1990, when public opinion polls already showed that high proportions of Russians backed the right of republics to secede from the USSR. While Gorbachev imposed an economic blockade on Lithuania in 1990, Yeltsin signed bilateral economic agreements between Russia and the Baltic States to break the boycott. While Gorbachev sanctioned the use of brute force to suppress the Baltic freedom movement in the winter of 1991, Yeltsin called for Gorbachev's resignation. Yeltsin and his entourage successfully staked their political careers on a sense that the Russian nation was ready to turn inward, to take care of its own problems, and to retreat from its traditional role of helping to sustain the Soviet empire.

After the coup failed, Yeltsin initially appeared to support the building of a new, albeit sharply reduced, central state structure for a union of sovereign states. In the end Yeltsin was won over to the anti-Union, anti-imperial camp by arguments that Russia stood a better chance of attaining democracy and prosperity if it decided to go it alone. The overwhelming Ukrainian vote for independence on December 1, 1991, also convinced Yeltsin that it was folly to press for the renewal of a Union state.

Yeltsin and his allies sensed the democratizing power of the movements that pressed for national self-determination in the republics. Yet because Russia inherited the bulk of the military of the former Soviet Union, and because the military elite was steeped in an ideology that aimed to preserve the multinational, Russian-dominated state, Yeltsin was careful not to take the lead in pressing for an end to the USSR. Such a role could well have eroded the strong backing he had earned among younger officers in the June 1991 presidential election. By playing the anti-imperial game skillfully and carefully and waiting for Ukraine's vote for independence to seal the fate of the Soviet Union, Yeltsin earned the trust of the USSR's military leaders.

The year 1992 signaled a period of intense nation-building. As 1992 drew to a close, fifteen new states moved to establish their own military forces, put their own economies in order, introduce their own currencies, and determine the shape of their economic, political, and security relationships. Without question, these opportunities would not have been there if not for the patriotic movements that had emerged in the late 1980s. Communist collapse and imperial disintegration were, in the end, inextricably linked. Without the mobilizing power of nationalism, the fall of the Soviets and of totalitarian rule would not have occurred, and the reemergence of civil society and the prospects for democratic transformation of the old Soviet order would have been at best remote.

Chapter Two

The Rulers and the Ruled: The Economics of Inequality

Citizens of the USSR of different races and nationalities have equal rights. Any direct or indirect limitation of the rights of citizens or establishment of direct or indirect privileges on a racial or national basis . . . is punishable by law.

SOVIET CONSTITUTION, ARTICLE 36 (1977)

Scholars and experts will long debate the root causes of the collapse of the Soviet Union. Yet there can be no question that one of the principal reasons for the unraveling of the totalitarian empire and the reemergence of nationalism described earlier was the Soviet Union's pattern of social and economic inequity.

Great movements of people arise from fundamental social causes. Certainly the mass opposition movements of the non-Russian peoples could not have emerged on the scale they did in the late 1980s and early 1990s without firm roots in profound social, economic, cultural, or political inequalities. Yet the reality of social and economic injustice had long been among the Soviet Union's darkest secrets, buried by the strictly controlled Soviet press and the USSR's politically manipulated academic community. However, in the endless flow of government statistics published in the USSR, there was clear evidence of profound national and even racial inequities at the core of daily Soviet life. Not only did the state-run Soviet media keep this reality from broader public awareness and out of public discourse at home, but Western Sovietologists also paid little attention to the profound ethnic and racial inequalities among the peoples of the USSR. When similar inequities in the United States began to be widely reported and subjected to extensive and vigorous debate in the early 1960s under pressure from the growing civil rights movement, interest in such inequities in the USSR began to wane among Western scholars, who became more interested in uncovering the sources of Soviet stability.

In the context of the fall of the Soviets, gross inequities among the republics and peoples that made up the USSR are now understood to have been one of the main causes of national upheaval and of imperial disintegration. The seven-decades-long experiment launched by the October Revolution claimed as its aim the promotion and safeguarding of the equality of peoples—rights guaranteed by the Soviet constitution. Yet this laudable goal proved very far from realization. Not only did the Communist experiment fail to create equality among the nations of the USSR, but, under Mikhail Gorbachev's rule, such inequity had in some instances widened. In broad relief, inequities between Russians and non-Russians in the USSR were significant and their consequences far-reaching.

Non-Russians, particularly the Turkic peoples of Soviet Central Asia and the smaller nationalities in the autonomous republics of the Russian Soviet Federative Socialist Republic (RSFSR), found themselves at a profound cultural, economic, educational, and social disadvantage. Despite the many economic privations confronting most citizens of the Russian republic, it paid to be Russian in Gorbachev's USSR.

The upsurge in non-Russian national discontent that swept the Soviet Union in the Gorbachev years brought long-simmering national problems of the Soviet Union into the international news headlines. In turn, the Western media and Soviet affairs experts from the United States and Western Europe sought to account for this unprecedented outburst of nationalism, a force that in recent years had been all but ignored. In its early stages, the nationalist upsurge that began in 1987 was interpreted as a series of isolated phenomena. While group enmities were frequently reported as the products of historic animosities and local political misrule, the persistence of these phenomena confounded Western commentators, who could not account for the wave upon wave of non-Russian protests. Few answers were offered by Soviet academics, because the issue of nationalism in the Soviet Union has long been relegated to the domain of linguistics experts and ethnographers. Some commentators put forth spectacularly wrong judgments on the root causes of growing non-Russian protests and national conflicts, ignoring the essential motivation of the mass protests—the imperial nature of the Party-state system and its social and economic injustices. With time, some press commentators began to draw on the analogy of empire in order to explain the ongoing manifestations of nationalism. While British journalists, particularly mindful of the experience of the twilight of their own empire, began to employ a few references to colonialism and exploitation, few commentators went much beyond examining population statistics and demographic trends to take a look at the economics of ethnicity in the USSR.

For anyone interested in probing, the evidence of inequality was easy to find. During a visit to Yugoslavia in March 1988, Gorbachev himself admitted to a group of reporters that the upsurge in national unrest could be attributed to the fact that the Soviet south had "been neglected for a long time" by past Party leaders. Because glasnost had given the Soviet press some breathing room, reporters slowly began to be more explicit in their discussions of the "nationalities question" as a product of economic and social dissatisfaction. Still, official Soviet explanations only hinted at the dimension of the problem and shied away from analyzing in detail the systematic pattern of advantages enjoyed by ethnic Russians—both those who resided in the Russian republic and those who occupied disproportionately privileged positions in the fourteen non-Russian republics.

There can be no doubt that economic factors were central to the growing discontent within the Soviet republics. The 145 million ethnic Russians who represented approximately half (50.8 percent) of the Soviet population were the beneficiaries of significant advantages in virtually all spheres of life. A Soviet statistical handbook, issued in 1987 to commemorate seventy years of Soviet power, provides ample evidence of this pattern of advantage, as do statistics contained in 1979 and 1989 census data and other statistical handbooks. The following patterns of inequality come from these Soviet sources and point to the reasons why the USSR unraveled and why, in the wake of its unraveling, the legacy of inequality continues to complicate economic and political relations among the successor states.

The RSFSR was the USSR's largest republic with a population of 147 million, of which 81.3 percent were Russians. Although it accounted for about 50 percent of the Soviet population, in 1986 the fixed assets of the RSFSR accounted for 61 percent of the USSR's fixed assets in construction, industry, and agriculture. Per capita, by the beginning of 1987 there were 46.5 percent more such fixed assets invested in the Russian republic than in the non-Russian republics. Under Mikhail Gorbachev, trends in capital investment did nothing to counter this disparity. Within the planned economy, there was over the years an implied policy of allocating an increasing proportion of resources to predominantly Russian regions, frequently at the expense of non-Russians. In 1986, Gorbachev's first full year in power, new capital investments in the RSFSR rose to 62.4 percent of all Soviet capital expenditures—and in absolute terms were 66 percent greater than for the non-Russian republics.

Some argue that these inequities were largely the consequence of historic differences in the patterns of development of the various republics, traceable to the legacy of czarist rule. While this may have been true in the first decades of Soviet rule, the socioeconomic landscape after two-thirds of a century of central economic planning could only be regarded as explicitly Soviet, a deliberate effort to retard the economic growth of some of the republics. In Ukraine, for example, decisions made by the central planners in Moscow took away more than was provided, and there was evidence of economic plundering. In a 1977 study, Zenon L. Melnyk, professor of finance at the University of Cincinnati, demonstrated that some 20 percent of national income was transferred each year from Ukraine to other parts of the Soviet Union—a level that was "unprecedented in international economic relations." Such income transfers were one reason why Ukrainians and other non-Russians became ever more determined to press for the economic accountability principle of *khozraschet*, by which each republic hoped to openly demonstrate the disadvantages conferred on non-Russians. In time, however, even such tinkering with the system proved unacceptable, and the non-Russians denounced with growing vehemence the inequities of the pricing, investment, and allocation decisions of the five-year-plan economic system. Non-Russian popular fronts, therefore, were nearly unanimous in their belief that all economic decisions and control over natural resources should be turned over to the republics.

Equally culpable were the USSR State Planning Committee (Gosplan) and the Ministry of Finance, whose commodity price structuring had been to the non-Russian republics' economic disadvantage. The republics argued for policies that would link Soviet pricing to the international market and create internal market mechanisms. At the Congress of the Ukrainian nationalist movement, the Rukh, held in Kiev in September 1989, Volodymyr Chernyak, an economist and member of the USSR Congress of People's Deputies, reflected a growing sentiment among the non-Russian movements when, in his economic keynote speech, he coined the slogan From a Free Market to a Free Ukraine.

In the last years of Soviet rule, television viewers grew accustomed to a steady flow of news reports on the economic hardships faced by the residents of Moscow and other Russian centers. There is no question that millions upon millions of Russians lived and continue to live in appalling conditions. The strike in July 1989 by hundreds of thousands of coal miners in such regions of Russia as the Kuznetsk Basin and in Vorkuta vividly demonstrated the misery of everyday life. While such sharp images of indigence should have conveyed the even more disastrous economic status of many non-

Russians, official statistics indicated that in broad economic terms, ethnic Russians clearly came out on top in the Soviet Union.

Although prices throughout the USSR were centrally determined and identical under Soviet rule, blue- and white-collar workers in the RSFSR earned over 11 percent more than their counterparts in the non-Russian republics. This national wage gap widened even farther in the Russians' favor among collective and state farm workers. Not only did the Soviet system enable Russians to earn more, it also enabled them to purchase more. While retail trade statistics measuring per capita purchases of foodstuffs, clothing, electronics, automobiles, and other consumer goods showed a 30 percent advantage for residents of the Russian republic, the difference throughout the Union was probably even greater, for in the non-Russian republics ethnic Russians received a disproportionate share of the better-paying and influential jobs and greater opportunities to settle in the urban centers, where they were able to take advantage of cultural, educational, and social amenities less available in the underdeveloped rural regions.

The Urban Advantage

Anyone who traveled through the former Soviet Union could see the vast disparities between urban and rural life. Housing in many rural communities was ramshackle, without running water, adequate heating, or telephone service. Most villages were far removed from decent public transportation and had no cinemas or cultural centers. In short, villagers lived in near total isolation. Consequently, leaders of the opposition non-Russian popular fronts—especially those in Central Asia—frequently raised the issue of urbanization, questioning why the cities and towns in their republics were so few in number and pressing for the advancement of their predominantly rural peoples. They also focused on equal opportunity and the extent to which their citizens were able to rescue themselves from the poverty of rural life by entering the industrial work force. "We need a proletariat," insisted Abdurakhim Pulatov, a leader of Uzbekistan's popular front, the Birlik (Unity) Popular Movement. His plea was not purely economic, but had important political implications as well. In an ideologically ordered society that regarded the industrial proletariat as its most progressive force, the absence of an urban working class placed more rural Uzbeks and other non-Russians at a distinct economic *and* political disadvantage.

Until it was banned in August 1991, the ruling Communist Party consistently emphasized that its policies were guided by the interests of the urban industrial working class. Because the Soviet working class was disproportionately Russian, the policies of the Party were biased in favor of the Russians. Statistics on urbanization reveal striking disparities among the republics. On the basis of figures from the 1979 census, 69 percent of the residents of the RSFSR lived in cities and towns, while 31 percent were residents of rural areas. In no other republic, except tiny Estonia, was there a higher degree of urbanization. Overall, the urbanization rate of the non-Russian regions was 53.6 percent, with the disparities being most pronounced in Tajikistan, Kyrgyzstan, Moldova, and Uzbekistan, each with a rural population of about 60 percent or more, and Turkmenistan, more than half of whose population is rural. Among the intermediate republics—with urbanization rates of between 50 and 60 percent—were Georgia, Azerbaijan, Kazakhstan, Belarus, and Lithuania. Among the more urbanized non-Russian republics were Ukraine (60.8 percent), Armenia (65.4 percent), and Latvia (67.7 percent).

This gap between Russians and non-Russians was greater still than statistics for each of the republics indicate: Among families in which all members come from one nationality (around 85 percent of all family units in the USSR), the urbanization rate was 90 percent higher among Russian families than their non-Russian counterparts. And conversely, among non-Russians, the rate of those living in the countryside was 220 percent higher than among Russian families. In 1979, around 77.4 million members of all-Russian families were living in urban centers, compared to 37.3 million non-Russians, while on the collective and state farms in the villages, the opposite was true: Non-Russian families outnumbered all-Russian families two to one (56.4 million to 28.2 million).

Even in the closed Soviet system, politics and governance were primarily urban phenomena. The urban populations have had and will continue to have the greatest influence on policies and politics within the new states that have emerged in the wake of the collapse of the USSR. Not only are all newspapers, major cultural institutions, industrial centers, and political organizations based in cities and towns, but the battles over the allocation of resources are also fought there. The dominance of the Russian population in most of these urban centers in the past assured that their voice was the best heard, both within their titular Russian republic and in most of the major urban centers of the non-Russian republics.

Now that the old totalitarian order has been sundered and many of the new states are moving toward a more pluralistic order based on power sharing and democratic governance, the influence of the urban masses will likely be further enhanced. Inevitably, urban democratic politics is likely to pit ethnic Russians against the non-Russian indigenous peoples of the newly independent states. This tension, resulting from policies pursued in the Soviet period, is likely to be a source of instability in post-Soviet life for decades to come.

Many other significant indicators of material well-being reflected the inequality for non-Russians that is the legacy of Soviet rule. In housing, for example, between 1971 and 1986 the number of new housing units built in the Russian republic was 43 percent greater than in the non-Russian republics. Even the amount of rubles spent to construct each housing unit was greater for Russians. The results of such long-term planning can be seen in one clear indicator of housing—square footage per capita. On average, there were about 161 square feet of housing space for every man, woman, or child in the USSR, or about one-third the average in the United States. This difficult housing situation is far worse in the Central Asian regions of the former USSR, where the housing situation is catastrophic. In Kazakhstan, there are 139.9 square feet of housing space per capita; in Kyrgyzstan, 121.6; in Uzbekistan, 118.4; in Azerbaijan, 113.0; in Turkmenistan, 109.8; and in Tajikistan, 93.6. While these data alone constitute a major housing crisis for the now independent republics, they reveal nothing of the often dilapidated state of such housing or the cramped conditions under which most people live, as they include in their calculations the areas occupied by kitchens, bathrooms, closet space, and internal hallways, as well as the shared spaces of the former USSR's numerous multifamily, communal apartments. But many non-Russians have taken matters into their own hands. According to detailed statistics published in 1986, there were 187.3 million square feet of housing built with private funds, about three-quarters of which was built in the non-Russian regions. Ukrainians, for example, built 300 percent more housing per capita than their Russian counterparts, while Lithuanians built 400 percent more and Uzbeks and Azerbaijanis, 500 percent. These data reveal two important facts: First, housing conditions were so appalling that they compelled non-Russians to build more shelter for themselves; and second, non-Russians were more inclined to take initiative than the more economically passive citizens of the Russian republic.

Discrepancies in health care between Russians and non-Russians were equally substantial in the twilight years of the USSR. Infant mortality rates within the non-Russian republics in 1986 were some 60 percent higher than in the RSFSR, where among children up to the age of one there were 19.3 deaths per 1,000 births. By contrast, the infant mortality rates in the non-Russian republics were significantly and sometimes drastically higher: Uzbekistan, 46.2 deaths per 1,000 births; Tajikistan, 46.7; Turkmenistan, 58.2; Kyrgyzstan, 38.2; Azerbaijan, 30.5; and Kazakhstan, 29.0. More significantly, while infant mortality between 1970 and the mid-1980s had shown an improvement of more than 17 percent in the RSFSR, infant mortality climbed in Uzbekistan by 50 percent, in Turkmenistan by 25 percent, and in Kazakhstan by 8 percent.

One important reason for these appalling discrepancies is the lack of adequate health care. Per capita, there are 19 percent more nurses and other medical personnel in the Russian republic than in the non-Russian republics, with the largest gaps evident among the Central Asians. The state of the environment also contributes to health-related disparities. Amid mounting political upheaval in the late 1980s and early 1990s, non-Russians complained about the cavalier attitude of central planners to the question of pollution in the non-Russian areas. Ukrainian activists in the Rukh, for example, noted that although their republic made up 3 percent of the territory of the USSR, fully 40 percent of all nuclear power plants were located there. Kazakhs complained that their republic has been turned into a nuclear weapons testing site, in close proximity to an important urban center, Semi-palatinsk, a region with a predominantly Kazakh population. And Uzbeks pointed to the disaster that had befallen the Aral Sea, an evaporating sewer poisoned with the toxins of insecticides used in the growing of cotton, a commodity that was produced almost exclusively in Uzbekistan against the will of the people. Such ecological catastrophes have endangered the health of the indigenous population and today pose formidable challenges for the newly formed states, some of whom seek aid to redress the effects of Soviet economic policies.

Alarming as the above disparities between Russians and non-Russians are, by far the most pronounced inequities inherited from the period of Soviet rule were to be found between the former Soviet north and the impoverished ex-Soviet south, which is populated predominantly by the Muslim, Turkic nationalities. The gaps between the white European peoples and the dark-skinned Asian peoples of the former Soviet Union are glaring. The USSR after all faced its own racial dilemmas. A Tass press agency report from September 16, 1989, admitted that in Azerbaijan "half the able-bodied population does not take part in social production."

Calculating poverty in the Soviet Union is a difficult matter, for poverty is obviously not only a matter of income. A purely statistical approach reveals nothing of the harshness of daily life and the drab misery in which most Soviet citizens lived in the late 1980s. In urban centers like Uzbekistan's capital, Tashkent, the indigenous population is crowded into tiny, dilapidated one-room dwellings, often without benefit of running water. In Baku, Azerbaijan, two hundred thousand Azerbaijanis live in a huge, jerry-built shantytown, a sprawling eyesore which the Communist authorities tried pathetically to hide by erecting a wall around it. And in the vast dismal countryside of Uzbekistan, Soviet rule meant that children whose families desperately needed the income broke up the harsh, chemically poisoned soil with sticks so that cotton could be grown and exported for hard currency. Of 56,000 inhabitants in the Kazakh town of Novy Uzen, rocked by ethnic violence in the summer of 1989, 21,200 had jobs and the official number of unemployed stood at 1,500. Tuberculosis was widespread, with approximately 2,500 cases reported in the city and the incidence of new cases steadily growing. There was no local newspaper or cultural facility. Telephone lines were restricted to government and Party offices and to members of the *nomenklatura*, the important Party posts filled only by the most suitable candidates. The inability of relatively well-paid Soviet coal miners to secure adequate housing, with water and gas heating, or to purchase such necessities as soap and detergent, was among the sparks that ignited the massive wave of strikes in Ukraine, the Kuzbas, and Kazakhstan in July 1989.

Nonetheless, in 1988 the USSR calculated the poverty level to be 78 rubles per month per capita. On the basis of that calculation, the USSR State Committee for Statistics determined that 41 million persons had incomes below 78 rubles per month, representing about 14.5 percent of the USSR's population. In the RSFSR, the percentage of those living below the poverty level stood at 6.3 percent (about 9 million residents). That meant that in the non-Russian republics the proportion of people living below the official poverty level was nearly 25 percent (32 million residents of the non-Russian regions). The poverty level in the Muslim, Turkic regions of Soviet Central Asia was truly alarming, standing at 36.6 percent in Tajikistan, 44.7 percent in Uzbekistan, and 58.6 percent in Turkmenistan. This pattern of poverty, published in *Izvestiya* in September 1989, once again highlighted the Russian–non-Russian dichotomy.

As the Soviet economy plunged into acute decline in 1990 and 1991, unemployment grew most rapidly in the Soviet south. In October 1989, an article in the Communist Party daily, *Pravda*, revealed that more than 3 million people had lost their jobs during the current five-year plan as a result of perestroika, and unemployment was expected to increase five-fold as perestroika took hold. *Pravda* also noted that for the last year for which statistics were available (1986), the highest unemployment rates were to be found in the non-Russian republics: 28 percent in Azerbaijan, 26 percent in

Tajikistan, 23 percent in Uzbekistan, 19 percent in Turkmenistan, 18 percent in earthquake-ravaged Armenia, and 16 percent in Kyrgyzstan. It was no wonder that such intense poverty and rampant unemployment created a social basis for ethnic violence.

Even among those lucky enough to find work, the gap between Russians and non-Russians was significant. By 1979, 31 percent of all workers in the RSFSR were employed in what was defined as mental labor and 69 percent in what was defined as primarily physical labor, while among the non-Russian republics, 27.4 percent of workers were engaged in mental labor and 72.6 in physical labor. Yet throughout the 1970s, Soviet planners deliberately continued to create greater opportunities for mental labor in the RSFSR where 483,000 new jobs were created in the intellectual sphere and only 459,000 involved physical labor. In the non-Russian republics, the trend was entirely different: 422,000 intellectual jobs were created and 601,000 jobs involving physical work appeared. The gap, therefore, had widened under Leonid Brezhnev, and there was no significant departure from this pattern under Mikhail Gorbachev.

The Politics of Culture

While social and economic disparities between Russians and non-Russians in the USSR were profound, Russian dominance in the fields of culture and education was even more overwhelming. Such inequities served to radicalize the indigenous intelligentsia and help to explain why writers, scholars, and scientists played a leading role in the proindependent popular fronts that blazed the trail toward statehood.

Of the 2.2 billion books printed in the USSR in 1986, 86 percent were in Russian but only 14 percent in the non-Russian languages. That meant that there were nearly 14 books in Russian for every Russian man, woman, and child, but only 2.4 books per capita in the native languages of the non-Russians. According to national rights activists, such figures were not a reflection of consumer demand but a statistical expression of the long-term policy of Russification. Similar gaps were to be seen in newspapers, magazines, films, and television production.

In the last years of Soviet rule in the Central Asian republics, the state of book publishing was nothing short of disastrous. A look at the yearly accounting of books and periodicals for 1987 reveals a culture decidedly out of balance. In Tajikistan, there were only 1.9 books, pamphlets, and brochures published for every resident. A closer examination reveals how even that statistic understates reality, for in Tajikistan, a republic with a population of 5.1 million, there were only 361 books or pamphlets published in Tajik and 469 published in Russian, while Turkmenistan (population 3.5 million) published 302 books and pamphlets in the native language versus 426 in Russian. Such an imbalance was particularly shocking given that in each of these republics well over 80 percent of the population was non-Russian. In Kazakhstan, where the number of Russians is about equal to the number of indigenous Kazakhs, Soviet rule meant that there were nearly three times as many titles published in Russian as in Kazakh.

In the realm of culture, however, there was an even more conspicuous imbalance. Ukraine, the second most populous republic, had traditionally been the target of the most relentless assimilatory and Russificatory policies, and its culture has paid the highest price. In the last years of Soviet rule, only 81 percent of Ukrainians considered Ukrainian their mother tongue. After the Belarusians, this was the lowest proportion among the fifteen nations with their own titular republics. The reason why Ukrainians might have been drawn to Russian culture can be understood if one considers some striking statistics from the late 1980s: For this nation of more than 44 million, there were just over one hundred magazines published in Ukrainian. By contrast, in the RSFSR alone, Russians had fourteen times as many periodicals to choose from in their native language as the Ukrainians did. In book publishing, Ukrainians were similarly far behind. In their own republic, the books published in Russian outnumbered those published in Ukrainian by almost four to one.

The cultural argument for statehood was implicit in these discrepancies. Compared to book publishing in the neighboring countries of Eastern Europe, in the years before the collapse of the Soviet Union, Ukraine (population 52 million) lagged far behind its less populous neighboring states of Poland, Czechoslovakia, and Hungary. Although they were under Communist rule until 1989, Poland published five times as many books as Ukraine each year; Czechoslovakia issued four times as many; and Hungary, with a population of about one-fifth that of Ukraine, produced six times more titles with a print run that was 60 percent greater. This lack of variety constricted Ukrainian readers, forcing them to seek out the Russian-language press and therefore drawing the non-Russian intelligentsia into the habit of reading, writing, and thinking in Russian. This cultural policy consequently sent Ukrainian children to Russian-language schools.

Such trends created a growing gap between educated non-Russians and non-Russian workers and peasants. Until national rights movements emerged in the late 1980s, the native culture in this context seemed like something second-rate, inferior—linked to the less intelligent and badly educated workers and rural inhabitants.

Cultural monotony crippled the magazine world as well. The USSR published approximately 5,000 different periodicals. Of those, 4,245 appeared in Russian but only 774 in non-Russian languages—an advantage of nearly six to one. The restrictions and limits on non-Russian publications are all the more glaring when one takes into account how little variety there was in the Soviet press in general. Before the explosion of cultural activity that accompanied the decline of the Soviet order, there were in 1987 but ten weekly magazines published in Russian, and only one Ukrainian-language weekly magazine. There were no other non-Russian weekly magazines published anywhere else in the USSR.

Statistics on newspaper publication reveal a similar pattern. Of the nearly 5,000 newspapers published in the Soviet Union, more than 90 percent appeared in Russian. The RSFSR produced only 97 different daily newspapers for a population of 147 million, while Uzbekistan, a non-Russian republic with approximately 20 million inhabitants, had only 4 daily newspapers.

Even in the period of glasnost, the Soviet ideologues preferred to cling to the concept of "gigantism," which comforted them with the knowledge that each day 25 or 50 million readers were reading precisely the same periodical. For Mikhail Gorbachev, who viewed himself as the architect of a fundamental transformation of consciousness, the relative uniformity of the means of information meant that his message of glasnost and perestroika could be hammered home without significant dissent. Traditionally, such centralization simplified censorship and made the task of the Communist propaganda apparat all the more simple.

When it comes to books on commercial, agricultural, and industrial topics, the gaps in the fare offered Russians and non-Russians are even more astonishing. In 1987, there were more than 2,500 different titles on transportation published in Russian, while only 90 appeared in non-Russian languages. Of titles dealing with machine building, three were thirty times more published in Russian than in non-Russian languages, and of industrial construction texts, one hundred times more. On agricultural topics, more than 4,000 Russian-language books were published, while 1,000 appeared in non-Russian languages—an apparent concession to the overwhelmingly non-Russian rural population.

Films, too, did not escape this pattern and tended to be dominated by Russian-language products. In Ukraine, one writer asked in 1989, "Why do film studios have to request funding for each film from Moscow?" and lamented upon the great delay and cost of translating films into Russian. He complained that Kiev's once-renowned Dovzhenko Film Studio and its counterpart in Odessa had been almost completely Russified. The Ukrainian cinema, he concluded, "is a fiction." To that writer's indictments could be added the fact that in Ukraine as in other non-Russian republics in the late 1980s, the most popular films—relatively new imports such as Francis Ford Coppola's *The Cotton Club* or *The Conversation*—were available usually only in Russian versions. As a rule, no provision was made for dubbing these films of intense public interest into native non-Russian languages.

Only the Georgian republic managed to protect its own developed film industry, producing, among others, Tengiz Abuladze's celebrated condemnation of totalitarianism and Stalinism, *Repentance*. The national identity of the studio also meant that filmmakers in the Georgian capital of Tbilisi played a key role in aiding their country's popular front and other dissident groups. The building of the Georgian Cinematographers' Union was, throughout most of 1989, the nerve center of the country's burgeoning national rights movement.

Soviet rule, even under the more relaxed regime of Mikhail Gorbachev, meant Russian dominance in education and popular culture as well. The enforced acculturation of children into the Russian-dominated Soviet culture was achieved through schooling and television. Typically, in most of the non-Russian republics, there were three television channels, two of which were usually Russophone, and the last, while devoted to local affairs, was frequently filled with Russian-language programs.

The pattern of Russian dominance began in grade school, permeated all stages of the educational system, and was reinforced by the mass media. Graduate students, whether Russian or non-Russian, were required to write their advanced-degree dissertations in Russian, further promoting Russification of the non-Russian peoples.

Sometimes, the fulfillment of this requirement could prove quite absurd. In Moscow, in the summer of 1989, we met a young Ukrainian screenwriter studying at Moscow University's prestigious film school who had begun writing a screenplay about life in a small western Ukrainian town. Although one of his themes was the gradual encroachment of Russian language and culture onto a formerly pure Ukrainian setting, he was for a long time prevented by teachers and school officials from writing any part of the script in Ukrainian. "The whole point would have been lost on a viewer. The rule rendered my subject nonsensical. How can you accurately convey the sense of place, the local color, and the underlying conflict without using the Ukrainian language?" said the young man. At last, the authorities relented, agreeing to pass him provided that he wrote a Russian-language synopsis. But his success was one of a handful of exceptions. Ironically, had he been a student in Ukraine before independence, he would have been compelled there also to write his dissertation screenplay in Russian.

The Russian advantage carried over into the sciences. More than two-thirds of all scientists and scientific workers in the USSR were to be found in the Russian republic. In secondary education, Russians enjoyed further advantages. Adjusted for population, the RSFSR had 20 percent more secondary school students than Georgia, 30 percent more than Azerbaijan, 20 percent more than Ukraine, 30 percent more than Uzbekistan, 12 percent more than Lithuania, 75 percent more than Tajikistan and Turkmenistan, 25 percent more than Armenia, and 30 percent more than Estonia. There was not a single republic that did better than the vast Russian republic in secondary or higher education. Overall, there were roughly 20 percent more students in the RSFSR than in the almost equally populous non-Russian republics. The gap in higher education was even greater: The RSFSR had more than one-third more college and technical school students per capita than the non-Russian republics. Indeed, the proportion of college and technical school students in the Russian republic population exceeded that of the fourteen other republics in proportions that ranged from 10 to 70 percent.

Government statistics confirmed the systemic superiority enjoyed by Russians and their language. Although "bilingualism" had become the Soviet buzzword in nationalities policy, only 3 percent of all Russians had bothered to learn to speak any of the non-Russian languages, despite the fact that some 20 percent of all Russians lived in the non-Russian republics. By contrast, nearly half of non-Russians could speak Russian. "Bilingualism" clearly was one area in which the educational advantage of the Russians did not appear to yield concrete results. Now, as newly independent non-Russian states move to introduce the indigenous languages into the work of the state and of commerce, their Russian populations will begin to face obstacles in advancement and promotion. This legacy of Soviet rule will, likewise, serve to inflame interethnic tensions and make language policy a vexing problem that will test the tolerance of the newly sovereign governments in the years ahead.

With all the intense pressure generated by Soviet rule to assimilate, particularly among Ukrainians and Belarusians, it was astonishing that so many non-Russians continued to cling to their mother tongue. By 1989, more than 95 percent of all Uzbeks, Kazakhs, Georgians, Lithuanians, Tajiks, Turkmenians, Kyrgyzes, Latvians, and Estonians regarded their own language as their mother tongue. Among the 6.5 million Tatars (who lived in a territory inside the RSFSR), the rate of identification with their own language was 85 percent; among Armenians, many of whom lived outside their republic, it stood at 91.6 percent; among Ukrainians, it was only 81 percent; and among Belarusians, it was at a USSR low: 70.9 percent.

With growing ferment among non-Russians, new concessions began to be granted by the central government in the areas of education and language. Additionally, in the years leading up to the collapse of the empire, the indigenous peoples rediscovered a renewed sense of pride in their ethnic roots, and in many long-Russified cities the indigenous languages began to make a comeback in everyday use.

Now that these peoples have won back their state independence, the above figures will undoubtedly climb in the years ahead. Most of the newly independent states had established the indigenous language as the state language in their constitutions. Other republics went even further, and enacted laws to define and enforce the constitutional changes.

The abiding pattern of generations of Soviet and Russian imperial policy will be difficult to overcome. After all, in no realm of personal and professional lives did non-Russians enjoy a significant advantage. Even in an area as innocuous as leisure time, Russians came out well ahead. In the 1980s, on a yearly basis, and adjusted for population, 33 percent more citizens of the RSFSR were able to take vacations in state-run resorts than were their counterparts from the non-Russian republics.

A Matter of Respect

The economic, social, and cultural disparities that were products of the Soviet imperial system became important elements in the arguments for statehood made by the nationalist and proindependence movements that emerged in the late 1980s. These democratically oriented movements frequently made their case for state independence, autonomy, or sovereignty in terms of self-interest. While the argument can be made that inequality is, in the end, a matter of perception and that many of the people are better off now than they were before Soviet rule, the rush toward self-determination and decentralization that typified the trends of recent years is perhaps the most convincing verdict on Soviet society. In a society whose one firm ideological pillar had been its profession of social equity, it was clearly a matter of time before non-Russians began to take the ideology at its word.

Over the years, Soviet authorities justified cultural imbalances by claiming a utilitarian need to publish, educate, and develop a mass culture in a language that was understood by virtually everyone. But the need for standardization and dissemination of information can easily be overcome without sacrificing cultural diversity; the polyglot culture of the European Economic Community (EC) seems to have solved that problem through publication of multilanguage editions, promotion of multilingualism in the educational system, and extensive use of translators and interpreters. While these measures may have increased costs and paperwork, they have kept intact the spiritual essence of diverse peoples, thereby encouraging them to be productive and creative. Linguistic diversity in the EC has not proved an obstacle to cooperation nor to integration, and its success will not be lost on the leaders of the fifteen new states that have emerged out of the ruins of the old Soviet empire.

Non-Russian democratic activists and cultural dissidents attributed the broad range of imbalances to the true nature of the Soviet state: a continuation by other means of the centuries-old Russian empire. The policies of centralization and Russification, given explicit expression during the Brezhnev years, in the end became a powerful source of discontent within the cultural and political elites of the non-Russian republics. Dissent was voiced even by those non-Russians who were integrated into official structures of the system and were an integral part of its political establishment. This was a natural outcome of a system that had stacked the deck in favor of Russians and Russian speakers. The inequity created by centralism led to pent-up discontent that sundered the unity within the Party, state, and armed forces, for inequity, as events of recent years have shown, has great potential for fueling mass unrest and political activism. The nationalism that shook loose the USSR was based in part on a demand for the recutting of the economic pie in the hope of a more equitable arrangement.

In its last years the central Soviet press began to acknowledge the verity of the demand for economic equity. In a November 2, 1989, issue of *Pravda*, K. T. Turysonov, a secretary of the extremely conservative All-Union Central Council of Trade Unions, put it this way: "Nowadays, there is recurrent talk that social justice is not observed in the distribution of consumption funds. . . . Prices and wages in our country are deformed. This has its effect. . . . Sometime in the mid-1960s, our economists put forward the thesis that the equalization of the economic level of the republics had been achieved. Economic strategy was elaborated on the basis of this premise. In actual fact, there had been no economic equalization. For example, vast regions of the RSFSR to the East of the center, and parts of Kazakhstan and Ukraine, possessing tremendous natural resources and having become the nation's pantry, are at the same time regions that have been done out of their fair share socially."

The average non-Russian is not to this day fully aware of all the statistical disadvantages that confront him as an individual and which challenge his newly-independent state. For decades, opportunities for travel within the USSR were severely circumscribed by both regulations and economics, and a heavily controlled Soviet press did not address these sensitive issues. But by the late 1980s, the openness engendered by glasnost allowed some of the issues of equality to permeate the Soviet media and at last be depicted forthrightly in the print and broadcast media. The potent slogans of economic reform and glasnost became appropriate banners under which non-Russians rallied in behalf of sovereignty and, later, independence and statehood.

The inefficiencies that issued from the old imperial order also affected the ordinary Russian citizen, whose life was less than idyllic and whose position was far from privileged, for the material benefits for the working class of any empire are rather modest. At the height of the British Empire, Friedrich Engels described the immense poverty of working-class Manchester. Today, working-class Vologda or Ekaterinburg is hardly the locus of privilege. As Mikhail Heller has written about the Russians: "They live impoverished, poor, hungry lives. In the Smolensk region, in the heart of Russia, sixty-five years after the Revolution, it is impossible in the winter to travel from one village to another. But that is because the Russians have to feed the Afghans and build roads in Nigeria and Kampuchea." The USSR also had to maintain a vast security system and a world-class military-industrial complex.

No set of statistics can fully measure the quality of life. A number of non-Russian cultures preserved traditions and styles of conduct, work habits, and other features to create a more pleasant life-style and a sense of community. Certainly, the average visitor to a city like Kiev in Ukraine or Tbilisi in Georgia was struck by their relative prosperity, by the dignity with which shopkeepers maintained their places of work, and by the greater variety of available goods. But these often were the by-products of industrious national cultures and not the legacy of policies promoted by the state.

It was clear in the last years of the USSR that when the Soviet state intervened, as it did in all spheres of life, it usually did so against the interests of non-Russian cultures. It was for this reason that most of the popular fronts were united in the belief that the non-Russian republics would fare better under self-government. With greater control over the allocation of their own resources and a decisive say in the setting of prices for natural resources and finished products, they argued, non-Russians would inevitably better their lot. Now, with statehood at hand, they will find the economic and social landscape was infinitely more complex and contradictory than they believed.

Still, there can be no doubt that the post-Soviet order, even an order in which the rickety Commonwealth of Independent States evolves into a durable structure, will permanently reverse the trends toward centralization that occurred under Brezhnev and persisted in the years of Gorbachev's rule. Under Brezhnev, 53 percent of all industrial output was controlled exclusively by the central, all-Union ministries. Paradoxically, under Gorbachev—his rhetoric of decentralization notwithstanding—this all-Union control grew from 57 percent in 1986 to 61 percent in 1987, when an additional 33 percent of industrial output was produced under the shared jurisdiction of central and republic ministries, which de facto meant central control. By 1987, as nationalist and separatist sentiments mounted, only 6 percent of all Soviet industrial output was under the jurisdiction of localities and republics.

According to the draft program on economic power sharing issued in 1989 with the concurrence of the Politburo of the CPSU, the proportion of local and republic control over industrial production was to have risen dramatically in all the republics: from just 4 percent to more than 25 percent of such output in the RSFSR; from 5 percent to more than 40 percent in Ukraine; from 7 percent to about 50 percent in Belarus; and from around 10 percent to between 50 and 75 percent in the Caucasian republics, the Baltic States, Soviet Central Asia, and Moldova. While this formula for the devolution of economic power was a step forward when compared to the centralized system then in place, it was rejected in late 1989 by the USSR's Supreme Soviet as too conservative.

Although this legislative rejection may well have been evidence of Gorbachev's growing understanding that such halfhearted measures would not have fundamentally altered the centrally controlled state apparat at the root of the USSR's economic crisis, Gorbachev in 1990 rejected the Shatalin Plan, a radical attempt at reducing the power of the center and making the republics the masters of their own economic home. The rejection of the Shatalin Plan may in retrospect come to be viewed as Gorbachev's fatal mistake, for in failing to give real political and economic power to the republics, the Soviet president left the ruling elite incapable of resisting the growing force of nationalism in the republics. Moreover, through his relentless support of political and economic centralism under the guise of federalism, Gorbachev fueled an ever-widening movement pressing for independence in the non-Russian republics and, under Boris Yeltsin, in Russia itself. Moreover, when independence-minded republics like those in the Baltic States enacted legislation that promoted the devolution of central control, these met with immense bureaucratic barriers and administrative hostility from the central authorities in Moscow, the most clear-cut of which was the economic blockade of Lithuania in 1990.

In 1991, the final year of the Soviet empire, the state press and propaganda responded to the upsurge in national assertiveness by promoting new myths about the advantages of the interrelated USSR economy, thereby sowing uncertainty and fear among non-Russians while raising the alarm among Russians and mobilizing support for the unity of the land of the Soviets. This propaganda line contrasted markedly, however, with growing press admissions that the non-Russians had been given a raw deal economically.

In a period of economic decline and resultant economic austerities, the fight for the reallocation of limited resources became a fight over the distribution of hardships, thus awakening resentment among the more privileged strata, who were disproportionately Russian. Because the unraveling of the Soviet Union came in a period of economic stagnation, mounting shortages of consumer goods, growing inflation, rising unemployment, and declining living standards, powerful forces emerged to fight to preserve the imperial status quo. The struggle over slices of the economic pie led to heightened resentment by the economic have-nots, while the more highly skilled, ethnically Russian, urban haves came to view growing regional and national economic and cultural assertiveness as a direct challenge to their interests, particularly in the non-Russian republics, where some 25 million Russians still live. Russian fears also helped fuel ugly racist and chauvinistic impulses. These trends led Gorbachev to resort to repression in December 1990, and emboldened the hard-liners who represented imperialist interests to proclaim a state of emergency in August 1991.

In the wake of the fall of the Soviets, anxious Russians also were forming the bedrock of movements resisting all forms of economic and political change. But Russian anxieties were also fueling a countervailing Russian turn inward. Such a Russian rejection of the burdens of an empire was associated with the election in June 1991 of Boris Yeltsin to the presidency of the Russian republic.

Rising Russian Resentments: A Front Against Democracy?

Yeltsin's 1991 victory notwithstanding, a pattern of Russian conservatism and resistance had emerged in the Baltic republics, where Russians created interfront organizations in a struggle to protect their privileged status and the supremacy of their language. In many instances, these antidemocratic fronts were offered material support by the discredited segments of the Party apparat and by the declining, state- and Party-controlled trade unions of the All-Union Central Council of Trade Unions. That dinosaur of the old order was, in the days before its disintegration, engaged in a campaign to revive its flagging fortunes by fighting for the preservation of the Soviet Union while advancing conservative slogans masked by demagogic populist appeals. The struggle was over much more than living standards or culture; it was a struggle for political power and national dignity.

In the last years of Soviet power, non-Russians were pressing on a variety of fronts: economic, cultural, educational, and political. But the net effect of their challenge was to widen the fissures in the last remaining empire and to pose a profound challenge to the integrity of the Soviet state. At the same time, because that challenge was led for the most part by non-Russians who came from the most talented and best educated segments of their societies, their movements were likewise the main forces for the kind of economic and political reform Gorbachev professed to support. Yet the Soviet leader proved incapable of co-opting some of these forces on behalf of his own agenda for decentralization and economic change. His was a high-wire tightrope act; and with every eruption of nationalist mass protest, it proved to be a high-wire act performed on a thin rope. The implications of economic inequity that played a critical role in the fall of the Soviet Union are certain to play a growing role in post-Soviet political life.

The very idea of economic self-sufficiency for the republics that made up the USSR was met with enthusiasm by non-Russians, but generated a high degree of trepidation among many leaders and citizens of the RSFSR. In October 1989, the then hard-line chairman of the Council of Ministers of the Russian republic, Aleksandr V. Vlasov, denounced what he called the growing tendency toward "autarky" in economic life. Speaking at a session of the Supreme Soviet of the RSFSR, Vlasov, who was also a nonvoting, candidate member of the Politburo of the CPSU, expressed worry over what economic self-financing would mean to the giant republic:

> Almost two-thirds of the republic's territory is in the far northern zone or equivalent regions. Gigantic reserves of natural resources, which are of great importance for bringing into circulation throughout the whole country, are concentrated here. However, the severity of natural and climatic conditions and the remoteness from developed regions causes a significant increase in the cost of building and operating enterprises and facilities of the social sphere in that zone. . . . The intensive development of new regions is unthinkable without concentrating the efforts of all the union republics.

Vlasov expressed the growing worry of Russians that the RSFSR could confront severe economic difficulties if left to its own devices, noting that even within the republic, great climatic and environmental variations had made "the standardized leveling approach to territorial self-financing in the context of the Russian Federation . . . totally unacceptable." He went on to issue a wide-ranging attack on greater economic self-determination for the republics that made up the USSR, saying in the standard Marxist-Leninist terminology of the time that it could "lead to a disruption of the objective processes of the socialization of production, the all-Union division of labor and specialization, and coproduction within it." Terming this process an "unfortunate" reality, Vlasov charged that an "inclination toward regional isolation" was mounting and with it "a manifestation of regional egoism and an aspiration to escape one's obligations to the country and the republic." He expressed the view that the then Communist-led government of the RSFSR was "resolutely against the transformation of our state into a union of national states." But Vlasov's warnings did not carry the day. In late May 1990, he was defeated in his bid for the chairmanship of the parliament of the Russian republic by Boris Yeltsin. In a stunning victory, Yeltsin was elected chairman of the Russian republic by a bare majority on May 29 on what amounted to a Russian patriotic platform.

Yeltsin immediately proclaimed his intention to fight for Russia's political and economic sovereignty. By June 1990, the Russian parliament had proclaimed this sovereignty, plunging the USSR into the murky seas of struggle over the proper division of power between the republics and the center.

In the context of the interrelated, irrational system that developed as a result of seventy-four years of Soviet rule, virtually all the republics have something to fear in the rigors of the free market. While economic accountability may well be beneficial in the long run for many of these new states, in the short run it can create as many problems as it solves. As the economic debate mounts in the post-Soviet period, the true basis of economic relations may reveal the Russians to be among the most uneasy, as they face the danger that their beneficial economic arrangement with the other Soviet republics has come to an end.

Party and State: Russian Predominance

What created the immense social, economic, and cultural disparities among the republics? A glance at the Soviet power structure in its waning years offers some possible explanations why the non-Russians tended to lag behind in almost all indices. For all but the last two years of Gorbachev's rule, power in the Soviet Union was exercised above all through the Communist Party, 60 percent of which was made up of ethnic Russians. The proportion of Russians increased as one moved up the power structure to its very pinnacle—the ruling Politburo and the Party's executive arm, the Secretariat.

By January 1990, nearly five years into Mikhail Gorbachev's tenure, of the twelve voting members in the Politburo, only three were non-Russians (Eduard Shevardnadze, a Georgian; Nikolay Slyunkov, a Belarusian; and Volodymyr Ivashko, a Ukrainian), and only one member of the Politburo (Ivashko) represented a non-Russian republic (Ukraine). In part, this state of affairs reflected Gorbachev's decision to make leadership appointments on the basis of individual abilities. While this was a decided improvement over the formalistic past practice, according to which as many as seven of the top Party leaders of the republics were given positions on the Politburo, the de facto acknowledgment that the republics had nothing to offer the central leadership was a comment on both the caliber of the Party apparat in the republics and the way the interests of the peripheries were regarded in Moscow.

The situation was even more bleak for non-Russians in the seven non-voting candidate members of the Politburo, for only one of them was non-Russian (the Latvian, Boris Pugo, the coup plotter who committed suicide in August 1991). Within the Secretariat, which ran the Party's day-to-day affairs, of the twelve secretaries only three were non-Russians. In the Central Committee, the principal policy-making body between Communist Party congresses, the situation was remarkably similar. As Radio Liberty's Ann Sheehy, who specializes in nationalities issues, observed in 1990: "Owing to the large number of personnel changes that have occurred since the present Central Committee was elected, the non-Russian republics are less represented than at any time in the recent past."

In the Central Committee, which in September 1989 was charged with the ratification of potentially far-reaching policies on ethnic and national issues, only about 15 percent of full (voting) members came from the Party organizations of the non-Russian republics, and only half of the Communist Party first secretaries from the fourteen non-Russian republics even had a place in the Central Committee as full (voting) members. They included the first secretaries from Ukraine, Belarus, Moldova, Kyrgyzstan, Kazakhstan, Tajikistan, and Turkmenistan.

Although the Communist parties of the non-Russian republics by 1990 faced a profound crisis of authority and confidence, this underrepresentation nonetheless elicited a great deal of unease among non-Russians, including those within the opposition popular fronts. Because of the Party's role for most of the Gorbachev period as the leading force in Soviet society and because of its vast prerogatives in the control of education, culture, and the media, this representation gap was a source of significant tension, especially within the indigenous Communist Party organizations. It served to further alienate the Communist elite from Moscow and had the unintended effect of pushing them further away from Gorbachev. And at a time of growing national assertiveness, the Party organizations in the non-Russian republics drifted farther from the control of a center in which they had little voice. Of course, there was a countervailing factor at work here—the principle of democratic centralism. Although each republic was allowed to maintain its own Party structures, until they began to unravel in the early 1990s, they were all subordinated to the commands of the central organization, the CPSU.

The tension and discontent occasioned by such subordination came to a head first in Lithuania, where, in October and November of 1989, the Communist Party of Lithuania began to assert, against great central pressure, its intention to withdraw from the CPSU. And in December the Communist Party of Lithuania did so, reconstituting itself as an independent, sovereign political entity. The move, motivated by the Lithuanian Party's desperate desire to maintain some measure of public support in a republic increasingly swept up by the forces of democratic change and nationalism, was the first strike at the heart of the imperial structure of the Communist state. Its effect, however, was to make the CPSU an even more ethnically Russian entity. The growing disaffection that began in the Baltic States quickly spread to other republic Communist parties, including the Russian Communist Party. By 1991, the recently established Communist Party of Russia had become a redoubt of hard-line nationalists who mobilized growing resistance among Party loyalists to Gorbachev nationalities policies that they believed were not sufficiently firm.

In the ministries, which until the August 1991 putsch had run the central Soviet economic complex, and where fundamental decisions concerning the allocation of resources were made, the level of non-Russian representation and participation was even lower than in the Communist Party. When on June 10, 1989, Soviet Prime Minister Nikolay Ryzhkov announced a new presidium of the Council of Ministers of the USSR, consisting of three first deputy chairmen and ten deputy chairmen, there was not a single non-Russian among them. The twelve men and one woman nominated for these top spots held the key positions in a Soviet system that was moving increasingly toward greater reliance on governmental and not Party structures. The responsibilities of these key government leaders were enormous in the twilight years of Soviet rule. Most of these officials chaired the critical committees and bureaus that determined the allocation of key resources, established prices and set the agenda for what remained highly centralized and planned Soviet economic projects.

Included in this roster were the chairmen of the USSR State Planning Committee (Gosplan), the State Commission for Food and Purchases, the State Commission for Military-Industrial Questions, the State Committee for Science and Technology, the bureau that supervised the Fuel and Energy Complex, the State Commission for Economic Reform, and the State Committee for Material and Technical Supply (Gossnab), the vital agency that provided enterprises access to needed supplies and equipment. By 1990, as Gorbachev began shifting power from the Communist Party to the presidency, he created a presidential council, a consultative body with extensive executive functions. Here, too, the predominance of ethnic Russians was apparent, as they represented eleven of the sixteen members of the council, including one Ukrainian and one representative of the Turkic population.

The rapid growth of national consciousness and assertiveness in the late 1980s meant that by 1990–91 this state of affairs could no longer be ignored by the now more open Soviet media. More and more voices in the republics raised the question of how responsive a Moscow-centered, ethnically Russian elite could be to what for them were distant, detached, parochial concerns. In an August 24, 1989, interview published in the daily *Komsomolskaya Pravda*, economist Professor E. Bagramov reflected growing popular concern about the unrepresentative nature of the higher decision-making bodies of the Soviet system when he forthrightly observed: "The Politburo . . . is selected . . . not on national grounds but according to political and professional qualities. But bearing in mind that this question has major internal repercussions in the republics and that it meets with different interpretations abroad . . . I think a future party congress must choose a Politburo composition that will more fully reflect the CPSU's multinational structure." In the last months of Soviet power, Mikhail Gorbachev attempted to do just that, but by then the authority of the Party had plummeted and its power had been shifted to the organs of government so that it was widely interpreted as a feeble effort to respond cosmetically to the growing clamor of separatist movements in the republics.

Under the czars, the Russian empire's development had been a decidedly unequal affair, and it was to destroy this inequitable "prison of nations" that the Bolsheviks claimed to have launched their revolution. But, in the last years of his life, even Lenin, who had ruthlessly crushed independent Ukrainian, Georgian, Azerbaijani, and Armenian states, grew increasingly concerned with the reemergence of Russian chauvinism under the new Soviet order. Hoping to correct a potential imbalance, he urged the preferential treatment of the non-Russian nationalities to close the gap in their level of development. Lenin's views on power sharing, advanced in the last year before his debilitating stroke and eventual death in 1924, were quite explicit. While the new USSR constitution was being discussed, Lenin had written the following note to his colleagues on the Politburo: "We must *absolutely* insist that in the Union TsIK [then the Soviet legislature], the presidency shall go in turn to a Russian, Ukrainian, Georgian, and so forth. *Absolutely!* Your Lenin" (Lenin's italics).

For decades, not only was this instruction ignored, but it had positively been traduced in the upper reaches of state power. Lenin's formula for power sharing in a multinational state, as advanced in his famous "Theses on Autonomisation," bore almost no resemblance to the USSR of the modern era. In that essay, dictated in December 1922, the father of the Soviet system lashed out at what he saw as the growing danger of "the Great Russian chauvinist." Lenin worried that he and his colleagues had not structured the delicate multinational balance of the USSR with sufficient care to create "a real safeguard against the truly Russian bully." Lenin also was careful to note that the advantaged nations, the "great" nations, as he called them (including the Russians), not only must observe a "formal equality of nations" but also must take affirmative steps leading to "an inequality of the oppressor nation, the great nation, that must make up for the [advantage] which obtains in actual practice."

Although he insisted on the unity of the "union of socialist republics," Lenin made clear that the unity was not to hamper the national development of the non-Russians, whose national language rights, he insisted, must be subject to the "strictest" protections. He even speculated that it might prove necessary to retain the "union of Soviet socialist republics only for military and diplomatic affairs, and in all other respects restore full independence to the individual People's Commissariats." Such a decision, he felt, should be made by the non-Russian republics alone.

As Gorbachev attempted to revive Leninist traditions of internal Party debate, he may also have contributed unwittingly to the upsurge in non-Russian demands. During the 1920s, Lenin listened to the nationally conscious Communist leaders from the non-Russian republics who pressed for the expansion of education in native languages, argued for increased economic resources to overcome centuries of czarist exploitation, and demanded some local autonomy in decision making. This trend, known as national communism, was ultimately uprooted by Stalin's Great Purge of the 1930s. The very term "Great Russian chauvinism" was effectively banished from the Soviet political lexicon as a Soviet taboo, as was any discussion of a turn toward a confederal arrangement.

Seventy years after the Soviet founder's musings on the question of national rights, the selfsame issues that troubled Lenin in his declining years rose with new force to the surface of Soviet politics. Paradoxically, although Gorbachev consistently tried to cast himself in Lenin's mold, he shied away from quoting the explosive analysis that underlies Lenin's view of relations among the various peoples of the USSR. Still, the trends that led Lenin to issue warnings in 1922 did become a permanent feature of the Soviet power structure, and Russian dominance in the Party and state apparatus went unquestioned.

Ethnic Russian dominance in the upper rungs of the Party-state establishment undoubtedly had a dramatic effect on the distribution of material and cultural resources in a state that touted its egalitarianism. This dominance offered evidence of something approaching a classic imperial arrangement, with most of the non-Russian republics playing the role of pliant colonies—cash cows for a centrally determined pattern of resource allocation *and* redistribution. Of course, this economic inequity did not affect all the non-Russian nations equally. The Baltic States enjoyed a higher standard of living than the RSFSR. Yet this could well have been been attributed in part to their geographic advantage (proximity to the West), their later incorporation into the USSR (which meant that traditions of private ownership and the work habits of an entrepreneurial culture were still a part of national consciousness), and their already having attained a higher standard of living than their Soviet counterparts at the time of their forcible incorporation in 1940.

Even in the RSFSR, the gap between Russians and other indigenous peoples was profound. Increasingly, glasnost led to exposés of the alarming poverty that afflicted the smallest of the USSR's one hundred national groups, those helpless peoples who live in the autonomous republics, or oblasts—territorial units that in principle were intended to preserve the identity and interests of indigenous peoples. Yet even these self-styled minority preserves increasingly came to be Russian-dominated centers where indigenous cultures were in decay and economic exploitation was rampant. This is not to say that a degree of economic progress was not achieved—albeit at great cost to human life and accompanied by the merciless destruction of tradition and culture in the period of Soviet industrialization and collectivization. Even if one accepts the paternalistic benevolence of Soviet intentions at face value, ought not a nation have the right to assess its own best interests? And if it was the stated purpose of communism to eliminate the inequities between nations and to reduce the gap between town and country, then seventy years was a sufficient period in which to assess whether the Soviet experiment in equality was a success.

In light of a broadening debate over the allocation of wealth and resources in the Soviet economic system, it was equally appropriate to ask whether trends toward economic equality were growing. In the last days of Soviet power, the evidence was that they were not. Poverty was on the rise in the Soviet south, the environmental crisis was accelerating, and capital investments in the non-Russian republics declined in the early Gorbachev years.

There was no question that the inequities integral to the Soviet system provoked independent activism and a plurality of interest groups that were in turn, the rudimentary building blocks of a civil society that began emerging in the republics. Such inequities were also contributing factors in the decision of many indigenous Communist elites in the non-Russian republics to make a break with the center and to seek their political survival through the advancement of the interests of their republics.

Profound gaps in the spheres of culture and mass media can be and are being altered in the newly independent post-Soviet states through the introduction of indigenous state languages, increased subsidies for national press, television, radio, and culture, and through reform of primary, secondary, and higher education. The number of places for Russians and other Slavs in universities and other centers of higher education is already declining in Kyrgyzstan, Turkmenistan, and Uzbekistan.

The economic disparities between the republics, however, posed a range of far more complex issues. The immense gap in development and incomes between the Slavic and Baltic states on the one hand and the Central Asian republics on the other is likely to affect their economic and political relations in the years ahead. If radical economic reforms take root, the European republics are likely to be drawn increasingly into the economic orbit of the developed industrial West. Such a course is likely not only for the Baltic States, which remain outside the Commonwealth of Independent States, but also for Ukraine and Moldova.

By contrast, Russia's interest in the substantial Russian populations in Central Asia is likely to color Russia's economic decision making. Yet even here there is a radical downward trend due in part to emigration—largely to European Russia—and in part to the high birthrates among the indigenous peoples of Central Asia. Between 1989 and 1990 alone, the percentage of

Russians in Central Asian republics declined sharply. In Tajikistan it fell from 7.6 percent to 6 percent, in Uzbekistan from 8.3 to 7 percent, in Turkmenia from 9.5 to 9 percent, in Kyrgyzstan from 21.5 to 21 percent, and in Kazakhstan from 37.8 to 37 percent.

Nevertheless, for the foreseeable future Russia will be required to engage itself deeply in the economic affairs of the neighboring Central Asian states. Such an engagement may well involve economic subsidies to prop up these impoverished and potentially unstable states. In turn, Central Asian republics such as Uzbekistan and Kyrgyzstan, which are predominantly rural and where poverty rates are high, will likely seek a close economic relationship with Russia and other more economically advanced and resource-rich republics. Central Asian leaders also recognize that until new generations of their peoples acquire the education and technical skills needed to run a modern economy and provide basic technological and medical services, a climate must be created to stem the crippling outmigration from the region of qualified ethnic Russians and other Slavs.

The newly independent states adopted a variety of strategies as they sought a way out of the economic dead end that Soviet rule bequeathed. Kyrgyzstan's leaders appeared to be interested in transforming their republic by developing an electronics industry, but in the first year of independence it became clear that the republic was not making progress in this direction and was relying largely on such traditional economic endeavors as tobacco production and sheep raising. Nor did Kyrgyzstan attract Western investment or substantial levels of Western aid. By the summer of 1992, *Izvestiya* had reported that the Kyrgyzstan government was running a 6 billion ruble deficit—with receipts of 11 billion and expenditures of 17 billion.

Ironically, it was Turkmenistan, which is firmly in the grip of a hard-line nomenklatura leadership, that of all post-Soviet republics appeared to be headed along a path of self-reliance. The republic's vast cotton production and its huge natural gas reserves provided a huge source of hard currency earnings ranging annually in the billions of dollars. By contrast, with its small population of 3.5 million and its underdeveloped economy, Turkmen leaders did not face the burdens of converting from a large military-industrial complex and could slowly begin to expand their economy.

The legacy of centuries of Russian colonial and later Soviet rule is a highly diverse and complex set of interrelationships among the republics. Such interrelationships are likely to lead many of these republics into working within the context of the Commonwealth of Independent States, primarily in its economic dimensions, as a means of managing a transition to more diversified economies.

The high level of interrepublic trade was an issue at the heart of the difficult move toward full sovereignty. In Belarus, it called for greater economic cooperation between Moscow and Minsk. In Ukraine, it resulted in a conscious policy by Ukrainian leaders to deliberately move to drastically reduce trade with Russia while seeking out new relationships with such states as Turkey and Iran, and such former Soviet republics as Azerbaijan and Turkmenistan.

During their first months of independence, virtually all republics faced the consequences of a continuation of the severe breakdown in economic life that had begun in 1990. In the first four months of 1992, throughout the Commonwealth of Independent States the national income stood at 84 percent that of 1991; industrial output, 87 percent. Inflation also raged out of control, with prices for consumer goods increasing by 477 percent in Turkmenistan, 599 percent in Ukraine, 678 percent in Russia, and 820 percent in Moldova. Meanwhile, incomes lagged behind with an increase of 488.5 percent. The national income declined least in Russia, Belarus, and Turkmenistan and most in war-torn Armenia and Moldova. Production of manufactured goods and raw materials was down throughout all republics.

In part the economic crisis was a legacy of colonialism. Many of the new states refused to export their raw materials to the European republics. Thus, Turkmenistan stopped natural gas shipments to Ukraine for several months, while Uzbekistan refused to ship raw cotton to Russian textile mills, resulting in mass shutdowns. And in part the crisis was occasioned by the decline in trade and the disruption of transportation due to civil wars and conflicts raging in the Caucasus and Moldova.

In the context of mutual suspicions and a belief by the citizens of virtually all the republics that under Soviet rule they were being exploited for the benefit of other republics, economic relations promised to be highly tense in the foreseeable future. But in an increasingly diverse post-Soviet setting there was virtual unanimity on one point: The leaders of the newly independent states were not eager to return to the kind of senseless economic development (and, for many, colonial exploitation) that had typified the Soviet period. Many in the newly free republics understood that economic collapse had begun long before—in the period of Soviet rule.

Chapter Three

Ukraine: The Pivotal Nation

Nobody listens to a people that loses its word.

FRANÇOIS MITTERRAND

For centuries, it was Europe's secret nation. With a population of 52 million, a territory about the size of France or Texas, and a history of dogged resistance to foreign rule, Ukraine dimly existed on the fringes of Western consciousness. As the Czech writer Milan Kundera wrote: "Over the past five decades forty million Ukrainians have been quietly vanishing from the world without the world paying heed."

The word *Ukrainian*, in Russian and Ukrainian, is derived from *okraina*, meaning "the borderland" or "the frontier." It is here in antiquity that the easternmost of the European Slavic peoples settled and shaped their nation. Because it is a borderland between East and West, Ukraine's evolution was convulsed by a series of invasions and occupations by Tatars, Mongol hordes, the medieval Lithuanian principality, and by Poland, Russia, and the Nazis. Yet Ukraine is far more than a borderland. Here the rich and highly developed medieval culture of ancient Rus emerged, bringing Christianity and monotheism to a series of warlike tribes that had roamed the vast plains of the Ukrainian steppe, engaging in a cult of sun worship.

Russians, Belarusians, and Ukrainians regard Ukraine's capital city, Kiev, as the cradle of their Orthodox Christian civilization. Kiev had enjoyed a precarious history of intermittent autonomy alternating with Russian or Polish rule. In the seventeenth century, the city was home to the Ukrainian cossack hetman, and was the de facto capital of the independent cossack state. By the eighteenth century Ukraine had developed an advanced culture that was producing many of the czarist court's leading government functionaries, writers, theologians, and musicians. Under Russian imperial rule, the city's distinctive Ukrainian identity was undermined, as the czars flooded

Kiev with Russian merchants, soldiers, and administrators, displacing the indigenous elite.

Ukrainian history is filled with dualities and ironies. The Ukrainians were a separate, distinct people, yet they were constantly told that they were merely an appendage of the Russian empire, inextricably linked through a common faith and a similar language. These two contradictory views created a divided consciousness that tugged at the loyalty of Ukraine's educated elite. Equally significant was Ukraine's dual status of frontier outpost and wellspring of religion and civilization. And no less significant to Ukrainian identity was the fact that its lands were frequently partitioned, with the result that the Catholic western Ukraine is more clearly linked to the traditions and values of the European West, while the Orthodox eastern Ukraine was, for centuries, influenced by the frequently violent and aggressive rule of the Russian empire. Thus, even as Ukrainians struggle to build their new independent state, they must also settle the question of their own national unity.

Over the centuries, Ukraine has been a much contested prize. It is an exceedingly rich land, with vast mineral resources, a moderate climate, access to the Mediterranean sea-lanes, and a rich soil. It is here that the humus-rich black earth, the chernozem, is found. And it is from this bountiful soil that Ukraine derived its famous reputation as the breadbasket of Europe.

But its greatest resource is its people. At once stubborn and warm, tough and friendly, they have determinedly clung to their traditions and kept the ways of their ancestors. Nevertheless, centuries of foreign domination have left a deep mark on Ukrainian national consciousness, producing an incomplete culture that is bottom-heavy in its emphasis on folk tradition, yet has very few great writers, sculptors, and artists in its pantheon.

Of all the non-Russian nations of the former USSR, the Ukrainians are by far the most numerous. Some 44 million strong, Ukrainians constituted around 16 percent of the Soviet Union's population. Independent Ukraine (in which about 38 million Ukrainians live) has a population of 52 million, 21 percent of whom are Russians, 1 percent Belarusians, and 1 percent Jews.

The economic, strategic, and geopolitical weight of Ukraine made it the jewel in the crown of the Russian and, later, the Soviet empire. The eminent British historian Norman Davies has explained the Ukrainian contribution to the Russian empire: "There is Moscow and Ukraine—all the rest is window dressing." The size and location of this republic and the size of its population made Ukraine the decisive factor in the non-Russian people's struggle for sovereignty.

There are, for example, more than twice as many Ukrainians as there are Lithuanians, Estonians, Latvians, Georgians, Armenians, and Azerbaijanis combined. As important as Ukraine was economically and geopolitically to the Soviet Union, its significance stemmed as well from its persistent resistance to foreign domination.

A History of Unrest

Over the centuries, the Ukrainian national identity has withstood the fierce onslaughts of the Tatars, Turks, Russians, Poles, and Nazis. The leading exponents of Ukrainian culture, men like the nineteenth-century poet Taras Shevchenko, died in exile far from their native soil and society. In the late nineteenth century, scores of prominent and nationally conscious Ukrainian scholars escaped the czars and lived in exile in Vienna and Geneva. Thousands later fled the Communist takeover, and tens of thousands from the intelligentsia—some 80 percent of Ukraine's writers and artists—fell victim to Stalin's terror. The attempt to behead the Ukrainian nation by destroying its small, talented, and politically dangerous intelligentsia was a practice inherited from the czars by the commissars of the new Soviet order.

Under Stalin, the physical eradication of the Ukrainian intelligentsia was accompanied by an equally monstrous phenomenon: the replacement of writers, thinkers, and artists by the totalitarian equivalent of intellectuals who produced trite and hackneyed works. While many refused to bend and were broken in the ensuing maelstrom of Stalin's Great Purge of the 1930s, others submitted to the demands of the totalitarian state. Talented writers like the revolutionary Ukrainian poet Pavlo Tychyna surrendered their creative integrity to the rigors of Stalinist aesthetics. Other writers, like the heretical Ukrainian national Communist Mykola Khvylovy, perished in 1932 at their own hands as their revolutionary ideals crumbled before their very eyes and Stalin's march against Ukrainian patriotism revealed the Kremlin dictator's true hand. Others, like the filmmaker and novelist Oleksander Dovzhenko—best known for his pathfinding 1930 film *Zemlya (Earth)*—were virtually prevented from making films, and kept quiet records of the ensuing years of pain in intimate memoirs that only now are beginning to see the light of day.

Not only was the flower of Ukrainian culture destroyed in the face of Stalin's rigid censorship and Brezhnev's Russification, so too were its distinctive traditions and the principal source of national identity: the Ukrainian language. Before independence, in many Ukrainian cities (as in the coal-mining center of the Donets basin), there was not a single Ukrainian-language school. And the Ukrainian university system was largely Russified, requiring that even dissertations on Ukrainian literature be written in Russian. The Soviet state's attempts to construct difficulties for Ukrainian speakers were so manifold that it was impossible to purchase typewriters with a Ukrainian script. Because of this stultifying cultural environment, nearly one in five Ukrainians regarded Russian as his native language.

According to leaders of the independent Ukrainian Language Society, by 1990 less than half the Ukrainian population spoke Ukrainian on a regular basis. In western Ukraine, the language was dominant in both urban and rural areas, while in the central and eastern parts, Ukrainian was heard mainly in the villages and on collective farms, and in the larger cities it was spoken by a distinct minority. In daily discourse, as a language of commerce, in the work of the Soviet Ukrainian government, in higher education, and in science, the Russian language had replaced native Ukrainian. The alarming state of the Ukrainian language reached crisis proportions in the view of activist Ukrainians, particularly those in the Ukrainian Writers' Union, which became a center of the Ukrainian nationalist movement, the People's Rukh, commonly known as the Rukh (the Ukrainian word for "movement").

Today, the blue-and-yellow flag of the independent state that emerged in 1918 from under the rubble of the czarist empire once again flies atop Kiev's administrative and government buildings. Created by Western-oriented leaders, the independent state maintained a precarious control over Ukrainian territory in the face of invading promonarchist Russian forces and the overwhelming numbers of the Red Army, until it finally fell in 1921. With the defeat of the independent state, the Soviet Ukrainian flag was raised. Resembling the Soviet flag, it featured a huge red field with a golden yellow hammer and sickle confined to one corner. Crowded out of this Soviet pattern, occupying a precarious place on the margins, was a hint of sky blue, a remnant from the blue and yellow colors that had symbolized independence.

Like the blue stripe crowded out of the flag, Ukrainian nationalism was marginalized but not destroyed. Despite intense repression, nationalism manifested itself through nearly seventy years of Soviet rule. A Ukrainian form of national communism emerged in the 1920s, with Party leaders seeking greater autonomy, resisting the centralizing tendencies of the Russian-dominated central Party apparatus, and promoting a blossoming of Ukrainian culture. These phenomena alarmed Stalin and by 1930 the first show trials of Ukrainian artists and intellectuals began. Stalin's forced famine of 1932–33 claimed from 4 million to 7 million victims, who starved as a result of a brutal policy of forced grain confiscation and collectivization.

The tenacity of resistance to collectivization was not to be found in Russia proper, demonstrating a significant historical difference between Ukrainians and Russians: Communal landownership, the norm in Russian areas freed from serfdom in the nineteenth century, had been virtually nonexistent in Ukraine. The principal aim of the forced famine was to break the back of the Ukrainian peasantry, the traditional bedrock of the national movement. In the words of the eminent Russian writer Lev Kopelev, Stalin's "destruction of the peasantry" amounted to no less than "pulling out the living roots of national historical existence."

During World War II, the Ukrainians were dealt a further blow. With its population caught in a vise between two totalitarian empires, Ukraine lost nearly 6 million people, 4 million of them civilians, including nearly 1 million Ukrainian Jews. In Kiev, where one in five citizens died during the 788 days of Nazi occupation, Soviet monuments to the war dead abound, memorializing only Hitler's victims, not Stalin's.

In the postwar period, Ukrainian nationalists continued an armed struggle against Communist rule in substantial numbers until 1949. The long-standing resistance waged in western Ukraine during and after World War II would not have been possible without the support of large segments of the Ukrainian population. Their intense opposition to Soviet rule, collectivization, and the suppression of the Ukrainian Catholic church was met with mass deportations to Siberia and Soviet Central Asia of more than half a million Ukrainians during and after the war. The Ukrainians had fought on bravely and resisted for so long because they mistakenly believed it was only a matter of time before the Western democracies would be forced into inevitable war with Soviet totalitarianism.

But Ukrainian quiescence was short-lived. The 1960s and 1970s saw the emergence of a dissident Ukrainian democratic movement that began the long struggle that would culminate in statehood. Artists, writers, and scholars joined in testing the limits of official tolerance to independent thought. An extensive underground literature, called *samvydav* (Ukrainian for "self-published"), emerged, urging greater cultural freedom, resisting the Soviet policy of Russification, and reclaiming a history suppressed by decades of Communist censorship and distortion. Even this largely cultural expression of national identity proved too much for the Soviet authorities, and a generation of Ukraine's most talented writers and artists soon found themselves behind bars or the barbed wire of the Soviet gulag.

Resistance to centralization and domination by Moscow manifested itself also within the Ukrainian Communist elite, who began publicly denouncing the extensive recentralization of economic power that occurred in Brezhnev's early years. Although Brezhnev had been a Communist Party official in the Ukrainian city of Dnipropetrovsk, when he assumed the reins of power in Moscow he alienated rather than allied himself with the Ukrainian Communist elite by keeping a tight rein on them and "trampling" on their ambitions. The Ukrainian apparatchiki did not take this well, but they were in no position to correct the imbalance. As Canadian historian Bohdan Krawchenko described it, the Kremlin "succeeded in making that elite 'more Ukrainian than Soviet.'"

In 1972, Moscow's fear of Ukrainian separatism and a possible emergence of a Tito-like "national communism" had evolved into an extensive purge of the Ukrainian Party and cultural elite. First to go was the Ukrainian Party's First Secretary, Petro Shelest, a crusty, plain-spoken tyrant who, in a style reminiscent of Khrushchev, tried to reach out to the people by defending Ukrainian culture against Russian domination and reclaiming Ukraine's colorful past. In a book prosaically titled *Ukraine, Our Soviet Land*, he proposed a heretical rendering of Ukrainian history, reaching back to the cossack age to paint a picture of an independent Ukrainian state guided by protosocialist principles. It was a historical telling that coincided with his Communist beliefs, yet because it glorified the anti-Russian cossacks, the book was a heresy that sealed his fate. Soon thousands of other high-ranking Party, government, press, educational, and cultural workers were purged. Russification was stepped up and Moscow's central control once again firmly established.

The Shelest era, 1963–72, did indeed prove worrisome for the Kremlin, for under Shelest, Ukrainian Party leaders were increasingly outspoken in their calls for national rights and economic self-determination, and were joined by writers, artists, and filmmakers who were producing bold new texts that celebrated Ukrainian culture and "separateness." As these cultural figures began to speak in increasingly bold tones and to become more and more politicized, they were joined by scholars and educators who reinterpreted the past from a distinctly Ukrainian perspective.

In 1972, Shelest, who had imprisoned many Ukrainian nationalists, was himself judged a crypto-nationalist and purged from the Soviet Politburo and later from the post of first secretary of the Communist Party of Ukraine. The scale of the Shelest purge was immense. Thousands of Party officials were stripped of power, and thousands of figures in the cultural establishment were removed from their posts as the iron hand of Brezhnev's centralized rule reasserted itself in Kiev and Ukraine. The purge also ensured that only the most backward, pro-Stalinist cadre remained in the Communist Party, a condition that was to plague Mikhail Gorbachev in his efforts to bring significant reform to a republic vital to the Soviet economy.

In the late 1970s, reeling from more than a decade of severe and sustained repression of the Ukrainian cultural establishment and of the alternative second culture alike, Ukrainian opposition acquired a decidedly more radical tone. Clandestine nonviolent activity supplanted the open, dissident activity of the 1960s and early 1970s. A document written by the Ukrainian Patriotic Movement made explicit the change in orientation and the radicalization of the Ukrainian opposition. It argued: "The spiritual and cultural climate here in Ukraine and in the USSR has become a horror for all civilized people. . . . The USSR has become a military–police state with wide-ranging imperialist intentions. . . . For more than sixty years the so-called government in Ukraine has been implementing this policy of national genocide." These anonymous and embittered dissidents declared their desire "to secede from the USSR, and lead our nation out of Communist imprisonment."

While the Ukrainian Patriotic Movement had only a handful of members, it represented the views of significant numbers of Ukrainians, for Ukrainian dissent has never been confined to the intelligentsia or to small dissident groups. In 1979, for example, tens of thousands of Ukrainians took part in a demonstration in the city of Lviv at the funeral of a popular Ukrainian composer, Volodymyr Ivasyuk, a kind of Ukrainian John Lennon who was murdered under suspicious circumstances that implied KGB involvement. His funeral became the occasion for a demonstration of pent-up national dissatisfactions at which Ukrainian dissidents delivered impromptu speeches to the thousands of participants.

Another major form of Ukrainian discontent was worker opposition. Soviet rule had seen a profound transformation in Ukrainian social structure. In 1939, only 29 percent of Ukrainians were industrial workers, 13 percent were white-collar workers, and 58 percent were collective farmers. By the 1970s, 47 percent were industrial workers, 16 percent white-collar workers, and 37 percent collective farmers. This movement of the labor force from farms and villages into factories and cities carried with it a concomitant improvement in their education and standard of living, and for many years was an important safety valve for potential discontent.

However, the second generation of urbanized Ukrainians that emerged in the 1970s was far less likely to be satisfied with its standard of living and more likely to be filled with rising expectations. One consequence of this trend was an upturn in mass unrest and independent trade union activism by Ukrainian workers. Dozens of strikes occurred in Ukraine in the 1960s,

1970s, and 1980s. In the years before the massive strikes by Ukrainian coal miners in the summer of 1989, worker unrest was manifesting itself in Kiev, Kharkiv, Odessa, Sevastopol, Pryluky, Kerch, and Dnipropetrovsk.

Industrial unrest ranged from city-wide work stoppages to strikes of small work brigades involving a handful of workers. Such strikes focused predominantly on quality-of-life issues such as housing, work conditions, and wages, yet some also contained elements of resentment against Russian rule. Surprisingly, in the vast majority of cases, the Soviet response was to act quickly to improve conditions and satisfy immediate demands. Only subsequently were strike leaders rounded up, arrested, and incarcerated in psychiatric prisons. In the Gorbachev years, strike movements operated with much more freedom and made more and more political demands.

The system of totalitarian repression, combined with widespread national oppression, kept the abiding force of Ukrainian national identity hidden for more than six decades, creating a double burden that made the Ukrainians a quintessentially hidden nation.

After Chernobyl

In the aftermath of the Chernobyl nuclear accident of April 26, 1986, the secret nature of the Ukrainian people and politics was further underscored when the *New York Times*, the *Washington Post*, and the three major American television networks ignored the national dimensions of the catastrophe. Had an environmental accident occurred in, say, Northern Ireland, it would be unthinkable for the press to disregard the implications for nationalism and separatism.

The Soviet authorities exploited Ukraine's rich and colorful traditions not only to calm the fears of neighboring republics and states, but to convey an image of cheerful normalcy for a region in the midst of a vast crisis. Only five days after the Number 2 reactor at Chernobyl had exploded spewing dangerous radiation clouds into the air, and with radiation levels dangerously high in nearby Kiev, an hour's drive from Chernobyl, Soviet television broadcast scenes of May Day celebrations that included smiling Ukrainian folk dancers, twirling and jumping in the acrobatic tradition rooted in the cossacks of the steppe. Viewers saw the sunny faces of Kiev's cheerful Ukrainian children dressed in traditional, intricately embroidered costumes and marchers carrying flowing red banners in honor of the socialist holiday.

But it was a different story for the children of top Party officials, who were quickly evacuated from the city as the radiation clouds approached. On that grim May Day, Ukraine's national culture was once again exploited for propagandistic ends. Despite the outward scenes of normalcy and good cheer, in their homes and in the city's streets the citizens of Kiev were angry and sullen as a growing state of unease enveloped the city. Their government was still not telling them about what they had learned of only through Western radio broadcasts and by word of mouth. Kievans were aware that the danger had not passed, but the formally independent Soviet Ukrainian government could not act on its own but only wait, as in all crises, for the word to arrive from Moscow.

The invisible wounds that Chernobyl has inflicted weigh heavily upon the consciousness of Kiev's residents. But horrible as the wounds are, they are but the tip of the iceberg of the ecological catastrophe that befell this once bountiful land.

The environment of the now-independent Ukraine is a vast, poisoned wasteland. According to David Marples, a leading Canadian expert on Ukraine's ecology, the eastern Ukrainian industrial cities of Dniprodzerzhinsk, Mariupol, Cherkassy, and Zaporizhia are suffering from contamination owing to the release of phenols, hydrogen sulfides, and ammonia into the atmosphere. In Dniprodzerzhinsk, a heavily industrialized city of 279,000, there are alarming rates of infant mortality, and up to one-quarter of school-age children suffer from pathological illnesses. An outdated and aging industrial infrastructure dumps pollutants into Ukraine's rivers. One, the winding Dniester, is virtually ruined, and another, the Dnipro, Ukraine's longest river, is disastrously contaminated, the consequence of a chemical plant's operating without a unit for the biochemical cleansing of water.

In southern Ukraine, once-verdant fields are in danger of disappearing—the result of salinization. By 1990, in the industrial city of Zaporizhia, industrial pollution stood at one hundred times acceptable levels, and had been doubling every three years.

In the town of Narodichi, less than forty miles from the power plant, thirty mutant farm animals were born in 1989. On various farms near the reactor, pigs with deformed skulls and calves without heads continue to be born. In a region ranging from thirty-one to fifty-six miles from the reactor, more than half of all children suffered from thyroid gland diseases. Moreover, the number of cancer cases near the nuclear plant doubled. In 1992, six years after the Chernobyl nuclear accident spewed radiation onto the picturesque Ukrainian landscape, many still-populated Ukrainian villages were unfit for humans.

For Ukrainians, the Chernobyl disaster was more than an ecological catastrophe; it was evidence of a centralized political system that denied its people a say in how their own nation was run. As a result of decisions made in far-off Moscow, Ukraine, which made up 3 percent of the vast Soviet territory, had the most nuclear power plants and produced 40 percent of the former USSR's nuclear power. "The concentration of all this nuclear power in an area with one of the USSR's highest population densities was sheer madness," observed Dr. Yury Shcherbak, once the leader of Ukraine's Green World Society and later independent Ukraine's Minister of the Environment. "We used to be silent and indifferent. Some of us believed, others didn't but were afraid to speak. Chernobyl taught us that silence is impossible," he said.

These days such newspapers as Kiev's daily *Vechirny Kiev* regularly remind readers that the Chernobyl legacy is still with them. The newspaper's back page shows readers an ominous, gloomy map of Ukraine, with large chunks covered with dark crosshatching, other regions covered in gray, and the distinct minority depicted in lighter tones. It is a map of warning: The dark regions represent the areas in which mushrooms and fruits are dangerously contaminated and must not be gathered and eaten under any circumstances. In the gray areas, all such gathered foods are to be subjected to radiation checks. Only the light-toned areas are free of contamination.

Chernobyl was for Ukraine and the Ukrainians a terrible catastrophe and an important impetus to political action, leading to a steady upswing in environmental activism that helped the golden-domed metropolis of Kiev awaken from decades of silence.

In Golden-Domed Kiev

Until the failure of the August 1991 putsch, the banning of the Communist Party, and Ukraine's rapid march to independence, the republic's capital showed few outward traces of a Ukrainian presence. In the shops and offices that lined the city's vast boulevards, Russian signs predominated. In the workplaces, Russian-language slogans urged workers on to greater productivity and discipline, and later through the struggle for perestroika. Seven times more copies of Kiev's Russian-language daily were printed than of its Ukrainian counterpart.

The beautiful city of Kiev—from its once elegant Khreshchatyk boulevard to the Podil, the city's low-lying Old Town—has been touched by Soviet vulgarity. Everywhere there are signs of an intruder. Classical revival architecture has been cheapened by its proximity to coarse, poorly built Stalin-era architectural monstrosities built to house the city's numerous ministries, research institutes, and government offices.

Despite the encumbrances of the despised era of Soviet rule, the Khreshchatyk's tradition shines through. In midsummer there are dozens of cafes, dispensing pastries, cakes, and apple turnovers. Children with their parents and grandparents politely queue up to buy Pepsi-Cola or Fanta, or a modest treat: vanilla ice cream, albeit at now inflated prices. But while Khreshchatyk has seen better times, the people still walk with a spring in their step and happier countenances than in Moscow. The shops are more cleanly kept; the meager shop window displays, more artfully arranged than in the Russian north. There is none of the oppressive air of Moscow. Although a boulevard in the Soviet style, there remain enough traces of the past. Even the street's name is redolent of history.

Khreshchatyk is derived from the Ukrainian word for "baptism." Legend has it that the boulevard courses over a long-gone stream in which Ukraine's first Christians were baptized in 988, when Grand Prince Vladimir (Volodymyr in Ukrainian) accepted Christianity from Constantinople. Through the centuries, Kiev's Russians and Ukrainians built splendid monuments to the glory of Christ. The city became a great center of ecclesiastic and later academic learning, with strong intellectual links to Constantinople and Mount Athos. Far from the obsessive power struggles, intrigues, and narrow-mindedness of Moscow, the imperial Russian capital, Kiev's Ukrainian identity and remoteness had inoculated its centers of learning and made of them impressive sanctuaries for free inquiry. The rulers of the city built impressive cathedrals with huge, glistening cupolas. Basilicas and monasteries rose along the riverbank of the winding Dnipro, the broad mother of rivers down which the Scandinavian warriors came a millennium ago—the Varangians, with names like Askold, Dir, Helgi (Oleh in Ukrainian), and Ingvar (Ihor in Ukrainian).

As the centuries passed, more and more gold cupolas peered through the deep green trees that populate the city's gentle hills. Today's Kiev still bears the traces of this past. But hidden under garish façades of Stalinist architecture and buried under acres of pavement are the remnants of dozens of magnificent churches and monasteries eradicated forever by the horror of the 1930s. It was then that the Communist planners, inspired by the ideals of a new socialist industrial order, pitilessly bulldozed the comforts and glories of the past, denouncing the ancient and traditional architecture as "meandering in the past." It was, said the commissars, a "peculiar" architecture inspired by "Ukrainian peasant homesteads," "the Jesuitic style of the baroque," and "the Russian empire style." All this was unacceptable, too nationally specific, too Ukrainian for the new internationalist order.

After all, said Stalin's zealous aesthetic partners, "Kiev was the site and citadel for various counterrevolutionary nationalistic groups. . . . It was not by chance that the manifestation of class ideology was especially striking in Kiev's architecture." And so a great master plan was born, a plan that would transform the central plazas and expanses of the city by eradicating the evidence of the old, defeated order. The instructions were given, the architectural plans drawn, and the dismantling of the past began.

A few brave souls tried to save the architecture. At a time of relentless repressions, this handful of daring men and women risked their lives in raising a faint voice of protest. Their voices were ignored. The structures, the commissars adjudged, were "insignificant." Among those "insignificant" monuments were such works as the Church of Saint Basil, built in 1183 as one of the last Byzantine churches of medieval Kiev, and later rebuilt in the late seventeenth century to repair the damage caused by heavy artillery fire in the struggles between Ukrainians and the Russian imperial troops; and the Collegiate Church of the Madonna of Pyrohoscha, built in 1132, the first brick structure in Kiev. In all, more than thirty houses of worship and monasterial complexes were destroyed, and with them countless belfries, convents, refectories, and cemeteries—the bulk from the seventeenth and eighteenth centuries, priceless rarities of baroque and rococo style. The golden altar gates—the *ikonostasis*—the friezes, frescoes, mosaics, elaborate porticoes, and articulated golden domes were scavenged and taken for the collections of Saint Petersburg's Hermitage, Moscow's Tretyakov Gallery, and other museums in Russia. So enthusiastic were the architects of the new order that they had planned even to tear down Saint Sophia, the most revered of all ancient Rus's churches. Such zeal, however, proved even too fanatical for Stalin, who overruled the Ukrainian commissar Pavel Postyshev.

A walk through the remnants of one of old Kiev's vanished glories—the former Mykhaylivsky Monastyr, the Monastery of Saint Michael of the Golden Domes—can still bring a chill. The complex, built by Grand Prince Svyatoslav II from 1108 to 1113, and renovated and enlarged in the seventeenth-century baroque style, included a massive church—the second largest in the city—a belfry, a monastery, a narthex, and tombs. Saint Michael's occupied one of the most scenic parts of the city, a rise on the right bank of the mighty Dnieper. The brisk winds that whistled through its courtyards must have added a note of solemnity and gravity of those who toiled and prayed there—to the faithful, a majesterial reminder of the power of a nature and world created by God.

Now all this is gone. The demolition was completed within a year, commencing in the spring of 1935—the entire process captured by photographers for the proud Party commissars. Part of the complex today is taken over by a massive building that houses the agencies of the Kiev government. Originally, the structure was home to the Central Committee of the Communist Party of Ukraine. It stands today as a looming, artless edifice with a monumental, sculpted flag and immense columns that wind in an arc facing toward the city's center, overlooking the ground where Saint Michael's once stood.

But the grand design, like much of totalitarianism's grandiose human project, was never fully realized, and so today there are large, empty patches of land. The wounds of those times weigh heavily on Kiev and Ukraine—and not only on the city's architecture but also in the numerous killing fields that dot the Ukrainian landscape. The repressed memory of the dark, bloodstained reign of Stalin has given way to the rebirth of national dignity, mobilizing hundreds of thousands of Ukrainian citizens, like the people of the village of Bykivnia.

The Poisoned Land

Located near Kiev, Bykivnia's forest long held a dark secret. Under its soil, carpeted with thick grass and red mushrooms, lay buried the corpses of thousands upon thousands of men, women, and children. For many years, a wooden fence kept the area undisturbed, but after a time the fence fell down and vandals dug up the soil to extract gold from the teeth of the skeletons. A few years ago, Soviet Ukraine's Communist authorities placed a plaque here: In Eternal Memory to the Victims of the German Fascist Occupation, the inscription read.

Later, the villagers learned of plans to build a railway station on the site of the mass graveyard. The sacrilege galvanized the elderly men and women of the village, who broke their silence of fifty years and protested the perversion of truth, telling anyone who would listen the true story of Bykivnia, of how beginning in 1936 Stalin's secret police, the dreaded NKVD, drove into the area then cordoned off by barbed wire and dumped truckload after truckload of bodies—the victims of unspeakable horrors. In the summer of 1989, under pressure from the Memorial, an anti-Stalinist organization in Kiev, Ukrainian Communist authorities were forced to acknowledge the inconvenient truth: In Bykivnia's forest were the remains of up to three hundred thousand victims of Communist repression—Bykivnia held the largest mass grave of Stalinist terror.

Today, the men and women of Bykivnia walk more proudly, having paid their debt to the memory of Stalin's victims. But for them as for most Ukrainian villagers, life in their now independent state remains grim and hard. Over the last three decades, millions of peasants have streamed out of the villages into the ill-prepared and overcrowded cities of Ukraine. In recent years, the migration from village to town has numbered more than two hundred thousand per year. And in the last two decades, more than fifteen hundred villages have been completely depopulated and stand now as eerie ghost towns. The village—long the treasure trove of Ukrainian culture, the conservative bearer of its tradition, and the firm bastion of its language—is fast disappearing.

In the villages that remain, and where about 30 percent of the Ukrainian population still lives, there are fewer amenities than in the grimy coal-mining towns of Ukraine's Donets basin. More than one-third of Ukraine's villages have no medical facilities whatsoever. For those that do, 70 percent are in truth medical stations situated in what the Kiev writer and Peasant Democratic Party leader Serhiy Plachynda calls "derelict flophouses." One-third of the isolated villages of the Ukrainian countryside have no cultural facilities, not even a place to put up a film projector for the screening of some twenty- or thirty-year-old propaganda relic.

A mere one in twenty of Ukraine's villages are linked to gas mains. A visit to the village of Muzhyliv in western Ukraine underscores the desperate state of rural life. The village, now a state farm, has been reduced to a grim latticework of muddy tracks and modest three-room houses. In the 1930s, it was a thriving village of private land holdings—the center of a robust community of highly motivated young landholders, many of them drawn to the cause of Ukrainian independence. Because the village was a hotbed of proindependence sentiment, Stalin's postwar Ukrainian satrap, Lazar Kaganovich, orchestrated the forced exile of hundreds of thousands of Ukrainians to remote, barren areas of Kazakhstan and Uzbekistan, where they were stripped of their native churches and schools, denied the use of their language, and compelled to grow cotton on chemically polluted tracts of land.

For those who remained, life was not easy as the village's infrastructure began to collapse under the weight of collectivized agriculture. Today, most of the young men and couples have left the farm for urban life, and despite the revival of nationalist ideas in the village, the knowledge of private, independent farming has all but vanished along with enthusiasm for privatizing the land. "We've gotten used to the way things are," says Maria, a retired collective farmer in her sixties. "What could I possibly do with the land on my own, without the men? Things might get worse if we were left each to fend for ourselves."

According to political and environmental activist Serhiy Plachynda, not only is the village in decline, "Ukraine is rapidly losing its land. At present there are eighteen million hectares of eroded lands and another two million are so oversaturated by chemicals that no efforts are being made to recultivate." The country's imposing, even majestic rivers, the Dnipro and Dniester, are extremely polluted by chemicals and nuclear contamination. That pollution has direct consequences for the health of the rural population, since around 90 percent of the republic's villages have no water mains. The water supplies that reach the villages are therefore frequently toxic. According to leaders of the Rukh: "The water pollution in . . . the Ingulets irrigation system exceeds the permitted norm by a factor of twenty-seven and in the Danube-Dnipro irrigation system, by a factor of fifty."

Rampant industrial mining of uranium has placed Ukraine first in the world in oncological illnesses and cancers. In late 1988, parents in the historic city of Chernivtsi, near the Romanian border, panicked when scores of children ranging in age from six months to fourteen years began to lose thick clumps of hair and to suffer hallucinations. While the origins of the mysterious disease were never fully established, the illnesses were traced to poisoning from thallium, a bluish white metallic chemical used in rat poison and in the manufacture of antiknock compounds for engines. As the crisis in Chernivtsi mounted, a massive chemical explosion in Uman, a city southwest of Kiev, reminded Ukrainians that factories continue to expose local residents to great dangers.

The Ukrainian national revival that began in 1988 was driven by the multidimensional cultural, environmental, economic, and political devastation of Soviet rule, provoking a wide-ranging investigation into past crimes that recovered some of the "blank spots," as they are euphemistically referred to, of the Stalin era. Independent activism helped to uncover the fact that the carnage through which the Ukrainian nation has passed in this century was second only to the nightmare of European Jewry. In all, 4 million to 7 million Ukrainians perished as a result of Stalin's forced famine of the early 1930s. Another 1.5 million fell victim to the Stalinist terror and the gulag archipelago, and 6 million Ukrainians died in World War II, bringing to nearly 12 million the number of lives snuffed out in less than two decades.

The Voices of a People

The blue-and-yellow Ukrainian flag, banned by the Soviet state, staged a stunning comeback in 1989 throughout the country amid a growing wave of marches and protest demonstrations that swept through Ukraine. It flew at the head of mass marches and meetings in Kiev, Lviv, Chernivtsi, Ivano-Frankivsk, and Ternopil, and by April 1990 had been raised atop the city hall of Lviv, the consequence of a stunning electoral triumph by nationalist candidates. Now the flag is an omnipresent symbol of independence and statehood.

The most spectacular manifestations of nationalist ferment were the demonstrations in western Ukraine that routinely attracted as many as two hundred thousand participants, and the rapid rise of the Rukh, which held its founding conference in Kiev in September 1989. The organization grew to more than seven hundred thousand members, and by 1990 had become the most popular political organization in the country. Equally threatening to the center of power in Moscow was the rapid rise of an independent workers' movement led primarily by the miners of the Donbass and the coal-mining region of the Lviv oblast.

By 1989, the leading lights of the official Ukrainian Writers' Union began to speak out for their nation's freedom. Ivan Drach, a poet, screenwriter, and essayist elected to head the Rukh, became not only one of the leading spokesmen for the national revival that swept Ukraine, but also a lightning rod attracting the venom of the Party's crude progaganda attacks. Once an enfant terrible of Ukrainian letters, today Drach is a balding, plumpish man in his mid-fifties with the remnants of a once-thick head of hair radiating in cascades from a bald pate. One dissident writer, who regarded this former conformist with suspicion, was delighted by Drach's political conversion to patriotic activism. "He has been seized with a visible passion. Even his poetry has been energized and elevated. He is a man transformed."

From 1989 until the proclamation of Ukrainian independence after the August putsch, Drach received streams of visitors in his ornate office on the top floor of the stately four-story building that was home to a rich local industrialist in the days before the Bolshevik Red Army captured Kiev, and now houses the Writers' Union. The huge room in which Drach still works contains a porcelain heater, a modest desk, and an imposing conference table cluttered with letters that flood in weekly from supporters around the country. For well over a year, until the Rukh moved to more formal, if less commodious, offices, Drach's office was a beehive of political activism.

A longtime member of the Communist Party, Drach had traveled on a long political odyssey. In March 1990, in the wake of the Rukh's impressive election showing (nearly two-thirds of its candidates were elected to consititute more than a quarter of the Ukrainian Supreme Soviet), Drach resigned from the Party and threw in his lot with a new proindependence force, the Ukrainian Democratic Party. Drach's transformation was coincident with the growth of a national rights movement. Spurred on at first by a small, isolated band of brave dissidents, many of whom served terms of imprisonment ranging from three to twenty-five years, Ukraine's modern-day intellectuals took up the verbal sword.

In 1989, the early days of his movement, Drach spoke only of a limited agenda: "We want to safeguard Ukrainian culture, to repair the damaged environment, and to create the conditions for open expression." In the years after Drach and his fellow writers boldly published a draft for a Ukrainian popular movement for restructuring in their 110,000-circulation weekly, *Literaturna Ukraina*, the Rukh helped inspire a mass movement in every way as serious and determined as those in the Baltic States, Armenia, or Georgia. In 1989 and 1990 demonstrations by as many as two hundred thousand were held in the western Ukrainian city of Lviv.

The protest wave stretched from the Polish border in the west to the southeastern industrial town of Dnipropetrovsk and spilled over into the coal mines of the Donbass in the republic's eastern reaches. In January 1990, hundreds of thousands of Ukrainians linked hands in a three-hundred-mile human chain that joined Kiev and Lviv in commemoration of the 1918 proclamation of a Ukrainian state.

At the inaugural congress of the Rukh in September 1989, about a thousand delegates from around the country gathered. They were hardened veterans of the gulag archipelago, sturdy and remarkable men like Levko Lukyanenko, then a sixty-two-year-old lawyer who had spent twenty-six years in Soviet prisons and concentration camps and who later headed the Ukrainian Republican Party. They were the tough leaders of the coal miners' strikes of July and August 1989; patriotic Communist Party members elected by a wave of popular discontent in the March 1989 elections to the USSR's Congress of People's Deputies; ecological activists outraged by the collapse of their once unspoiled environment; and cultural activists from the Ukrainian Language Society concerned about the decline of their mother tongue.

Despite the changing atmosphere in Moscow, the Rukh faced daunting problems, not least among them their lack of access to what was then a

Communist Party–controlled press. Still, one sign that the movement was emerging as a serious political force was the presence of Communist Party ideological chief Leonid Kravchuk at the Congress of People's Deputies, who less than three years later would come to power as president on a political program of state independence credited to the Rukh. Another sign of the Ukrainian movement's coming of age was the presence at the Rukh Congress of six leaders of Poland's Solidarity, including Adam Michnik, editor in chief of Poland's largest daily newspaper, *Gazeta Wyborcza*; Bogdan Borusewicz, then chairman of Solidarity for the Gdansk region and later head of its parliamentary faction; and Zbigniew Janas, member of the Polish parliament, who then headed the Polish trade union at Warsaw's sprawling Ursus tractor factory.

Michnik, a close adviser to Solidarity and one of the architects of the political opening in Poland, electrified the Rukh delegates with a strong condemnation of Russian imperialism and colonialism. "You as Ukrainians and we as Poles know the face of Great Russian chauvinism," he said. "We know how much harm it has brought to the Russians themselves. No nation can be happy if it degrades and oppresses other nations. Poland is with you! Solidarity is with you!" Michnik said to thunderous applause. "Long live a democratic and free Ukraine!"

Michnik's well-received remarks proved not to be the fanciful ravings of a revolutionary run amok, but the eloquent formulation of a new, emerging realpolitik, in which democratic movements throughout Eastern Europe provided each other mutual support. It was a prescient expression of confidence in the possibility of a new, decentralized, and democratic landscape that eventually replaced the postwar Soviet empire.

Although by late 1989 it was clear that while the Ukrainian language and Ukrainian identity were staging a large-scale comeback, they had a long way to go before Ukrainians would win their cultural and political struggle for independence.

In Lviv

If Kiev became the political center of the Ukrainian national revival and the battleground of a struggle between the Ukrainian and Soviet cultures, Ukraine's heart was in Lviv, an ancient western Ukrainian city with a rich history and a great sense of local pride. If Kiev contains the influences of ancient Constantinople's orthodoxy, Lviv, a Catholic city, is decidedly Central European, eclectic in its architecture, Western in its manners and tone.

Traditionally a multinational city, populated at the turn of the century in roughly equal proportions by Ukrainians, Jews, and Poles, today Lviv is overwhelmingly Ukrainian and its roots are evident everywhere. The city's most ancient structures were built in the thirteenth century by Armenians, whose influence continues in the name of a street that dissects the cobbled streets of Old Town—the Virmenska, the Ukrainian word for "Armenian." Farther on, a statue of Adam Mickiewicz, the Polish national poet, stands as another reminder of the city's ethnically diverse past.

The city's architectural splendors range from the structures of the ancient Rus of the late thirteenth century to the Gothic traditions of the fourteenth through sixteenth centuries. There are the Church of the Bernardines and the Boims family chapel, designed by Italian architects who invested the city with the flavor of the Italian Renaissance, the splendid baroque seventeenth-century church and convent of the Order of the Barefoot Carmelite Nuns, which until 1990 was given over to the use of the Komsomol, the Communist Youth Movement; the ornate, rococo Saint George's Cathedral, once again the province of the long-outlawed Catholic Ukrainian Uniate church; and the looming, glorious Dominican church with its Latin motto: *Soli Deo, Honor et Gloria,* which housed Lviv's Museum of the History of Religion and Atheism. Lviv's Democratic city council is likely to return it to the faithful. There are reminders of Central European influence in the remnants of the art nouveau style that captured popular tastes at the turn of the century. And there are reminders of the city's entrepreneurial past, including the former offices of the Land Credit Association, with its Empire-style façades and bas-reliefs that depict mythological scenes and angels. There is, too, the former five-story home of the Dniester Insurance Society, which employed 1,200 agents and insured 250,000 Ukrainians until Soviet authorities closed it down in 1939. Gone, too, are the vast network of consumer cooperatives with exotic names like the Narodna Torhivlya (People's Exchange) and the Maslosoyuz (the Butter Union), and the stores and savings and loans organized by the Prosvit (Enlightenment) Association, which brought literacy, volunteerism, and economic improvement to prewar Galicia.

Lviv is inextricably linked to the history of Europe, for here Poles, Jews, and Ukrainians coexisted for hundreds of years. Today, however, the dynamism of its past is a distant memory. The city's center is suffocating under mounting air pollution, and architectural landmarks are dilapidated. The streets are soot-laden, and the walkways of the once splendid parks are full of gaping holes. But while the aesthetic lines of Old Town's highly stylized and developed architecture have been crowded by the dead-end culture of totalitarianism, at least the city's Soviet rulers shied away from the monumentalism that dominates and distorts many other post-Soviet cities.

Since the summer of 1988, when mass demonstrations swept Lviv, signaling a Ukrainian patriotic awakening, Lviv's youth have seen an explosion of political activism and cultural innovation. Typical of this new generation is Ihor Hryniw, a research scientist in his early thirties. A former Komsomol leader and now a member of New Ukraine, a centrist faction of parliament, Hryniw is today clearly comfortable with the language of free-market liberalism.

His ground-floor flat is larger than most, with high, molded ceilings, a throwback to the old, elegant prewar Lviv. He is an avid collector of Ukrainian folk art, and although he has adopted the tidy habits and elegant manners of prewar Lviv, Hryniw is hardly living in the past. The youth movement he led before election to parliament, the five-hundred-member Lev (Lion) Society, was at the center of the city's political and cultural awakening. Taking its name from Lviv (the City of Lions), the Lev Society organized thousands of Ukrainians in protests calling for pollution controls to protect the decaying historic center of the city and sent cultural expeditions down the Dniester River in western Ukraine to uncover and restore abandoned village churches. Another of the group's missions was to save from extinction an arcane form of black pottery. Having mastered the techniques of molding and firing from elderly village craftsmen, several of the group's members are now thriving entrepreneurs selling highly popular and profitable folk art. A splendid collection of the black jugs, bowls, and cups clutters Hryniw's stylish old china cabinet.

"In a society in which the state and Communist Party claimed to initiate everything, we revived genuine private sector volunteer activities for the first time since communism was installed," Hryniw proudly notes. With the Lev Society's active support, Hryniw was elected in March 1990 to the Ukrainian parliament on a slate backed by the Rukh and began to use his parliamentary tribune to advance Ukraine's independence.

Andriy Panchyshyn is yet another young activist, a kind of Bob Dylan of the new Ukraine who has performed to packed audiences throughout the country as part of the Ne Zhurys (Don't Worry) ensemble, who had taken their name from a popular 1930s Lviv jazz band. The folksinger performed at dozens of factories and mines before thousands of gritty, worn, but enthusiastic young workers and students. There is a sharp edge and a clear political subtext in his ironic and sardonic ballads. In the days before independence he sang of Stalin's anti-Ukrainian satrap, Lazar Kaganovich; lamented the persistent lies that emanated from a local Lviv radio station nicknamed

"The Liar"; and poked merciless fun at a bumbling, unnecessary KGB. One of his bitter, sardonic songs was in the form of a classified ad for the Ukrainian language, offering up the "lost mother tongue" for sale to the highest bidder. Panchyshyn's concerts often turned into large political rallies, with the blue-and-yellow flags of the independent Ukraine unfurled and the cheerful crowds emotionally singing the then-banned national anthem, which begins: "Ukraine has not died yet."

Among the young people of Lviv, the past lived as a golden age. Satirical musical ensembles abounded, and even modern cabarets like those of the Ne Zhurys hearkened back to the past in a movement known as Lviv retro. In Lviv of 1989–90, young women dressed in the long skirts of the 1930s, and young men wore leather coats, trilby hats (*kapelyukhy*), and reed-thin ties in the fashion of that era. The ambience of the prewar city had made a strong comeback. In nightclub cabarets, ensembles performed the dance hall numbers of the Depression era. Crooners murmured the love songs of the 1920s and 1930s. Nightclub performers aspired to near total authenticity. "Alo-eh, alo-eh," they sang, re-creating the aloe facial cream jingles of Lviv's bygone radio days.

One student in his mid-twenties explained the popularity and abiding fascination of this subculture: "It's quite simple really. It's the last period before communism. It's a way of retreating from our . . . Red nightmare."

The revival of a politicized alternative culture spread out from Lviv. Sister Vika, a Lviv local, became Ukraine's most popular alternative musician. Dressed in black with a cropped punkish haircut, Vika's aggressive rap songs satirized the Soviet order: "I don't want sausage; don't want butter; don't want fancy dining; / All I want is for the Kremlin's star to keep on shining." Vika's music exported anticommunism, Ukrainian patriotism, and the Ukrainian language to such Russified redoubts as the coal-mining Donets basin. By 1991, most of Ukraine's alternative youth culture was proindependent and adopted as its language of protest the long derided Ukrainian language. Hundreds of avant-garde rock bands and rap artists were suddenly singing in the native language, and because pressing for independence had long been taboo, independence became the main aim of the protest culture. Among the young, suddenly it was hip to be Ukrainian.

Youth radicalization became manifest in October 1990, when after a general strike and a demonstration by more than one hundred thousand in Kiev had failed to topple the government, the students made a try. Hundreds of them launched a hunger strike and built a tent city in what was then called Lenin Square, galvanizing democratic activism around the country.

After two weeks, the students had forced the resignation of Prime Minister Vitaly Masol, a Brezhnev era holdover, and exacted a promise—not kept—that a referendum on dissolving the parliament would be held within one year.

In the months that followed, as Mikhail Gorbachev launched a wave of repression in the Baltic States, Ukraine's Communist leaders also attacked the Democratic opposition, beginning with an incident involving the radical parliamentary deputy Stepan Khmara. On November 7, 1990, as Khmara was walking in an underpass in central Kiev, a disheveled, distraught woman approached him, claiming to be one of his constituents asking for his help in apprehending a man who she said had just beaten and robbed her. Khmara and several of his colleagues from the Kiev Strike Committee stopped the alleged assailant, disarming him after a brief altercation.

The assailant turned out to be a KGB officer; the victim, a former criminal turned KGB informant. The entire incident was caught by KGB video for broadcast on Ukrainian television in selectively edited form to depict a violent deputy assaulting an officer of the state. The radical Khmara, who had recently called for legislation to ban the Communist Party, was quickly stripped of his parliamentary immunity by his Communist colleagues in the legislature, arrested in the parliament, and imprisoned on charges of assaulting a security officer and of exceeding his rights.

In the state-dominated society, Democrats began to encounter mounting administrative difficulties. The main opposition groups faced endless obstacles in publishing their newspapers, obtaining office facilities, and reaching the public through radio and television. Propaganda attacks were launched to portray the moderate Democratic opposition as an erratic band of extremists.

If the authorities expected the Khmara case and other forms of harassment to have a chilling effect on the opposition, they were soon disappointed. Their actions became a rallying cry for Democrats. By April 1991, after dozens of Ukrainian coal mines had shut down in a protracted strike and Khmara was released from prison as one of the strikers' demands, he remained under a legal cloud and was soon rearrested, only to be released with eight other political prisoners after the failed August 1991 coup.

The coup and its collapse left the Ukrainian Communist Party in disarray. Implicated in collaborating with the State Committee on the State of Emergency, the Party was outlawed as a criminal organization by the Ukrainian parliament. On August 24, parliament proclaimed Ukraine a sovereign and independent state, subject to confirmation by a nationwide referendum on December 1, 1991.

The Growing Rukh

The collapse of the coup was the main factor in the rapid acceleration of the movement toward Ukrainian statehood. Communists, who still controlled most of the levers of power in Ukraine, understood that amid a rising wave of anticommunism and mounting sentiment for state independence, their only salvation was to adopt the program of their proindependence Democratic opposition.

By late 1991, all across Ukraine the intense patriotism that first emerged in western Ukraine had gained millions of new converts, making significant headway in the countryside and in former cossack strongholds like Zaporizhia, where in the summer of 1990 and 1991, the Rukh had conducted massive Woodstock-style festivals of cossack culture. As many as half a million participants thronged to these cultural and historical celebrations, where songs, dances, peagantry, and speechmaking resurrected the traditions of self-rule represented by the region's seventeenth- and eighteenth-century cossacks, rekindling local pride and support for Ukrainian statehood.

But perhaps the most important headway was made in the Russified redoubts of Dnipropetrovsk and Donetsk. The city of Donetsk and the surrounding region form the heart of Ukraine's coal-mining industry. In July of 1989, the region was gripped by a massive coal miners' strike involving more than 250,000 workers. Although initially the strike committees were suspicious of all overtures from the nationally conscious Rukh and sought to limit its demands exclusively to workplace issues, by September 1989 the miners had sent representatives to the Rukh Congress, where they voiced opposition to the leading role of the Communist Party and began organizing themselves for upcoming local elections.

In advance of the March 1990 elections to the Ukrainian Supreme Soviet, a number of coal miners worked out the contours of a broad coalition that would unite them with Ukrainian nationalists and national rights activists and less nationally conscious proponents of radical economic reform. More important, the miners had come into contact with the nationally conscious miners of the Galician-Volynian coal-mining region. As the USSR's economy began its steep decline, more and more miners from the Donbas—Ukrainians and Russians alike—warmed to the idea of a sovereign Ukrainian state. By the fall of 1991, some of the mines in the Donbas had endorsed the nationalist Rukh candidate Vyacheslav Chornovil for president. Chornovil, the governor of Lviv oblast, won 23 percent of the vote in a field that included three other veterans of the Democratic movement. And while it was true that the embrace of the slogan of Ukrainian independence by much of the former Communist nomenklatura contributed to that outcome, there was no question that independence would not have come without the sustained struggle of Democratic forces like the Rukh. In the months following the independence vote, Ukraine moved quickly to demarcate its sovereignty, creating its own army, moving to establish its own currency, introducing the Ukrainian language into state structures and the educational system, and securing diplomatic recognition from more than one hundred countries.

The young Ukrainian state is now a strategically significant factor in post-Soviet Europe. The Ukrainian armed forces, over 500,000-strong in 1992, are continental Europe's second largest military—nearly 50 percent larger than Germany's *Bundeswehr* and larger than the combined armed forces of Britain and France. The Ukrainian military is two and a half times larger than the entire complement of U.S. forces in Europe. Ukraine's weight in post-Soviet politics is a consequence of its large population and territorial expanse (it is Europe's second largest state), by its geopolitically vital location on the Black Sea, and by the presence of tactical and strategic nuclear weapons still on its soil. And while the emergence of the new state has not been free of conflicts and controversies, most significantly with Russia over the disposition of nuclear weapons and control of the Black Sea Fleet, Ukraine's statehood has been achieved without bloodshed or major upheaval.

After centuries of colonial anonymity, Ukraine has begun to make its mark on world affairs. Formerly relegated to a secondary status by the West, Ukraine rapidly emerged as a forceful and critical actor in defining the contours of post-Soviet Europe. Although Russia and its president, Boris Yeltsin, had taken the lead in the defeat of the August 1991 coup and in the disintegration of the Communist Party, it was Ukraine and its president, Leonid Kravchuk, that provoked the unraveling of the Soviet empire.

It was Ukraine's resolute decision not to sign Mikhail Gorbachev's Union treaty that precipitated the collapse of the USSR and led to the creation of the Commonwealth of Independent States, which, according to Belarusian President Stanislav Shushkevich, had been cobbled together hastily as a loose confederation primarily to satisfy Ukrainian concerns. Although a founding member of the Commonwealth, Ukraine has turned out to be its most reluctant partner.

From the outset of his term in office, Ukraine's newly elected president, Leonid Kravchuk, pursued a policy aimed at ensuring a weak Commonwealth. With many of its political leaders viewing the new Commonwealth as a transitional structure to carry out a divorce between the former Soviet republics, Ukraine consistently opposed attempts to create permanent coordinating structures and blocked efforts to build a large central bureaucracy, insisting that all coordination efforts be handled through bilateral and multilateral discussions among independent states.

In its first months, the main theme of Ukrainian statecraft was to define the contours of state sovereignty and to assert and test that sovereignty at every turn, all the while reminding the former republics of the Soviet Union and the rest of the world that the Commonwealth of Independent States was neither a state structure nor a subject of international law. At the March 1992 summit of member states, hosted by President Kravchuk in Kiev, Ukraine rejected all but four of the eighteen treaties and agreements proposed. Kravchuk was explicit in his intentions: "I would like history to record one day that Kravchuk was one of those that did much to break up the empire, that Ukraine played an enormous role in that."

Ukraine's resolute military policies in early 1992 led to the fragmentation of what had been the world's second most powerful military. Kravchuk's belief that a unified military endangered sovereignty triumphed, and the Ukrainian position has not only won the support of Moldova, Azerbaijan, Belarus, and Uzbekistan, each of which is forming its own army, but has also forced Russia to create its own armed forces, thus defining the military structure of the post-Soviet world.

The creation of the Ukrainian armed forces began in earnest on December 6, 1991, when the Ukrainian parliament adopted a Law on the Armed Forces and a Law on the Defense of Ukraine. By December 12, just four days after meeting with Russian President Boris Yeltsin and Belarusian parliamentary chairman Stanislav Shushkevich to create the Commonwealth, Kravchuk signed a decree appointing himself commander in chief of all nonstrategic military formations on Ukrainian territory.

The Ukrainian Ministry of Defense became perhaps the most revolutionary part of the new state. The work of the ministry had already begun in September 1991, when Konstantin Morozov, a forty-eight-year-old colonel-general in the Soviet Air Force, resigned his commission to take the post of minister of defense. Of Russian and Ukrainian heritage, Minister Morozov rapidly moved to Ukrainianize the military, assembling a mix of military professionals and advisers, many from the Democratic nationalist Rukh movement and the radical Union of Ukrainian Officers. Ministry staffers from the Democratic movement were responsible for such matters as educational programs and military-industrial conversion.

Because Minister Morozov began his ministerial duties ex nihilo with only two aides, he was free to shape an institution to his needs. Unlike most Ukrainian ministries, everyone in the newly minted Ministry of Defense was new; thus the ministry did not inherit the stultifying array of long-standing nomenklatura functionaries or the many time-serving apparatchiki that still populated most other Ukrainian ministries and agencies. Morozov's institution emerged as the most dynamic part of the Ukrainian government.

In its early days, with the USSR still formally intact, many regarded the prospects for a Ukrainian military force as a hopeless folly; however, Minister Morozov had received strong technical assistance from the Union of Ukrainian Officers. Created in 1990, the officers' group worked closely with the proindependence camp and many of its leaders were active in the Rukh. By the beginning of 1992, the group had fifteen thousand officers and ten thousand reserve officers in its ranks.

While the agreement establishing the Commonwealth emphasized that "member states . . . will preserve and maintain under joint command a common military-strategic space, including unified control over nuclear weapons . . ." this formulation did not preclude a subsequent agreement in which Ukraine would begin setting up its own army on January 3, 1992. The main instrument for creating the Ukrainian military was a new oath of allegiance that pledged soldiers "to defend the Ukrainian state, to stand firmly on guard for its freedom and independence." The oath was to be taken by all servicemen serving in Ukraine, and by the Black Sea Fleet based on Ukrainian territory. After oath-taking was impeded in Ukraine's Carpathian, Kiev, and Odessa military districts, the Russian commanding officers were dismissed and replaced by ethnic Russians born in Ukraine.

Thereafter, with the exception of the Black Sea Fleet, the oath-taking process encountered few significant obstacles and spread like wildfire. As with commanding officers, troops that refused to take the loyalty oath were transferred for service in other republics or demobilized into the reserve. Within the first two weeks of January, 250,000 troops in Ukraine had taken the oath; by early April, some 450,000. In mid-March 1992 Ukraine extended the loyalty oath to components of the Commonwealth's stategic forces, thus adding to the military repatriated Ukrainian officers and conscripts. According to the deputy commander of the Ukrainian Air Force, 55 percent of the troops that fly strategic aircraft and 95 percent of those responsible for refueling and other auxiliary functions had taken the pledge. According to *Izvestiya,* tens of thousands of Ukrainian officers and recruits applied for a return to their homeland. And President Kravchuk insisted he was ready, if necessary, to absorb the 400,000 Ukrainian citizens who served in military units outside their republic. To underscore Ukraine's territorial integrity and the independence of the armed forces, Ukrainian defense officials on several occasions denied Commonwealth military leaders access to Ukraine's military bases.

The troops in Ukraine's new army were educated in the spirit of Ukrainian patriotism. Military academies rapidly developed curricula that emphasized the struggle for Ukrainian statehood, including the seventeenth-century period of cossack rule, the period of Ukrainian independence from 1918–21, and the activities of the anti-Communist, anti-Nazi Ukrainian Insurgent Army. A sweeping new education program was developed for officers, NCOs, and conscripts.

The task of transforming Soviet troops into a Ukrainian force, elaborating a new mission, developing a new threat assessment, preparing for defense conversion, and managing a substantial demobilization are daunting tasks for any defense establishment. It was especially true for a military that was unsure precisely how many troops were on its territory. The most reliable estimate of Ukrainian troop strength (700,000) did not include border forces and the new national guard. A census and an inventory of materiel were undertaken. And while the Ministry of Defense did not have complete figures on equipment and inventory, Commonwealth military officials suggested that Ukraine had wound up with much of the most advanced weaponry and technology in the Soviet arsenal. And when Kiev declared its intention to scale back Ukrainian armed forces to 200,000–300,000 over a period of five years—well within the level accepted by most European powers—Ukrainian defense officials did not see this reduction as a weakening of the country's defense capabilities but as an opportunity to make technological improvements that would yield a military whose firepower matched that of 1992 force levels.

No aspect of Ukrainian policy attracted greater attention than its position on nuclear weapons. In April 1992, parliament reconfirmed Ukraine's intention to be a neutral, non-nuclear state. By May 1992, all 4,000 tactical nuclear weapons had been removed, while 176 strategic intercontinental ballistic missiles with more than 1,600 warheads remained on Ukrainian soil. Presidents Kravchuk and Bush met in Washington in May 1992 and agreed that Ukraine would rid itself of all nuclear weapons by the end of the decade—an agreement that appeared to supplant earlier statements that the republic would remove all strategic nuclear weapons by 1994. By mid-1992, there was increasing sentiment within the Ukrainian political establishment to keep nuclear weapons. While the consensus within parliament and among major political groups was to proceed with missile destruction, heightened Russo-Ukrainian tensions could in the future reverse this attitude. Moreover, by late 1992 Ukraine's government sought security guarantees and economic assistance in return for its ratification of the START 1 Agreement and non-nuclear status.

In the first months of independence, the pace of Ukrainian economic reform did not match that of military reform. Ukraine's efforts at economic change seemed consistently to lag behind developments in Boris Yeltsin's Russia. Significantly, such reform-minded Ukrainian officials as Deputy Prime Minister Volodymyr Lanovy noted that this was probably inevitable: "Ukraine . . . is unprepared for independent implementation of the reforms because its economy is not under full control of the state. . . . It is part of the economy of another state and is still regulated largely from Moscow."

A major agricultural and industrial center of the former Soviet Union, Ukraine accounted for 16 percent of the USSR's economic output in 1990, producing 25 percent of its meat and meat products and 21 percent of its dairy products. Of foods exported to other Soviet republics, Ukraine provided 80 percent of pasta, 55 percent of vegetable oil, 46 percent of canned vegetables, and 30 percent of flour. On the industrial front, Ukraine produced 56 percent of the USSR's rail cargo cars, nearly 50 percent of iron ore, 41 percent of rolled steel, 35 percent of ferrous metal, 33 percent of televisions, 31 percent of harvesters, 25 percent of computer and automation equipment, 23 percent of coal, and 22 percent of both tractors and bricks.

Thus, the unavoidable issue for Ukraine was that its economy was still largely intertwined with those of other former Soviet republics, most notably Russia. Arguing that the new state could not gain control of its economy and implement price reforms so long as Moscow controlled the printing and distribution of rubles, Kiev has permitted the circulation of coupons as a substitute currency to allow the economy some autonomy until it can introduce its own currency—the Canadian-printed *hryvnia*—hopefully in 1993.

On March 24, 1992, President Kravchuk's presidential advisory body, the Duma, issued a report on the "Fundamentals of Ukrainian National Economic Policy." Prepared by the president's State Counselor Oleksander Yemelyanov and endorsed by an overwhelming vote in the parliament, the report emphasized that financial, monetary, and pricing policies continued to be managed "from afar," thus making Ukraine incapable of making serious independent decisions on economic matters. To prevent being drawn into a single, Russian-dominated economic complex, Ukraine was to take the following steps:

- "withdrawal from the ruble area and the swift introduction of a separate currency";
- "a gradual reduction in imports from countries in the ruble zone through the introduction of an austerity policy";
- "a reorientation toward new markets";
- a payment system for freight and commodities transported through Ukraine based on international norms, including taxes and charges "for all foreign facilities using Ukraine's transport infrastructure";
- and control over "customs tariffs and foreign economic activity along the length of the Ukrainian state border."

Yet while President Kravchuk and most Ukrainian leaders stated that they favored fundamental reforms, they were divided about the specifics of such an economic program. Some were deeply critical of Russia's approach to reform. As Volodymyr Chernyak, an economist from the Rukh coalition, put it: "Neither in Russia nor in Ukraine is it possible to follow the classic International Monetary Fund scheme. You cannot free prices as the cornerstone of reform." Kravchuk had also emphasized that Ukraine could not survive the radical shock therapy approach that had been tried in Poland. "We have to learn from the experience of other East European states," he told us in Kiev on the eve of his election. "Ukraine will take its own path."

With the March 1992 elevation of New Ukraine democratic bloc member Volodymyr Lanovy to the post of deputy prime minister, the economy appeared poised for rapid reform. The Ukrainian parliament passed laws setting the stage for major privatization initiatives for the commercial sector and small enterprises. Current joint ventures were given a legislatively protected right to repatriate their share of profits tax free for five years; foreign stakes in new joint ventures were made exempt from taxes for the first three years of profitability; and local governments were allowed to privatize housing and land.

When he ran for Ukraine's highest office, Kravchuk had relied on the strong support of the collective and state farm managers. But after his election, he appeared to have declared war against these entrenched interests: "We can no longer tolerate a situation where a vast [agro-industrial] administrative apparatus, having exhausted its usefulness, is preserved in its primitive form." He appointed a new Minister of Agriculture with close links to the Democratic bloc in parliament.

Progress was also made on the question of the USSR's hard currency debt. Until March 1992, Ukraine resisted attempts to take collective responsibility for Soviet obligations, regarding the debt problem as an infringement on state sovereignty. In the end, Ukraine's initial hesitancy was overcome and the republic agreed to assume responsiblity for 21.13 percent of the USSR's $82 billion debt, with Russia agreeing to take responsiblity for the balance owed by the republics.

No matter what sort of reforms they pursued, one major economic issue, energy, promised to vex Ukrainian leaders in the years ahead and complicate the drive toward sovereignty. Ukraine was dependent on 42 percent of its energy needs, a shortfall that had traditionally been met by Russia. In all, Ukraine needed 66 million tons of oil and 4,061 billion cubic feet of natural gas, but produced only 8 and 20 percent of these needs, respectively. To reduce this dependency and to prepare for Russia's introduction of higher energy prices, Ukraine planned to reduce its output of electricity by nearly 20 percent, going from 270 billion kilowatt hours in 1990 to 220 billion kwh in 1992. Yet despite such economies, Ukraine remained extremely dependent on Russia to satisfy most of its oil and natural gas needs. Seeking to diversify their energy sources, Ukrainian leaders reached an agreement with Iran and Azerbaijan to construct new oil and gas pipelines.

Despite the lofty rhetoric of fundamental reform that emanated from Kravchuk and Prime Minister Vitold Fokin, by the summer of 1992 Deputy Prime Minister Lanovy had become discouraged by the government's unwillingness to quickly implement a program of economic change, charging that an entrenched old-line apparat was torpedoing reforms. Lanovy became increasingly vehement in his criticism of the policies of his prime minister—the former head of Ukraine's State Planning Committee. In July 1992, Kravchuk dismissed Lanovy, raising anew questions about Ukraine's commitment to democratic change.

One year after the August coup, the man at the heart of Ukrainian statehood and at the center of the formation of the Ukrainian state remained something of a mystery. Kravchuk, a former director of the ideology department of the Ukrainian Communist Party and ideology secretary of the Ukrainian Communist Party in 1989–90, became a fierce advocate of Ukrainian statehood.

In the months before the December 1, 1991, referendum and presidential election, analysts in Russia and Ukraine suggested Kravchuk was playing to growing nationalist sentiments in a bid to secure high office. Once he took office, it was said, Kravchuk would move quickly to shape some sort of union with the other republics. Nothing was further from the truth. In the aftermath of the failed August coup, President Kravchuk moved consistently to secure Ukrainian independence. Polls published in January and February 1992 by Russia's influential newspaper *Nezavisimaya Gazeta* judged him to be the most influential politician in the Commonwealth of Independent States. While many traced Kravchuk's political transformation to high opportunism, others pointed to the fact that he was born into a peasant family of Orthodox believers in the Volyn region of traditionally nationalist western Ukraine. Still others suggested that Kravchuk had learned to appreciate the trappings of statehood, the ceremonial aspects of high office, and the power that comes from legitimate popular support.

Whatever the motives, Kravchuk was unwavering in the Ukrainian march toward statehood, although in the sphere of political reform he was a study in contradictions. While opening up Ukrainian mass media and stopping the intrusive surveillance of the old security apparat, Kravchuk's personnel policies showed a predisposition to trust those who worked within the Communist apparat. Even in the case of his many appointments of ministers and advisers from the Democratic camp, virtually all were former Communists. In March 1992, after the parliament granted Kravchuk sweeping powers to reform local governments, three-quarters of those he appointed as local presidential representatives were former apparatchiki, including numerous former regional and local Party secretaries. Democratic activists from the Rukh and New Ukraine movements charged that this practice slowed change and stymied the many local legislatures and governments now in the hands of elected Democrats. "We call it a velvet putsch," said one Kiev city council leader.

By the second half of 1992, politics in Ukraine was characterized by a proliferation of small parties. Nevertheless, Democratic forces had coalesced around two major camps: the Rukh and New Ukraine. The Rukh remained strongest in western Ukraine and in such urban centers as Kiev and Kharkiv, where it claimed seven hundred thousand members and pointed to the millions of adherents who had taken part in mass actions in behalf of statehood. Led by former political prisoner Vyacheslav Chornovil, who finished second to President Kravchuk in the December 1 presidential race, the Rukh divided into two wings: the Chornovil-led majority that emphasized its role as a Democratic opposition and a minority that believed the Rukh should offer active support to Kravchuk as he worked to consolidate Ukrainian statehood. Chornovil managed to maintain unity between these two poles by defining the Rukh as a "constructive opposition" that backed the president when he advanced Ukrainian statehood, yet criticized him when he resisted basic democratic and economic reforms. "We live in what at the grass-roots level is still a Communist society," Chornovil argued in July

1992, noting that in the collectivized countryside and in many cities and towns, local authorities were the selfsame apparatchiki who had actively backed the August coup. Now that statehood had been won, Chornovil suggested, the major task was to build a thriving civil society and to shape a democratic Ukraine.

Chornovil's approach was echoed by leaders of the New Ukraine movement. Unlike the Rukh, which was led primarily by long-standing anti-Communists, New Ukraine was created by activists who emerged from the Democratic platform, a reform faction that split with the Communist Party in mid-1990. New Ukraine offered strong support for Ukrainian statehood, but because many of its members were ethnic Russians or Ukrainians from Russophone regions, it deemphasized the patriotic sloganeering and symbolism of the Rukh, placing its emphasis on economic reform and the strenghtening of civil society. New Ukraine included in its ranks representatives of the proreform wing of industry, the emerging business community, segments of the academic community, and the scientific intelligentsia. It had two wings: liberal proponents of a free market and Social Democrats. New Ukraine's leader Volodymyr Filenko believed this dichotomy would not result in divisiveness: "As in Eastern Europe, differences between the liberals and the Social Democrats will not emerge until a considerable amount of privatization has occurred."

According to close observers of the Ukrainian political scene, neither New Ukraine nor the Rukh would capture a majority in new parliamentary elections. The Rukh would enjoy strongest support in western and central Ukraine, while New Ukraine, with its substantial presence of Russophone leaders, would draw significant support in eastern and southern Ukraine.

The dividing lines between the Rukh and New Ukraine indicate the differences that remain between the regions of Europe's second largest state. Indeed, there are cultural and political differences between the Catholic Uniate west, where nationalist sentiments are passionate, and the Orthodox east, with its high proportion of Russians and Russian speakers. Still, the evolution of the Ukrainian independence movement successfully traversed the breach. By forging a nonethnically defined sense of inclusive Ukrainian patriotism (defined as support for a Ukrainian state) and by wooing Ukraine's Russian, Jewish, Polish, and Hungarian national minorities, the Rukh and other anti-Communist movements avoided the divisive ethnopolitics that plagued other non-Russian republics. The democratic nationalists in the west tempered their nationalism and argued for Ukrainian statehood in pragmatic, economic terms, thus avoiding dividing the country into hostile camps while also setting the stage for cooperation between the Rukh and New Ukraine.

While ethnic relations between Ukrainians and Russians remained calm in the first year of Ukrainian independence, state relations between Russia and Ukraine were tense, as high-ranking Russian leaders began a pattern of aggressive statements questioning current Russian-Ukrainian borders. In December 1991, President Yeltsin's then press secretary Pavel Voshchanov suggested that the border issue was yet to be resolved. After a quickly improvised high-ranking Russian mission to Kiev tensions were defused, but the gauntlet was picked up again in late January by Vladimir Lukin, then chairman of the Russian parliament's Foreign Relations Committee and now Russian ambassador to the United States, who wrote a widely publicized memorandum suggesting that to secure control over the Black Sea Fleet, Russia should question Ukrainian patrimony over Crimea, a region ceded to Ukraine in 1954. Such a maneuver, argued Lukin, would help respond to the growing clamor on the part of the Russian nationalist right, while at the same time pressuring Ukraine into abandoning its claim on the fleet.

The publication of the Lukin memorandum and a subsequent resolution by the Russian Supreme Soviet asking for an investigation of the circumstances of Crimea's transfer to Ukraine provoked outrage in Ukrainian circles. Soon after these challenges to Ukrainian territorial integrity, Kiev revealed that it had suspended transfer of tactical nuclear weapons to Russia. While Ukraine's action was accompanied by assurances that these weapons were being dismantled under international supervision, the decision had come in the context of Kiev's growing unease about Moscow's intentions and so must be seen as part of the perennial Russian-Ukrainian dispute.

In April, relations again worsened after an unauthorized visit to Ukraine by Russian Vice President Aleksandr Rutskoy and State Counselor Sergey Stankevich, who traveled to Sevastopol for highly publicized meetings with the Black Sea Fleet. Rutksoy, who regularly criticized Yeltsin's policies and attacked the putative surrender of "historical Russia," pronounced the Crimea and the Black Sea Fleet to be Russian, provoking Kravchuk into a decree on April 6 that placed the fleet under Ukrainian jurisdiction. One day later, Yeltsin followed suit, proclaiming Russia's takeover of the Black Sea Fleet. Cooler heads prevailed on April 8, as the leaders rescinded their decrees and established a joint parliamentary commission to resolve the lingering disagreement over the fleet. In the summer of 1992, Ukraine and Russia appeared to have narrowed their differences at a successful summit between Presidents Yelstin and Kravchuk.

The Russian officials' ill-considered and provocative remarks conformed, in the eyes of Ukrainian leaders, to a pattern of Russian conduct that had plagued their republic for centuries—a relationship of domination—and they were determined not to let history repeat itself. While Kravchuk and other Ukrainian officials understood that Russian President Yeltsin never questioned Ukraine's current borders, and Yeltsin aides confirmed that the Russian president was committed to honoring a 1990 treaty that confirmed existing borders, nevertheless Ukrainian officials watched an increasingly shrill ultranationalist opposition to Yeltsin and questioned his durability in office.

While most of the tension initially surrounding the Crimea was fanned by the dispute over the Black Sea Fleet, the Crimean question could well survive Russo-Ukrainian rapprochement. A large and well-financed Crimean Republican Movement had agitated for independent statehood for the peninsula, gathering more than two hundred thousand signatures in an effort to force a petition on the question of Crimean independence in 1992. While a reliable poll conducted in February 1992 showed public sentiment in the Crimea to be fragmented—with 42 percent supporting Crimea's remaining an autonomous republic linked to Ukraine, 15 percent favoring a return to Russia, 22 percent supporting a sovereign Crimean republic within the Commonwealth of Independent States, and 8 percent in favor of complete state independence—public opinion remained highly volatile.

Although Russia was the central preoccupation of Ukrainian foreign policy in its first months of statehood, nevertheless the new state moved with alacrity to signal the contours of its foreign policy, focusing primarily on the desire to secure full-fledged membership in democratic Europe. Ukraine has made it clear that it seeks eventual membership in the structures of the European Community. As a vehicle toward that end, it seeks membership as the fifth partner in the Vysegrad process through which Poland, Hungary, and the Czech and Slovak republics attempted to coordinate their entry into democratic Europe. A cornerstone of Ukrainian policy was the insistence on the permanence of existing international borders.

Ukraine was an important presence in Central and Eastern Europe, sharing land borders with Poland, Hungary, the Czech republic, Slovakia, Romania, Russia, Belarus, and Moldova and the Black Sea coastline with Turkey, Bulgaria, Romania, Russia, and Georgia. Of these, relations with Poland and Hungary were strongest. Poland had been first to recognize Ukraine's independence and in recent years activists from the Solidarity movement have offered technical and material assistance to the Rukh, while Hungary had been first to solidify a close relationship through a visit to Kiev by its president, Arpad Goncz, and through a military cooperation agreement with its neighbor. Ukrainian relations with the Czech and Slovak republics were cordial. With the exception of Russia, of all the states bordering Ukraine, Romania loomed as the greatest potential danger, its parliament having made territorial claims on southern Bessarabia. Ukraine took steps to defuse the question by staying out of the conflict in Moldova's Slavic Dniester Moldovan Republic. Unlike Russia, which pursued a vigorous policy in support of ethnic Russians and Russian speakers, Ukraine secured its borders, noting that the territorial dispute was a matter for Moldova to resolve. By respecting Romanian and Moldovan borders, Kiev apparently hoped for eventual reciprocity.

Another focal point of Ukrainian foreign policy is its relations with countries with a substantial Ukrainian diaspora, including the United States, where there are 750,000 Americans of Ukrainian ancestry; Canada, where 700,000 ethnic Ukrainians live; and Brazil, with a diaspora of more than 200,000. There are also a quarter million Ukrainians in Poland and substantial Ukrainian communities in Britain and Australia. A further focus is Israel, which was quick to recognize the new Ukrainian state. Relations that had warmed between the two countries in the months before Ukrainian independence were crowned in October 1991 in a solemn week-long commemoration of the tragic massacre of Jews in Kiev's Babi Yar.

While an embattled Boris Yeltsin was forced to dismiss pro-Western democrats from his government and Russian reform appeared to be stalling in late 1992, a quiet revolution in Ukraine put in place a coalition government in which the dominant posts were held by democratic nationalists and reformers from the Rukh and New Ukraine coalitions.

The momentous changes in Ukraine occurred in late October 1992, with the naming of Leonid Kuchma, the director of Ukraine's high technology missile production plant, Pivdenmash, as the country's new prime minister. Kuchma, a design engineer by training, had been a part of the New Ukraine democratic reform bloc. He replaced Vitold Fokin, the former head of the Ukrainian SSR's state planning ministry and an opponent of radical economic reform.

In his first weeks in office, Kuchma made it clear his government would differ from his predecessor's. He announced a wideranging anti-corruption campaign, and backed it up with revelations about how Ukrainian officials had sold cheap Russian petroleum on the open market for huge personal profits.

Further evidence of Kuchma's intentions was the formation of a government team in which democrats controlled key economic, social, trade, and cultural portfolios.

The fall of the retrograde Fokin government had been a byproduct of rising social discontent, including a transport and miners strike in early September 1992, a rapidly accelerating inflation rate that had reached 30 percent per month by the autumn of 1992, an 18 percent decline in agricultural production, and a severe energy crunch exacerbated by Russia's unwillingness to sell Ukraine cheap oil. Another factor was a split between Ukraine's cautious President Leonid Kravchuk, and its increasingly democratically-oriented Parliamentary Speaker Ivan Plyushch. Plyushch, a former Communist leader from Poltava, had reshaped himself as a Ukrainian patriot. He further had broadened his political horizons through foreign travels, including two visits to the United States. He also had developed a good working relationship with leading Ukrainian democrats from the Rukh and New Ukraine.

Amid growing fragmentation in the once monolithic political bloc of apparatchiki, Plyushch saw an opening and won the support of some of Ukraine's industrial directors. "In circumstances of acute economic crisis," Rukh parliamentary leader Les Tanyuk told us in Kiev in November 1992, "industrialists and managers had two choices: either to engage in criminal activities with the aim of quick personal enrichment or to take the plunge and support radical economic reform." Enough of them had chosen the latter, opening the door to the Kuchma team.

When we met with First Deputy Prime Minister Ihor Yukhnovsky in Kiev in late November 1992, the democratic activist who had opposed President Kravchuk in elections one year before was optimistic if soberminded. "I am convinced that the Prime Minister will remove any ministers or officials who block radical reforms. This will not be a repeat of the last year."

Nevertheless, Yukhnovsky, a highly respected physicist, was clear about the new team's mission: "We are a government of the condemned," he stressed. "We will be called upon to press ahead with painful economic reforms. And we will have strong opposition from the entrenched interests of the old order."

As 1993 appeared on the horizon, economic experts under Deputy Prime Minister Viktor Pynzenyk, a member of the Rukh parliamentary bloc from Lviv, worked out a program designed to rein in a budget deficit that stood at 44 percent, mapped out a program of privatization of shops, apartments, and industrial enterprises, and sought to solve Ukraine's widening energy crisis.

The significance for the West of these events in Ukraine could not be overemphasized. With a population of 52 million, an independent Ukrainian state, rooted in the West, could emerge as an anchor of stability in Eastern Europe and a check on imperial and hegemonic impulses that were reemerging within wide segments of Russia's political establishment.

Certainly the changes that had occurred in Ukraine as 1992 drew to a close were among the most auspicious of any in the new post-Soviet states.

While Ukraine is eager to be accepted by industrial democracies—as suggested by its shipments of tactical nuclear weapons to Russia and its declared commitment to nuclear nonproliferation—it still has a long road ahead to attain the status of a full-fledged democracy. The revolutionary forces that secured Ukrainian independence must now ensure democratic and economic renewal. They must do so in the face of mounting resistance from large segments of the Old Communist nomenklatura.

Chapter Four

The Baltic States: Vanguard of Independence

The Soviet Union turned to secret diplomacy and accepted the imperialistic principle of the assigning of spheres of influence to powerful States. . . . The Soviet German treaties decided the fate of other States, turned independent States into military protectorates and then forcibly incorporated them into the USSR.

FROM A STATEMENT ON JULY 20, 1989,
BY THE COMMISSION OF THE CONGRESS OF
PEOPLE'S DEPUTIES OF THE USSR TO EXAMINE
THE HITLER-STALIN TREATY OF 1939

In the struggle for independence and freedom from the Soviet Union, the Baltic States are the unacknowledged champions who cleared the way for other republics. Lithuania, Latvia, and Estonia, ranged along the coast of the Baltic Sea on the peripheries of the Soviet Union, were among the last to be incorporated. Annexed in 1940 during World War II, after having existed as independent states since 1918, these three republics were the most immediate reminder to the outside world of the true imperial nature of the Soviet state. Reports of repression of the Baltic people were not as easy to suppress as those farther east of the edge of the Iron Curtain. Emigré organizations and political refugees made sure that the world would not forget the plight of their compatriots.

Nevertheless, for almost fifty years the people of Lithuania, Latvia, and Estonia existed in a twilight zone. No democratic state would sanction their annexation by the Soviet Union, but neither would any foreign power support their desire for independence. When tens of thousands of people were deported to Siberia in the nightmarish exodus that followed the consolidation of Soviet power in the late 1940s and 1950s, there was no murmur of protest from the West. While the United States never recognized the Baltics' incorporation into the USSR, it did little over the years to provide diplomatic backup to its routine assertions of Baltic sovereignty, trotted out once a year for the Captive Nations Day commemoration. The Baltic States seemed continually to slip off the agenda whenever the two superpowers had real exchanges, and remained nations lodged on the periphery of the Western world's consciousness. They were equally remote and unknown to the other peoples of the vast Soviet empire.

The Baltic States were the first to test the limits of glasnost and perestroika. Step by step, they gained the possibility to proclaim their desire to regain independence. By 1989, the Baltic States had succeeded in gaining permission to celebrate the anniversaries of their original declarations of independence. In each state the date was commemorated with the mixture of solemnity, barely repressed jubilation, and yearning for true independence that had characterized their movements for years.

In Estonia, the celebration of national independence first gained in 1918 was held on February 24, 1989. As in the other Baltic States, the date was charged with significance. Public commemorations had been banned for years, as was the flag of independent Estonia. But on that day in 1989, for the first time in over forty years, the blue, black, and white national flag of independent Estonia was raised on the Pikk Hermann tower in Tallinn. The people cheered hoping that the red flag of the Estonian SSR, which was taken down, would never again be seen flying from the ancient tower on Toompea Hill in the center of the city.

A ceremony such as the one that took place that February, attended by officials of Estonia's Communist Party as well as prominent members of the Estonian Popular Front (Rahvarinne), would have been unimaginable one year earlier. Then, mere possession of the flag of free Estonia, a symbol that was banned for its anti-Soviet associations, was liable to provoke arrest; and the thought of hoisting it atop the Pikk Hermann had been just a dream. But many incredible things took place in that year of miracles.

On the day the flag of a free Estonia was raised, Hirve Park below was filled with tens of thousands of people looking up to the looming Pikk Hermann. As all eyes fixed on the blue, white, and black flag, the words of Estonian Popular Front leader Edgar Savisaar rang out: "We raise this flag as a fighting flag and we declare that under it we shall have next autumn a new Estonian parliament, a parliament elected in accordance with the will of the people and in the hands of the right men. . . . We are building a new Estonia."

Similar pledges were made in Latvia and Lithuania that year, but for the next two years, the republics that had come this far now seemed to be marking time. The sheer force of the people's will was not enough to secure the legal recognition and international acceptance of the independence that they felt in their hearts. The obstacles to independence lay in the Kremlin's consistent policy of refusing to countenance the secession of the Baltic republics and the failure of the West to defend the majority sentiments among the people.

The August 1991 coup in Moscow came just as the three Baltic States were preparing to commemorate the signing of the Molotov-Ribbentrop Pact on August 23, 1939. The treaty signed between Hitler and Stalin on the eve of World War II contained secret protocols dividing Europe into spheres of influence between the two dictators. For years, the Baltic nations had identified the secret protocols as an act that had brought the Red Army into their states, leading to their annexation by the Soviet Union. The commemoration had been held in secret for many years, but for the previous two years, public events had finally been staged without too much harassment from the Soviet authorities. Even though Lithuania had formally declared independence by 1991, and Latvia and Estonia had pronounced themselves to be in a transition toward independence, the tough struggle had prepared people for more conflicts ahead.

While the people of Estonia, Latvia, and Lithuania were making the final round of arrangements for the forthcoming commemoration of the Molotov-Ribbentrop Pact, the shocking news came through. On the morning of August 19, 1991, almost as soon as the State Committee for the State of Emergency in Moscow had announced its intention of "restoring order" in the country, tanks began to roll in each of the Baltic States. Unlike most of the other non-Russian republics, where the coup plotters had apparently counted on local KGB forces to bring the local authorities under their control, they knew that outside force would be unavoidable in the Baltic States. There was no doubt the people of the Baltic States would resist all attempts to bring them back under Moscow's control, whoever occupied the Kremlin.

Soviet troops were already in a state of alert in Lithuania. Since the military crackdown of January 1991, Lithuanians had become used to arbitrary and unannounced movements of Soviet troops, and shared a silent dread of a full-scale occupation that would set them back fifty years. On the morning of the coup, the television and radio center in Kaunas was quickly occupied by Soviet troops. The television and radio center in Vilnius had been under the control of Soviet troops since they had stormed it as part of the crackdown in January. Tanks were on their way to the parliament in Vilnius. In Estonia, tanks were on the move in Tallinn, and the predominantly Russian-populated northeastern region of Estonia was preparing to welcome the regime in Moscow and disassociate itself from the nationalists in the republic's capital. Latvia was one of the few places where the emergency committee was given a resounding vote of confidence by the local Communist Party. For months prior to the coup, the tension between the pro–Soviet Union Latvian Communist Party and the proindependence Latvian parliament had been mounting. Alfreds Rubiks, the first secretary of the Central Committee of the Latvian Communist Party, who had conducted a vicious campaign against his pro-independence compatriots, was clearly delighted by the new regime in Moscow. Like the Latvian-born Boris Pugo, one of the principal coup plotters, Rubiks stood in singular dissent against the overwhelming majority of his fellow countrymen in his fervent support for continued rule by Moscow over the tiny Baltic state.

The response to the coup by all three Baltic parliaments was similar: In Latvia and Estonia, the "transition" phase to independence was abruptly ended and full, unconditional independence declared as they joined Lithuania in severing all links to the Soviet Union. All three parliaments issued statements calling upon the population to obey only the laws and decisions of the legally elected representatives of the people. Hundreds of thousands of people prepared, as they had done in previous months, to stage mass rallies to protect their parliament or to launch political strikes and a campaign of civil disobedience.

The sequence of events after the first two days of the coup is now well known. Once it became clear that the coup plotters had not succeeded in bringing key sectors under their control, and that thousands had come rallying to support Boris Yeltsin, the parliamentary leaders in the Baltic States felt vindicated. Moreover, the coup had received only lukewarm responses from leaders in other republics who might have been expected to give their unequivocal support. An important factor that contributed to the rapid collapse of the coup was a profound split within the Soviet military-industrial complex, a split that was cemented by the condemnation by virtually all foreign leaders.

Suddenly the independence of the Baltic States took on a new aspect. The obstacles posed by Moscow's intransigence on the issue that had seemed insurmountable just a short time ago, suddenly evaporated as the tragicomedy of the coup unfolded. In a rapid turnaround, international support for Baltic independence suddenly came flowing in unsolicited. The bungled coup had been the decisive event that finally closed the door on fifty years of Soviet rule in the Baltic States.

The Baltic States' struggles for independence had put them at the forefront of all movements for democracy and independence in the crumbling Soviet Union. The "national awakening" that took on a specific form in the Baltic States and spread throughout the Soviet Union was one of the principal factors in the disintegration of the Union. The peaceful and measured way in which it evolved, however, was in large measure a result of the example set by the Baltics. That is the reason why the three tiny states on the western periphery of the Soviet colossus were so much in the news, and why they were important at that crucial time. Although they occupied an area that covered less than 0.8 percent of the USSR's total territory, and the population of the three indigenous ethnic groups amounted to less than 2 percent of the Soviet population, the three Baltic States nonetheless became the vanguard for national movements in the other Soviet republics.

The Baltic States were the last to be annexed into the Soviet Union, and their three peoples were among the least Russified, retaining a high degree of continuity in their language and culture. The fierce resistance against Soviet control for cultural freedom underpinned the struggle for economic freedom and political independence. Under perestroika, the Baltic States tried to break away from centralized economic control to exercise more autonomy over their economies and over their cultural politics, creating with their measured approach a model for the other national republics. These three republics had the best memory of independence and of the operation of a democratic, multiparty system and free-market economy. Their proximity to Western Europe and links with a lively emigré community in the West provided them with moral and material support through the years of repression.

By the beginning of 1989, each of the Baltic States had its own mass movement with a popular front membership numbering in the hundreds of thousands: Sajudis in Lithuania, the Popular Front of Latvia, and the Estonian Popular Front, Rahvarinne. Some people believed that the idea for popular fronts originated in Moscow and that they were modeled upon the popular fronts that existed in Eastern Europe just after World War II, to be used essentially as a ruse by the new, illegitimate Communist power bloc to co-opt and mold a disgruntled population. But the explosion of enthusiasm and national activity within and around the mass-based popular fronts of the late 1980s dispelled illusions that Moscow could be dictating the agenda and swept aside concerns of possible manipulation.

Although the popular fronts were the principal independent organizations to flourish at that time, each republic also began to develop a vibrant, independent civil society made up of many political, cultural, ecological, or other issue-oriented groups. There were numerous independent publications, some published officially, some still unofficially. The people's religious lives were rapidly reviving, and there was a resurgence of activity among different minority groups within each Baltic republic. Some of the more radical groups already in existence prior to the creation of the popular fronts experienced a new lease on life and carved out an area for themselves either in cooperation with the mass movements or independently. Even the Lithuanian, Latvian, and Estonian Communist parties were forced to respond to the new situation, as many Party members developed a double allegiance, belonging to both the popular front and the Party. In Lithuania at the end of 1989, this process had advanced so far that the Communist Party determined that the only way it could regain the loss of prestige and influence was to break away entirely from the CPSU. By an overwhelming majority, its leading members voted to constitute an independent Lithuanian Communist Party, and to join in the general national movement to separate from Moscow and to restore an independent Lithuanian state. The Estonian and Latvian Communists soon followed the Lithuanian example, thereby setting a precedent for the Communist parties in other republics.

From Uzbekistan to Azerbaijan to Ukraine, the leaders of the newly emerging democratic movements recognized the important role of the Baltic States as a model for organization and political thinking. But that had not always been so. Until glasnost made some information available about the dissident movement in the Baltic States, they were known as the most prosperous republics in the Soviet Union; but in a climate of repression and intense censorship, little was known about their struggle for independence among the other nations of the USSR. Most Soviet citizens still believed the myth created to strengthen control over the newly acquired states: The Baltic republics, the story went, had been part of the Soviet family at the end of World War I, and the intervening years of independent statehood—between 1920 and 1940—were merely an anomaly. Soviet historiography perpetuated the notion that the only desire of the proletarians of Lithuania, Latvia, and Estonia was to reunite with the Soviet state, a goal that finally was achieved in 1940, the argument went, when Soviet power was restored.

The Baltic nations regarded the secret 1939 Hitler-Stalin pact as the root cause of their subjugation throughout the postwar period; and campaigned energetically to expose the illegal nature of the act that brought the Red Army into their territories. They argued that if the protocols could be proved to have been against international law, and perhaps even Soviet law, then the legal basis for their remaining within the USSR would be weakened. On

August 23, 1989, the people of the Baltic States staged a remarkable event in protest against the continuing injustice of their incorporation within the Soviet Union, when 2 million people joined hands in a human chain that stretched through the three capital cities—from Tallinn to Riga to Vilnius—to denounce the Hitler-Stalin treaty. Television coverage showed miles upon miles of people: grandparents, teenagers dressed in parkas and blue jeans, families with young children, some dressed in their national costumes, many carrying their national flag, holding hands and standing peacefully in united opposition to the politics that had brought their countries into the Soviet Union.

Perhaps in anticipation of the mass demonstration, and under pressure from the articulate and vocal Baltic deputies, the USSR's Supreme Soviet established a twenty-six-member commission during that summer to investigate the Molotov-Ribbentrop Pact of 1939 and its secret protocols. The commission was diverse and included respected scholars, ranging from the liberal historian Yury Afanasyev to the Kremlin's old propaganda hand Valentin Falin, and was headed by Aleksandr Yakovlev, Gorbachev's chief ideologist and most trusted Politburo ally, and included eleven Baltic members. On July 20, 1989, the commission and its working group submitted their conclusions charging that the Hitler-Stalin treaty did indeed have a secret protocol that had violated the "sovereignty and independence of a number of third states." The documents also concluded that the secret protocols were an aberration and in no way reflected the will of the Soviet people, who, moreover, had been misled by Stalin's sudden change of policy toward Nazi Germany, revising in one stroke of the pen the Soviet's "relentless struggle against fascism." The commission's findings were not widely publicized at the time but even where they were, they were generally accompanied by the new line from the Soviet government, which went as follows: Even if the Molotov-Ribbentrop Pact had been a violation of Leninist norms, the incorporation of Latvia, Lithuania, and Estonia into the Soviet Union was accomplished through the voluntary actions of their parliaments. Such reasoning severed any connection with the treaty itself.

Despite this setback, and its untenable leap of logic, the Baltic republics intensified their struggle, step by step, using legal and peaceful means to regain their sovereignty and independence. By establishing the illegality of the treaty under international law, they were, however, merely establishing a fact that was already widely known and accepted abroad. The insistence on establishing a legal basis for challenging their annexation showed their commitment to a peaceful, nonviolent disengagement from the Union.

Estonia

Estonia, with its population of 1.5 million, the smallest of the three Baltic States, covers a mere 17,413 square miles, but is nonetheless larger than Denmark, Belgium, and Switzerland. It stretches about 150 miles from north to south and 210 miles from west to east. While ethnic Estonians number just over 1 million, the smallest ethnic group in the USSR to have had its own republic, these courageous people built a reputation far greater than their number. Estonia, the mouse that roared, the David that challenged Goliath, was for many crucial months at the forefront of the Baltic drive for more autonomy.

The Estonians were the first to establish a popular front, in April 1988; the first to declare their own language the official language in the republic, in June 1988; the first to declare republic sovereignty, in November 1988; and in January 1989, the first to adopt legislation setting rules governing the use of Estonian as the state language. From then on, Estonian was to be brought into use in all official business and by all officials and individuals in positions of authority, who, the law said, were to be given four years to learn the language and comply with the regulation.

The Estonian language is similar to Finnish and, because it is part of the Finno-Ugric family of languages, Russian and English are more closely related to each other then they are to Estonian. Its structure offers a clue to the Estonian national character. "Estonian has no future tense," a member of the Estonian Popular Front informed us, "that is, no future tense in the abstract. We have to think in terms of 'What is possible must be done today,'" she explained, trying to be helpful. "Maybe that is why Estonians consider things very carefully before acting. The whole of our culture is based on this approach."

Perhaps that is why the Estonians found it so difficult to believe in communism, with its promise of enticing benefits to be attained some time in a radiant future. The Estonian language is just one sign of the cultural gulf between the Estonians and the Slavic giant on their doorstep. Most Estonians spoke Russian only grudgingly and with a distinct accent, even the young people who had been obliged to study ten years of Russian and had never known a time when Estonia was not "occupied," as they refer to the period under Soviet rule.

Tallinn, the capital, is a fairy-tale town. The streets are cobbled and the buildings that surround the Old Town square have the uneven look that comes with centuries of wear. The Old Town hall on one side of the square dates from the fourteenth century. At the top of the hill, where Pikk Hermann and the other remains of the city's old fortress are located, sits the Upper Town, offering a view of the Baltic Sea shimmering in the distance. The Upper Town itself was the ancient fortification; today it is still home to several government buildings and an ocher-colored Russian Orthodox church.

For many years, Tallinn's dreamy tranquility remained unbroken. Public commemorations of important events were not even contemplated for fear of arrest and incarceration. But gradually, as repression grew more relaxed, the nascent national movement became more bold. The first public demonstration against the Hitler-Stalin treaty took place on August 23, 1987. Although the authorities had officially sanctioned the meeting, they nonetheless caused difficulties by changing the venue at the last moment. One of the people at that demonstration retold the story: "Who would have thought it possible? As we stood there we were afraid of what the future might hold. . . . We were being photographed and watched by the security police, we thought it would only be a matter of time before they set the dogs on us. . . . We were so surprised by the turnout. We had to move into the park as there were far too many people to continue the meeting where we were. . . . Nobody even thought to bring a megaphone; we didn't realize we would need it. People brought their own banners, and stood and listened to the impromptu speeches. We never expected the people to support us in this way."

Although the organizers expected only a hundred or so brave souls to turn out to support them, two thousand gathered in Tallinn's Hirve Park to register their resentment against the pact that had brought independent Estonia into the Soviet Union.

Tunne Kelam, our source for this information, later became chairman of the Congress of Estonia. He was also a founding member of the Estonian National Independence Party, created four months after the demonstration against the treaty, even though some of the group's leaders had already fallen victim to Soviet reprisals. Tiit Madisson, a charismatic young organizer of the demonstration, was expelled from the country almost immediately, and within the next month five of his colleagues joined him in forced exile. For many years, those who considered themselves Estonian patriots had worked clandestinely and concealed their identities to avoid the gulag. There were only a few people courageous enough to sign the declaration of intent to establish the Estonian National Independence Party in January 1988. The party remained small and was regarded as a minority party, honest people prepared to suffer for their views. But its members enjoyed a moral authority and tacit support unrivaled by the other new groups, Kelam believes. Many people who might have wanted to join were still afraid of losing their privileges should they take the step into overt opposition that the party represented. Their apartments, and their jobs at the university and at prestigious journals, could have been taken away.

Demands for independence and sovereignty in Estonia were at first the domain of the courageous dissidents and, later, the brave group around the Estonian National Independence Party, but they soon spread to become the everyday slogans of the Estonian Popular Front, and were taken up even by the Estonian Communist Party. Such was the rapid growth of confidence and patriotic feeling in this republic.

Rahvarinne, the Estonian Popular Front, was formed a few months after the Estonian National Independence Party in the summer of 1988. On April 13, Edgar Savisaar appeared on Estonian television on the program *Let's Think Once More* and proposed the creation of a "popular front in support of perestroika." During the summer, hundreds of thousands of Estonians became accustomed to attending mass meetings of one kind or another: 170,000 gathered to see off the delegates to the Nineteenth All-Union Conference of the Communist Party of the Soviet Union in Moscow, the first such conference since June 1941. Weeks later, many more—almost one in every three Estonians—participated in the Estonian Song Festival, held once every five years. This was the summer of Estonia's "Singing Revolution," when the Estonian people united in thoughts of their homeland. By the end of the summer, there were 250,000 who supported the Estonian Popular Front, which was formally constituted at its first congress on October 2, 1988.

Rein Veidemann, then the editor of the progressive literary journal *Vikerkaare* and one of the original seven members of the Estonian Popular Front's executive committee, lives in an apartment block that was once specially reserved for literary critics and writers at the center of Tallinn's Old Town. As he is a mere editor and literary critic, the apartment he shares with his wife and child is by no means the largest—the best were set aside for the novelists and poets, he explained.

"The Estonian Popular Front was formed to support perestroika," Veidemann explained, offering us the ubiquitous sandwiches of Baltic sardines. "The front was formed to mobilize the people to put up an opposition to the bureaucracy. But more practically," he added, "the Baltic peoples were beginning to lose hope; the Popular Front has renewed our hopes that our aspirations will be achieved. The political school behind this move was the school of democracy."

In the middle of 1989, the Estonian Popular Front was the leading force in the Estonian republic, enjoying the support of 50.3 percent of Estonians and 35.2 percent of the entire population. The Communist Party of Estonia mustered only a 16.2 percent popularity rating in the same poll, with only 7.2 percent among Estonians. The moderate view expressed by Veidemann represented a consensus of opinion among Party and non-Party members of the popular front. Most Estonians believed that there should be a variety of forms of ownership of land and property, including the "independence to own private property," as one member put it.

Discussions on land reform and farming occupy a special place in the minds of most Estonians and so take on a special intensity. Here they rely on elements of Estonian mythology and the essence of Estonian national consciousness that is so hard for the outsider to grasp. An Estonian ethnographer offered this insight: "We Estonians have occupied this piece of the earth for over five thousand years. It is not an easy place to live; it is not naturally fertile and it has rejected many of the peoples who tried to conquer it by force—the Swedes, Germans, the Russians—only we Estonians, with our hard work, patience and persistence, have managed to eke a living from this land. And from this hardship developed the bond that now holds us to the land. That is why we defend its interests so fiercely."

Estonians have always been people of the land; they never developed any significant urban presence as the towns always belonged to the Germans, Russians, Swedes, or whoever ruled over the territory at the time. The Estonians' special relationship to this tiny strip of territory, pushed into the extreme northeast corner of the landmass dominated by Russia, is a strong element in their sense of national consciousness. Stalin's campaign of collectivization left searing memories for many Estonian farmers, who were not easily herded into the Sovietized system of farming and consistently defied orders from the center, only to be vindicated by higher yields and better-quality products.

The Estonian attachment to the earth was one factor that helped to launch the national movement, when in 1987 the Estonian government secretly consented to the USSR Ministry of Fertilizer Industry's plan to conduct phosphite mining in eastern Estonia. The plan was publicized by the journalist Juhan Aare, and the Estonian public rose in outrage, for not only are these lands among the most fertile in Estonia, but they also constitute the source for Estonia's major rivers. The pollution of Estonia's water supply and the prospect of phosphite mining laying bare the country's best arable land galvanized the public into a protest campaign.

During that campaign, ideas began to form and groups of intellectuals and others got together to broach the wider problems facing their nation, putting Estonia's specific problems against the general background of economic and ideological crisis in the USSR. The Estonian Green Movement was launched at this time and soon became by far the most popular group among Estonians. The Greens worked out their own specific agenda, but defined it broadly to accommodate many diverse trends. The first commitment was to protect the environment; the second, to help protect a distinct life-style for Estonia and the Estonians. These points were based on the premise that the only way to protect nature is to protect the rights of individual nations.

For a time, it looked as if Moscow might use Estonia as a laboratory where new Soviet reforms could be tested. Private cooperatives were encouraged, but they were not greeted with much enthusiasm. Many Estonians considered them to be just one more way in which the Russians could take advantage of them. As early as September 1987, Estonia's economists worked out a plan for restructuring Estonia's economy, to make it more self-financing and thus more independent of Moscow's control. The acronym for the Estonian economic plan, IME, means "miracle" in Estonian. But they were still working in conditions that were duplicated in each republic: 90 percent of Estonia's industries were directly administered from Moscow. The misnomer of republican self-financing, or *khozraschet* as it was called in Russian, referred only to the 10 percent of the economy not controlled directly by the all-Union ministries.

By the late 1980s, most Estonians were not interested in the intricacies of self-financing and relationships with Moscow. One Tallinn housewife summed up the frustration of everyday life: "We were much better off when we were independent. All we want now is to have a market economy and to be able to get back to Europe where we belong. Imagine how I feel every day when I switch on the TV and watch the commercials on Finnish television, for washing powder, yogurt, shampoo—all the things that are normal in a normal society, but here I have to stand in line, or know someone who can save me something. In 1940, Estonia had the same standard of living as Finland, and now, Finland's is seven times higher!" The tantalizing proximity to Finland was a perpetual and irksome reminder of Estonia's predicament. Three channels on Finnish television were easily received in Estonia and there was no difficulty with such a closely related language.

One of the predominant features of the recent national democratic revolution in the Baltic States was the prominence of songs and national symbols. Having lived under a regime that made an industry out of its monopoly over the political songs and symbols as part of its control over everyday life, the Latvians, Lithuanians, and Estonians, more than most, understood the significance of symbols. A song could convey an entire opposition ideology without a word being spoken, and the act of displaying a flag or a national emblem was a way of showing a determined rejection of all that was Soviet. The songs and symbols of the national struggle took on an almost sacred significance in the Baltic States that was emulated later in other republics.

The solemnity surrounding the use of symbols was exemplified on two days in Tallinn. February 23, 1989, was the last time the Day of the Soviet Army and Navy was officially commemorated in Estonia. That day the Estonian SSR flag—a sheet of red, pulled through with a thin wavy blue line—was decreed to be flown from flagpoles on every building and storefront. The appearance of this flag all over Tallinn was particularly irksome to Estonians; one of their main demands at that time was the withdrawal of the 150,000 Soviet troops stationed in the tiny republic—one soldier for every ten people. But the following day, February 24, the anniversary of the 1918 declaration of independence, the Soviet flags were replaced in huge numbers by the clear white, blue, and black of the national flag, colors that more accurately reflect the Estonian soul. At that time, the Estonians had adopted the prewar national flag only as their national flag, leaving the Soviet version as the state flag. As long as they considered their state to be under Soviet occupation, most Estonians applauded the decision to keep the two flags with separate functions, demonstrating that they did not consider the national flag with all its connotations of national independence as the appropriate Estonian flag—yet.

Trivimi Velliste, a man with long-standing service in the Estonian patriotic movement, shares the view that political symbols are very important to Estonian national identity. He was one of the founding members of the Estonian Heritage Society, the organization largely responsible for restoring the Estonian tricolor. The heritage society was the organizer of the heritage festival where the still-banned flag was publicly displayed in large numbers for the first time in Tartu in April 1988. It was impossible for the Estonian authorities to do anything about it once it had occurred. From then on, they grudgingly accepted the public display of the flag and eventually made it legal. The event also led to a summons from a high-ranking Moscow official for a discussion with Velliste: After an hour of discussion, the official recommended that the Estonian flag should be kept in a museum. But it was already too late for that solution.

The heritage society took up many of the interests that Estonians could engage in without taking a step over the boundary of what was political and therefore under the close scrutiny of the authorities. Similar groups were taking up these kinds of interests all over the Soviet Union. Within a couple of years the society amassed more than ten thousand registered members in more than two hundred local clubs. In addition to the society's usual activities of restoring monuments, preserving graveyards, and collecting historical memoirs, the summer of 1989 brought a minor coup, when the heritage society sponsored the restoration of the statue of Konstantin Pats, the last president of Estonia before World War II. Velliste reported on its progress; it had been the subject of some interest from a Canadian film crew: "They went to look at it being made. There were many dusty Lenins lying around, too, but work on the Pats statue took priority." The statue was unveiled on June 25, 1989, in the presence of thirty thousand spectators exactly fifty years to the day after the original unveiling, and forty-nine years after its destruction by the Soviet regime.

Together with the Estonian National Independence Party and others that favored full independence for Estonia, the heritage society determined a way to resolve the problem of Estonian sovereignty. On February 24, 1989, they launched a campaign to register all citizens of pre-1940 Estonia and their descendants, through a network of citizens' committees, to establish a Congress of Estonia that would be the only authentic representative body empowered to decide the fate of Estonia. A year later, 850,000 people had registered—around 93 percent of the total of those eligible to be citizens of the Estonian republic under those criteria. Registration was also accepted from thousands of non-Estonian residents wishing to become citizens.

When voters went to the polls in the last week of February 1990, they elected a congress of 499 delegates: 109 unaffiliated; 107 supporters of the Estonian Popular Front; 104 supporters of the Estonian Heritage Society; 70 supporters of the Estonian National Independence Party; 39 from the Estonian Communist Party; and others. This congress was the largest independent body in the history of the Soviet Union to have been elected with no relationship to the central powers in Moscow, and set a precedent that other republics tried to follow. For the first time, the Estonians demonstrated that if it were not possible to work through the established channels to change the system, then sometimes it was necessary to step outside the system.

The Congress of Estonia held a moral and a certain kind of legal authority in Estonia and established a dual leadership for a while. The Estonians rendered unto the Kremlin what was supported by the Kremlin—the Supreme Soviet—but continued to look for leadership to the Congress of Estonia in matters concerning the national heritage. The dual leadership lasted until well after the Moscow coup and the final proclamation of independence.

Latvia

Latvians and Estonians share a problem that will continue to haunt them and will shape their politics for some time to come. Both nations run the real risk of soon becoming a minority in their homeland. Estonians number only 61 percent of the republic's population and their current low birthrate does not give cause for optimism for the future. Latvians have the same worry. According to the last census, Latvians make up barely half of the population of Latvia, which numbers 2.6 million. The real and imagined fear of national extinction added a particular intensity to the Latvian and Estonian national movements.

The imbalance in population was accomplished by a systematic policy of immigration into the formerly independent states. A short drive through the center of Riga, Latvia's capital, reveals an attempt to Sovietize the Latvian landscape as well as the population. Riga is the largest city in the Baltic States and has a population of almost a million, only one-third of which is Latvian. The city's broad roads and massive Soviet architecture indicate the heavy hand of Gosplan, the former State Planning Committee of the USSR. Vilnius and Tallinn preserved much of the attractive architectural style that set them apart from other Soviet cities, but in Riga only the Old Town shows evidence of the city's former role as a thriving port and a commercial center of the Hanseatic League.

Riga was founded at the beginning of the thirteenth century as a Catholic church mission and home of the Livonian Brothers of the Sword. An influx of Westphalian nobles and immigrant peasants brought to the area a strong German presence that it has never entirely relinquished. The architecture of the old city reveals the connection with the Germans. The two huge churches that stand next to each other in the Old Town look solid yet airy inside and are sparsely decorated according to the later Lutheran tradition. One of them, the Cathedral Church built at the beginning of the thirteenth century, houses the largest pipe organ in the world, which is used for concert performances. For many years it was a concert hall, but now it falls under the jurisdiction of the small but influential Latvian Lutheran church. The cobbled, traffic-free streets of the Old Town are lined with houses, shop fronts, and cafes that are coming alive to make Riga once more a vigorous and colorful place.

Outside of the Old Town, Gothic and Teutonic architecture gives way to Soviet-style monuments and buildings. Until recently teams of Young Pioneers regularly changed guard at the monument to the Latvian Riflemen, goose-stepping and swinging their arms in the exaggerated gestures required of this particular Soviet ceremony. The monument was dedicated to the battalion of Latvian marksmen that helped Lenin to secure the revolution at a crucial point in 1917, and then went on to fight in the civil war on the side of the Bolsheviks. By manipulating the history of the Latvian Riflemen, revering their memory and giving them a prestigious place in Soviet history books, the Soviets tried to gain the support of a primarily hostile population. However, Latvians generally looked for their heroes elsewhere.

Our guide in Riga is eminently suited to take us through the recent history of his country. Eduards Berklavs was a Communist youth leader before World War II in independent Latvia. After the Soviet takeover, he quickly rose through the ranks of the Party to become first secretary of the Riga City Party Committee and a deputy chairman of the Latvian Council of Ministers, but fell afoul of the Party leadership at the end of the 1950s for his pro-Latvian policies and received a reprimand from Khrushchev himself. He was sent into exile in Siberia for his so-called mistakes. When he returned, he became an ordinary worker. He turned to writing protest letters to the Communist Party and government and was expelled from the Party for his trouble in 1972. This stocky, white-haired man with thick, heavy-rimmed glasses is once more in the vanguard of change, but this time as a leader of the Latvian Independence Movement, which counted more than ten thousand members almost as soon as it was established in 1989.

Before the Soviet takeover of Latvia, there were never more than 250 members of the Communist Youth League in the underground in Latvia, and no more than 500 to 600 Communist Party members. According to Berklavs, "It's patently clear that these kinds of forces could not even contemplate overthrowing the Latvian government, which had, after all, its own army. . . . When the tanks rolled into Riga on June 17, 1940, we Communists were as surprised as anyone else." The Latvian Communists were invited to a meeting in an apartment in the Old Town, but were soon informed by a liaison from the Soviet embassy that a government had already been formed.

Berklavs explains that Latvia was singled out for industrial development in the 1950s, which meant importing not only technology and hardware, but also large numbers of Russian workers. Once he saw that the large-scale immigration was changing the very fabric of the country, Berklavs used his position of power to try to impose limits. "There were people coming in at the rate of two to three thousand a month," he recalls. "The situation was getting out of hand. In Lithuania, they resisted immigration, and they are much better off today. But here in Latvia . . . we managed to stem the flow for a while. Then they branded me a 'bourgeois nationalist'—me! a son of poor workers who had never owned anything in his life—and you know what happened to me after that."

In the center of Riga, in the middle of the wide boulevard that leads into the Old Town, stands the highly esteemed Freedom Monument. A column topped by a female figure, The Lady of Liberty, who holds three stars with arms outstretched to the sky, the monument was constructed in 1933 during the period of Latvia's independence. During the Soviet period, it was reviled by the official media as a symbol of the bourgeois regime, but secretly venerated by a population struggling for its national rights. For much of that time, it was as if the monument were invisible; people were afraid to openly acknowledge its existence, although its powerful presence was felt throughout the city. Sporadic demonstrations took place there, and from time to time the area was cordoned off or closed to traffic. Nevertheless, the monument grew to symbolize the freedom Latvians craved, and existed as a permanent reminder of the people's aspirations. Today the monument is once more the focal point of attention, having seen a new wave of nationalist activity since it became a place for regular gatherings, and some of the repressions that followed. Now it is most often used to provide a dignified backdrop to the many commemorations of freedom and independence that are held here.

Lithuania

Lithuania is the southernmost of the three Baltic States and the farthest inland. It is also the largest and the most ethnically homogeneous of the Baltic States: 80 percent of its 3.6 million people are Lithuanian. Of the former non-Russian republics of the USSR, only Armenia has a higher percentage of the titular nationality as its native population. Lithuania's geography also reveals a different historical evolution than its two Baltic neighbors. Unlike the port cities Riga and Tallinn, Lithuania's capital, Vilnius, is located some distance inland, reflecting its past role within a larger land-based kingdom.

At the beginning of the fourteenth century, when Latvia was a thriving realm of the Livonian Knights and Estonia was ruled by Denmark, Lithuania constituted one of the largest areas of land in Europe. While the areas to the north of Lithuania were participating in the world of the Hanseatic League, Lithuania, blocked by the Livonian Kingdom to the north, had expanded its territories southeastward toward the Dnieper River. Gedymin (1316–41), the real founder of Lithuania, made Vilnius the capital of the new state. The state remained heathen—one of the last in Europe—until Jagiello, Gedymin's grandson, married Jadwiga of Poland, thus linking the two states by a personal union and introducing Roman Catholicism as the state religion of Lithuania in 1387.

Pre-Christian influences have remained intertwined with Roman Catholicism in the distinctive Lithuanian culture. The Lithuanian language is believed to be derived from Sanskrit; it bears only a slim resemblance to any of the languages of the surrounding peoples, and is one of the most ancient languages in the region. It is written in the Latin alphabet and has the appearance of a medieval Latin gone wrong with its *ius* endings. You know you are in a country where time went its own way when you come across men named Ringaudas, Vaidotas, Sigitas, Zigmas, and Arunas, and women called Ginte, Angonita, Jurate, and Mirga.

Vilnius must have been a beautiful city, a Florence of the north with its stunning baroque architecture and pastel-shaded buildings. Many buildings in the Old Town are in need of repair, with plaster peeling and scaffolding around walls marked with rust and years of neglect. Some have been earmarked for restoration and stand surrounded by scaffolding bearing the plaque of PKS, the Warsaw-based firm that specializes in restoration, whose services are increasingly in demand in the Baltic States' historic cities. In the heart of the Old Town stand the buildings of Vilnius University, one of the oldest seats of learning in Europe, and a dynamo for Lithuanian culture and intellectual life. Many leaders of the Lithuanian reform movement were connected with the university in some way and many of the most active members were students, or people in their twenties or thirties.

Sajudis, the Lithuanian Popular Front, was formed at the same time as the popular fronts of Latvia and Estonia; it was conceived in the summer of 1988 and held its first congress in October. Of the three organizations, Sajudis had the most solid support from its population from its inception, bringing together most of the new informal groups under its umbrella. Only a few of the most radical groups remained outside Sajudis's organization, but their differences concerned only tactics and timing: The radical groups wanted full and unconditional independence for Lithuania immediately, while Sajudis determined to work through constitutional channels to ensure a stable transition and thus a stable democratic system.

Sajudis's constituency showed how far the system had broken down, as many were also members of the Communist Party, echoing the same refrain that was heard elsewhere in Eastern Europe: People stayed in the Communist Party to keep their jobs. One Sajudis Council member admitted honestly that many jobs, especially the more influential ones in the universities or in the Academy of Sciences, were virtually unattainable to non-Party people. In the past, there was no alternative employment, and there was no reform movement to join to attempt to improve the situation. For the first time, the popular fronts in the Baltic States provided a legitimate alternative for people who wanted to work for change without severing ties with the Communist Party. For a while, some members who still held dual allegiance justified their participation in Sajudis by explaining that the popular front's main goal, in accordance with its name, was to support and put into practice Gorbachev's policy of perestroika—the restructuring of society and the economy—to better meet the needs of the Lithuanian people.

The independence day commemoration held on February 16, 1989, was one of Sajudis's first major triumphs. For the Lithuanians, as well as the Estonians, it was the first time in some fifty years the day was officially celebrated. It was declared a national holiday and hundreds of thousands of people took to the streets to participate in the planned events. The main ceremonies were held in Lithuania's two major cities: Kaunas, the capital of the independent state between the wars; and Vilnius, the present-day capital, which was located within the boundaries of Poland at that time. Each event of the official commemorations would have been a pretext for arrests and harassment in the old days, but in 1989 officials and ordinary people alike took part without incident or obstruction.

On that day, every Lithuanian city was festooned in the yellow, green, and red colors of the Lithuanian flag. In Vilnius, the balcony from the Sajudis office's inner sanctum, where the leaders sit and receive foreign visitors, was the perfect vantage point onto Gediminas Square and Vilnius Cathedral. At around noon, people began to converge on the square, emerging silently from the surrounding side streets as if beckoned by an invisible Pied Piper: young people, old people, people in groups, a lone Lithuanian striding along with a full-sized national flag unfurled across his shoulder. The day's proceedings were about to begin with a solemn Mass in commemoration of the day, seventy-one years ago, when Lithuania's political leaders declared independence in Vilnius. The Mass was celebrated in Vilnius's baroque cathedral, which had just been handed back to the Catholic church two weeks earlier after having served as a state-run art gallery for years.

Hundreds of people gathered to watch the unveiling of a plaque on the building in Pilies Street, the main thoroughfare of old Vilnius, where the declaration of independence was signed in 1918. (The street was called Gorky Street until shortly before the event, but reverted to its old name, establishing a precedent throughout the non-Russian republics at that time, where the names of towns, streets, and districts were reverting increasingly to their original form.) The event proceeded with the recitation of verses by a renowned Lithuanian poet, and an exhortation for further struggle for the Lithuanian cause by an elderly participant in the 1918 events. Among the crowds, young people held their banners, some emblazoned with such slogans as Red Army Go Home or Stop Communism in Lithuania; others carried the ubiquitous flag. The ceremony concluded with a once banned song, the Lithuanian national anthem.

All through the afternoon, loudspeakers in Vilnius's main square relayed the proceedings of a historical conference on the struggle for independence to the people milling around, waiting for the evening's rally, the culminating event of the day that was attended by over two hundred thousand people. The proceedings began with a dramatic swearing of an oath: "Let there be the kind of Lithuania that her people want. Our goal: a free Lithuania. Our destiny: Lithuania. May God and all people of goodwill in the world help us." The flags paraded around the town during the day—the Lithuanian tricolor; the Estonian blue, white, and black; the Latvian deep red and white; and an occasional Belarusian and Ukrainian flag, brought by Lithuania's neighbors as an act of homage and solidarity—formed a sea of colored cloth around the speakers' platform. Leaders from Sajudis spoke first, followed by greetings from a representative of the Lithuanians in Canada, the Latvians and Estonians, and the minority Russians in the republic. Only the speaker from the Lithuanian Communist Party was given a lukewarm reception; the rest were welcomed with roars of "Freedom, freedom!"

The greeting from Sajudis, given by the organization's first president, Vytautas Landsbergis, captured the symbolism of the event. A musicologist by profession, his selection as president of the organization reflected the commitment of its members to deep-rooted, exclusively Lithuanian values. The Landsbergis family's fate has been interwoven with the fate of Lithuania for generations. Landsbergis's ancestors have long been involved in the struggle for Lithuanian independence: His father fought for independence in World War I and one of his maternal ancestors, of the Jablonskis family, was responsible for the development of the literary Lithuanian language. As he stood at the podium to address two hundred thousand people, his tone was clear, his message strong; one could imagine the spirits of his ancestors lined up in triumph behind him as he spoke of his nation's struggle for freedom and independence.

It is no wonder that this quiet man with a full dark beard and thick heavy glasses was elected the country's president when Lithuania finally declared its independence on March 11, 1990. In 1988, he was voted the most popular figure in Lithuania. An opinion poll gave him 78 percent of the vote and named him Man of the Year.

It was obvious from an early stage that Sajudis and the Lithuanian national movement would pose a major threat to the central powers in Moscow. Perhaps in anticipation of the need for a new strategy to deal with emerging national groups, the Communist Party's ideological watchdog, Aleksandr Yakovlev, paid a visit to Lithuania in August 1988. After his visit, Sajudis was given limited access to the official media. It began to publish the newspaper *Atgimimas* (*Rebirth*) in Lithuanian with a Russian-language supplement. The first twelve issues were published without censorship until early in 1989.

"The idea behind that move was fairly simple," explained a young editor of a mass-circulation unofficial bulletin. "The authorities thought they would wean the readership away from the unofficial publications—numbering around twelve at that time—and then once they had closed them down they would crack down on the one official paper. But it didn't work out that way. Our unofficial press is thriving." Such were the attempts to co-opt the new mass national movements. But the attempt failed. Independent publications continued to flourish until each of Lithuania's forty-four administrative regions had its own Sajudis-run newspaper and many informal groups had their own publications.

By early 1989, however, anyone visiting Vilnius could see that the growing national movement would be hard to co-opt. The city was buzzing with excitement. The Sajudis headquarters, three floors up in a corner building overlooking Gediminas Square, was the hub of activity. Packed with people, some manning the information desk, some visiting, some just sitting around, the office was decorated with the yellow, green, and red of the Lithuanian flag and with the representations of the medieval knight Vytautas on his steed emblazoned in red across one wall. Here and there hung decorations made out of bank notes that were the currency in prewar Lithuania. In the corner was an antique-looking East German Robotron computer, and a couple of telephones, each attached to a single line. Apart from these, and a television in the main office, there were no other items of technical equipment to suggest that this was the nerve center of an organization of hundreds of thousands, supported by a couple of million more people. The office was given to Sajudis after the organization's founding congress in November 1988. With only a few full-time staff, the office was nonetheless fully staffed every day and evening, with Sajudis officials stopping in when they could to catch up on business. For many of the young people, it was also a place that they felt was their own, a place where something was happening. Part carnival, part permanent campaign headquarters, the office provided a focal point for the people who were ready to coordinate the movement that would lead their nation to independence.

The support for Sajudis was almost universal and the scope of its activities truly awesome. It took the organization only three days in October 1988 to collect a million signatures to protest amendments to the Lithuanian constitution proposed by Moscow. The entire country mobilized: Bus drivers were entrusted with carrying petitions out to the villages and bringing them back signed. The outpouring of dissatisfaction was there to be harnessed, and, more than the other popular fronts in Latvia or Estonia, Sajudis skillfully united the entire spectrum of people in its movement from the merely discontent to the politically astute.

One reason for the remarkable unity of the Lithuanian national movement lay in the makeup of the Lithuanian population. Most Lithuanians are Roman Catholic and, like the Poles, have always looked to the Catholic church for refuge against the tyranny of Soviet rule. However, the Catholic church could not play as great a role in the resistance against totalitarianism in Lithuania as it did in Poland, for it was itself the victim of severe repressions, reviled for many years by the authorities and systematically suppressed because of its close links to Lithuanian nationalism.

The *Chronicle of the Lithuanian Catholic Church* was one of the longest-running samizdat journals in the Soviet Union. Begun in 1972, it helped to foster a sense of unity among Lithuanians and established the Lithuanian Catholic church as an alternative to the Party's monopoly over ideological thought and activity. Vilnius's baroque cathedral served as a storehouse and then as an art gallery under Soviet rule until it was returned to the Catholic church in February 1989, just two weeks before the independence day celebrations. Lithuania's Catholic clergy suffered exile and repressions: Archbishop Julijonas Stepanovičius of Vilnius was exiled for twenty-seven years in a remote village in Lithuania until his joyous return to the city in 1989; Cardinal Sladkevičius, the highest-ranking Lithuanian prelate (the See of Kaunas), was also exiled for twenty-one years until his release in 1982.

Father Vaclovas Aliulis of the Lithuanian Catholic church was a member of the first Sajudis Council—the only man of the cloth among the leaders of the reform movement at that time. Living and working in the *kurija* (church center) by the side of one of Vilnius's old churches set in the midst of the twisting roads and cobblestoned alleyways of the Old Town, Father Aliulis endured all the vicissitudes meted out to the Lithuanian Catholic church. He recalled the situation in the 1960s when the seminary for training young priests was allowed to accept only 25 students per year. Father Aliulis worked tirelessly from 1965 onward at translating and editing liturgical texts. By 1989, he was the editor of the first Catholic journal to be published legally in the Soviet Union.

Lithuania's independence movement aimed to be inclusive even though most of its members were of one nationality and one religion. Emanuel Zingeris, a leading force behind the revival of Jewish culture in Lithuania, was also a member of the first Sajudis Council. A mercurial figure and a mass of energy, he was always in motion between the Sajudis office, the newly established Jewish Cultural Center in Vilnius, and any number of other projects at one time. It is hard to picture it now, but before the war Lithuania was home to over a quarter million of Europe's Jews, who had lived there for centuries, developing a distinctive culture and speaking a variant of Yiddish that set them apart from their fellow Jews in the rest of Europe. The war swept it all away, the Communist power repressed what was left, closing down the remaining synagogues and rewriting the history books as if there had never been a Jewish population.

During the early 1980s, Zingeris tried to stage exhibitions of Jewish art and culture, but was threatened by the authorities and warned that there would be repercussions if he persisted. Today there are only some eight thousand Jews in Lithuania, and the rich and distinctive culture has all but disappeared. Many among the younger generation of Lithuanians are only dimly aware of the history of Jewish settlement in the Baltic lands, so well have the Soviet history books rewritten the past. Some of the remaining Lithuanian Jews took advantage of the relaxation under Gorbachev's administration to emigrate, but others, like Zingeris, decided that the prospects for a better future lay in cooperation with Sajudis and the struggle for an independent Lithuania.

One distinctive feature of the Lithuanian movement was the number of young people who were actively involved. Many were only in their teens and early twenties, and none could have known anything other than the day-to-day reality of life under the Soviet system. They were not old enough to have experienced the Khrushchev years, the formative years for many Russian and Ukrainian dissidents who led their national democratic movements. Few of them remembered even the Soviet invasion of Czechoslovakia in 1968. Yet their exuberance and determination were striking.

"We are all Lithuanian, and we want to be free," explained one young man in the Sajudis office, who struggled to speak English even though his Russian was much more fluent. "We feel in our hearts that independence is the only way." He looked around and received affirmative nods from everyone else in the room.

One young woman added further explanation: "It's not as if we were ever taught to strive for independence. It depends, from family to family, how much real history a person managed to learn. I don't remember my parents ever telling me directly that the Russians were bad, or that we should struggle against communism for an independent state once more. I'm not sure why we all feel so involved in this struggle. It's something that's always been with us; it's hard to explain."

By the end of 1989, there was no longer any question that independence was a platform supported by most Lithuanians. The certainty was echoed in the other Baltic States, establishing a new political landscape on which all groups were now obliged to work. Sajudis's leaders often found themselves in the paradoxical position of having to explain the necessity for moving in a gradual and systematic fashion, even though all were convinced that independence was the only solution.

The Lithuanian Communist Party saw that the situation in Lithuania had changed and that its authority now stood to be challenged. In a series of moves that was echoed within Communist parties in other republics, the Lithuanian Party decided to chart a new, more independent course, realizing that the only way to retain any of its former influence was to join the inexorable move away from Moscow. Under the leadership of Party First Secretary Algirdas Brazauskas, who, treading a delicate tightrope between the warnings from the Kremlin and the increasing pressure for independence from the Lithuanian population, convened a special congress of Lithuania's Communist Party. The delegates voted by an overwhelming 855 to 160, with 12 abstentions, to reconstitute themselves as an independent Party, separate from Moscow, with its own programs and statutes. In its Declaration of Independence of the Communist Party of Lithuania, the goals of the new Party were described as Lithuania's "independence, a democratic society and the implementation of the ideals of humanistic socialism."

Lithuania had been the first Soviet republic, on December 7, 1989, to follow in the footsteps of Poland, Hungary, East Germany, and Czechoslovakia, in formally dropping the guaranteed leading role of the Party from its constitution and thus opening up the political field for a multiparty system. Facing an open competition with Sajudis candidates and other parties, the Communist Party could not risk being trounced at the ballot box once more, as it had been in the elections to the Congress of People's Deputies in March 1989. The only way to remain alive was to declare independence from the CPSU and stand with, if not at the head of, the independence movement. Brazauskas's popularity ratings shot up, and suddenly the Communist Party became a contender for political power. For a short while, patriotic Party people in the Baltic States felt they could use their Party posts to further their national activities. Nowhere was there a sense of the reverse: that the newly revived national feelings were seeking to resurrect Marxist-Leninist ideology.

In the face of the growing assertiveness of the Baltic Communists, Gorbachev himself decided to pay a visit to the wayward Lithuanian republic in January 1990. A top-level delegation was convened, led by Vadim Medvedev, the Kremlin's top ideology watchdog, to prepare the visit of the president and his wife. By any account, the purpose of the visit was not clear, especially as the Lithuanian Party had already made its break with Moscow—the horse was out of the stable. Nonetheless, Gorbachev spent three days in and around Vilnius, debating, cajoling, and coming up short with Communists, workers, and even people on the street. The visit was highly publicized on Soviet television, but the overwhelming impression was one of a peaceful, mass movement, totally in disagreement with the president and leader of the CPSU. The most interesting of Gorbachev's statements during his visit indicated that the Kremlin might be prepared to accept Lithuanian demands. Instead of ruling out secession from the USSR, Gorbachev prevaricated, stating that the process should be regulated and that new laws were under discussion to provide the framework for such a move.

Roads to Independence

The year and a half that followed Gorbachev's visit to Lithuania was the peak of the Baltic struggles for independence. Although each state's independence movement had developed in a slightly different way, depending on local circumstances, many of the obstacles they faced were the same. By early 1990, Lithuania had taken the lead. On March 11, events took a dramatic turn, when the newly elected Lithuanian parliament voted Vytautas Landsbergis president of Lithuania and at the same time voted to secede from the USSR. The name Lithuanian SSR was changed to the Republic of Lithuania.

The move to reestablish independence took place just days before Gorbachev was voted wide-ranging powers and promoted to the position of president of the USSR by a vote in the Supreme Soviet. Faced with the reality of the declaration of independence, Gorbachev made his intentions clear. Within hours of the Lithuanian decision, tanks were rolling through the streets of Vilnius, and Soviet soldiers had seized buildings belonging to the Communist Party and had forced their way into the offices of the republic's procuracy and leading newspapers. At the same time, young Lithuanian army conscripts who had deserted their posts in the Soviet army seeking refuge in Lithuania were brutally rounded up in a surprise raid in the hospital in which they were sheltered.

Lithuania's declaration of independence should not have come as a surprise to Gorbachev and his leadership in Moscow, although their immediate reaction suggested a total lack of policy alternatives for this event. The new Lithuanian government pointed out that most of the parliamentarians in the Supreme Council, as they now preferred it to be called, were elected on a proindependence platform. But in the tense weeks that followed, the war of words escalated as officials in Moscow claimed the Lithuanian government had perpetrated an illegal act. The Lithuanian government countered that the Soviet occupation of Lithuania in 1940 was the illegal act; they were merely reinstating the legal existence of a republic that had been on hold for fifty years.

Several ultimatums were issued from Moscow instructing the Lithuanian Supreme Council to rescind the declaration of independence; foreigners, including young people of Lithuanian parentage from North America who had come to help Sajudis, were ordered to leave. Lithuanian requests for negotiations were swept aside as Gorbachev took decisive action and imposed an economic embargo on the republic. The embargo was reinforced by a blockade, which effectively prevented goods being delivered from Poland or via the sea route on Lithuania's east coast. The new Soviet law on secession was rushed through the Supreme Soviet in Moscow, establishing a procedure so lengthy and cumbersome that many national democrats began to refer to it as the "antisecession law."

There was little sympathy for Lithuania in Moscow even among liberal Russians, including members of the Interregional Group of Deputies. For several weeks the situation looked desperate. On April 26, Stanislovas Zemaitis, a Lithuanian national, set fire to himself and burned to death in Moscow in protest against the Soviet government's refusal to recognize Lithuania's declaration of independence. In his suicide note he wrote: "Lithuanians will not live in a Lithuania that is not independent."

Lithuanian deputies were dispatched around the Soviet Union to seek assistance from democratic groups and deputies in other republics; and in the international arena, Lithuania urged recognition of its new status, particularly from the United States and other countries that had for years professed a policy of nonrecognition of the incorporation of the Baltic States into the Soviet Union. The delegations received a positive response from the newly elected Moscow City Soviet and the Democratic bloc in Ukraine among others, but Lithuania's request for assistance from the governments of the Western democracies met with a cold shoulder. However, the leaders of the fledgling democracies of Eastern and Central Europe were not so reticent in their support for Lithuania's independence. President of Czechoslovakia Vaclav Havel invited Vytautas Landsbergis for a two-day visit to Prague. The Polish Sejm adopted a resolution of support for Lithuanian independence and sent a high-ranking delegation of Solidarity parliamentarians headed by Bronislaw Geremek to Vilnius for talks. Asked in an interview what he would say to Mikhail Gorbachev about Lithuania, Solidarity leader Lech Walesa stated: "I would say what I said a long time ago: The only solution is to dissolve the Soviet Union. And then you can establish ties founded on completely different principles—free will, freedom. You cannot try to prevent an unavoidable trend by force because this dissolution must come."

While Moscow continued its coercive tactics against Lithuania, and the tense standoff dominated headlines in the West, the two other Baltic States quietly planned their own moves toward independence. On March 11, 1990, the Congress of Estonia was convened and, following its own interpretation of international law with impeccable logic, declared that there was no need to proclaim independence as independence had never formally been given up by the citizens of Estonia. The newly elected Supreme Soviet of Estonia voted to cooperate with the Congress, and voted on March 30 to announce the continuing de jure existence of the Republic of Estonia. A provision was made for a transition period that would lead to full independence for the republic. On May 4, 1990, the newly elected Latvian Supreme Soviet followed Estonia's lead and declared Latvia's incorporation into the USSR illegal, adopting a resolution that called for a period of transition leading to full independence for the republic.

Gorbachev's response to these events was unequivocal: The declarations were judged to be in contravention of the Soviet constitution. And as long as Lithuania continued to uphold its declaration of independence there would be no negotiations and the economic blockade would continue. Feeling the pressure, but buoyed now by a sense of solidarity, the three republics signed an agreement reestablishing the Baltic Council of the interwar period to coordinate their moves toward independence.

The blockade against Lithuania lasted until the end of June. During that time, gasoline was rationed, buildings went unheated and without hot water, newspapers reduced their output, and hospitals ran short of medicines.

Finally, the Lithuanian Supreme Council came to an agreement with the Soviet government to hold a 100-day moratorium on the declaration of independence, so that new talks could be held.

For the rest of the year, the situation in all three Baltic States was one of stalemate characterized by arbitrary actions from the Soviet side and an inability to move further toward independence by the Baltic States. Although the embargo against Lithuania was formally suspended, deliveries of natural gas and coal were often interrupted or not fulfilled. Deliveries of other goods were suddenly canceled; for example, Latvian farmers were informed in November that they would no longer receive cattle feed. In Estonia, plans toward economic sovereignty were suddenly challenged in July when a conglomerate was formed bringing together the major heavy industries, defense related enterprises, and technical institutes into an independent industrial-economic complex that would bypass the republic's administrative agencies to deal directly with Moscow.

Pressure mounted from Moscow to bring the Baltic States back into the fold. Despite the initial agreement with Lithuania to negotiate on the terms of secession and independence, Moscow's negotiators soon made it clear that the main item on the agenda was the signing of a new Union treaty. Latvia and Estonia were given similar notification. Lithuania, following the mandate of its Supreme Council, stood by the notion that an independent state should not embark on discussions of a Union treaty. While the stalemate continued, the people of the Baltic became used to irregular troop movements, sometimes without any prior notification.

After months of inconclusive discussions the Kremlin's policy came abruptly into focus. Even though Eduard Shevardnadze's resignation from the post of Soviet Minister for Foreign Affairs on December 20, 1990, gave a signal that the Soviet leadership was moving toward dictatorship, nobody believed that the crackdown would come in the Baltics. The sequence of events that lead to the armed attack by Soviet troops in Vilnius on January 13, 1991, is now well known. A well-planned strategy had been put into place: A shadowy National Salvation Committee of Lithuania had been formed, in its own words, "to take all power and avert the economic crisis and a fratricidal war." Troops were called in to assist the National Salvation Committee in this task. The attack on the television studios and broadcasting tower left fifteen dead and over one hundred wounded. The coordinated assault continued and for the next few days Lithuanian parliamentarians maintained an around-the-clock watch within their building, defended by sandbags, crowds of people, and young volunteers, some armed only with hunting rifles.

A similar scenario was being played out in Latvia. As in Lithuania, an anonymous, Communist-controlled National Salvation Committee was formed purportedly to prevent the restitution of "bourgeois dictatorship." Its aim was to dissolve the parliament and the government. The "Black Berets," or OMON (Otryady Militsii Osobogo Naznacheniya), the Special forces of the USSR Ministry of Internal Affairs, had been active in Latvia for some time. They had already taken over the press building and were clearly aiming to topple the government. On January 20, the OMON stormed the Ministry of Internal Affairs on the pretext of carrying out a request from the salvation committee. After a ninety-minute gun battle, five people lay dead, including the well-known Latvian filmmaker Gvido Zvaigzne.

Reports on the events in Moscow reverted to official disclaimers and one-sided explanations that smacked of the standard propaganda fare of Brezhnev's time. The crackdown showed all the indications of having been a carefully planned and executed attempt to take over power in the two republics, even down to the timing: The rest of the world was preoccupied by the beginning of the war against Iraq in the Persian Gulf. The close association of defense minister Dmitry Yazov and internal affairs minister Boris Pugo suggests in retrospect that these future coup plotters were perfecting a plan that could be put into general use against national and democratic forces anywhere in the Soviet Union.

Neither Gorbachev nor any member of his leadership would offer a firm rebuttal to the violence, and official investigations revealed only that nationalists had somehow provoked the Soviet troops. The continued presence of the OMON and other troops led to other sporadic attacks and random killings for the next few months, the most appalling taking place at customs posts newly established by the Baltic States along their borders.

The August 1991 coup in Moscow finally brought an end to the months of tension and uncertainty in the Baltic States, each of which wasted no time in taking advantage of the turmoil in Moscow to break free of the Soviet Union finally and conclusively. The state of euphoria was increased by the procession of foreign countries now ready to recognize their independence, including the Soviet Union.

The dramatic turnabout in events was welcomed by Latvia, Lithuania, and Estonia, who more than the other republics of the Soviet Union, were ready to take up the new demands of independence. Their peaceful struggle for freedom had already helped them to strengthen the fabric of civil society in each state, resulting in the formation of well-organized citizens' groups, the establishment of parliamentary procedures, and a rudimentary respect for the rule of law.

The Baltic States have fared better than other republics in establishing their statehood and are making valiant efforts to introduce free-market economies and a stable political system. But there are some problems, created by the Soviet system, that will continue to require attention for some time to come. The presence of former Soviet troops on the territory of the newly independent states for months after the dissolution of the Soviet Union resulted in strained relations with the new Russia, and emphasized the unanticipated problem of minority rights for the indigenous Russian population.

For years, the Baltic States have felt themselves on the verge of extinction. With a catastrophically low birthrate—Latvians had the lowest birthrate in the USSR, closely followed by Estonians and Lithuanians—these small nations felt precariously close to being obliterated. Soviet migration policies, which brought thousands of Russians into the formerly independent nations during the 1950s and 1960s, were reinforced by a policy of Russification, leaving each Baltic nation anxious about its very existence. The need to reassert a national identity and presence was the imperative that gave the national movements a sense of urgency not encountered in other republics. It was not surprising then that when the opportunity finally came to redress the balance, many saw it as a way to legislate extra advantages for the indigenous ethnic group by restricting citizenship. Amid cries from the Russian Federation's parliament about the "violation of human rights" against the minority Russian population, each republic debated the optimal way forward.

In Lithuania, where the titular nationality is a healthy majority, citizenship was extended to all residents. But in Estonia and Latvia, where the native population is barely in the majority, the new citizenship laws were discussed for months. In both Estonia and Latvia, there was general agreement that all citizens of the interwar republics and their descendants should have their citizenship restored. In Estonia, legislators finally came up with a procedure for naturalization that demanded only two years' residence and minimal competence in the language. In Latvia, where the Latvian population makes up barely 52 percent, some legislators were in favor of imposing a sixteen-year residency requirement. As well as the legal aspects of integrating a large non-Baltic minority population, the two newly independent states will continue to face the cultural implications of their new, and perhaps unanticipated, multiethnic status for some time to come.

The Baltic States have embarked on a long-awaited road to independence and statehood. In the tumult caused by the dissolution of the rest of the Soviet Union, the history of their noble struggle may be buried by the weight of broader concerns. But there are many who will remember that the peaceful tactics of nonviolent struggle in the Baltic States were the model and inspiration for national movements throughout the Soviet Union.

One year after the Moscow coup and the broad recognition of the Baltic States' independence, there were indications that the struggle for reform and statehood might not be without certain reversals. When the citizens of Lithuania went to the polls to elect their first post-Soviet parliament in October and November 1992, the results brought a decisive victory for the candidates of the Lithuanian Democratic Labor Party, the former independent Lithuanian Communist Party. Of the 141 seats in the new parliament, the former Communists gained over half, with the Sajudis coalition winning less than one fifth. This new turn of events meant the return to leadership of Algirdas Brazauskas, chairman of the Democratic Labor Party and the stepping down of Vytautas Landsbergis. In an interview immediately after the results were announced, Landsbergis blamed shortcomings and splits within Sajudis for the defeat. Other democrats pointed to the concerted effort by the DLP campaign to win over the Russian-speaking population by reassuring them of a new, more conciliatory policy toward Russia. Although Brazauskas was quick to declare the change of political leadership a normal event in a democratic society, Landsbergis questioned whether the new majority party would make Lithuania's national interests a priority and above the interests of "another country." With this reference, Landsbergis made clear his concern over the possibility of a reversal of Lithuania's sovereignty through concessions to Russia.

The September 1992 elections in Estonia brought a different result. The majority of seats to the State Assembly (*Riigikogu*) was won by the pro-reform *Pro Patria* coalition, which included the Estonian Conservative Party, the Estonian Christian Democratic Party, the Estonian Christian Democratic Union, the Estonian Liberal Democratic Party, and the Republican Coalition Party. The election for president held at the same time was inconclusive in the first round, showing a close race between Arnold Ruutel, a former member of the Estonian Communist Party Central Committee who had gained much popularity over the previous two years, and Lennart Meri the candidate of the *Pro Patria* coalition. In the case of such a close race the vote is given over to the parliament, thus the majority party candidate Meri finally was elected President of Estonia.

As the Baltic States recede from the focus of attention for the western public, and Baltic politicians settle down to the pedestrian requirements of everyday politics, it should never be forgotten that this was where the mighty Soviet Union began to crumble. For years to come students of history will study how the term "national rebirth" took on a countenance in the Baltic States that combined both culture and politics, and how the relentless struggle of the Baltic people against all odds finally drove in the wedge that sundered the Soviet empire.

Chapter Five

The Caucasus: Region of Conflict

When will the blood cease to flow in the mountains?
When the sugarcane grows in the snows.

CAUCASIAN PROVERB

The turbulent, mountainous Caucasus region, lodged squarely between the Black and the Caspian seas, has been viewed in the past as a gateway from Russia in the north to the lands of the Middle East, and depicted by poets and writers like Lermontov and Pushkin as a region of mystery and passion. During the Soviet period, the region was best known by Moscow's more prosperous housewives as a good source for fruit, vegetables, and wine. In the period when the Soviet Union was breaking up, this region became a microcosm for all the tensions, conflicts, and contradictions of the empire.

The Caucasus is where Europe and Asia meet, where three major nations and a number of ethnic groups coexist, and where Islam and Christianity share a spiritual frontier. For the people of the Caucasus, the period under Soviet rule is a mere blip in the region's history, stretching back through the mists of time to the mythological era when Jason and his Argonauts landed in Colchis, in present day Georgia.

The land encompasses a diverse terrain. Among the peaks of the Caucasus mountain range, Mount Elbrus rises to over eighteen thousand feet above sea level. The lush and comfortable resorts of Sochi and Sukhumi are among the most popular around the Black Sea, and Georgia's vineyards have long been renowned for their wine and champagne. On the other side of the mountains are the oil fields of Azerbaijan that used to produce nearly ten percent of the USSR's total output of oil. The Armenian towns of Spitak and Kumayri (formerly Leninakan) were at the epicenter of one of the century's most devastating earthquakes in December 1988. All this is located in less than 78 thousand square miles, encompassing the three Caucasian republics of Armenia, Azerbaijan, and Georgia.

Each of the republics has been the scene of dramatic events over the past five years. In Armenia a mass movement early in 1988 marked the first time that crowds numbering in the hundreds of thousands took part in peaceful demonstrations on the streets of a major Soviet city. Despite previous declarations from Gorbachev and assurances from the Soviet press, these demonstrations showed that the Soviet Union was on the verge of momentous change and started a trend in mass street gatherings throughout the USSR. The Armenian movement went on to create a broad, more structured proindependence movement that challenged the Soviet system, then matured to take over positions of power in the newly independent republic.

In the same period, Georgia experienced both tragedy and good fortune. In April 1989, Tbilisi was the scene of a brutal attack by the authorities on a gathering of people praying in front of the government building. The use of sharpened shovels and lethal chemical gas sent tremors of dissent through the Soviet establishment and galvanized the entire Georgian population, both Communists and dissidents, to support the drive for independence. Georgia was the second republic after Lithuania to declare independence from the Soviet Union in April 1991, and the first to hold popular elections for the post of president.

After this auspicious start, Georgia went on to become the first republic to demonstrate that the relationship between independence and democracy is a fragile one fraught with potential contradictions, and the first republic to run its democratically elected president out of office by force. These events brought about a state of civil war on the streets of Tbilisi for a while, and led to the return from Moscow of the same Party boss who was promoted to first secretary of the Communist Party of Georgia in 1972. "From Shevardnadze to Shevardnadze," as one prominent Georgian philosopher ruefully put it. Interethnic disputes also formed a part of Georgia's problems at this time, especially in South Ossetia, where the population, feeling itself continually under fire, eventually expressed its desire to reunite with the North Ossetians across the border in Russia.

With perhaps one of the most rigid regimes in the USSR, Azerbaijan's movement for independence was slow to take off, but when it did, it brought hundreds of thousands of people out into the streets. Interethnic strife has played a major part in political life in Azerbaijan, however. The demands of the Armenians living in the mountainous enclave of Nagorny Karabakh, an autonomous region within Azerbaijan, have colored the political attitudes of Communists and Democrats alike, complicating the movement for independence with an added dimension. The growing openness in Azerbaijan has also awakened the nation's Turkic sensibilities, much more than in the republics of Central Asia. The growing relationship between Turkey and Azerbaijan is likely to become a new axis for many political and cultural trends in the future and will promote the rapid reintegration of Azerbaijan into the world economy.

Relations between these three distinct and ancient peoples, now numbering a total population of around 15.6 million, have not always been easy. The Russian czar Alexander I annexed part of Georgia in 1801, and by 1810 had consolidated his rule over the country. The annexation of the rest of the Caucasian region was complete by 1829, after a war against Persia, when the Armenian territories together with the city of Yerevan were signed over to Russia. The Azerbaijani principalities in the region were conquered by Russia at the same time.

The nineteenth century was a period of uneasy coexistence between the Georgians, Armenians, and Azerbaijanis. As long as czarist domination persisted, borders remained fluid or nonexistent and ethnic groups intermingled. Azerbaijani Turks, as they were known, lived in Armenia, and Armenians lived in Azerbaijan and Georgia. Of the three peoples, the Georgians were the most geographically compact, occupying a well-defined area in the western Caucasus. Nonetheless, Tbilisi, or Tiflis as it was then called, had a distinct Armenian character because of the predominance of Armenians in the urban merchant class at that time; and up until the recent strife between Armenians and Azerbaijanis, there was a strong Armenian presence in Baku, the capital of Azerbaijan.

When the Russian empire disintegrated in 1917, major political groups consolidated primarily along ethnic lines in the Caucasus. For a time after the October Revolution, the three Caucasian nations maintained a federation, but by the spring of 1918, internal dissension had made that arrangement untenable and each state in turn declared its independence. Independence did not last long, however, as one by one the national states that had broken free of the czarist empire were reabsorbed into the new Soviet state. Under Soviet rule the three Caucasian nations became part of the many nations and peoples that make up the USSR. Although none of the three nations came into the union as enemies of Russia, their subjection to Soviet nationalities policy through the years has only fueled the desire for independence from the Russian-dominated state in the north.

Georgia

The Georgia of popular imagination is a land of dancing ensembles whose dark-eyed women glide like clockwork dolls and whose mustachioed men perform an array of acrobatic feats on tiptoe to the sound of pounding drums. This perception is not entirely inaccurate, for Georgians are renowned for their aristocratic bearing. The women are celebrated for their looks, not pretty but striking; and the men usually wear a beard, a mustache, or a five o'clock shadow—these are definitely the marks of manliness here.

Georgia is the birthplace of Stalin, about whom many Georgians remain ambivalent—at once proud and critical. It is also the birthplace of Eduard Shevardnadze, who secured a special status for the Georgian republic when he was allowed to run the Party and its administrative organs as the republic's Party boss from 1972 to 1985 with little direct interference from Moscow, as long as Party discipline was preserved and nationalism kept in check.

But the Georgians also have much to be proud of. Mtskheta, the ancient capital of Georgia a millennium ago, was at the junction of important trade routes that ran from east to the west down the river Mtkavari, and from the north to the south down the river Argvi, then onward to Armenia and Iran. The old Jvari Church sits atop a precipitous peak just outside the town, and below it in the center of the town is the huge Svetitskhoveli Cathedral, built in the eleventh century and the spiritual center of the Georgian Orthodox Church. It is a breathtaking edifice, stunning in its simplicity, yet aesthetically complex with its asymmetrical construction. Dressed in long black raiments and conical, black hats, priests walk by as if the tourists were not there. The cathedral draws many native Georgian visitors, as it is the burial place of a number of Georgian monarchs.

Tbilisi, the present-day capital of Georgia, is a one thousand five hundred-year-old city with a population of more than 1 million. Deriving its name from the Georgian word *tbili*, which means "warm," the city is home to a district of sulphurous springs and is located in a picturesque basin surrounded on three sides by mountains that treat the city's inhabitants to many spectacular sunsets. Tbilisi, a city of citadels, cathedrals, castles, and cable cars, has a long history as a center for trade, commerce, and intellectual life. Its various districts reflect three distinct periods in Georgia's history: the period of the Georgian kingdom, the nineteenth century under czarist rule, and the last seventy years under Soviet rule.

The city bears few traces of a Russian or Soviet presence. Signposts and street names are written in Georgian, which uses a beautiful and unique looped script. Although Georgian script looks similar to Armenian script, the structure of the language itself resembles no other living language, which makes the Georgians proud to say that their language is the only authentically Caucasian language. A billboard prominently displayed on one of Tbilisi's main thoroughfares had been used until recently for political purposes, showing Georgia's evolution over the past few years. In Brezhnev's day, it displayed a large picture of the venerated general secretary, dressed in a dark suit in the winter and a light suit in the summer. When Gorbachev took over, the portraits disappeared, to be replaced by sayings from the new leader and exhortations for more effort toward perestroika. Soon after the tragic events of April 9, 1989, all semblance of lip service to the regime in Moscow was abandoned, and the billboard began to display a series of quotes from the medieval Georgian poet Shota Rustaveli, attractively illustrated with a Georgian-style folk pattern around the border.

At the same time, the paraphernalia of Georgian independence became visible everywhere on the streets of Tbilisi. Independent vendors peddled a variety of pins, flags, and other items bearing the distinctive cherry red flag with the white and black square inset. Newsletters and the literature of independent groups could be bought for a modest price. The Georgians' growing national assertiveness literally changed the city's appearance. Young people walked down Rustaveli Avenue, Tbilisi's main artery, carrying the national flag, reveling in an act that would have provoked immediate arrest not long ago. Many of the monuments erected in the Soviet period were dismantled one by one. A statue of Sergo Ordzhonikidze, Stalin's right-hand man in the conquest of Georgia for the Bolsheviks and an officially venerated figure, was pelted with rotten eggs and vegetables for months. After repeated, futile efforts by the authorities to keep it clean, the local government finally gave in and ordered its dismantling. Such was the fate of many official edifices of the Soviet era.

A walk down Rustaveli Avenue today conveys a very different atmosphere. Independence—declared in April 1991—is now taken for granted. There are some who do not know now whether to regard it as a blessing or a curse. At one end of the avenue crumbling buildings and piles of rubble remind people that just a short time ago this was the scene of intense street battles between the supporters of President Zviad Gamsakhurdia and the armed opposition. Many still do not comprehend how patriotic Georgians could have gone from the heroic defense of Georgian ideals on the Bloody Sunday of April 9, 1989, to the fratricide and ignominious flight under fire of Georgia's first democratically elected president.

Hardly anyone who witnessed the tragic event in Tbilisi in 1989 could have imagined where it would lead. Bloody Sunday, as it is now referred to, stunned and shocked the Georgian people, and provided a compelling reason for resistance to Soviet rule for those who had hitherto stood on the sidelines of demonstrations. There were some who claimed a knowledge of ulterior motives by the authorities on that night: a secret plan to force the crowds to enter the government building as if in a spontaneous, storming surge. Troops from the Ministry of Internal Affairs armed with sharpened shovels and lethal C-S gas had flanked the crowd on three sides, leaving open the side toward the government building, and were ready to force the crowd inside. A telegram addressed to Moscow from the then first secretary of the Georgian Communist Party, Dzhumber Patiashvili, explaining how the troops were obliged to put down the rioting masses when they broke into the government building, had already been drafted. But the plan backfired. The crowds refused to be incited and remained calm, most of them on their knees praying in front of the building. Nineteen people, mainly women, were killed and many more injured when the troops attacked. Many of the victims died of chemical poisoning, and countless others were hospitalized suffering severe side effects.

Months after the horrible tragedy, passersby could still detect a faint whiff of chemicals in the air, even though the stone slabs and turf in front of the government building had been pulled up and a fence erected to block off the site from public view. In October 1989, the Georgian Supreme Soviet issued a report, concluding that the military operation in Tbilisi "had the appearance of a deliberately planned slaughter carried out with extraordinary cruelty." A committee of the Supreme Soviet came to a similar conclusion, implicating high-level officials in Moscow who had made key decisions on the operation, among them Defense Minister Dmitry Yazov, and Politburo members Yegor Ligachev (who had criticized Gorbachev for being "too liberal") and Viktor Chebrikov. Across the street from the site of the massacre, the Kashveti Church has become a memorial sanctuary and, even now, candles are set up there to honor the dead in the age-old Georgian religious tradition.

For the Georgians, Bloody Sunday was a national tragedy that marked a watershed in their history, mobilizing the entire population behind the movement for independence. Shaken by the wanton violence against their own people, the authorities ceased to obstruct and prosecute the activities of independent groups and associations. Hardly a Georgian could be found who did not condemn the events of April 9 and come to the conclusion that independence was the only way forward for the Georgian nation.

The Union of Cinematographers building about half a mile up Rustaveli

Avenue from the scene of Bloody Sunday became a meeting place for intellectuals and reformers in the summer of 1989. The filmmaker Eldar Shengelaya, peoples' deputy and supporter of Georgian rights, had given over the use of his offices in the union building to the informal groups for their meetings. (Georgia's filmmakers have always been somewhat independent. Tengiz Abuladze's film *Repentance* was one of the first to reach a mass audience with its explicit criticism of Stalinism shot in a Georgian setting.) It was there that we first met Zviad Gamsakhurdia, riding high on a wave of popularity and adulation. His dark eyes and brooding good looks identified him as a true son of Georgia. Even though his hair had turned grey since his first independent activities, he was in 1989 a popular hero whose time had come.

Georgian nationalism runs in his family. His father, the renowned Georgian writer Konstantin Gamsakhurdia, was expelled from the Georgian Writers' Union in the early 1930s as Stalinism moved into high gear. In the 1950s, he was once more singled out for attack for "idealization of the past" in his works—a code phrase for attempting to present history as it was, rather than as the Party had dictated it should be written. The young Zviad suffered these indignities along with the rest of his family.

Until a few years ago, Gamsakhurdia was a virtually unknown figure despite many years of human rights activity. As a teenager, he was arrested for distributing proindependence leaflets and served a short sentence. In 1972, then a teacher of American literature and English language, he made a protest against the poor state of Georgia's architectural monuments. When it was discovered that precious Georgian religious artifacts were missing, Gamsakhurdia pressed the authorities into an investigation that eventually led them to the wife of the Georgian Party chief Vasily Mzhavanadze.

In 1974, Gamsakhurdia and his colleagues regrouped to defend human rights, and in 1977, to monitor violations of the Helsinki Accords, which the USSR had just signed. He was arrested with his longtime friend and colleague, the human rights campaigner Merab Kostava, and sentenced to five years' incarceration. The authorities did their best to make sure that news of the arrests was kept away from the Georgian public. Gamsakhurdia's plight was known mainly in the West, publicized through links he had established with Russian dissidents in Moscow. When the case finally came to trial in the summer of 1978, Gamsakhurdia made a public recantation of his purported crime, admitting he had been led astray. His sentence was commuted to two years of internal exile not far from Georgia. His standing in the dissident community was considerably diminished as a result of this act, even though recantations made under duress were not uncommon in those days. This odd incident seems to have been largely forgotten a decade later in the rush of cheering crowds.

In the summer of 1989, he displayed the characteristics of someone who has discovered the solution to all problems. He had a brisk businesslike demeanor and his sentences were clipped and precise. True to the Georgian character, there was no room for equivocation in what he said: "The Georgian government is Moscow's puppet. . . . There are no Marxists in Georgia; even in the Party they are all businessmen, hiding behind Marxist and Communist ideas. It's a party of businessmen." He paused, to make sure we got the message.

It was clear that he saw independence as the only way forward for Georgia and that he believed there was widespread support for the idea—in "practically the whole of Georgia," he stressed. But even at that time he foresaw that Georgia's path toward this goal would be different: "The Baltics have their own way, a parliamentary way. . . . This is possible for them as they have nationally conscious people in the Communist Party and in the government. Ours are corrupt and antinational."

Gamsakhurdia's assessment of the national question in the Soviet Union at that time was bluntly argued: He professed to know that the interethnic conflicts in Georgia, whether with the Abkhazians or with the Ossetians, were orchestrated from Russia as part of "Moscow's imperial policy." Many thoughtful dissidents had also voiced similar opinions. But in retrospect, there was a certain tone in the way Gamsakhurdia discussed this subject—a suggestion of paranoia together with an oversimplification of the problem and a reluctance to consider its complexities—that should have given a signal of the ominous character traits of the future president.

We witnessed his popularity and how he could play to the crowds, by accompanying him for half a day of campaigning in Tbilisi in 1989. He was eagerly awaited at the Stalin Rail Carriage Repair Factory. Not allowed to hold the meeting indoors, Gamsakhurdia addressed the workers outside in a small amphitheater decorated with panels depicting scenes from working life. More than two hundred people in tattered and shabby overalls stood and sat on the steps awaiting his arrival even though he was more than half an hour late. The assembled workers cheered and applauded as he strode up to the platform to join his colleagues from other radical groups. He was the center of attention, the main speaker, and his message to his growing constituency of supporters was clear: He wanted their support for a one-day token strike that would be a part of the strategy toward establishing his ideal. The crowd broke into tumultuous applause as he built up to the conclusion: "Long live a democratic, independent, Christian Georgia!"

Gamsakhurdia was unquestionably the leader of the opposition movement, even though there were many other factions and groups. Most, however, were radical and inclined toward dramatic gestures and rousing rhetoric. There was little evidence then or later of the meticulous, careful planning of strategies and moves that had characterized the national movements in the Baltic States. Georgia's youth were swept up in the maelstrom of nationalist activity, even though they, more than any group, had little to guide their energy and enthusiasm. Alienated from the Communist Party, they found themselves instinctively drawn to the independence movement. What they lacked was the accumulated knowledge of world affairs that only exposure to uncensored information can provide. For generations, the Georgians have been isolated from events in the rest of the world, without even a significant diaspora like that of their neighbors, the Armenians, to give them a window on a different way of life and a vision of a different way of organizing things. It was no wonder then that in discussions with any group of young Georgians one would be likely to hear, "Georgia should be only for the Georgians!"

Sitting around in their offices in the summer of 1989, in a building of faded splendor off Rustaveli Avenue, the young Christian Democrats were one of the new political groups springing up at that time. The group's emblem in the sign of a cross was emblazoned on a wall-poster next to a stylized poster of the Georgian national flag. As they interrupted each other to voice their opinions on a broad range of topics, their youthful enthusiasm brought forth a string of expressions couched in the language of democracy. But behind the rhetoric, there was not much evidence that the easy references to Western values and institutions were deeply understood or more than a reservoir for anti-Soviet slogans.

The infectious enthusiasm for independence and the shortage of democratic ideas, especially among the youth, may be seen partly as the result of Georgia's location and historical development. Situated on the peripheries of the Western world, Georgia never had a Magna Carta, nor the same traditions of justice and law that developed in Western Europe. The Georgians lived under constant threat of being conquered by Persia or Turkey. Nonetheless, a rudimentary understanding of democracy and social and political rights evolved through the years between the Georgian nobility and the peasantry. After Georgia's annexation by the Russian empire, the Georgian nobility that was not gradually absorbed into the imperial social structure became so impoverished as to be virtually indistinguishable from the rest of the Georgian population. The social contract broke down and responsibility for creating the foundation for a modern democratic tradition passed to the Georgian intelligentsia in the nineteenth century, one of whom was Ilya Chavchavadze, who proposed the preservation of Georgia as a homogeneous agricultural society based on respect for Georgia's language and historical traditions, and a political system that extended voting rights to peasants. But the development of the Georgian national democratic tradition was squashed, as were many other national democratic movements in the nineteenth-century Russian empire, by restrictions imposed by an increasingly conservative czarist government. In the twentieth century, democratic movements were hardly given a chance to develop before the independent Georgian state constituted under the leadership of the Georgian Mensheviks was brought under Bolshevik rule.

Among the radicals in 1989 there were some forces for moderation. Nodar Notadze, a philosopher at the Academy of Sciences and a relative latecomer to the ranks of the organized opposition, was (and still is) the leader and spokesman for the popular front, outlining their support for an independent Georgia through a gradual approach. He admitted that this strategy was more difficult for Georgians to grasp than the goal of unconditional independence clearly articulated and publicized by radical dissidents for many years.

In the summer of 1989, Georgia's political groups gathered for earnest discussion of Georgia's future. Almost all groups were represented: the newly formed Georgian Popular Front, the Ilya Chavchavadze Association, the National Democratic Party, the radical Association of Saint Ilya the Righteous, and several others. Discussions proceeded at an amicable yet determined pace. Although there was no disagreement on the fundamental issue of independence, the moderates, such as the Georgian Popular Front, were in favor of participation in the elections and work through constitutionally established channels. The radicals in the Association of Saint Ilya the Righteous and the National Democratic Party favored a boycott. The inability of the Georgian opposition to find a firm middle ground was already apparent. Anxious crowds gathered outside the building day and night throughout the summer. Still suffering from the trauma of Bloody Sunday, they gathered to hear the latest news, to give each other moral support, and to feel a sense of solidarity with their fellow countrymen at a time of crisis. Across the road, the statue of Shota Rustaveli joined them in silent vigil.

A respected Georgian philosopher Merab Mamardashvili was troubled by the widespread radicalization of the national movement after the massacre. Sitting in his study in a comfortable Tbilisi apartment that summer, we knew we were listening to one of the wisest men in Georgia. As he sucked on his pipe he pronounced: "Georgians are so taken with the idea of freedom that they have lost the ability to think rationally."

Mamardashvili had walked the fine line between official approval and banishment for his pursuit of philosophical truth, teaching himself English and other languages to have access to the philosophical traditions outlawed by Soviet philosophy. He dealt deftly with terms such as "liberty," "democracy," "perestroika," and "bureaucracy." He believed there was no bureaucracy in the Soviet Union in the strict sense of the word: "A bureaucratic system is predictable and runs according to set rules. This we do not have. Gorbachev has brought into use all the words in the European political lexicon, but their meaning," he shook his head with regret, "bears no relation to reality." As he expressed his fears for the future of his country, he felt powerless to divert the mounting swell of nationalist feeling onto a path that would ensure a peaceful evolution toward democracy. Since his tragic death from a heart attack in November 1990, his words have attained a prophetic ring of truth.

The year following the massacre saw a steady, inexorable drive for more autonomy and independence. The Communist Party essentially withered away under the relentless onslaught by the radical opposition. All the elements for the incendiary series of events that followed were already present. First and foremost, even though Georgia had always enjoyed a certain kind of maverick independence despite repression and Russification, the level of understanding of democracy remained abysmally low at all levels of society. The lack of a developed civil society and lack of access to the works of intellectuals grappling with the same problems in Central Europe made Georgia all the more isolated and vulnerable. The passion stirred up by anti-Communist slogans mixed with appeals to the noble Georgian spirit was usually taken as a positive force in itself. Throughout the opposition movement, there were few voices speaking out for tolerance and coalition building, even fewer who understood the need for strengthening the opposition's moderate forces to have a workable center. No one, it seems, considered the importance of evaluating the role and power of institutions; in fact, there appears to have been a wholesale lack of respect for the institutions of democratic government. There was little consideration for either the checks and balances in different parts of the government, or the powers given over to the presidency.

Gamsakhurdia entered the hustings for the presidency with several long-standing opponents already ranged against him. The opposition movement in Georgia in the 1980s had developed from a number of groups that had generally been organized around an individual leader. Personal rivalries often led to faction fights, causing groups to split when there appeared to be few real grounds for disagreement. The elections to the Georgian Supreme Soviet, originally scheduled for March 1990, speeded up the formation of parties. Pressure from the opposition forced the postponement of the elections and gave time to introduce some changes in the election law to allow multiparty participation for the first time.

Two of Gamsakhurdia's main opponents at that time, Georgi (Ghia) Chanturia and Irakly Tsereteli, formed their own parties, the National Democratic Party and the National Independence Party, respectively. For some time prior to the elections, the various groups within the opposition had debated whether any election held within the structures created by the Communist Party could be legitimate. A group of parties, including Chanturia's and Tsereteli's, coalesced around the condemnation of the whole process as illegal and urged a boycott of the elections in favor of establishing a truly representative body in the form of a national congress, along the lines of the alternative institutions formed in Latvia and Estonia.

The group of parties around Gamsakhurdia, calling themselves the Round Table, determined early on to take part in the elections despite residual misgivings about the holdover structures of the Communist regime. The exchanges between these opponents became increasingly acrimonious as the elections approached, exacerbated by mysterious acts of violence against both sides. Two of Gamsakhurdia's bodyguards were killed in the offices of the Round Table, Chanturia was wounded in a gun attack, and a bomb was planted in the offices of Tsereteli's party.

The elections held in October 1990 brought the Round Table a landslide victory, securing 155 seats out of 250 in the parliament, and electing Gamsakhurdia chairman of the Supreme Soviet. Although the Communists won 64 seats, the second largest bloc, they decided to form a coalition with the Round Table to support them on almost all issues. Any opposition to Gamsakhurdia was either politically weak—the popular front headed by Nodar Notadze gained only 12 seats—or completely outside the system of government. In one case, the opposition was not merely a disgruntled group but a fully armed paramilitary force, the Mkhedrioni (Horsemen) under the command of Dzhaba Ioseliani, which was associated with Tsereteli's National Independence Party.

When the first presidential election took place in May of the following year, even though there were five other candidates, Gamsakhurdia swept to victory with 86 percent of the vote. But what happened next has all the makings of a bad fairy tale. Knowing that he could not be challenged in the parliament and basking in the genuine adulation of the people, Gamsakhurdia embarked on a series of highly questionable political acts. The new Law on the Presidency allowed him almost unlimited powers. With his personal representatives already in place, he suspended the powers of local governments and postponed the local elections, abolished the autonomous status of the South Ossetian Autonomous Region, made access to the media more difficult for his opponents, and arrested and imprisoned several of his opponents. While allegations of ill treatment and human rights abuses flourished, very little progress was made in economic and political reform. Then there were the rumors of luxury cars and presidential perks for Gamsakhurdia's family.

It may never be known whether Gamsakhurdia deliberately set out to establish an authoritarian regime, or whether he simply had no aptitude for the difficult task of taking Georgia through a transition to democracy—or whether, as some have suggested, his newly acquired power merely exacerbated a proclivity toward mental instability.

Interethnic conflicts in Georgia grew steadily worse during Gamsakhurdia's presidency. Abkhazians, who live in what was an autonomous Soviet republic within the borders of Georgia, have maintained an uneasy relationship with the Georgians for many years, occasionally putting forward proposals for leaving the Georgian republic to join the Russian republic to the north. Georgians object, as they consider the territories of Abkhazia and the Abkhazians themselves to be part of the traditional Georgian heritage. Gamsakhurdia's failure to take a realistic approach to interethnic problems also exacerbated tension between South Ossetians and Georgians. The Ossetians' demands for more autonomy were met with suspicion and then repression by the president. Finding no road to reconciliation, the Ossetians finally escalated their demands to ask for reunification with their compatriots in North Ossetia, just across the border in the Russian republic. These disputes had the effect of mobilizing the rest of the Georgian population in support of the leadership for a while in a way that talk of peaceful democratic change did not. With no incentive to seek a peaceful settlement in any ethnic dispute, Gamsakhurdia's administration tended to define a maximal pro-Georgian position, thus ensuring a continuation of the deadlock.

As soon as it became clear that the coup in Moscow was doomed, Gamsakhurdia's opponents took advantage of his initial hesitation in condemning the coup (some accused him of complicity with the coup plotters), and his ill-advised decision to disband the national guard. Refusing to comply with his commands, a large segment of the guard took its weapons and withdrew out of Tbilisi under the leadership of its commander, Tengiz

Kitovani. On September 2, 1991, a demonstration was organized by Gamsakhurdia's political opponents led by Chanturia, and when scuffles broke out, the police opened fire on the crowd, injuring several people. This action moved the disparate segments of the opposition to work together.

More protest demonstrations led to more repression by Gamsakhurdia, and a spiral of desertions began from the government as members left one by one to join the opposition. Gamsakhurdia showed no willingness to cooperate with his former colleagues or even to negotiate their differences, charging, in ever more hysterical tones, that opposition to him was inspired and organized from Moscow, that he was surrounded by spies and traitors. Even the moderates turned to active opposition demanding that steps be taken to move away from the presidential system toward a parliamentary one. Gamsakhurdia retaliated by suspending the law on political parties and by arresting some members of the opposition. Showing himself completely unable to cope with protests from many sides, he resorted to busing claques of adoring peasant women into Tbilisi to chant in his support in street demonstrations.

The demonstrations were interspersed with exchanges of fire between the armed opposition and the remaining Gamsakhurdia loyalists. The exchanges escalated until, in mid-December, when the other republics of the former Soviet Union were in the process of creating the new Commonwealth, the opposition issued the president an ultimatum to resign. For lack of any acceptable alternative, Gamsakhurdia fled to the government building protected by the remaining loyal guard.

What followed was a two-week siege, through which, with characteristic bravado, Gamsakhurdia boasted he could hold out. He was proved wrong, however, as he staged a dramatic undetected escape from the building in early January 1992, to seek asylum across the border in Grozny, capital of the self-proclaimed republic of Chechnya, under the protection of his colleague, General Dzhokhar Dudaev.

With Gamsakhurdia out of the way, a military council was quickly established from the ranks of the opposition. Once the situation had become more stable, the council issued an invitation to Eduard Shevardnadze to return to Georgia to help in the reconstruction of the state. Shevardnadze accepted and arrived in Tbilisi to a warm welcome in March 1992. He immediately took up the post of head of the newly established State Council and set about bringing the country to order. In the meantime, Gamsakhurdia had not been deserted by his supporters. Seventy parliamentarians gathered in Grozny to convene a rump parliament that condemned the new State Council as an illegal body and called upon the population to support a campaign of civil disobedience.

Under Shevardnadze's leadership, Georgia was admitted into the United Nations and began to enjoy some confidence from the world community once more. Despite his stature as a statesman and experienced politician, however, he found it impossible to avert the counterstrikes from Gamsakhurdia's supporters, which included the kidnapping of several high-ranking officials.

Georgia continues its tradition of ambivalence toward its leaders. Even though Gamsakhurdia was out of the way, he was still close enough to provide an embarrassing reminder of how the first democratically elected president in any republic of the USSR squandered the trust of his people. And although Shevardnadze continues to be lionized in the West, the Georgians have mixed feelings for their leader, whom they cannot forget contributed to Georgia's subjugation. But then, the Georgians still have not reconciled their sentiments toward the most famous Georgian in history, Joseph Stalin.

By the end of 1992, Shevardnadze was back at the helm of Georgian government in his new position as Chairman of the parliament. Elections in October brought him a new mandate and majority support in a new parliament which was made up of some twenty political parties. Despite the number of parties, many Georgians were unable to tell the difference between them, and one thoughtful observer characterized it as a parliament suitable for the "End of History" with neither strong opposition nor a convincing body of support for the government.

In the chilly twilight of the winter evenings, as the inhabitants of Tbilisi contemplated their fate in the absence of hot water and heating because of the lack of fuel, many must have pondered the events of the past months, and wondered what the uncertain future might hold.

Armenia

Armenia, the state to the south of Georgia, has over the past five years traversed a spectrum of emotions, from elation to despair. The Armenians were the first of the Soviet nations to take to the streets in mass demonstrations of hundreds of thousands. There had already been demonstrations in the Baltic States and even on Red Square itself, but the rumored number of demonstrators in Armenia's capital city of Yerevan in February 1988 surpassed anything ever seen before in the Soviet Union.

A disbelieving world waited for concrete news of what was happening. Western reporters based in Moscow were banned from traveling to the area; telephone communication was cut off and trips suddenly canceled. But the resourceful ex-political prisoner Sergey Grigoryants, editor of *Glasnost*, the unofficial bulletin of news and opinion and himself part Armenian, procured a videotape of the demonstrations in Yerevan and passed it on to the Western news media for rebroadcast. The scenes were unbelievable: a sea of dark-haired heads stretching into the distance filled the screen. Hundreds of thousands of Armenians sitting peacefully or swaying in unison to one chant. Unofficial estimates put the number of people on the streets at more than a million.

It was February 1988, almost two years before the pictures of thousands in the streets of East Germany and Czechoslovakia stunned the world. In a little-known part of the Soviet Union, the Armenian nation was experiencing its own baptism by fire in the streets of Yerevan, as almost a third of the population of the Armenian SSR took to the streets in peaceful protest over an area of land officially called the Nagorny Karabakh Autonomous Region. A little-known place even for the average Soviet citizen at that time, Nagorny Karabakh is a territory about the size of Long Island located in the Republic of Azerbaijan. It has been a source of dispute between the Azerbaijanis and Armenians since it was first given over to Azerbaijani jurisdiction by Stalin in 1923, despite its predominantly Armenian population. Armenians regard Nagorny Karabakh as historically a part of ancient Armenia, and refer to the territory by its old Armenian name, Artsakh. In czarist times, the region was at the center of important cultural developments for the Armenian nation, but territorial boundaries in 1923 were drawn so as to prevent any contiguous border with the Armenian republic.

For years, the Armenians who lived there felt themselves cut off from their people in the Armenian republic and claimed discrimination at the hands of the Azerbaijanis. The painful issue of Nagorny Karabakh was raised time and again with the Soviet authorities. Moscow's continuing lack of response gradually bred anti-Soviet sentiments in an Armenian population that had traditionally welcomed Russian protection. Underground groups formed on this and other issues; people were arrested and imprisoned. Through the years the population swung between silence and sporadic outbursts of anger and mass demonstrations. Finally, in the period of Gorbachev's glasnost, when the Nagorny Karabakh Supreme Soviet passed a resolution for independence from Azerbaijan, many in Armenia thought it would be a simple step for Moscow to confirm this move. Throughout 1987, small groups of Armenian activists, enjoying more relaxed conditions under glasnost, collected signatures on a petition demanding the return of Nagorny Karabakh to Armenian control, while a similar movement stirred in Nagorny Karabakh itself.

Although the demonstrations in Yerevan started a wave of mass peaceful protest among the nations of the Soviet Union that grew and finally involved millions of people, signaling the disintegration of the empire, the issue of Nagorny Karabakh has remained unresolved. While Armenia has reaped the reward of its leadership among the nations of the former USSR—it has gained its independence—Nagorny Karabakh remains a dominant theme in Armenia's internal politics and international relations. With hundreds dead and thousands of refugees on both sides, the problem looks further from resolution than ever.

For the Armenians, who trace their origins from the dawn of civilization, the current troubles are a continuation of hundreds of years of struggle, eclipsing even the association with the Russians to the north. Yerevan is reckoned to be one of the world's oldest cities—more than 2,800 years old. Armenia was on the map of the Middle East as early as the sixth century B.C., when it was one of the most powerful states in the region, stretching across lands that are now part of Turkey, Syria, Iraq, and Iran. Although not always an independent state, Armenia maintained a precarious existence between Persia and Rome up until the ninth century, when it fell to the Turks. During the wars over her territories between Mongols, Turks, and Persians until the nineteenth century, Armenia remained a culturally unified entity. Christianity and the Armenian church were the most important elements that sustained the strong sense of identity among Armenians, wherever they eventually ended up. The Armenian Apostolic church is separate from both Byzantium and Rome, and the Catholicos Vagzen I of All the Armenians of the monastery in Echmiadzin is the head of the church and spiritual leader of the nation.

The Armenians were unusual, even within the USSR, as part of a nation that has found itself scattered all over the world. An Armenian diaspora has existed since the Middle Ages, when the population scattered at the hands of foreign invaders. Today the Armenian nation stretches from Los Angeles, to Moscow, to Syria and other parts of the globe. When Armenia was part of the Soviet Union, only 66 percent of the population of 4.6 million Soviet Armenians lived in the republic, although the republic itself was the most ethnically homogeneous with more than 90 percent of the population native Armenian. Yet, wherever they are, the Armenians' sense of identity has always remained strong.

Armenians all over the world share a heritage that reflects their history of survival. Their collective memory combines stories from biblical times as well as the sufferings of the twentieth century. Every Armenian knows, for example, that after the flood Noah's Ark came to ground on Mount Ararat, which then was located at the center of the Armenian state, but now is located at new coordinates in the northeast corner of Turkey, clearly visible from Armenia. For Armenians, whose national consciousness has been impregnated with anti-Turkish feelings as a result of a history of animosity between the two peoples, the current dispute with the Azerbaijanis only reinforces their constant dread of their neighbors on both sides.

The horror of the 1915 massacre of Armenians at the hands of the Turks is a haunting memory shared by all Armenians. The massacre, often cited as the first genocide of modern times, decimated the Armenian population in the Anatolian region of Turkey, killing up to 1.5 million people of all ages. The motivation for the atrocity, according to some historians, lay in the pan-Turkic ideal of uniting the Turkic peoples from Constantinople eastward through Central Asia. The 2.5 million Christian Armenians in eastern Turkey were in the way of such a scheme. The Anatolian Armenians were also considered a security risk by Turkey, which was at war with Russia. The proximity to their Armenian and Christian compatriots just across the border in the Russian empire was felt to endanger the success of the Turkish war effort.

A monument to the genocide stands in a quiet place on a hill overlooking Yerevan as a perpetual reminder of the nation's struggle. Above the hustle and bustle of the city, the beams of concrete curve inward over the eternal flame of remembrance like the petals of an enormous flower, forming a chamber that protects it yet also leaves it open, still vulnerable to the outside world: a metaphor for the Armenian nation's survival through misfortunes both manmade and natural.

In the twentieth century, the Armenians have been a nation struggling to retrieve their lands and their dignity. After World War I, when the Ottoman Empire was broken up to form Turkey, Syria, and other countries in the Near East, the new Bolshevik regime in Moscow protested vigorously against the proposal to form an Armenian state between Lake Van and Mount Ararat in the traditionally Armenian territories of eastern Turkey—a proposal that was supported by Woodrow Wilson. Any hope for the return of their ancestral lands, despite the brutality they had suffered there, was thwarted. Thus, the only territory left to the Armenians was the tiny tract of land within the Soviet Union where Armenians had formerly lived under the protection of the Russian czars. Once a state that bordered three seas, the

Armenian republic has been shaved down to a landlocked state with access to none.

Today's independent Armenia has inherited the borders of the Soviet republic; its territory amounts to just 11,500 square miles, about the size of the state of Maryland. Neighboring Georgia takes up 26,000 square miles, slightly larger than West Virginia, and Azerbaijan occupies 33,500 square miles, the size of Maine. The Armenians' predicament, the lack of land to accommodate their people, has been added to their storehouse of national grievances. The old tragedies cannot be remedied, but for seventy years under Soviet rule the territorial predicament remained unresolved, despite the fact that the snow-covered twin peaks of Mount Ararat appeared on the Soviet Armenian emblem.

The mass meetings of February 1988 began to have an impact on Armenian politics, bringing a new group of leaders into the public eye and sending a tremendous burst of national consciousness through the population. Among those leaders were people who now find themselves in positions of power in Armenia: Levon Ter-Petrossian, president of Armenia; Ambartsum Galestyan, mayor of Yerevan; Ashot Manucharyan, chief advisor to the president on national security; and Paruir Hairikiyan, who took an active part in the 1988 demonstrations and continues his activity in opposition.

Hairikiyan described the process of natural selection of leadership from the people who came up to speak to the demonstrators: "Various orators gave speeches. But in time, these speakers would pass through a filter—the filter of public opinion. If someone spoke nonsense he was hooted and jeered. These people would not come back to speak. If a speaker spoke truthfully and intelligently, he was applauded. It was a case of natural selection. The nation elected who should speak. . . . Out of this process a leadership emerged, a leadership selected by the hundreds of thousands who gathered to protest. This was a remarkable phenomenon. It cannot adequately be described in words. In the end, the nation was opting, more and more, for self-determination, for the right to determine one's own fate."

It is hard to believe that this dark-haired, bearded man with deep brown eyes and passionate convictions had spent seventeen years in prisons and labor camps by the time he was thirty-eight years old. He has been an Armenian rights activist since he was a teenager. His imprisonment without a formal charge and without a trial at the height of the demonstrations in 1988 became a cause célèbre, and demands for his release were included in chants taken up by the crowds in Yerevan. Human rights activists in Moscow soon joined the chorus. The authorities were at a loss what to do: In

July 1988 they unceremoniously stripped Hairikiyan of his citizenship, expelled him against his will, and sent him to Ethiopia. Living in forced exile in the United States, he finally returned in the summer of 1991, to take part once more in the struggle for democracy and independence in his country.

The Nagorny Karabakh problem has continued to exert influence on the Armenian independence movement in many different ways, adding fuel to the growing nationalist feelings by provoking violence. Just after the Yerevan demonstrations, Azerbaijanis went on a rampage in the industrial city of Sumgait, near Baku, killing thirty-two people, twenty-six of whom were Armenians. Intellectuals in Baku were reluctant to believe that Azerbaijanis, unprovoked, could have perpetrated what became known as an anti-Armenian pogrom. Yet in January 1990, Armenians in Baku were hunted down in the same fashion. These ugly scenes of murder and violence set the scene for the unfolding events that left many dead on both sides of the border as well as in Nagorny Karabakh itself.

As the movement for self-determination for both Armenia and Karabakh grew throughout the year and tensions between Armenians and Azerbaijanis increased, another tragedy struck. On December 7, 1988, an earthquake measuring eight points on the Richter scale devastated an entire town and the region around it not far from Yerevan. Original estimates of twenty-five thousand dead were later revised upward to forty thousand. Houses built according to the poor designs and with inadequate materials in the last twenty years collapsed like a pack of cards, leaving thousands of people wandering around piles of rubble searching for loved ones in the freezing cold of winter.

Sensing a crisis of confidence, Mikhail Gorbachev, then President of the Soviet Union, dramatically cut short a US-USSR summit in Washington to rush to the scene of the disaster. When he got there, he succeeded only in making a tense situation worse when he expressed his exasperation at finding an unresponsive and angry Armenian population still insistent on raising the Nagorny Karabakh issue at this moment of tragedy. The disordered and slow-moving relief effort organized by Soviet officials did little to raise Gorbachev's already flagging prestige.

The loss of faith in Moscow's leadership and the new intensity of national feelings became evident in the aftermath of the earthquake. Rumor spread that Armenian orphans were to be taken to the Russian republic to be cared for. There was an immediate outcry and the informal movement headed by the Karabakh Committee organized a relay of women to guard and take care of the orphans, just as it had already mobilized a relief effort for victims far sooner than any planned by the Soviet authorities.

The Karabakh Committee had become the moral authority and the principal political force in Armenia throughout that year. Arising out of the February 1988 demonstrations as an informal group, its leaders, including Ter-Petrossian, became the spokesmen for the aspirations of the Armenian people. The committee began to organize within Armenian society and quickly became an alternative source of authority to the long discredited Communist Party in Armenia. The committee's credibility was further enhanced by the arrest of its leaders and their incarceration without trial. By mid-1989, the Karabakh Committee had gained such prestige and trust among the population of Armenia that its members decided to transform the committee into a broader opposition group, the Armenian National Movement, that would address a range of political and social issues affecting Armenia.

For several months in 1989, Moscow removed the Nagorny Karabakh enclave from Azerbaijani jurisdiction and exercised direct rule from Moscow through a special commission, experimenting with a new constitutional amendment giving the Presidium of the Supreme Soviet new authority to introduce "special forms of administration" to protect the safety of Soviet citizens. But the territory was then returned to the jurisdiction of Azerbaijan without any noticeable progress in resolving the conflict. By the end of 1989, relations between Armenians and Azerbaijanis reached a low point and the conflict looked poised to break out into full-scale war between the two nations. Both Armenians and Azerbaijanis had armed, and skirmishes had taken place along the border and around the Nagorny Karabakh region. The two sides seemed irreconcilable, and Soviet troops sent into the region on Moscow's orders were ineffective in countering guerilla tactics.

Armenia suffered for months under a blockade when essential and consumer goods were prevented from moving through Azerbaijan into Armenia. For many items this was the only route. In the meantime, the Armenian National Movement was gaining strength under the leadership of Ter-Petrossian. At the same time, armed militia groups were being formed, reflecting the sheer frustration of the Armenians at their state of powerlessness and inability to effect change, either in their relationship to Nagorny Karabakh or their defense against the blockade and continuing attacks from Azerbaijan.

In March of 1989, Armenians went to the polls along with all the citizens of the Soviet Union to elect for the first time a limited number of representatives to the Congress of People's Deputies. In a move that may have appeared unusual, the Armenians voted overwhelmingly for Galina Starovoitova, an ethnographer from Saint Petersburg. The election came as a surprise for the Communist authorities, who had not taken her candidacy seriously until it was too late. Since her election, Starovoitova, an expert in nationality affairs, has been a tireless defender of Armenian rights, both in the republic and in Nagorny Karabakh.

By the time of the elections to Armenia's own Supreme Soviet in May 1990, however, there were many signs of fatigue among the population. The frustration and anger of the intervening year had turned to apathy and emotional exhaustion. On the day of the vote the turnout numbered less than 50 percent, and a clear majority was gained in only 74 of the 259 electoral districts. But in one bright spot, the former dissident activist Paruir Hairikiyan was elected to the parliament even though he was still in forced exile, unable to return at that time to take up his seat.

The Communists gained as many seats as the Armenian National Movement, and the inconclusive election results delayed the emergence of a steady leadership until August, when Ter-Petrossian was elected as the first non-Communist chairman of Armenia's parliament. Together with his new team he immediately set about forging new policies for domestic affairs and Armenia's relations within the USSR. They determined that Armenia would take a legal path toward independence as soon as the opportunity allowed. Even the Communists within the parliament supported this policy, having determined that they would also break with the CPSU. Ter-Petrossian also undertook control of the independent militia forces that had been established outside a number of governmental structures. An ambitious program of privatization was proposed and multiparty politics given the green light.

While privatization has helped to ease the difficulties caused by the Azerbaijani blockades, in one way or another Nagorny Karabakh has continued to affect Armenian politics. The naturally cautious Ter-Petrossian has come under attack for not being aggressive enough in defending Armenian interests in Nagorny Karabakh, and for an apparent alliance with the Communists in the early days of his administration. When plans were being made in Moscow for an all-Union referendum on the preservation of the Union, Armenia opted to boycott the referendum and instead hold a vote on independence. Even so, when the Soviet government in Moscow laid down a complicated set of rules and procedures for secession from the USSR, Armenia was the only republic that chose to comply, setting a date in September 1991 for a referendum on the question of independence.

The August 1991 coup in Moscow barely made an impact in Armenia. While the parliament was naturally anxious about the outcome of the events, Ter-Petrossian hesitated only briefly before voicing his support for Yeltsin and condemnation of the coup plotters. The new turn of events made no difference in the strategy toward independence, and the referendum re-mained on schedule for the following month. The outcome could not have been in any doubt, but the postcoup euphoria and rush of other republics declaring independence brought the Armenians out en masse for the vote. An overwhelming majority voted in favor of independence for Armenia. One month later, Armenians went to the polls again, this time to elect a presi-dent. Ter-Petrossian won with over 80 percent of the vote.

Starting along the path of building a truly independent state, Armenia confronted many continuing problems. The warfare in Nagorny Karabakh escalated without any resolution in sight and after the dissolution of the USSR, it became an issue for the international community as a dispute between two sovereign states. In the new alignment of states, Armenia has once again found itself in a potentially threatened position, lodged between two Turkic neighbors. Traditionally, the Armenians had looked to the Rus-sians for protection against the threat from the surrounding Muslim popula-tion, but today's Russians have thus far disappointed them and the old debate has been reopened: Should Armenia work toward an accommoda-tion with Turkey or should it strive to strengthen relations with Russia?

Confronting this problem head on, one of Ter-Petrossian's first appoint-ments was taken from the Armenian diaspora. A Los Angeles business-person, Raffi Hovannisian, was invited to take up the post of minister of foreign affairs, thereby firmly establishing Armenia as a new player in the Western world.

Azerbaijan

Azerbaijan is the odd man out in the trio of major nations in the Caucasus. Wedged between the Black and Caspian seas with its Christian neighbors Georgia and Armenia, it differs from its neighboring republics in that it is a predominantly Muslim country. Although many Azerbaijanis assert their Caucasianness—and occasionally claim to be the original inhabitants of the entire region—their culture attaches them more to their Muslim cousins in Central Asia. Like the other two Caucasian states, Azerbaijan has also un-dergone a period of turmoil in the past five years. The Communist regime in this republic, considered one of the most rigid in the Soviet Union, made every effort to retain power, often supported by assistance from Moscow. Azerbaijan had always been an important asset to the central authorities because of its mineral resources.

Baku is the most important city in the Caucasus because of its proximity to the oil fields that were exploited first by the Russian czars, then by the Soviet regime in Moscow. The oil rigs, some distance out in the Caspian Sea, are not easily discernible from the city's center, but everywhere there is evidence of the culture that has evolved through the centuries because of the presence of oil. The name Azerbaijan is believed to have derived from the word *Adurbadagan*, which means "land of flames." Baku's coat of arms bears three torches on a field of sea waves.

In ancient times, according to the mythology, the people of this region were fire-worshippers, prone to experience spontaneous manifestations of their god in unexpected places. The science behind the belief is hardly mysterious. Near the village of Mahomedly there is a rock that has allegedly been burning since the time of Alexander the Great. The escaping methane that keeps the flames alight must truly have seemed a miracle to the fire-worshippers. Azerbaijan is also the birth place of Zarathushtra and historical bastion of Zoroastrianism which vied with Christianity until Islam supplanted them both in the middle of the seventh century and became the dominant religion under the Arab caliphate.

The oil wells of the Baku region were jealously guarded even in medieval times. As well as being used for lighting, heating, and medicinal purposes, the oil was used in warfare by special detachments of flamethrowers right up until the spread of firearms in the sixteenth century. By the mid-nineteenth century, the first deep borehole had been drilled and an oil processing plant had been established near Baku. Today, downtown Baku bears the signs of a nineteenth-century boomtown. European-style houses and streets fan out from the walls of the old city, and the wide promenade constructed along the seashore in the 1860s lends the atmosphere of a British seaside town. On summer evenings, *Bakintsy* (the people of Baku) stroll up and down the promenade while young men play snooker on specially constructed tables and their elders play chess, or they sit in one of the *chaykhanas* (teahouses), drinking tea Turkish style, in small glasses with sugar cubes, discussing the events of the day.

On a hill in the southwest corner of town there is a grand reminder of Azerbaijan's former slavish relationship to Moscow. The magnificent house on the hillside was built by former Party boss Heidar Aliev for a one-day visit by the then general secretary, Leonid Brezhnev. Many people speak of the "legacy of Heidar Aliev" in the same derisive tones now reserved for Brezhnev's period of stagnation. Aliev was the only Azerbaijani to have broken into the predominantly Russian Party leadership in Moscow. The existence of the house was a badly kept secret for many years. Neither the high walls nor the barbed wire surrounding the house could prevent the stories of its lavish interiors and fabulous decorations purchased for hard currency that went to adorn the one-day wonder. People had heard of the sixteen-foot-high mirror specially made in Austria and the intricate and equally expensive light fixtures. No one knows whether Brezhnev was impressed. Today the house serves as the Palace for Weddings, and is open to the public. Every half hour or so, a wedding party pulls up outside the entrance and the band that sits on the doorstep strikes up a nuptial march as the couple enters. On the hillside beyond the house is the enclave where Baku's Party elite used to live, in apartment blocks within walking distance of the Central Committee and the Republican Party offices. This district was set apart from the rest of the city, as if to symbolically keep the Soviet-style architecture and crumbling workmanship away from the true heart of the city.

It was one of the misfortunes of Soviet town planning that the largest open space in the center of the average Soviet city was usually the square in front of the statue of Lenin, originally constructed for local May Day and October Revolution parades suitably near the Party building so that portly Communist Party dignitaries would not have to walk too far to mount the dais. The statues of Lenin are now largely gone and the open spaces carry a history of large demonstrations that were key in shaking and eventually toppling the old regime.

In Baku, what was Lenin Square is now a widened roadway that comfortably accommodates half a million people. The guidebook, written at a time when it was not even conceived that this would one day be the capital city of a separate country, describes it as being "as large as Moscow's Red Square and Leningrad's Palace Square put together."

For eighteen days in November 1988, the square became the site of a continuous demonstration by thousands of protesters. At its height, the crowd swelled to half a million. Many who were there described it as a turning point for the normally conciliatory Azerbaijanis, who had stood by and watched throughout the year as the situation in Nagorny Karabakh grew steadily worse and the Azerbaijani Party leadership seemed powerless to assert authority over the enclave that legally lay within its jurisdiction. Frustration with the leadership spilled over into other national and political issues to fuel the protests. The Azerbaijanis had been subjected to the same kind of nationalities policy as other nations in the former Soviet Union, including Russification and the debasement of their own history and culture. But the Azerbaijanis had never formed dissident groups or taken part in the human and national rights movement. Deviation from the official line was generally limited to the closed circles of intelligentsia. For the masses of the population, the corruption and abuse of power by Communist Party officials in Azerbaijan was the crucial factor. By the mid-1980s, these were so apparent as to have eroded any confidence by the population. This widespread discontent provided fuel for the protests.

The November demonstration was joined by Azerbaijani refugees from Armenia who had nowhere else to go. The protest finally came to a head at 4. A.M. on December 4, 1988, when a reduced contingent of demonstrators (women and children, except for the refugees, had been sent home) were left facing four lines of armed soldiers. All the while, the Afghan veterans in the crowd made sure that all refugee women and children were in the protected area in the middle. The *spetznaz* troops, the specially trained Soviet troops often brought into ethnic areas, were armed with clubs. Lashing out at the protesters, they cleared the square with an official total of three dead and thirty wounded among the civilian population. The demonstration had mobilized the population, including the workers, who had put forth their own leader, the twenty-six-year-old Nemat Panakhov.

Emboldened by the people's response, Azerbaijan's fledgling popular front, the Khalq Jibhasi, began to strengthen its organization and press for registration. Within a few short months the membership had grown to more than seventeen thousand. In April 1989, the leaders of the front went to meet Abdul-Rakhman Vezirov, the first secretary of the Communist Party in Azerbaijan. "He was not happy to see us, and questioned us on why we wanted to set up the front," said Leyla Yunusova, who was then one of the leaders. So enraged was the Party first secretary that he threatened that if they had been in Stalin's time he would have had them all shot. He was especially incensed by her comments. "As a woman—in fact I was the only woman in the delegation," she pointed out, "according to Azerbaijani tradition, once he had insulted me the men were obliged to defend my honor." Harassed when they tried to meet, and refused an office and access to the media, the popular front leadership nonetheless continued to gain support.

The Azerbaijanis were latecomers to the popular front mode of organization. There was an impression in the West at that time that was shared by dissidents in Moscow, that the Muslim regions could not sustain a Western-oriented, prodemocratic movement; that Islamic fundamentalism would be the way forward for the mass of people in Central Asia, beginning with the Azerbaijanis. But the reality appeared to be very different. The urban intelligentsia and the leaders of the popular front were looking toward the West—even though this often meant toward the Baltic States—for their ideological inspiration. In fact, the first draft program of the front was very similar to the programs of the popular fronts in the Baltic States.

As a result of these demonstrations, Baku was brought under martial law from January to September of 1989. At the designated curfew hour everyone scattered homeward and anyone left on the streets listened nervously for the sound of tanks. Despite these adverse conditions, the Azerbaijani Popular Front continued its work. Unlike the popular movements in Ukraine and the Baltic States, the Azerbaijani Popular Front was made up of individuals and was not an umbrella for a number of civic and political organizations. Neither was there an attempt by the Azerbaijani authorities to either co-opt or compromise with the front. For these reasons, it found itself in head-on opposition to the republic's Communist leadership with no intermediary institutions.

Most of the Azerbaijani Popular Front's demands were similar, however, to those of other republics, reflecting the desires of most of the population to have a leadership that would be responsive to the people. The popular front objected to the way the deputies to the Congress of People's Deputies were selected in March 1989. Their complaint was the standard one in the non-Russian republics: The candidates who might have represented the true interests of the people had been blocked from standing for nomination.

In August 1989, the Azerbaijani Popular Front organized a number of successful mass demonstrations. Up to six hundred thousand people gathered on several occasions that month to put pressure on the Party leadership to support the front's demands, which included recognition of the front as an official organization, release of arrested members of the pan-Turkic Birlik society, a revision of the March elections, greater local autonomy, and continued control over Nagorny Karabakh. On September 4, the Azerbaijani Popular Front called a successful general strike that brought the republic's transportation and industry, including the precious oil industry, to a standstill for over a week. The republic's Party leaders finally gave in and agreed to recognize and register the popular front and consider its demands.

Apart from their grievances over the lack of representation, many Azerbaijanis felt that their interests were not adequately represented in Moscow. Moreover, there was the distinct perception that Armenian influence predominated in the Soviet Union's capital. Meeting up with foreigners, Azerbaijanis would reel off lists of Armenians with influence in Moscow, then bemoan the fact that the media and press were dominated by the Armenians and an Armenian interpretation of the news, especially on the Nagorny Karabakh issue. The visit of Andrey Sakharov to the Caucasus in December 1988 brought no joy for the Azerbaijanis, many of whom believed he had taken the Armenian side before he had heard them out.

Throughout most of 1989, Baku's inhabitants, many of whom were only dimly aware of the refugees that had flooded into the city since the troubles started, experienced the Nagorny Karabakh dispute and the tensions with the Armenians only secondhand. But perhaps it is the Azerbaijani character that discouraged them from sharing the grim facts with strangers. Azerbaijanis, so the traditional wisdom goes, do not shout their misfortunes from the rooftops, but keep it in the family.

Gradually, most Bakintsy began to find out about Khutor, one of several shanty towns on the edge of the city that had become so overcrowded with Azerbaijani refugees from Armenia that the authorities built a wall around it to shield it from view. More than two hundred thousand people were living in these conditions in mid-1989, with more arriving every month. Whole families shared small cramped rooms in the jerry-built dwellings, or *samostroiki*, as they were called in Russian. Many had been forced to leave their homes in Armenia at short notice, often having been called into the local Party offices and informed that, Party membership notwithstanding, the authorities could no longer ensure their safety if they stayed. Most Azerbaijanis left behind a lifetime's accumulation of possessions; some had to abandon newly built homes; others in their haste left behind vital documents, such as the *trudovaya kniga* (Soviet work book), without which it is difficult to secure work. Without residence permits and other documents required by the Soviet system, many new arrivals found it extremely difficult to find work and to gain access to services such as hospitals and polyclinics. Many still suffered the trauma of being under attack by armed Armenians, being airlifted out by Soviet troops in helicopters, and barely escaping with their lives. With only a one-time fifty-ruble handout from the authorities, many of the displaced Azerbaijanis were angry, but resigned to the attempt to rebuild their lives somehow in these desperate circumstances.

The appearance of refugees from Armenia and also from Nagorny Karabakh began to politicize Azerbaijanis around an issue of national pride, much in the same way Armenian political life had been gradually and imperceptibly politicized by the same issue. Early on in the dispute, Azerbaijani intellectuals had put forth numerous theses on the Azerbaijani origins of Nagorny Karabakh. They pointed out that *Karabakh* is a Turkish word meaning "dark vineyard" or "garden," and underscored the area's significance as the home of many cultural figures, writers, and musicians, such as Uzeir Hajibeyli, composer of the first Muslim operas and of the national anthems of both the Azerbaijani Republic and the Azerbaijan SSR.

January 1990 brought a sudden escalation in the violence between Armenians and Azerbaijanis. Armed clashes occurred along the border between the two republics and armed men on both sides took to the hills in and around Nagorny Karabakh, prepared for prolonged guerilla warfare, having procured sophisticated arms and in some cases even armored cars and helicopters. In several cities, radicals from the popular front seized power, while unrest mounted in Baku.

Baku had historically been an ethnically mixed city, home to Armenians, Jews, Russians, and many other nationalities, but what happened in that month cleared the city of its population of Armenians, which had at one time been estimated at close to two hundred thousand. In mid-January, groups of Azerbaijanis began a targeted campaign of violence against Armenian families, causing most of them to abandon their homes and friends and flee from the city.

After several days, during which police and troops reportedly stood by and refused to intervene, the authorities finally gave the go-ahead for a military crackdown in Baku. KGB troops were brought in from outside the republic together with regular army and navy forces to assist the Ministry of Internal Affairs troops already in the republic. As a result, 150 innocent bystanders—mainly Azerbaijanis—were killed.

Thousands turned out for the funerals of those killed and a massive show of civil disobedience shut down transportation and industry for days in Baku. Once again, as in Georgia, the use of troops served only to activate broad masses of the population against the Soviet system, and encouraged the idea that secession was the only solution.

Although reports later emerged of good-hearted Azerbaijanis protecting their Armenian friends, the violence was in fact an anti-Armenian pogrom. What remained unclear, however, was how the violence began. Gary Kasparov, world-famous champion chess player and former Aremenian resident of Baku, who witnessed the events, assessed that there was some prior knowledge of the pogrom by the authorities and a purpose behind their instigation: "Provoking these events led to the creation of a situation in Baku that would permit tanks to crush the movement for independence in the republic. That is, to strike not against those responsible for the pogroms but against those who were demonstrating for changes in the republic, for an end to Azerbaijan's dependence on Moscow, for a chance to sell their oil and cotton."

Two years later, in the summer of 1992, Kasparov's suspicions were proved correct. Marshal Dmitry Yazov, minister of defense at that time, had already gone on record as confirming that the military crackdown was necessary to prevent a government takeover by Azerbaijani nationalist forces. The July 1992 investigation launched by the Azerbaijani parliament discovered that Evgeny Primakov (now head of Russia's External Intelligence Directorate) had been the main organizer and instigator behind the tragedy.

A state of shock and feeling of deep inertia prevailed for months after the crackdown, and Baku remained under martial law. In the rising swell of grief and protest, the moderate members of the Azerbaijani Popular Front, who had launched the movement with a platform of struggle for democracy, representative government, and a free press, left to join Azerbaijan's Social Democratic Party, feeling that their measured approach to political change had been swept aside. And although Party First Secretary Abdul-Rakhman Vezirov lost his post and was replaced by Ayaz Mutalibov, one thing remained the same: Rather than crumbling in the wake of the crackdown, the Communist Party retrenched and regained something of its strength. The only issue that continued to arouse a popular response was Nagorny Karabakh. Under the leadership of Mutalibov, the Communist Party sought support by recasting itself in a more nationalist mold, purloining parts of the popular front's platform. Nobody was surprised when the elections to Azerbaijan's Supreme Soviet in September 1990 brought in an overwhelming Communist majority, with only a handful from opposition groups.

Mounting opposition to the Communist regime throughout 1991 was countered by the Azerbaijanification of the Party, and by Mutalibov's calculated distancing of himself and his Party from Moscow. On one point at least, there was agreement between both sides: Moscow had failed to make any progress in restoring Azerbaijani rule over Nagorny Karabakh.

When the August 1991 coup occurred in Moscow, Mutalibov was in Iran on an official visit preparing to return in time for the presidential elections scheduled for September 8. When the State Committee for the State of Emergency seized power, Mutalibov was reported to have expressed in an interview with an Iranian news agency his satisfaction at Gorbachev's removal from power. But by the time he returned to Baku, his initial statement had been retracted and he was voicing support for Boris Yeltsin. Despite attempts at denial, Mutalibov's stand brought people out into the streets in a new wave of demonstrations calling for his resignation.

In a dramatic move to shore up his popularity, Mutalibov convened an emergency session of the Supreme Soviet, in which he simultaneously supported the unanimous vote for a declaration of independence for the Azerbaijan SSR and resigned from the Communist Party. The following week, running unopposed in Azerbaijan's first popular presidential election, he won a large majority despite mass demonstrations organized in Baku by the popular front.

By early 1992, Mutalibov's popularity was in serious decline, partly because of his enthusiastic support for membership in the Commonwealth of Independent States at a time when the majority favored real independence, and largely because he had failed to secure any advantages in Nagorny Karabakh in the face of increasing Armenian successes. Mutalibov's resignation in March came under pressure from the Supreme Soviet, which revoked its decision two months later and tried to have Mutalibov reinstated. But his one-day return to power was cut short when the Azerbaijani Popular Front forcefully seized power, and the old-guard president finally fled to Moscow amid mass demonstrations by anti-Mutalibov protesters.

The political situation began to stabilize, and a plurality of parties and candidates emerged in preparation for the first multicandidate presidential elections. On June 8, 1992, Azerbaijani Popular Front president Abulfaz Elchibey was elected president of Azerbaijan in an election that was generally considered to be free and fair. A philologist who spent two years in prison for his views during the Brezhnev era, Elchibey is generally considered to be a moderate who makes no secret of his pro-Turkish leanings. It is thought he was Turkey's favored candidate.

From the beginning of his tenure, he made it clear that Azerbaijan would follow a path similar to Turkey's by instituting a secular Islam. Although Islam is important in Azerbaijan, its character has always been somewhat different from that of the other Central Asian states. The Caucasus region is still considered a stronghold of Sufism, with many holy places very close to Baku and on Azerbaijan's northern border, where Sufism and mysticism have traditionally been strongest.

It is also unlikely that Iran's influence will pull the Azerbaijanis along the fundamentalist track. When Iran's Hashemi Rafsanjani visited Baku at the beginning of July 1989, he was greeted by a disappointing turnout of around three thousand at Baku's Tazapir Mosque. Although Azerbaijan's Muslims are predominantly Shiite and traditionally Shiites and Sunnis worship separately, both are accommodated at this mosque, decorated with both Sunni and Shiite symbols. Rafsanjani's cool reception had less to do with religious differences than with old wounds. The Azerbaijani population in Iran (estimated to be anywhere between 9 million and 17 million) suffered waves of persecution under the Shah's regime and at the hands of Ayatollah Khomeini's functionaries.

There are some groups in Azerbaijan that consider reunification with "Southern Azerbaijan" inevitable at some point in the near future, but young intellectuals in Baku, while still considering their cultural traditions to be Muslim, are at the forefront of the revival of language and traditions. They draw a distinction between themselves and the older generation, as one young historian put it: "Our parents still think of themselves as Muslims, but we—the younger generation—we consider ourselves to be Turks."

Chapter Six

Central Asia: The Muslim Factor and the Turkic Continuum

When a caravan turns around, the last camel becomes the first.

PROVERB OF TURKMENISTAN

Long before the dissolution of the Soviet Union, discerning travelers in the region that was then called Soviet Central Asia could have predicted that major changes would soon be inevitable. Propaganda and reality were worlds apart in the final years of the USSR: Far from making the area a region of full employment and prosperity, seventy years of Soviet rule had merely given Central Asia crushing poverty and blatant colonial status. Seventy years of atheist policies had failed to eradicate the Muslim faith, the strongest bond that unites the people in this region. Seventy years of cultural and linguistic engineering and campaigns to convince the people of the superiority of Russian culture and language failed to expunge the dominant Turkish cultural influence.

In 1989 one would often hear heartfelt sentiments: "The Uzbek intelligentsia has always regarded its culture as part of a broader Turkish culture. Our history is tied to the history of the Kyrgyz and the Kazakhs. . . . In the 1920s and 1930s, we understood each other and could read the same texts. The languages are very close. You could even say that Kyrgyz, Kazakh, and Uzbek are dialects of one great language."

Central Asia—the heartland of the Muslim faith in what was the USSR—is now made up of five independent states: Uzbekistan, Kazakhstan, Turkmenistan, Kyrgyzstan, and Tajikistan. Previously thought of as the "soft underbelly" of the Soviet empire, today the newly independent states in this region form a contiguous bloc of Muslim states with a population of 60 million that stretches from Turkey to China, and reaches into the Russian Federation to the north, where the Tatars and the Bashkirs form a Muslim bloc at the center of the new Russian state. The strategic and political importance of this new alignment of states has not yet been fully realized by the world community, nor has its economic potential yet been assessed.

Kazakhstan is the largest state in terms of territory—almost 1.1 million square miles—and has a population of 16.5 million. Uzbekistan has the largest population, 19.9 million. Kyrgyzstan, on the border with China, has a population of 4.3 million. Turkmenistan, which borders Iran and Afghanistan, has a population of 3.5 million; and Tajikistan, the republic that borders on Afghanistan and China, has a population of 5.1 million. All of the major Muslim groups are Turkic peoples, except the Tajiks, whose ethnic origins can be traced to Iranian roots.

Although the Muslim population of the former Soviet Union was surpassed only by those of Indonesia, Pakistan, India, and Bangladesh, the Muslim factor was the least familiar piece in the jigsaw puzzle of nations and peoples that found themselves within the Soviet empire. Without a strong presence in Moscow and without a significant emigré community in the West to publicize their existence, the plight of the Soviet Muslims was never fully revealed to the rest of the world. Information emanating from Moscow promoted a view of these peoples as mysterious and exotic with impenetrable traditions and esoteric agendas. Today, these formerly hidden nations are just beginning to appraise their own potential in preparation for rejoining the international community.

The rich and ancient cultures of Central Asia did not adapt well to Sovietization. The ideology of Marxism-Leninism never took root in this region. Throughout the long Brezhnev years, local Communist Party officials mouthed the expected Party line in exchange for being left to exercise power virtually unrestricted, as long as they fulfilled their obligations to Moscow. The Communist regimes in each republic evolved into a characteristic amalgam of forces: They maintained the required structure for Party organizations that followed the principle of democratic centralism, but often the actual lines of authority followed the traditional Central Asian patterns of clan hierarchy. All major political and economic policies, however, were decided in Moscow and the Central Asian republics became little more than colonial appendages. The region was reduced primarily to a producer of raw materials and its governments to colonial administrators.

The August 1991 coup in Moscow did not appear to take the leaders in Central Asia by surprise. In fact, the leaders of Tajikistan, Uzbekistan, and Turkmenistan waited in silence to see whether the State Committee for the State of Emergency would succeed in installing itself as the new legitimate government. Following their natural inclination to accept without question any orders coming from Moscow, they may have been relieved to learn that a strong hand was finally being restored in Moscow after the seeming chaos of the final phase of Gorbachev's perestroika that had disrupted the familiar patterns of corruption and nepotism. Glasnost, in the form of investigators from Moscow, had exposed many cases of corruption involving high-level officials, especially in Uzbekistan, where thousands were arrested during the 1980s.

Viewed from Tashkent, Ashgabad, and Dushanbe the coup must have seemed far away, and the forces supporting and opposing it of little consequence to the future of Central Asia. Even if the Central Asian leaders were aware of what Yeltsin's challenge represented, there was simply no precedent for opposing, endorsing, or reacting in any independent way to changes at the top of the Soviet state hierarchy, regardless of which way they came about.

Kazakhstan and Kyrgyzstan were clearly against the coup from the outset. The Kazakh president, Nursultan Nazarbaev, astutely anticipated the outrage expressed around the world in support of Gorbachev, and threw in his lot, albeit cautiously at first, with the opposition to the coup. Nazarbaev, more than any of the other Central Asian leaders, had staked his career on support for Gorbachev.

The reaction of Kyrgyzstan's president, Askar Akaev, was the most decisive and statesmanlike. Fearing a similar coup in his own republic, he immediately dismissed the Kyrgyz KGB chairman and sent loyal Ministry of Internal Affairs troops to barricade the radio and television center, the telegraph office, and the Central Committee building. He immediately sent a telegram of support to Boris Yeltsin and had Yeltsin's appeal broadcast and published in all the newspapers. He was the only republican leader to attempt to organize an interrepublican effort against the coup plotters, while also seeking assistance for his republic at the United Nations.

No sooner were the other Central Asians reconciled to the failure of the coup and the return of Gorbachev than a new dizzying progression of events began in the power struggle between Yeltsin and Gorbachev. Once again, fundamental changes in Central Asia were being dictated by events in Moscow. In the months between August and December 1991, the Central Asian states marked time, uncertain whether they would be called upon to sign a new Union treaty or whether some other form of association was being planned. The only sure trend was toward sovereignty. With the exception of Kazakhstan, the Central Asian republics followed the other Soviet republics by declaring independence and holding presidential elections.

It was not until December, when Ukraine's citizens voted overwhelmingly for independence in their referendum, that the new politics of the post-Communist era began to emerge. The sudden formation of the Commonwealth of Independent States in meetings between the leaders of the three Slavic republics, without the participation or notification of the Central Asian states, abruptly put a new cast on events. Once again, fundamental changes in the region were being driven by the Slavs. The absence of any consultations or even any warning by the leaders of Russia, Ukraine, and Belarus about the formation of the Commonwealth, and more importantly, of the dissolution of the USSR, left the Central Asian leaders bewildered and unprepared.

Kazakhstan's Nursultan Nazarbaev reacted quickly. Of all the Central Asian leaders, he recognized that Kazakhstan stood to lose most, both politically and economically, from a split with Russia. He worked quickly to broker the entrance of the Central Asian states into the Commonwealth. Within days of the meeting of Slavic leaders in Minsk, the Central Asian leaders met in Ashgabad and reached unanimous agreement to participate in the new Commonwealth. On December 21, at a historic meeting hosted by Nazarbaev in Alma Ata, leaders of all five Central Asian states, joined by Armenia, Azerbaijan, and Moldova, agreed to take part in the Commonwealth that had been formed by Russia, Ukraine, and Belarus on December 8.

The Commonwealth brought the Central Asian republics in on an equal basis with the other republics, leaving them nominally free of Russian control for the first time in more than a hundred years. Suddenly an entire vista of new possibilities and dangers opened up for the Central Asians, who were now obliged to rethink their relationship with the huge Russian state to the north.

The Russians were not always the dominant power in this region. The territory in Central Asia was once part of the Mongol empire where Genghis Khan held dominion—an empire that stretched as far as the medieval principality of Moscow. The Russians were one of the few Christian peoples of Europe to experience the "Tatar Yoke" from the thirteenth to the fifteenth century, a period of domination by Mongols who converted to Islam. This period left a deep imprint on the Russian psyche and on Russian-Muslim relations. Although the newly centralized Muscovite state began to drive back the Muslim conquerors in the sixteenth century, the two states coexisted for a time in an uneasy balance of power. During the sixteenth and seventeenth centuries, important Muslim territories, including Kazan, Astrakhan, and western Siberia, were conquered and incorporated into the Russian empire. It was not until the mid- to late nineteenth century that Central Asia, or Turkestan as it was known, was finally conquered. Tashkent fell in 1865, followed by Bukhara and Khiva in 1873. And in 1875 the Russian army invaded the Kokand Khanate. Last to be taken over were the Turkmen territories.

The October Revolution and Bolshevik victory brought about a distinct turn of fortune for the Muslims. Although the czars had not encouraged Islam, the religion was left more or less unhindered under their rule. Lenin's new atheistic state, on the other hand, sought to eliminate Islam as part of a policy of the wholesale destruction of religion. Much of the history of those first years under Soviet rule was lost to the population of Soviet Central Asia. During the 1920s, when Bolshevik rule was being consolidated in the former territories of the Russian empire, fervent young Bolsheviks went into Soviet Central Asia to promote the Bolshevik creed on a mission to spread enlightenment and dispel years of illiteracy and backwardness. Official records of the era abound in pictures of Kazakh herdsmen marveling at the phenomenon of an electric light bulb, and of Uzbek women seeing the light of day for the first time after emerging from behind the Muslim veil.

An independent Muslim approach to communism looked possible in the early 1920s when Muslim intellectuals, under the leadership of Mirsaid Sultan Galiev, one of the highest-ranking Muslims in the Communist Party hierarchy, embarked on redefining the Communist doctrine for the Tatar and Turkic peoples who had just thrown off the tyrannies of czarist rule. Sultan Galiev hoped for a system that would not only provide for the welfare and economic prosperity of the Turkic peoples of Russia but would also be a blueprint for revolution for their Turkic brothers still oppressed by imperialist powers beyond its borders. He had a bold vision of all Muslim peoples living together in a kind of Turkic commonwealth within the new socialist order. But Stalin had a different vision and called for Sultan Galiev's arrest and expulsion from the Party in 1923 on charges of "nationalist deviation." Stalin made it very clear that national communism would have no independent role to play in the newly established Union of Soviet Socialist Republics.

Under the Bolsheviks, the new system gradually reverted to the old, familiar practices of Russian domination and great-power chauvinism. But instead of leaving the people to worship and educate their children in the age-old traditions, as czarism had allowed, the Bolsheviks began to systematically wipe out the old faith and to indoctrinate the people into a new way of life, with an aim toward clearing Soviet Central Asia of its indigenous religion, history, literature, and culture.

The people's disillusionment soon turned to active opposition. Some groups of Muslims had taken to the hills in Ferghana as early as 1918 to form an armed resistance in response to the crushing of their autonomy. The

Basmachi, as they were known, became an effective fighting force that proved a formidable challenge to the Red Army until 1923. Guerrilla fighting and anti-Soviet opposition continued until at least the end of the 1920s. The history of the Basmachi movement was never taught in Soviet schools and is only now being revealed to three generations of Central Asians.

By the end of the 1920s, the new Soviet leadership had put an end to the Muslim national Communists' plan to preserve the unity of the Muslim region. Plans to codify a language for all Turkic territories came to an abrupt halt as Muslims were divided into thirty-six separate nations, and literary languages were established—and sometimes invented—for each. At the same time, the Latin alphabet was introduced to replace the Arabic script that had been used throughout the region for centuries. In 1939, another alphabet change, this time to Cyrillic, was forced on the people, further distancing the Central Asians' ties to their rich culture, traditions, and history.

The New Politics in Central Asia

The sudden dissolution of the Soviet Union left the Central Asian republics facing unanticipated problems. The national democratic movements that in other republics had played an important role in the disintegration of central power were not strong enough to challenge the power of the local authorities and take over the government. Although there were sentiments for independence among some of the opposition groups, they were by no means widespread. Many of the political leaders had not planned beyond an indeterminate desire to be rid of control from Moscow; they had not considered any practical steps toward establishing a viable statehood. Political independence was thrust upon the Central Asian states, who had neither asked nor struggled for it.

One of the major differences between the Central Asians and the other peoples of the former Soviet Union was the absence of a widespread notion of national consciousness before the Soviet era. The Uzbek, Turkmen, Tajik, Kyrgyz, and Kazakh nations, it could be argued, were essentially formed under communism, although the intellectual elites of each were the descendants of rich and ancient cultures. The idea of nationhood and the concept of a nation state with its essential element of popular sovereignty had originated in Europe and was alien to their culture and traditions. There was little in the historical experience of the Central Asian peoples—apart from the past seventy years—to prepare them for independent statehood. They now faced the dilemma of establishing viable nation states, where the consensus on national identity is so recent as to be still open to question.

The difficulty of determining identity in Central Asia adds a step that other states have already resolved. Without the intercession of the Bolshevik revolution, the process of state formation in Central Asia may have taken a very different path. There was a strong movement among intellectuals to recreate a larger Turkestan even under the Soviets, in parallel with the community of Muslim believers in the spiritual sphere. However, with only a few distinguishing characteristics to determine differences between ethnic groups and tribes, the borders of republics were drawn by Stalin primarily to promote political expediency. Although the forced differentiation of peoples that took place under Stalin was largely artificial, there is today an increasing tendency, especially among the urban intelligentsia, to identify themselves voluntarily as Uzbek, Tajik, or Turkmen. Enforced nationhood and census-taking that required the registration of a government-approved ethnic identification has had an effect. Other factors such as Russification and discrimination have helped to consolidate a genuine national consciousness. Uzbeks, for example, attribute the rise of national feeling to the sense of victimization and resentment felt during the grueling investigations of corruption conducted from Moscow.

On the other hand, Islam continues to play a major unifying role throughout the region, pulling people toward a different set of loyalties and self-identification. Its importance to the Soviet Central Asians' identity cannot be overestimated; it was the force that held them together and provided cultural and spiritual nourishment when they were under pressure to Sovietize. More than nationalism, Islam was often the vehicle for anti-Communism in this region. The Soviet authorities also played the Islamic card by exaggerating the threat of Islamic fundamentalism to both obscure the real nature of the opposition and to raise the level of anxiety in the West over the spread of an ideology considered as undesirable as communism. The demise of communism has not dispelled this fear in the West even though the prospect of a full-fledged Islamic revolution in any of the new states is extremely remote. The Islamic Rebirth Party formed in 1990 as a region-wide political movement is unlikely to gain a mass interrepublic following even though it does have strong support in individual republics.

The region's Turkish heritage has recently reemerged as another unifying force. Young Central Asians are beginning to rediscover what their ancestors always knew: that from the Kazakhs and Uigurs in the northeast to the Tatars, Turkmen, and Azerbaijanis farther west, they are part of a Turkic continuum that, when aroused, could provide a powerful counterweight to the Slavs. Increasingly, the Turkic peoples are becoming aware of their common heritage and are seeking to bridge what they regard as an artificial gulf imposed upon them by the policies of Stalin and his successors. The combined population of Turkic peoples of the former Soviet Union is more than 50 million and rapidly rising. The newly established contacts with Turkey provide renewed incentives to drive forward the sense of reviving strength and cultural unity.

The new politics in Central Asia is being played out against a backdrop of shifting populations. Russians have been leaving to return to Russia since the late 1980s in the wake of widespread concern that the Slavic population would be forced to learn the indigenous language once each republic passed a law on its use as the official state language. Then, as violence broke out in parts of Uzbekistan and Tajikistan, local Slavs began to feel threatened even though the violence was not aimed at them. In 1991, one hundred thousand people—mostly Slavs—left Tajikistan and sixty thousand left Uzbekistan. The striking feature of the remaining indigenous population is its youth. Half of Uzbekistan's population is under the age of thirty, and all the Central Asian republics have maintained a consistently high birthrate for decades. Children born in the 1960s are now establishing their own large families. No government has yet considered the repercussions of supporting a large, young, and unskilled population, as the predominantly Russian engineers, doctors, and other professional people leave in increasing numbers.

In the absence of central control from Moscow, it is possible to observe an increasing differentiation between the Central Asian republics. Each state is rapidly developing its own profile in domestic as well as international affairs. Kazakhstan, the most European of the states, stands apart from the others in many respects: It was the only one with nuclear weapons when the USSR dissolved and the only one with developed industries. Kazakhstan's president is eager for his state to rank in importance alongside Ukraine and Russia. But despite his declared support for privatization and a free-market economy, Nazarbaev has made few real changes in the distribution of political power. Kyrgyzstan, however, shows encouraging signs of moving toward democracy under the enlightened leadership of President Askar Akaev. The opposition openly criticizes the government without harassment, although there have been several laws passed restricting criticism of the president and the freedom of speech in other areas. Islam is unlikely to play a major role in politics in either this state or Kazakhstan. But as Uzbekistan and Tajikistan struggle to determine a new status for themselves, the influence of Islam is becoming a factor in political discourse, as is the influence of territorial clans, especially in light of their strong financial support for the political elites. Turkmenistan, once considered the most backward and insignificant republic, is now coming into its own and has become something of a maverick among the Central Asian states. Like the heir to a large trust fund bequeathed on the death of a guardian, Turkmenistan has found itself suddenly wealthy and is testing its potential influence in the region, now backed by its inheritance of oil and mineral wealth.

For all the new prospects confronting the Central Asians now, there is a sense in which the new politics is a return to the old. The struggle for power and influence in Central Asia has traditionally been played out between rival clans or families, with Moscow, the longtime intruder in this arena, serving as an outside adjudicator. The forced adoption of Marxism-Leninism as the framework for political discourse merely provided a new vocabulary for what was often, in fact, the old politics. Now that Moscow is no longer a factor, many of the old rivalries and traditional power struggles are reviving.

This may explain why after the coup, the dissolution of the USSR, and the humiliation of the Communist Party, the old conservative elites remained in power in all the Central Asian states with the exception of Kyrgyzstan, where all Communist Party formations and activities were banned. In the other republics, the leaders slipped out of their Communist Party garb and donned something more Central Asian, while the Party simply underwent a change of name—in Tajikistan and Kazakhstan it became the Socialist Party; in Uzbekistan, the People's Democratic Party; and in Turkmenistan, the Democratic Party—a scheme that has enabled essentially the same people to maintain their positions within the legislative and executive power structures.

For most of the Central Asian republics, independence has been greeted by the ruling elites as the opportunity to take control over the institutions of power that used to be in the hands of people in Moscow. In the absence of a widely appreciated understanding of democracy, the developing structures of government have tended to work against increasing the participation of the population in the political process. The appointment of presidential prefects in Kazakhstan was followed by the appointment of directors of the executive branch in Kyrgyzstan and Uzbekistan, and in Turkmenistan local councils were replaced by People's Councils, thus strengthening the vertical ties to the republican elites.

The strategic significance of the new bloc of nations has not been lost on other Muslim states in the region. Barely had the new states found offices and personnel for their brand-new foreign ministries than they were being courted by envoys from Turkey, Iran, Saudi Arabia, and Pakistan vying for their loyalty in what will evolve as a new alignment of powers in the Middle East. Within a few weeks of the collapse of the Soviet Union, Turkey had signed economic protocols and opened up embassies in each of the republics, while also extending funds to establish an ambitious satellite linkup in each republic so that Turkish-language broadcasts could quickly begin. Iran has provided funds for education and the building of mosques, and Saudi Arabia has made investments in an attempt to woo the Central Asians.

Foreign policy has also taken on political significance in the choice of alphabets. For years, Central Asian intellectuals complained that the Cyrillic alphabet was incompatible with the sounds and inflections of their languages; now, there is an opportunity to make a change. In the first few weeks of independence, Tajikistan opted to revert to the Arabic script, bringing the new state closer to Iran, while Azerbaijan and Uzbekistan veered toward the Latin script, bringing them closer to Turkey.

But the battle for influence has only just begun. As the Central Asian republics throw off the structures of a command economy and one-party state, they are faced with an array of political systems and state models to follow. In the Muslim world alone there is a wide choice between a secular state as in Turkey, ranging through various degrees of adherence to the faith in political life, to the strict regime practiced in Saudi Arabia.

The Uzbeks

The Uzbeks were the third most numerous ethnic group in the Soviet Union after the Russians and the Ukrainians, numbering close to 16 million, but their numerical strength was never rendered into an equivalent access to political power at the highest levels of government. All major decisions relating to Uzbekistan's economic development were decided in the offices of Gosplan in Moscow. In the 1960s, there was even a plan to turn Uzbekistan into a model republic, an example of the success of the Soviet system and a hub for the other Central Asian republics. Three decades later, these promises have largely been forgotten, and newly independent Uzbekistan has inherited a crushing slate of problems ranging from a devastating level of poverty to a record of ecological disasters of catastrophic proportions.

Tashkent, capital of Uzbekistan, was once touted as the showcase of Central Asia, or gem of the Soviet south. But the reality marks a stark contrast. Tashkent's many wide boulevards are lined by large antiseptic government buildings and identical apartment blocks in an architectural monotony relieved only by plenty of parks and trees that provide shelter against the fierce, scorching summers. The earthquake of 1966 destroyed much of old Tashkent. The buildings constructed since show all the signs of the creeping stagnation of the Brezhnev era. Shoddily built from the outset, there are some buildings under construction that are already crumbling. Rows of apartment blocks have risen up among the rubble left by the earthquake, but there remain expanses of wasteland in the middle of the city, giving it a stark, Orwellian appearance. Parts of Tashkent are sensibly planted with trees and greenery, and the older parks are crisscrossed by *aryks*, small irrigation canals. Tashkent's statue of Karl Marx sits in the middle of just such a park, his sculpted facial features bearing more resemblance to Genghis Khan than to a German of Jewish extraction.

The combination of earthquake damage and socialist city planning has left Tashkent a city without a heart. Until recently, its shopping districts offered little in the way of goods. Few people carry shopping bags or containers of any kind as they move about town. Uzbek men wear the *tubateyka*, a square skullcap that sits on the back of the head, while Tashkent's female population adorns itself in the limited selection of dresses available to them—on any day, the same style of dress and fabric can be seen on hundreds of women.

Tashkent's Old Town is located in the vicinity of the old Chigotai Gate, once a part of the Old Silk Road, the most famous medieval trading route, which ran from the Black Sea in the west to China in the east. But there are no old or exotic buildings, no Eastern architecture harking back to antiquity. The road is a dust track and the buildings are barely above the wattle-and-daub stage; at a junction, a pile of rubbish lies smoldering.

There are fly-infested restaurants every few courtyards along, where Uzbeks eat shashliks cooked over an open fire at tables under canopies open to the street. In one restaurant, a large bathtub in the center serves as a sink for washing the plates. Traditional Uzbek green tea is served and Uzbeks go through an elaborate procedure of swilling out the teacups before drinking in order to "disinfect" them. Like many other of the Central Asia republics, Uzbekistan is often afflicted with epidemics. In the summer of 1989, one in five people carried hepatitis.

The roads are lined with buildings whose only entrance is onto the street. The typical layout of an Uzbek house includes an interior courtyard with a small patch of land on which herbs and small vegetables grow, and where perhaps a goat is tethered to a post. The building that surrounds the courtyard has a porch and rooms for the members of the extended family and their children. Prior to the earthquake, much of Tashkent looked like this. The new apartment buildings built after the earthquake were generally given over to Russians. Tashkent's Uzbek population, never city dwellers, has for the most part been only recently urbanized. Thus, the Uzbeks have no historical attachment to any major city, unlike the Tajiks, who point to the stunning architecture of Bukhara and Samarkand as a product of their long history of urban settlement.

One of the most serious problems Uzbekistan's leaders face is how to introduce a market system into an economy that was not only planned in Moscow but skewed toward the production of raw cotton to the virtual exclusion of any other crop or industry. Throughout history, the Uzbeks produced not only cotton but a wide variety of foods: rice and other grains; vegetables such as carrots, peppers, and radishes; fruits such as grapes, apricots, and melons; and walnuts and many other things. As recently as twenty years ago, people traveled to Uzbekistan to buy fruit and vegetables, but now they cost more here than in the bleaker, less fertile regions. The concentration on the cultivation of cotton—the monoculture, as it is called by Uzbeks—has led to innumerable social and ecological problems.

According to statistics for 1983, the USSR was the world's second largest cotton producer after China. Two-thirds of all cotton produced in the USSR came from Uzbekistan, which alone produced almost as much cotton as the United States in 1983. At that time the crop accounted for more than half of the agricultural output in Soviet Central Asia. Despite its key role in the production of such an important commodity, Uzbekistan did not reap the benefits. The cotton was grown and harvested in Uzbekistan, primarily using methods abandoned in the cotton-growing regions of the United States at the turn of the century. The raw cotton was sold for a pittance and exported out of Uzbekistan to be processed and made up into goods in other republics, which sold them for a far higher profit.

Ironically, Uzbekistan has never been an ideal place to grow cotton. Although the climatic conditions provide enough heat and sunlight, the lack of rainfall has meant that huge reserves of water must be diverted to the region from the rivers that used to run into the Aral Sea. The final stages of irrigation to feed each thirsty cotton plant and to prevent the soil from drying up in the arid heat are generally still performed by hand. The land itself is exhausted from the harmful chemicals, artificial fertilizers, and pesticides used to cultivate cotton. The traditional system of crop rotation, which prevailed until the 1940s, was replaced by continuous production of cotton. Harmful pesticides, long-banned in Western Europe and North America, were routinely used in Uzbekistan in quantities that exceeded even the norms allowed under the Soviet regime.

Irrigation has almost dried up the Aral Sea, one of the world's largest inland expanses of water, causing a huge imbalance in the region's ecosystem. The two great rivers, the Amu Darya and Syr Darya, that used to flow in to replenish the sea no longer reach its shores, their waters having been diverted years ago to irrigate the land to support rice and cotton. The resulting catastrophic drop in water levels in the sea has exposed miles of seabed, now made up of a mixture of salt, sand, pesticides, and defoliants. An ambitious plan to divert rivers from Siberia to flow into Soviet Central Asia was discussed for many years as a possible solution to the region's water shortage, but was abandoned in 1987 partly as a result of opposition from Russian writers and intellectuals.

The systematic poisoning of the land and the sea has been accompanied by an abysmal state of health. Cancers (especially cancer of the throat), anemia, and hepatitis ravage the Uzbek population. The average incidence of child mortality in Uzbekistan is around 47 per 1,000, but is closer to 100 per 1,000 in the region of the Aral Sea. Child mortality in this area is among the highest in the world. The environment is so polluted that mothers often contribute to the poisoning of their infants through their own breast milk.

The situation of women is particularly harsh, despite the fabled equality achieved under the Soviets. Mainly women and teenagers work the cotton fields where the pay is minimal, while the men try to find scarce higher-paying jobs elsewhere. Self-immolation, a common method of suicide among Central Asian women, is viewed by Uzbek intellectuals as a resort to sheer desperation over the hopeless conditions, high birthrate, and few opportunities for prosperity, contrary to the view put forward by some that it is a practice founded in cultural or religious traditions.

As recently as 1988, children were routinely brought into the cotton fields at harvesttime. For two to three months at a time, children of ten, eleven, and twelve years were deposited in the cotton fields for the entire day, without shelter in the scorching sun and often with little refreshment. In some areas, they were taken away from their homes and housed in barracks close to work while the harvest was in progress. Uzbekistan's new government offers little likelihood of an improvement in the situation of women and children, as any legislation on women's rights in the future is likely to be more restrictive to conform with the demands of Islamic law.

Mukhammad Salikh, formerly a secretary of the Uzbek Writers' Union and now president of the Democratic Party "Erk," has long been a leading spokesman for the Uzbek people. He is concerned about Uzbekistan's economic problems, and has spoken out on the subject on many occasions, despite the Uzbek authorities' disapproval. He is forthright in his assessment: "There is a direct link between the deteriorating ecological situation in Uzbekistan and the cotton monoculture," he told us. "We have lost not only our lands and waters, we have forfeited the health of our people. The land is ailing and also the people who work on it. Around eighty percent of Uzbeks live in *kishlaks*, traditional rural Uzbek settlements, where they work the cotton fields. This part of the population is basically in a state of ill health." Salikh recounts the list of Uzbekistan's grievances in a matter-of-fact way, not pleading for special consideration for the Uzbeks, but merely stating well-known facts and statistics.

Threatened with reprisals by the Soviet authorities for his outspoken-ness a few years ago, he was vigorously defended by student demonstrators and all charges against him were dropped. He went on record as speaking out against corruption in the ranks of Uzbekistan's Communist leaders, Rashidov and Inamdjon Usmankhodjaev, long before glasnost made it fashionable to do so. Asked in the summer of 1989 about Uzbekistan's new first secretary, Islam Karimov, Salikh adopted a tone of determined resignation: "He is said to have very democratic views, so we have hope for him. We'll see. We can only hope. Apart from hope, we have very little else."

By February of 1990, Salikh had become one of the founding members of the Erk Party, whose objectives were to work toward political objectives as far as possible within the legal framework of the state. Meeting up with these authors again in September 1991, Salikh demonstrated how his thinking had evolved: "Without independence [for Uzbekistan] there can be no other kind of independence, not economic, cultural, or any other." Erk's objective, he explained, was to pursue this goal as a parliamentary political party, while spreading its views to the broad masses of the population through the party newspaper and television.

In December 1991, Salikh ran as Erk's candidate in Uzbekistan's first free presidential election. As the only other candidate allowed to register for the race, Salikh gained only 12.4 percent of the vote against Islam Karimov's 85.9 percent. Although fraud was suspected, the overall outcome could have been predicted considering the opposition candidate's lack of access to the mass media and the Uzbek population's continuing preference for supporting the existing power. The Birlik (Unity) Popular Movement, based on a mass opposition movement, had not even been allowed to register a candidate.

Karimov's presidency began on an inauspicious note and heralded things to come. In January 1992, six people were reported killed in clashes between demonstrators and the militia when students gathered to protest against sudden price increases. When the government released the official version of what had happened, the students protested once more amidst a general demand for the resignation of the president.

By the summer of 1992, the situation in independent Uzbekistan looked little different from circumstances of three years earlier. The defeated Mukhammad Salikh, previously in favor of working with the existing regime, turned resolutely against such a path. After brutal beatings and the arrest of members of the Birlik opposition movement, he announced at a press conference that the Erk party would be joining Birlik in the underground to oppose the regime of Islam Karimov.

The "Unity Movement for the Preservation of Uzbekistan's Natural, Material, and Spiritual Riches," the Birlik Popular Movement—usually known by the Uzbek word for "unity,"*Birlik*—was founded in the summer of 1988 primarily in response to ecological concerns that simmered even then at the edge of people's consciousness: the growing concern over the devastation wrought by the monoculture of cotton and associated catastrophes.

Amidst looming ecological problems, Birlik was formed from a coalition of writers, professionals, and students who came together originally to help out the residents of an area that had formally been designated a recreational area to protest against the construction of a factory in their district. The authorities, as usual, had not consulted the residents of the area. Gradually, people began to coalesce around issues that concerned them. Students came out to demonstrate, and in March 1989 thousands of people attended a demonstration sponsored by Birlik in favor of making Uzbek the state language in the republic. By mid-1989, there were three hundred thousand members in the organization. Their primary concerns continue to be the social and economic conditions in Uzbekistan, a stand that has gained them a large following, even without any access to the mass media.

Abdurakhim Pulatov, chairman of Birlik and one of its founding members, is not a writer but an engineer. For him, social and economic issues are the most important items on the agenda for the Uzbek national movement. He is acutely aware of the poverty and hardships of everyday life for Uzbeks. "When people hear there is an organization for Uzbeks," he says, "they know immediately what its program must be; even without access to the media thousands of Uzbeks have given their support."

In the summer of 1989, Birlik managed to procure temporary office space on the ground floor of the Uzbek Writers' Union building. People drifted in and out in a continuous stream. The variety of people in the office at any one time was a reflection of the diverse membership of the movement. One woman volunteer in her midthirties told us she was the mother of four children. Having worked in a research institute for ten years, she now felt a need to do something to contribute to a better future for her children. Most of Birlik's leaders are in their early forties, thirties, or younger—the average age of the Uzbek intelligentsia. In Uzbekistan, there is no old intelligentsia. During Stalin's rule, anyone who could remember how to read the Arabic script was sent to prison, and usually never heard of again.

Many of the problems that brought people into the Birlik movement remain unresolved despite the fact that Uzbekistan is now an independent state. Feeling inadequately represented in the parliament, many Uzbeks bring their unanswered complaints to Birlik. Common grievances continue to be the poor state of health of the population, arbitrary exercise of power by the executive branch, and few cultural resources. Although Russification of Uzbek culture is no longer considered an urgent problem, the withdrawal of Russian dominance in television broadcasts and publishing has not resulted in a rich diversity of Uzbek-language materials. As in most of the other newly independent states, radio and television is still under the firm control of the government, while publishing, which has caved in to the demands of public taste, suffers under the restraints of a steep increase in the price of paper on the new free market.

Birlik's principal form of protest has been the organization of large demonstrations. In October 1989, demonstrations in support of greater official standing for the Uzbek language and against the official law that sought to limit the language's use brought out an estimated fifty thousand people. Pulatov was arrested along with around one hundred other demonstrators at one of the events. These tactics of street politics were at the root of the split with the Erk party in 1990. Birlik remained illegal and unregistered until shortly before the dissolution of the USSR, as did its offshoot, the Birlik Party, which remained unregistered and illegal in the summer of 1992. The Birlik movement continues to unite many of the opposition groups, such as the Islamic Rebirth Party, the Free Farmers' Party, Green Party, Tomaris Women's Association, and the Organization of Free Youth of Uzbekistan, whose combined membership in the summer of 1992 was estimated at close to half a million. The Birlik Party alone claimed a membership of ten thousand.

After months of frustration over the lack of response from the now independent government of Uzbekistan, Birlik planned to hold a demonstration in cooperation with the Erk party on July 2, 1992, on the day of the opening of the Uzbek Supreme Soviet session, to demand genuinely democratic elections. Many of the leaders of Birlik were arrested, to be tried for "forcibly resisting law enforcement officers." Pulatov had been severely beaten only two days earlier by several men wielding iron clubs as he left the city procurator's office. The deputy chief of city police and the deputy prosecutor reportedly stood by as the attack took place; Pulatov received such severe blows to the skull that he was reported near death.

The prospects for improvement in the political and economic sphere look bleak. Breaking out of the cycle of poverty and manual work is very difficult for the majority of Uzbeks, who must compete with Russians for the more highly paid jobs for skilled workers. Until very recently, fluency in the Russian language determined a person's access to work, and Uzbeks often failed to qualify for specialist courses in technical schools that were taught only in Russian. Out of the few thousand workers at the aviation factory in Tashkent in 1989, for example, only 12 percent were Uzbeks. The production of cotton has tied people to the land and, especially in the case of children, robbed them of a significant part of their education. Although some of the Russian workers have opted to leave, freeing up their jobs for Uzbeks, jobs requiring any level of skill cannot immediately be filled by unqualified workers with no experience. But the statistics on poverty in Uzbekistan paint a dismal picture: Around 45 percent of the population is paid a wage below the poverty level, and unofficial sources estimate the number of unemployed in Uzbekistan at close to 2 million, most of them young people.

In the Ferghana Valley, where many of the young people live, the combination of social discontent and mixed ethnic groups living in close proximity has led to outbursts of violence. In the summer of 1989, Uzbeks and Meskhetian Turks clashed in a rampage that lasted more than a week and left more than a hundred dead. The following summer, Uzbeks and Kyrgyz clashed near the city of Osh, leaving close to two hundred dead. Many theories have been put forth about the violence: Uzbekistan's chief of security blames "pan-Islamic" agitators for inciting the violence; some of the Uzbek intelligentsia suspect a well-planned provocation to crack down on informal associations, especially Birlik; more probable causes point to conflict over land and water rights.

As well as native Uzbeks, Tajiks, and Kyrgyz, the Ferghana accommodates two relative newcomers: Meskhetian Turks and Crimean Tatars. Originally natives of Georgia, the Meskhetian Turks were deported as a nation under orders from Stalin at the end of World War II on charges of "collaboration" with the German invaders. Stalin also lodged a charge of treason against the Crimean Tatars and had them deported in 1944 from their native Crimea. Many of these deported peoples ended up in various parts of Central Asia, primarily Uzbekistan, and although they are considered as Turkic cousins to their Uzbek neighbors, their differences and a higher standard of living often set them apart. To exacerbate the potential for confrontation, the region itself is divided between three countries—Uzbekistan, Kyrgyzstan, and Tajikistan—whose jurisdictions remain unclear.

Despite the sporadic outbreaks of interethnic violence, Uzbekistan's government, more than those in any of the other Turkic republics, has expressed an interest in turning the notion of a broader Turkestan into a reality. Although most versions of pan-Turkism have been rejected by the Turkic intelligentsia in the republics, especially the notion of a close political union, Uzbekistan's leadership has used the symbolism of a unified Turkic community of interests to bolster support among an Uzbek population that is increasingly conscious of its growing importance. But it is also aware that Uzbek claims to national heritage do not go back in history very far before they become subsumed into the prerevolutionary Central Asian identity. Uzbekistan has welcomed the interest shown by Turkey, a secular, Muslim state that has generated a relatively high standard of living for some of its people. And while Turkish-language journals are very popular in Uzbekistan, there is, as in most of the other Turkic states, a reluctance to enjoy the embrace of the newfound friend too far. As one Uzbek intellectual put it: "We did not cast off one big brother merely to acquire another."

Times are changing for the Uzbeks. A vista of choices has opened up on both a governmental level and an individual level, particularly for those who are financially secure. A publisher we met three years ago explained to us the inner conflicts being experienced by many in the Uzbek intellectual elite at that time. Living in a chic neighborhood of Tashkent, he acknowledged his good fortune. He referred vaguely to a time when he was not so well accepted by the powers-that-be in Uzbekistan, after he had made statements against the Soviet invasion of Afghanistan, where more than a million Uzbeks live. Nonetheless, he felt alienated among the predominantly Russian residents of the neighborhood, complaining there was no Uzbek-language kindergarten to which he could send his young son. Yet there was a sense of ambiguity toward his own culture. He and his wife are a modern couple, enjoying all the trappings of a comfortable urban existence, yet she did not take part in our discussions but drifted in and out of the room serving sumptuous dishes of *plov* and other Uzbek specialties, according to the traditional practice. The young girls of the family were, of course, nowhere to be seen. He and his family represent a growing trend among the Uzbek intelligentsia. For many years, they were weaned away from their national traditions and discouraged from identifying with the national minority population by the lure of a position within a new internationalist class, in exchange for loyalty to the dominant culture centered in Moscow. The benefits of this arrangement proved illusory for the younger members of the intelligentsia, who are now trying to fashion a new Uzbek identity for the future.

The overt return to tradition has been accompanied by a revival of religion in Uzbekistan, although, as in other Soviet Central Asian republics, Islam was never suppressed among the broad masses of the population. In the past few years there were numerous reports in the Soviet newspapers of respected Party officials, who had maintained a public face as atheists throughout long and successful careers, suddenly becoming unofficial mullahs on retirement. The staying power of Islam in this region was reinforced by the incorporation of its rituals into the national traditions of the people. The Islamic way of conducting circumcisions, marriages, and, particularly, funerals became partly secularized after 1917 in the transition to national tradition. A few years ago, the only existing translation of the Koran from Arabic into Uzbek was prepared before the 1917 revolution. The Muslim shariah law was maintained purely through its survival as an oral tradition that had been subsumed into the developing Uzbek national tradition.

When it became known not long ago that a local strongman had built himself a luxurious fortified estate in Uzbekistan, complete with slaves and a private prison, the republic became a target for thoroughgoing investigations into corruption. Supercops Telman Gdlyan and Nikolay Ivanov of the Soviet crime-fighting force uncovered corruption throughout the Soviet establishment, reaching formerly untouchable people such as Leonid Brezhnev's son-in-law. Even archconservative Yegor Ligachev was implicated, though never directly accused by the prosecuting team. As a result of their investigations, which became famous as "the Uzbek Affair," hundreds of Uzbek officials were dismissed from their posts and punished for wrongdoing, usually taking many other officials with them.

In spite of Uzbekistan's tarnished reputation, Uzbeks have a profoundly different side to their national character. Sherali, the most popular singer in Uzbekistan, professes to be a devout Muslim. His enormous success among both young and old may be attributed to the reviving interest in the Uzbeks' cultural heritage. To the accompaniment of the traditional eleven-stringed *tor*, he weaves lyrics by Alisher Navoyi, Omar Khayyam, and more recent Uzbek poets into renditions of his own poems. He is the Uzbeks' bard, the keeper of the ancient verses. The richness of the Uzbek cultural heritage that spans the centuries is revealed in these songs, which speak of the eternal themes of faith, love, and passion. Yet the descendants of that culture, the present-day Uzbeks, are a people now struggling for their very existence.

The Uzbeks may yet be destined for good fortune. Recent discoveries of oil have been made in Mingbulak, and information on Uzbekistan's extensive gold fields is also now available. The production of gold was completely controlled by Moscow until September 1991. It has been estimated that Uzbekistan provided around a quarter of the Soviet Union's gold. But even now, according to the opposition, the Uzbek government is turning over around 60 percent to Russia in exchange for essential supplies of food and oil.

As Uzbekistan's population continues to grow at a rapid rate, the dismal circumstances for the majority of the population and the lack of tangible improvement may make their existence increasingly untenable in the coming months and years. The Uzbeks have not yet had their democratic revolution, but their evolving sense of a need for real self-determination and the awareness of having been exploited can only encourage further changes.

The Kazakhs

The dissolution of the Soviet Union in December 1991 left Nursultan Nazarbaev, president of Kazakhstan, ill prepared to cope with the problems of independence and statehood. Even though Kazakh assertiveness had increased over the past decade, Kazakhstan, of all the Central Asian republics, is the least able to make a clean break with Russia. Travel to the region explains some of the reasons why.

Alma Ata, the capital city of Kazakhstan, is home to many Russians. It preserves the atmosphere of a colonial outpost of the czarist empire and the surroundings are a secret closely guarded by the people who live there. The air is clear and sharp and the stunning Tien Shan Mountains, higher than any others in the region, form an omnipresent backdrop to the cityscape. Close to the Chinese border, the city appears to have avoided much of the dismal construction and pollution that are the hallmark of most major cities of the Soviet era.

Vernyi (the Faithful), as the town was originally called, was founded in the mid-1850s with the arrival of 470 soldiers and officers to establish a fortified garrison outpost for the Russian empire. Russian and Kazakh families soon followed, and by the end of the decade the town had five thousand inhabitants and soon gained a reputation as one of the most lively market towns in Central Asia. People came from miles around to the five market squares in the town where there was trade in fruit, agricultural produce, wood, horses, livestock, and anything that needed to be bought or sold. The largely Russian population and the function of the town as a frontier outpost of the Russian empire resulted in having very few characteristics of a region populated mainly by the nomadic Kazakhs.

Alma Ata is filled with delightful parks and an occasional Russian Orthodox church. There is one surrounded by a park, with an onion-shaped dome made up of bright, multicolored tiles of pink, ocher, blue, green, and white. The city has not been subjected to the typical ravages of war and destruction, followed by reconstruction, as have the former Soviet cities farther west. The legacy of the Russian imperial presence in the late nineteenth century is all around and affects even today's relations among the nations.

Until they began moving into Alma Ata, the nomadic Kazakhs had invested little energy in constructing buildings and cities, traveling instead from place to place and living in their distinctively shaped yurts. During the period of Sovietization, many were forced into a sedentary life-style against their will.

Today less than half of the population of Kazakhstan is composed of native Kazakhs, the borders drawn in the 1920s having ensured the republic would have a mixed population. The southern and western regions are inhabited by the core Kazakh population, while in the territory to the north—the vast virgin lands of Communist myth—Kazakhs are the minority. Nonetheless, the latest statistics show that the Kazakh share of the population is increasing. The 1989 Soviet census showed the Kazakhs, for the first time in the postwar period, as the largest national group. The percentage of Russians in the republic has now dropped to 37.6 percent, and the Kazakh share has increased to 38 percent, an increase due partly to the higher birthrate among Kazakhs, but also to the minor exodus of Slavs migrating back to their ethnic homelands. In the last decade, more than 780,000 people—more than in any other republic—mainly Russians, have migrated out of Kazakhstan to take up jobs in European Russia where there is a labor shortage.

Prior to the breakup of the Soviet Union, Kazakhstan's borders were never considered an issue in interrepublic relations. But now that independent statehood is a factor to be taken seriously, both Russians and Kazakhs on both sides of the border are taking positions. Nationalist members of the Russian parliament have declared, not without justification, that the original border between Russia and Kazakhstan was drawn without taking into consideration the ethnic groups living in the region, and charge that the time has come to draw a real, solid border that will include the "Russian" population and territories within the borders of a Russian state. Both Yeltsin and Nazarbaev have thus far avoided making an issue of the matter, recognizing that a major change of borders could bring disastrous consequences. As long as both men are in power, the border will most likely remain unrestricted.

National consciousness in Kazakhstan is developing at a rapid pace. It was the Kazakhs in Alma Ata who staged the first major ethnic disturbance of Gorbachev's tenure in December 1986. News of the demonstration that turned into a riot swept through the Western press corps in Moscow, but direct information was difficult to come by as reporters were not allowed to travel to the scene. According to official Soviet accounts, thousands of Kazakhs had taken to the streets and had rampaged through the city in violent clashes with the militia, leaving two dead and many injured. The culprits were arrested and subsequently many young people were dismissed from their colleges and universities. Several people received very harsh sentences. One young man was sentenced to death, a sentence later commuted to life in prison.

The Soviet press at the time had reported that an armed gang of Kazakh youths—"hooligans, drunks, and other rowdies"—had damaged public buildings and attacked the militia. A young man present at the demonstration relates a different version of the events: "It was a peaceful demonstration, without excesses. Mainly young people gathered for three days on the square. There must have been a permanent contingent of around five thousand. But you can imagine, in December it is very cold in Alma Ata." The demonstration included both workers and students, who were already organized before the event. Faced with a potentially unruly crowd, the authorities tried to regain control by urging Party leaders to speak to the crowds; but that only made matters worse, because few of them could speak in the Kazakh language. Then some Russian and Kazakh workers began to fight and troops from the Ministry of Internal Affairs moved in, armed (according to eyewitness accounts) with heavy truncheons.

It was almost three years later that the Kazakhs finally began to press for an official commission to investigate the events. During the first historic session of the Congress of People's Deputies in the spring of 1989, the well-known Kazakh writer Olzhas Suleimenov raised the issue and compared the 1986 demonstration with the recent April 9 massacre in Tbilisi, Georgia. Brushing aside all the official information released on the demonstration, he confirmed that it had been peaceful, similar in its origins to the Georgian gathering, and urged a thorough and public review of the incident.

The immediate cause of the demonstration had been the replacement of longtime Party First Secretary Dinmukhamed Kunaev, a native Kazakh, by Gennady Kolbin, an ethnic Russian and supporter of Gorbachev. Kunaev had been in power since 1959—except for a two-year period, 1962–64, when he fell afoul of Khrushchev—and was closely identified with the Brezhnev clique. It was assumed that Gorbachev would soon move to replace him, as he had with several of the Brezhnev holdovers in the Politburo.

For the first time, it became clear that Gorbachev was either unaware of national sensibilities or had grossly underestimated the power of ethnic allegiances. It was the first in a series of blunders and miscalculations by Gorbachev that showed he had no plan for perestroika in nationalities policy. The Alma Ata riots were a rude awakening. From Gorbachev's point of view, Kolbin was the ideal choice for cleaning up a republic that still bore signs of functional stagnation. He was young and energetic and had proved his loyalty to Gorbachev and his policies in his previous appointments as second secretary in Georgia and Party leader in Kazakhstan's Ulyanovsk Oblast. But, as one Kazakh writer put it: "He was completely unaware of our customs, our way of life, our language. How could he understand our problems?"

The demonstrations of December 1986 left a deep impression on the development of Kazakh political consciousness. There is even a political party named the Jeltoksan (December) National Party after the events of that month. Although not a major player, the party was the only one to put up an alternative candidate to challenge Nazarbaev in the presidential elections of December 1991.

The development of national consciousness in Kazakhstan prior to 1986 took on a steady pace even though it was never overtly encouraged. Dinmukhamed Kunaev was not an enthusiastic supporter of Kazakh nationalism. He was nothing like his fellow first secretary, Petro Shelest, the Ukrainian Communist Party boss who lost his position in 1972 for allegedly supporting Ukrainian nationalism. Kunaev did not speak out in defense of Kazakh national rights, nor did he pen any historical works of nationalist subtext or seek to preserve monuments with particular significance for Kazakhs. Nonetheless, Kunaev's Kazakhstan appears to have been a much more livable place than other republics over the past twenty years or so.

This feat was accomplished by skillfully balancing the demands imposed from Moscow against the needs of the republic while at the same time maintaining a regime of strict control. Alma Ata, for example, boasts new housing complexes that are not the standard Soviet-built fare. In the districts at the edge of the city, new apartment blocks have been built on a fairly regular schedule. They are decorated with Asiatic motifs and look quite attractive from a distance against the backdrop of mountains. Certainly, public architecture here is more in tune with the surroundings, a rare treat compared with Moscow's monumental cinderblock projects.

Although Kazakhs benefitted under Kunaev's rule in some ways, in other ways they suffered the discrimination inherent in Soviet nationalities policy. As recently as 1989, even though Alma Ata's population was one-quarter Kazakh and rising, there were no kindergartens for Kazakh children, and Kazakh-language instruction in schools was often unavailable. Kazakh intellectuals at that time felt a long way from being able to retrieve their language and their history from under decades of Soviet restrictions. Caution was still needed in discussing historical subjects that did not fit with the standard history of the Soviet Union propounded from Moscow. There were few studies on figures such as the Kazakh Turar Ryskulov, a Bolshevik with nationalist inclinations who was active in the national Communist movement in the 1920s but whose life and ideas were barely known to his own people. He remained on the fringes of what could be officially discussed for many years.

Today, the restrictions have evaporated and studies on previously risky subjects such as the Alash Orda, a liberal nationalist Kazakh political party that formed an independent Kazakh government from 1917 to 1920, have reappeared. The major restrictions nowadays stem from financial difficulties: Paper for publishing books is scarce and expensive on the open market, and the existing state allocations are reserved for government-approved publications.

There has always been an underlying feeling of hurt national pride among Kazakh intellectuals based on perceived and real deprivations throughout their nation's history. In 1930, the Kazakhs outnumbered the Uzbeks, but today there are twice as many Uzbeks as Kazakhs. In 1932–33, the Kazakh population was cut down by a famine at the same time as the Ukrainian famine. A Kazakh demographer has calculated that between 2.5 million and 3 million Kazakhs perished at that time. The famine was followed by Stalinist repressions in 1938–39 and soon thereafter by the war. If the Kazakh population had not suffered such severe setbacks, it would, according to one Kazakh authority, number around 30 million today. Although their population is slowly increasing, the Kazakhs feel they have a lot of catching up to do.

Kazakhstan has its share of economic and social problems that flare up as ethnic conflicts from time to time. In the summer of 1989, Kazakhs clashed with immigrant workers in the western Kazakhstan town of Novy Uzen, a new town with a modern oil industry that has attracted many immigrant workers from outside Kazakhstan to earn high wages while many of the native Kazakhs remain unemployed. One writer clarified the situation: "It is easy to see what has happened. Next to Novy Uzen [New Uzen] there is Stary Uzen [Old Uzen], the old settlement. Its population is exclusively Kazakh, around sixteen thousand, and not even one telephone between them! In that area there is nothing but sheep and camels. Is it any wonder that the native population vents its frustrations every now and again?"

Many Russians consider Kazakhstan to be their homeland. The sheer beauty of Alma Ata often creates a deep-rooted sense of attachment that has drawn many people here over the years. The classical film directors Vsevolod Pudovkin and Sergey Eisenstein lived out World War II here. The Luna Park, with its landscaped flower beds, paths, and ornamental ponds, was laid out just two years after the first contingent of the czar's Russian soldiers arrived at the garrison in the 1850s. Its mature trees and elegant walkways exude an atmosphere of more bourgeois times. The only signs of Sovietization even in the 1980s were a small statue of Maxim Gorky, for whom the park was officially named, and a portrait of Lenin fashioned out of a hedge, tastefully tucked away to the side of a walkway. As with many formerly Soviet cities, the names of roads and districts have reverted to their pre-1917 versions. In Alma Ata, the district just north of the park is once more known as Tatarka, named after the Tatar settlement that was one of the three original districts of the garrison town.

Russians and Kazakhs work and live together in Alma Ata even though it was difficult until recently for Kazakhs to settle here. The rate of urbanization of the Kazakhs was deliberately held back. Kazakhs were discouraged from moving into the city: If they did manage to find work, they often gave up and moved back to their *aul* (country settlement) because they were unable to find anywhere to live.

Marat is one of the lucky ones. He, his wife, and two children share a three-room apartment with his brother, his wife, and their child. The kitchen accommodates only two adults standing and the bathroom is not much bigger. Marat's room is almost filled by a bed and the children's cots. The living room sofa doubles as his brother's bed at night. A beautiful handmade rug covers one wall. "It's a traditional Kazakh design," Marat explains, "a present from my family for our wedding." The two young families try not to be at home all the same time, and Marat hopes to make some money in business so that he can move out soon and leave the apartment to his brother, a doctor.

There is a reviving interest in Kazakh culture and language. The few urbanized Kazakhs, who had easily assimilated into a Russian cultural way of life, are now demanding better quality Kazakh-language education for their children, who are often still passed from one grandparent to another, to learn their native language. College-educated Kazakhs often study Arabic to try to regain something of their heritage. Together with the growing respect for their Kazakh heritage comes a growing commitment to the people and the place: "The Kazakhs," one youth leader pronounces, "are part of the great Turkic race which stretches from the Uigurs of northwest China to the Magyars of Hungary." The addition of Hungary to the continuum of Turkish peoples is somewhat unexpected, but the youth assures us that the Magyars migrated westward from the region around Alma Ata. "Almaty was the name of the old settlement here before the garrison town of Vernyi; *alma* is the Hungarian word for 'apple.' This was known as the City of Apples."

Kazakhs are not the only Turkic nation in Kazakhstan. There are close to two hundred thousand Uigurs living in Kazakhstan. The Kazakh-Chinese border divides the Uigurs from the main body of their people—estimates range between 5 million and 10 million—who live in the Xinjiang Province of China. Travel and immigration have once more eased, as the border, closed in the 1960s after the breakdown in relations between the USSR and China, opened again in 1988. Many families that had settled on the Soviet side of the border and were cut off from their relatives can now visit their families in China, and a renewed railway service between Alma Ata and Urumchi has now restored links with the Uigurs on the Chinese side of the border.

Kazakhstan's diverse mix of nationalities may prove a stumbling block to political integration in the future. Although Kazakhstan's two major ethnic groups—the Kazakhs and the Russians, at 6.5 million and 6.2 million respectively in the last census—clearly outnumber the others, there are substantial numbers of Germans (958,000), Ukrainians (896,000), Tatars (328,000), Belarusians (183,000), and Koreans (103,000). Some of the national groups living among the Kazakhs were deported from the native republics farther west on Stalin's orders during World War II, when their loyalty to the USSR came under suspicion.

One Ukrainian we met told us of his family's experiences when they were deported from western Ukraine in 1941. Several families were roused in the middle of the night and given half an hour to gather their belongings before being loaded onto wagons and deported eastward. The appalling living conditions in the early years helped to spread sickness and fatal diseases, often striking at the young children and the elderly, who rarely survived. Our friend was born just after Stalin's death when conditions had improved. Even though Ukrainians make up 5 percent of Kazakhstan's population, the former deportees are for the most part denationalized and no longer speak the language or know the customs. Some have become virtually indistinguishable from the Greeks, Uzbeks, Kazakhs, and others around them.

At least one of the civic groups in Kazakhstan has attempted to reflect the situation. The Adolat (Justice) society, one of the first informal groups in Kazakhstan, rapidly gained respect and recognition not only among Kazakhs, as it was established to expose the crimes of Stalinism and rehabilitate the victims, especially among those who were deported to Kazakhstan: Germans, Ukrainians, Meskhetians, Chechens, Crimean Tatars, and others. Adolat has steered away from an exclusively Kazakh agenda, although it does research and publicize suppressed issues in Kazakh history. From its inception, it was intended to provide a voice for all who live on the territory of Kazakhstan.

But for the most part, the postindependent political landscape in Kazakhstan looks decidedly monoethnic. There are few political groups or movements that span ethnic divisions. Kazakhstan never developed a national popular front movement such as those in the Baltic States, or even in Uzbekistan and Azerbaijan, because of the lack of a clear ethnic majority. Many groups were originally established to protect Kazakh national traditions and values, but one of the most successful based its appeal on protests against nuclear testing.

Nevada-Semipalatinsk was the chosen name for the movement, to signify protests against the nuclear testing in Semipalatinsk, in the north of Kazakhstan. Generally known as Nevada, the hope was to inspire a counterpart movement in Nevada, in the United States, to be called Semipalatinsk. The movement was launched in February 1989, when protests to the USSR Supreme Soviet from the Kazakh Writers' Union pointed out that the Soviet Union rated only twenty-eighth on the list of comparative standards of living in developed countries, and that the average life expectancy in Kazakhstan had dropped by four years—a state of affairs not remedied, they proposed, because of the expenditure of funds on nuclear arms. Headed by Olzhas Suleimenov, Nevada has provided a rallying point for Kazakhs throughout the republic. Kazakhs in Karaganda held demonstrations against the noise and pollution from the testing site, and at its height the membership was estimated at more than a million. Now that the testing site has been closed, Nevada's success has also led to a weakening of its appeal.

Olzhas Suleimenov has moved on to more political concerns. In an attempt to bring together groups and parties from different ethnic groups, Nevada became one of the founding members of the People's Congress of Kazakhstan. The founding congress was held in October 1991, and the organization was established on the basis of support for all nationalities and for reforms—that is, the reform path already outlined by the president. Nursultan Nazarbaev addressed the Congress as a keynote speaker and endorsed the platform.

The congress has not proved as popular as its founders had hoped, partly because it faces the same dilemma as Nazarbaev himself: how to establish a viable political base of support in the absence of motivating forces other than the ethnic factor. Nazarbaev's political career has flourished among Russians and Kazakhs, although he is not entirely trusted by either.

Other political parties and movements have had internal disagreements over whether to take an internationalist approach to their activities and membership. Azat (Liberation) is perhaps the most important group within the national democratic opposition. Established in April of 1990 and acting as a force for moderation, it too has been subject to internal divisiveness on the issue of ethnic priorities.

The Alash party has no such misgivings. Founded in April of 1990 with the same name as the Alash Orda party that existed 1917–20, this party is unequivocally Kazakh and pan-Turkic. Because of its radical mode of operation, focused primarily on demonstrations, hunger strikes, and sit-ins, this party comes in for tight surveillance and repression by the authorities and has lost many members to more moderate parties since independence. Its slogan in support of a unified, Islamic Turkestan—From Vladivostok to Istanbul—has attracted small but dedicated groups of followers in Tashkent, Baku, and even Yakutia.

Kazakhstan is the odd man out among the other Central Asian republics from several points of view. It is the least likely to develop a strong Islamic fundamentalist movement. The Kazakhs adopted Islam much later than many other Central Asians, and the religion never became as great a cultural force in their society as it did in the others. Because of their nomadic lifestyle and isolation from centers of Muslim culture, the Kazakhs developed a form of Islam that retained elements of their earlier beliefs. Even today, a walk around Alma Ata suggests a mode of life much more Europeanized than in the other Central Asian capitals. Until recently Alma Ata had only one small mosque, not lavishly adorned and barely distinguishable as a house of prayer but for the small minaret.

Kazakhstan is the only Central Asian republic with developed heavy industries, so it is not surprising that the only large and influential independent trade unions are located here. Among them are the Independent Miners' Union of Karaganda formed in May 1991, which grew out of a local strike committee formed in July 1989. Birlesu, which unites both individual workers, entrepreneurs, and groups, functions as a trade union defending its members' interests against the state-controlled sector. Birlesu's membership increased dramatically after the August 1991 coup to around 250,000 members, and it continues to grow as a political and social organization. Kazakhstan also has a revived Russian cossack movement. The Russian-speaking descendants of the Ural cossacks have formed into an organization that is pressing the Kazakh authorities for reunification with Russia.

As long as Nazarbaev can keep these varied forces under control, and as long as Russia makes no serious claims to Kazakhstan's territory, he may succeed in guiding Kazakhstan through a tricky transition period. Kazakhstan is in a good position to capitalize on its independence, with plentiful resources of oil, gas, and precious metals. One small sign of Kazakhstan's growing self-assertion has come out of negotiations with the Chevron corporation for the development of the Tengiz oil field. In early 1992, after three years of laborious discussion that involved interlocutors from Moscow and Alma Ata and were fraught with misunderstandings and lack of clarity on who should gain the benefits, the Kazakh side suddenly moved decisively to cut a deal that would be more advantageous to Kazakhstan than any of the previous proposals.

The Tajiks

The Tajiks are the only major national group in the Central Asian republics that traces its cultural roots to the Persians rather than the Turks, although they have much in common with their Turkic neighbors, the Uzbeks, Kyrgyz, and Turkmen. The Tajiks are one of the older sedentary peoples of Central Asia. The stunning architecture of Samarkand and Bukhara, now located in the Uzbek Republic, is a product of Tajik culture. Before the October Revolution, Central Asian intellectuals in this region were generally bilingual in Tajik and Uzbek, and the people lived side by side in the Muslim commonwealth without significant friction in their relations. In the early days of independence, Tajikistan opted to dispense with the cumbersome Cyrillic alphabet and revert to the Persian script, thus taking the republic yet one further step away from its Turkic-speaking neighbors, who are more inclined to opt for the Latin script.

Tajikistan shares its northwestern border with Uzbekistan, the southern with Afghanistan; to the east lies China and to the northeast, Kyrgyzstan. It has been estimated that there are as many Tajiks across the border in Afghanistan as there were in the former Soviet Union: In 1989, the Soviet census registered 4.2 million Tajiks. The Tajiks were the least Russified of all the Soviet Central Asians and were among the most religious. The Soviet invasion of Afghanistan added a powerful spur to their increasing assertiveness over the past decade. There was already strong anti-Soviet feeling among the Tajiks. Many of the Tajiks in Afghanistan are descendants of the Basmachi, who fought a guerrilla war against the Soviets in the 1920s. When Soviet troops marched into Afghanistan, they quickly realized their own Tajiks would have to be withdrawn from the force, as they showed themselves to be largely in sympathy with the Afghans. Throughout the 1970s, the border between Tajikistan and Afghanistan was considered a dangerous zone, prone to ambush from both sides.

Throughout the 1980s, there was a marked increase in religious activity in Tajikistan, partly attributed to the war. Attempts to discredit the unofficial mullahs usually boosted their credibility, and propaganda aimed at improving "atheistic upbringing" had no effect. If anything, the observance of Ramadan increased, and holy places of pilgrimage became even more popular. In 1986, under the influence of unofficial mullahs, informal groups in Tajikistan became the first to call for an independent Islamic state.

Unrest broke out in Dushanbe, the capital of Tajikistan, in February 1990 and a wave of violence swept through the city. In response to reports of violent interethnic clashes, tanks and troops were sent into the city. Officials claimed there were several dead and more than two hundred injured. The demonstrations began as rumors spread among the local Tajiks that Armenians escaping from the violence in Azerbaijan would be given on arrival preferential treatment for housing. Many Tajiks, struggling to find scarce housing in the city, were understandably incensed by the rumors. Thousands gathered to demand the resignation of the entire Communist Party leadership, and a broad range of economic and ecological improvements: jobs for the thousands of unemployed in the region; better housing; the return of all proceeds from the sale of Tajikistan's cotton; the closure of a dangerous aluminum plant; and an end to the sale of pork, which the predominantly Muslim population does not eat.

In the wake of the February demonstrations, Tajikistan's nascent political forces began to build up momentum. As in other republics, a popular front movement was already established—Rastokhez (Rebirth) People's Movement—and was growing in membership, primarily among the urban classes. A small Democratic party was established some months later. But the most rapidly growing party, the Islamic Rebirth Party of Tajikistan, drew its strength from the groundswell of reviving religious fervor, despite being banned by the republic's authorities. By the end of 1991, the party numbered about sixteen thousand members.

Months of continuous friction between the opposition and the government came to a head in August 1991, when Tajikistan's Communist leaders all but endorsed the emergency committee in Moscow. Confronted with demonstrations organized by the opposition forces, Kakhar Makhmanov, the president, offered his resignation. After a brief interim period, when the Communist Party was banned and many of the trappings of Soviet power were brought down, Rakhmon Nabiev was installed as president. Nabiev, who had been the republic's Party First Secretary, had lost his position in December 1985 when he failed to respond to calls for reform. Going against the trend that swept through the crumbling Soviet Union in those months, Nabiev won Tajikistan's first popular election for president on November 24 with almost two-thirds of the vote. His opponent, the popular film director Davlat Khudonazarov, gained only a third. For many months after, when mass demonstrations rocked Dushanbe, opposition leaders proclaimed their doubts about the legitimacy of that vote.

As the Soviet Union faded into the pages of history, the new year greeted Tajikistan as one of the newly independent states in Central Asia. For a couple of months, the republic enjoyed relative calm, perhaps reeling from the momentous events breaking out all around. In March, the demonstrations started once more, this time revealing a pattern that had not been so obvious in the earlier demonstrations.

In the absence of any clear understanding of democracy, and without the veil of Communist vs. anti-Communist politics to obscure reality, the traditional pattern of Central Asian politics once more became apparent. Even under Communist rule, the power structure reflected the traditional rivalry between the "north" and the "south." One of the factors underlying Nabiev's return to power was his strong base of support in the north, even though most of this supporters still clung to hard-line antireform positions. Support for Khudonazarov came mainly from the south, even though these supporters were mainly the Islamic Rebirth Party, backed up by the Qazi Kalon (Chief Judge) Qazi Hodja Akbar Turajonzoda, Tajikistan's highest ranking Muslim clergyman. In May 1992, antigovernment demonstrations in Dushanbe came to a head and forced an agreement between Nabiev and the opposition, proposing a Government of National Reconciliation to replace the Supreme Soviet by a Majlis (assembly) made up of both government and opposition supporters. In September, Nabiev was ousted.

By the end of the year, however, the Communist forces in Tajikistan had retrenched and with the help of Russian troops had managed to clear the capital Dushanbe of most of the armed opposition, clearing the way for the return to power of pro-Communist forces.

The Tatars

Among the Turkic peoples of the former Soviet Union, the Tatars are truly a hidden nation among hidden nations. Numbering around 7 million when they were part of the Soviet Union, the Tatars were the sixth largest ethnic group after the Russians, Ukrainians, Belarusians, Uzbeks, and Kazakhs. Even though there are differences among branches of the Tatar family— between Crimean Tatars and Volga Tatars, for example—the Soviet census often put all the Tatars in one category, thus robbing this large ethnic group of political recognition and central representation. After the disintegration of the Soviet Union, the Tatars found themselves again the only major Muslim ethnic group without a sovereign voice, surrounded by a state that sought to bring the republics into a federal relationship with the new center of power. Yeltsin's Russian Federation was no more eager to have the Tatars push for more autonomy than Gorbachev's Soviet Union.

And therein lies the point of tension that has colored Turkic-Russian relations since World War I. When the Tatar Autonomous Soviet Socialist Republic (ASSR) was created just after the Bashkir ASSR in 1920, it put an end to hopes for the formation of a large Tatar-Bashkir republic extending over the territory of the Kazan Khanate, the Middle Volga, and the Ural region. The formation of such a republic, uniting the closely related Tatars and Bashkirs, would have provided a strong impetus for Turkic unity. This expectation was quashed, together with any hope of Kazan's retaining its role as the cultural and political center for the Muslims of Russia. The newly drawn boundaries were calculated to separate the Bashkirs from the Tatars, and ensure that the Tatars would not be the majority in their own ASSR. The Tatar ASSR measured 68,000 square miles and the Bashkir ASSR, 143,600 square miles. Their capital cities: Kazan and Ufa.

Soon after the coup, the Tatar and Bashkir autonomous republics renamed themselves Tatarstan and Bashkortostan and increased their push for more autonomy. Although this was in step with the general trend of proindependence movements, it was a direct challenge to Yeltsin's newly assembled democratic government in Russia. It also posed the question whether the disintegration of the Soviet Union would stop at Russia's borders or whether it would continue into the core of the Russian Federation.

Even though one draft of the new Russian constitution began in a very magnanimous way, "We the peoples of the Russian republic," the democrats at the helm of Yeltsin's new state were uncertain how to go about integrating the peoples of the new Russian state into a workable polity. While the constitution writers in Moscow wrangled about the new form of state, Tatarstan's leaders were pressing for their own agenda. Although only 2 million Tatars live in Tatarstan, accounting for 48 percent of the population (Russians make up 43 percent), the republic determined to launch a campaign to hold a referendum. The republic's leadership felt confident that the Russian population would see the economic advantages of a looser relationship with Moscow. Tatarstan produces a quarter of Russia's oil output and is a major center for the defense and petrochemical industries.

Under the leadership of the Tatar president, Mintimer Shaymiev, the referendum was set for March 21, 1992, asking the question: "Do you agree that the republic of Tatarstan is a sovereign state, a subject of international law, building its relations with the Russian Federation and other republics and states on the basis of treaties between equal partners?" Even though the Tatar leadership issued a series of reassurances to the Russian government that the referendum was not the prelude to secession, the Russians reacted with alarm, accusing the Tatars of sowing the seeds for the breakup of the Russian Federation. In the weeks before the referendum, pressure was exerted in several ways to try to derail the referendum. The Russian Constitutional Court ruled the referendum to be unconstitutional; a number of prominent Russian politicians spoke out against referendum; and President Yelstin staged a last-minute appeal to the parliament of Tatarstan to reverse the decision on the referendum, and when that failed to have any effect, he went on the air on the eve of the vote to urge the people of Tatarstan to vote "no" to preserve the integrity of the Russian Federation.

The referendum went ahead and the "yes" vote won, with a majority of 61.4 percent in favor and 37.2 percent against. The rural areas, where most of the Tatar population lives, turned in a higher percentage of the "yes" vote, but in the capital, Kazan, 51.2 percent voted against.

The immediate casualty of Tatarstan's referendum was the Russian Federation Treaty, which had been scheduled for signing at that time. Even though Tatarstan had been one of the two constituent republics that had not initialed the original treaty (the other was Chechen-Ingushetia), the results of the referendum emboldened the republic in its negotiations with Russia and encouraged other republics to come forward with their misgivings about the Federation Treaty. The government of Buryatia announced objections and the Kabardino-Balkar Republic insisted on some changes before it would sign. Following suit, Yakutia also put forward some amendments for more favorable provisions on property, budget, and tax policy. Bashkortostan also declined to sign the treaty until serious issues involving property, mineral resources, and economic policies were solved. The leaders of Bashkortostan claimed that not enough protection had been included in the treaty to recognize the republic's declaration of sovereignty.

In the midst of discussions with Russia, a group of parliamentarians announced a plan to create a "Volga-Ural Confederation," with its own citizenship and legal structure, by uniting the territories of Tatarstan and Bashkortostan, with an open offer for the Chuvash, Udmurt, and Mordovian republics to join. Although the plan was roundly rejected by the majority of Tatarstan's legislators, it raised once more the specter of a unified Turkic republic carved out of the heart of Russia—a republic that Stalin and subsequent generations of Moscow's ruling elite had labored so hard to prevent.

The Turkic factor may yet be the challenge that upsets Russia most. Both in external relations with the new Muslim republics and as an internal problem, Russia is now faced with difficulties on both fronts. Russia's external relations with the Central Asian republics are fraught with difficulties. Although separation from Ukraine may involve more cultural and emotional factors, the separation from the Central Asian republics may prove more difficult in the long run. Perhaps it is not by accident that the Commonwealth of Independent States was originally planned to unite only the three largest Slavic republics. While Ukraine was adamant about separation from Russia, the Central Asian republics were initially lukewarm to the idea. A Commonwealth without Ukraine would skew Russia's relations decisively in the direction of Asia, with direct ties to a series of underdeveloped states.

It may yet take many years to settle Russia's relationship with the Central Asian states on an equal basis. The formerly colonial character of their relations has ensured a continuing Russian interest in these countries. Russia will continue to retain its interest in Uzbekistan's immense gold reserves, for example. And in the military sphere, disengagement will not be easy. Shortly after having taken over the portion of the former Soviet army on Uzbek soil, it was discovered to nobody's surprise that it would be impossible to employ Uzbek as the language of command as fully 93 percent of the officers understood only Russian.

These and similar problems will continue to plague relations between Russia and the Muslim and Turkic states. As long as there are no moves for changing the internal or external borders, the situation will most likely develop in a peaceful fashion, but if the desire for Muslim or Turkic unity becomes a real issue on the political agenda, there may yet be cataclysmic events in store in this region of the world.

Chapter Seven

Russians: Democracy or Empire?

Russia is a whole separate world, submissive to the will, caprice, fantasy of a single man, whether his name be Peter or Ivan, no matter—in all instances the common element is the manifestation of arbitrariness. Contrary to all law of human community, Russia moves only in the direction of her own enslavement and the enslavement of all the neighboring peoples. For this reason it would be in the interest of not only other peoples, but also her own that she be compelled to take a new path.

PYOTR CHAADAEV, WRITING IN 1854

With the collapse of the Soviet Union, the new Russian state represents the dominant power in Central Eurasia. Yet whether the Russian Federation respects the autonomy of its newly free neighbors or seeks to become the hegemonic power in its region will in large measure help determine whether the post-Soviet future is one of stability or dangerous tension.

In its first year in power, the Russian government led by President Boris Yeltsin crafted a policy designed to build statehood, while at the same time respecting the choice its neighbors made in opting for independence. This course, however, is hardly set in stone. And there is a growing chorus of voices in the new Russian state that seek to restore its status as a superpower.

To understand the predicament of those who seek fundamentally to reform the nature of Russian international conduct requires not only delving back into the history of the Soviet Union, and of the czarist empire that preceded it, but also understanding the nature of the Russians, and the ideas and cultural forces that have helped define them.

Under Soviet rule, the Russians—the self-styled "elder brother"—made up half of the population of the USSR. Although the USSR was said to be a state guided by the principle of an internationalism that conferred equality on all its ethnic groups, the special status of the Russian nation was celebrated in embarrassingly fawning national anthems of several of the USSR's republics. The Uzbek SSR's anthem, for example, began, "Hail Russian brother, great is your people," and the Azerbaijanian SSR anthem extolled, "The mighty Russian brother is bringing to the land the triumph of freedom; and with our blood we have strengthened our kinship with him." A non-Russian textbook from the mid-1960s put it more explicitly. "There is a Russian people. You have a leader."

Praise of the Russian nation flourished in the Brezhnev years, when what some writers have called "the Russian party" of chauvinistic Soviet bureaucrats in the Communist apparat, the cultural establishment, and the military wielded immense power. Although Russians represented a bare majority of the Soviet Union's population, it was not merely their demographic predominance that was at the core of the USSR's national tensions, but more the Russian national identity that defined national relations and, consequently, helped propel a resurgence of national assertiveness among the non-Russian nations.

But the preeminence of Russians within the empire—their relatively privileged political, cultural, and, in the end, economic status—came at a price. Soviet rulers deemphasized specifically Russian institutions within Russia, while at the same time making sure that each principal institution at the all-Union level was firmly under Russian control—an arrangement that came undone under pressure of the national awakening in the republics. Authentically Russian institutions did not emerge until the waning years of the Soviet Union, when in December 1989 Mikhail Gorbachev took a hesitant—some say reluctant—step, announcing the creation of a Russian Bureau of the Central Committee of the Communist Party of the Soviet Union and putting himself at its head. While there were Ukrainian, Lithuanian, Georgian, Armenian, and other Academies of Sciences, until 1990 there had been no specifically Russian Academy of Sciences.

With a population of some 145 million, the Russians are Europe's largest nation. Their titular homeland, the newly independent state of Russia (or the Russian Federation) occupies 6.6 million square miles—more than 75 percent of the territory that was the USSR. The Russian Federation is the world's largest state, consisting of eleven time zones separated from Moscow by as much as ten hours. The time gap between Moscow and the towns and settlements on the Bering Strait where the Chukchis live is greater than that between Moscow and Washington.

Russia runs some 2,500 miles from north to south and 5,600 miles from east to west. Geographic and climatic conditions vary accordingly. Winters are almost uniformly harsh, falling to below −90 degrees Fahrenheit in the tundras of Siberia. The immense, sprawling distances led to a great deal of local isolation and impressed Russia's rulers with the belief that this vast territory could only be governed sensibly by absolute control from the center. Unlike traditional nation-states that seek to consolidate their ethnic group within a single territory, the Russian state was shaped from the outset by the imperative of external conquest. As the Yugoslav dissident and historian Milovan Djilas has noted: "Russia did not follow the European path from nationhood to statehood. Muscovy came first—the Russian sense of nationhood came later. Hence the Russian people's obsessive fear that the state may disintegrate; that if the state loses its grip the Russian nation may be gravely weakened. . . . That the Communist system [promoted] centralization for its own reasons was a bonus and a happy coincidence."

The Russians have been a dominant force in Europe and Asia for two centuries. From a population of around 18 million in 1750 the czarist empire's population leaped to 68 million in 1850, then to 124 million in 1897, and 170 million in 1914. Russian numerical strength conferred certain advantages within the multinational Russian empire, providing military strength from a virtually limitless pool of recruits. The rapid natural growth of the population, combined with immense poverty, propelled the migration of the Russian nation and the expansion of the Russian state. After the period of the *ordynskoye igo* (The Tatar Yoke), Russians poured into the areas east of the Volga, and in the seventeenth and eighteenth centuries they expanded to the northern Caucasus and Siberia, later to the Altai country, then through Kazakhstan to Central Asia. Although in many of these settings they maintained relations with the indigenous peoples, the usual pattern of settlement was in growing urban clusters, usually fortress towns, which helped secure defense in frequently violent settings.

Having endured Napoleon's invasion, endless military intrigues, a civil war, two world wars, and long bouts with illness and famine, the Russian nation emerged with nearly double the population of the Germans, Europe's second largest national group. While this numerical advantage derives in great measure from the Russian nation's rapid population growth in the eighteenth and nineteenth centuries, it also has been aided by the Russian proclivity toward the absorption of conquered peoples in a process known as Russification that emerged as a conscious policy in the nineteenth century, persisted under Stalin's murderous reign, and was implemented with renewed zeal under Leonid Brezhnev.

An important factor contributing to an elastic Russian identity springs from its link to Christian Orthodoxy, a faith that provided a universalist impulse firmly linked to traditional cultural values and forms of expression.

Historically, for the Russian elite, any Slav who adopted the Russian language and converted to Orthodoxy was regarded as Russian. Yet this elasticity also led to significant confusions and evasions. Many Russians to this day deny the separate identity of the Ukrainians and Belarusians, seeing in them something less than distinctive nations, considering them peoples whose languages are vulgarizations issuing from their isolation from the Russian centers of culture and education.

The relationship of Russians to their Ukrainian and Belarusian neighbors reflects deep-seated ambiguities and tensions. It is undeniable that these three Slavic nations at one point in history shared certain traditions and influences. The Kievan state that emerged on what is now ethnically Ukrainian territory brought to the three peoples the Christian faith and the Cyrillic alphabet, but linguistic differentiation into separate ethnic groups began, according to Roger Portal and other leading historians, as early as the eleventh century. And certainly by the seventeenth century, Russians, Ukrainians, and Belarusians had evolved into distinct national groups.

The ambiguous attitude of the Russian imperial elite to its Ukrainian and, by extension, Belarusian subjects can be found in the patronizing writings of a leading nineteenth-century architect of Russian education policy, Mikhail Katkov, who wrote in 1864: "We love Ukraine in all her peculiarities in which we see the token of future riches and variety in the common development of the life of our people." Katkov, a leading defender of what Lenin called the "prison of nations," went further: "We love Ukraine, we love her as part of our Fatherland, as a living beloved part of our people, as a part of ourselves, and this is why any attempt to introduce a feeling of mine and thine into the relationship of Ukraine towards Russia is so odious to us." This remarkable explication expressed clearly the Russian proprietary impulse.

In their constant search for new frontiers, the Russians became the most relentlessly and consistently successful expansionist ethnic group in history, leaving an indelible imprint on the national consciousness and institutions. Russia had to become a highly centralized state to rule over the vast territory, control the diverse non-Russian peoples, and hold the empire in its thrall. All policies, cultural and political, issued from Moscow, making the Soviet empire, like its czarist predecessor, a "centralized despotism mightier than any other in history." The eminent historian Hans Kohn extended this pattern back to the nineteenth century: "The later Russian Empire differed fundamentally from the liberal, tolerant British Empire in its tendency to impose uniformity upon its immense domains, to Russify or later to communize them without any freedom of spontaneous development."

Czars and Commissars: Continuities in the Russian and Soviet Empires

The principal continuities between the czarist and Soviet empires were striking and convincing, especially as the borders of the two entities were remarkably similar. There also was a striking continuity in the realm of ideas. Where the czarist empire had a state religion in the Russian Orthodox church, the USSR had a state ideology with many of the characteristics of religious faith. Where the Russian empire suppressed competing religious groups, Soviet leaders repressed competing political movements that threatened their ideological and political monopoly. And just as under the czars the doctrine of the Third Rome, as posited in 1511 by the monk Philotheus in a letter to the czar, meant that Moscow was the center of the true faith and spiritual heir to the traditions of Rome and Constantinople, so under Communist rule Moscow became the center of international communism— the sole arbiter and bearer of Communist orthodoxy.

After the Bolshevik revolution, the Third Rome was supplanted by the Third (Communist) International. The late Russian essayist and political exile Boris Shragin wrote of other important continuities between the USSR and its czarist antecedent. "The idea of 'Holy Russia,'" he observed, "conferred a sort of plenary indulgence on the country, a clean bill of moral health despite the atrocities of its history and all it did or suffered." Likewise, he argued, the idea of communism's progressive mission justified immense inhumanities.

Another continuity in the Russian tradition was the close relationship of the state to the Russian Orthodox church, a link that endured until the collapse of the Soviet state. The modern day Russian Orthodox church was a pliant tool of Soviet foreign policy, willingly partaking in the USSR's agenda of nuclear disarmament, while refusing to speak out against the repression of democratic religious activists and the suppression of entire churches, and equally silent about violations of basic human and religious rights, never speaking out in defense of religious prisoners of conscience. Its hierarchy frequently collaborated with the Communist state, most notably in Stalin's effort to crush the Ukrainian Uniate Catholic church and the Ukrainian Autocephalous Orthodox church. Under the czars the mechanism of the church's subjugation to the state "in the name of God" was realized through the state-controlled Most Holy Synod; in the USSR, control was exercised through the Religious Affairs Committee of the USSR's Council of Ministers.

An impulse to militarism and expansionism was another characteristic of both states. In the case of the czarist empire, expansion was justified as a civilizing mission—the advancement of higher moral teaching and the promotion of a better living standard—an idea echoed in modern-day communism's claim that it represented the force of progress. Both empires were also committed to the Russification of subject nations.

Such continuities extended as well to the internal regime of both empires, in particular to the idea of communal judgment and communal responsibility embodied in the czarist empire's long-standing institution known as the *mir* (literally "world"), or *obshchina* (community) an ostensibly economic arrangement reinforced by the ceding of land not to individual peasants but to communities which administered the land, supervised the collection of taxes, and arranged the provision of draftees into the czar's army. But it had a second role that proved even more abiding. As emigré writer Boris Shragin argued, the mir strictly regulated private behavior, coercing individual peasants into proper conduct while retaining the right to exile unruly or unreliable members of the community, and was pliantly submissive to the local constabulary, thereby linking its coercive power to the means of livelihood and diminishing the sanctity of private property. Under the Soviet system as well, the workplace was a source of collective pressure on the individual, a kind of moral judgment seat whose mechanisms were more rigorously defined in a panoply of workplace collectives, comrades courts, and state-controlled trade unions. As an instrument of collective coercion, the workplace reflected the long-standing prerevolutionary institutions that were deeply immersed in the Russian tradition. Interestingly, in neighboring Ukraine, where even the czars recognized that such an arrangement was alien to the native spirit, land was ceded to the individual and serfdom was not as deeply rooted.

Others have pointed out that the practice of the psychiatric incarceration of dissidents, the existence of a powerful secret police, the use of state censorship, and the institution of forced labor all had their antecedents in the prerevolutionary Russian past. Just as Russian serfs were tied to the land and denied the right of free movement, so too under Soviet rule an elaborate internal passport system denied citizens the right to change workplaces or residences without state approval.

While Russian consciousness was inextricably linked to the powerful and oppressive state that predated it, a clearer sense of Russianness emerged full-blown in the nineteenth century by the proclamation in 1832 of the doctrine of Autocracy, Orthodoxy, and Nationality. Propounded by Count Sergey Uvarov—who later became minister of education—the doctrine sought not only to make the czar and the Russian Orthodox church the pillars of legitimacy, but also to extend to the masses the sense of national consciousness that permeated the elite.

Historian Hugh Seton-Watson argued that, in the 1880s, Russians, like other "leaders of the most powerful nations, considered it their destiny and indeed their moral duty to impose their nationality on *all* their subjects—of whatever religion, language or culture" (Seton-Watson's italics). Consequently, Russians sought to make over the non-Russian subjects into Russians. Russification accelerated under the rule of Czars Alexander III and Nicholas II, whose targets were primarily their Slavic subjects, the Ukrainians and Belarusians. The czarist court promulgated two ukases concerning the banning of the Ukrainian language in its printed form: the Ems Ukase and the Valuyev Ukase. But Russification was also applied to the subject Baltic peoples; to Poles, who came under Moscow's dominion; and to Jews, whose schools were closed down and who were banned from wearing their traditional clothing.

In the end, despite attempts by the czarist state to create a more modern notion of nationalism, these ideological ambitions soon encountered the weight of Russian history and of the Russian nation's close identification with the very structure of empire. Today, after the loss of empire and of patrimony over non-Russian republics and amid the birth of a specifically Russian state, Russians are confronting the question of identity. This process of self-examination is by no means simple. As the writer Grigory Pomerants has written: "The Russian Empire antedated Russian self-awareness, and therefore every territory that Russian soldiers set foot on is considered Russian. This can be seen in the national (not only the official) reaction to the Prague Spring [of 1968] and the subsequent Soviet invasion." If such an attitude were to persist, needless to say it would have profound consequences as well for the Russian view of their new democratic political institutions. In Pomerants's view: "To preserve the remnants of an imperial structure is to doom democracy. . . ."

The very idea of building a specifically Russian state is itself new, as Russians have never experienced a prolonged period in which they lived in an authentic, ethnographically homogeneous nation-state, their expansive state having predated the full-blown formation of the Russian national consciousness. The idea of a definite configuration of a Russia proper is a modern-day phenomenon, only today given shape in the form of the newly independent Russian Federation. Until the rise of Boris Yeltsin, most Russians did not identify with or feel particular loyalty to Russia, but rather to the broader USSR.

Mikhail Gorbachev's approach to Russian nationalism was inconsistent. Some Sovietologists and not a few Russian nationalists argued that overt Russian nationalist themes were dampened by the cool, more modern form of rule that typified the technocratically oriented Gorbachev *équipe*. They said that in the face of growing assertiveness among the non-Russians in the late 1980s, it appeared that the Russians were in danger of becoming a hidden nation. But this did not occur. As the 1990s began, a variety of nationalist and patriotic currents began to surface within the political culture. Inspired by the upsurge of non-Russian nationalism, there was among Russians a growing discussion in the press of their need to create specifically Russian institutions. Democrats and hard-line Communists began to embrace specifically Russian issues.

Early in 1990, as Boris Yeltsin and his allies from the Democratic Russia movement began articulating the idea of Russia's turn inward, toward solving its own problems, prominent leaders and important periodicals added their voices to the debate over the desirability of a Russian Academy of Sciences and Russian television and radio. Within the circles of the Communist Party, similar themes began to be sounded within the Russian Communist Youth League, and an RSFSR trade union confederation. The leaders of the moribund All-Union Central Council of Trade Unions had attempted to dampen growing enthusiasm for a specifically Russian trade union body on a par with the Ukrainian, Armenian, and other sections, proposing instead the creation of a Russian bureau attached to the AUCCTU. But these calls met with opposition within the trade union and the embattled leadership not only relented but, in a number of cases, linked itself enthusiastically with the most extreme Russian chauvinist forces, particularly those organized around the Workers' United Front.

Growing Russian discontent led to the establishment of the Russian Bureau of the Central Committee of the CPSU and later, in June 1990, to the creation of a Russian section of the Party. As soon as these specifically Russian movements were formed they became the locus of hard-line Communist activists who resented Gorbachev's efforts to enact political and economic liberalization. The leadership of the new Communist Party of the RSFSR was more reactionary than that of the CPSU, while the new leader of the trade unions, Ivan Klochkov, had been secretary of the Moscow Regional Communist Party. Initially, the newly established Federation of Independent Trade Unions was supported by Party hard-liners who attempted to counter Boris Yeltsin's growing popularity among the workers. Later they entered a temporary alliance of convenience with the Russian leader.

Whatever the initial motives, these developments helped to create a more precise sense of Russianness, a concept that for centuries has been full of ambiguities. The emergence of Yeltsin's specifically Russian, nonimperial patriotism was poised to play an important role in further stimulating the dissolution of the USSR. But the emergence of nationalism among the non-Russians also fed antidemocratic currents among the Russians. Through most of the Gorbachev years, while the Soviet state was unraveling, highly xenophobic and messianic ideas that had long been part of the Russian tradition resurfaced amid a broader Soviet identity crisis, their seeds having been widely sown in previous decades of Soviet rule.

While there was ample evidence concerning the many cultural and political advantages enjoyed by the Russians, who were *prima inter pares* within the Soviet empire, many Russians argued that the price of privilege was too high. In the view of many Russian nationalists, a Russian-speaking, ethnically Russian, but fundamentally totalitarian antinational ruling elite stood atop the Soviet Union, while opposition Russian nationalists argued that Russians and their culture had suffered more than anyone else under communism. There can be little argument that totalitarian ideology destroyed the Russian village, drained the Russian Orthodox church of much of its spirituality, claimed millions of Russian victims through repression, and subsumed Russianness into a bland version of national identity that could not be fully authentic lest it awaken the slumbering nationalism of the smaller nations in the Soviet Union. The price Russians paid for their empire was a loss of their own spiritual roots and national identity.

The Price of an Empire

In the past, Russian patriots had warned of the disadvantages of an empire. Writers like the great novelist and controversial social critic Aleksandr Solzhenitsyn argued for a new, retrenched Russia, a Russia shed of much of its empire. For them, the Russian empire had come at too high a price—the debasement and disintegration of Russianness. A Russia like the one proposed by Solzhenitsyn would look to its own Orthodox roots and traditions and would have no claims on the Catholics of western Ukraine, the Baltic nations, the vast and populous reaches of Central Asia, or the Caucasus. The empire had led to the degradation of Russia's own cultural traditions, Solzhenitsyn and some of his colleagues argued.

In the Moscow of the late 1980s, one got the simultaneous sense of imperial grandeur and of the corruption and disintegration at its heart. Moscow, under Mikhail Gorbachev, was a city whose streets were full of potholes, the concrete broken, the sidewalks covered with sludge. Endless miles of roadway were constantly torn up for repair work that never seemed to end or bring improvement. Housing, too, was decrepit. Most buildings looked as if they had not been painted for decades. The high-rise apartments in which most Muscovites lived were stuffy and dilapidated, their façades and stairwells crumbling. The elevators and hallways frequently reeked of urine, the result of endless drinking binges. Moscow's grim-faced, plodding citizens, many of them living on the verge of a desperate poverty, trudged along the cracking, muddy sidewalks. In winter as in summer, Muscovites dressed in poorly made, ill-fitting, tawdry, frayed clothes and appeared to the casual observer to be poorer than America's homeless. The steady decline in the value of the ruble had made Soviet society increasingly barter oriented. A common sight was of a woman hawking cheap digital wristwatches in an alleyway near the Lenin library, or a man carrying a mesh shopping bag filled with dozens of packages of butter, presumably to be traded for other necessities. This degrading descent into more primitive forms of economic exchange gnawed at the souls of young and old alike. For the average resident of the capital of what was then the Soviet empire, it took a long leap of faith to believe that there was any economic benefit from the empire. A young, thickset cab driver in his late twenties, a native Muscovite, expressed his resentments to us: "It's hard to live in Moscow. And yet the Asians and Georgians keep on coming. Where do they get their money? They come here, loaded with cash, and they go after our Russian women. Why don't they keep to their own?" These were hardly the comments of a self-confident citizen who felt he had directly benefitted from Soviet imperial rule.

Economic decline in turn sparked a fundamental debate about the nature of Russia and the Soviet Union. On the one side, it helped inspire an inward-looking democratic patriotism identified with Boris Yeltsin. On the other side, it provoked a new virulent form of Russian nationalism supported by opportunistic neo-Stalinists and anti-Communist proponents of an iron hand.

Many experts agree that through centuries of relentless propagandizing, the Russian psyche was adapted to the idea of an empire and that the very stability of the Soviet state depended in large measure on its capacity to satisfy the Russian public's support for an expansionist imperial structure. Amid economic decline and social discontent, in the USSR's waning days, the roots of legitimacy were to be found almost exclusively in the success of the empire and its superpower status. As Marxism-Leninism was increasingly identified with economic collapse and communism's crisis of confidence mounted, Russian citizens—and some leading Communist hard-liners—turned increasingly to the empire and Russian nationalism as the ideological pillars of legitimacy.

The turn to "great power" Russian nationalism was not without precedent in Soviet history. Stalin resorted to Great Russian nationalism when he faced the Nazi invasion. In the latter years of the Brezhnev era, too, there was a notable growth in Russian nationalist sentiments, often officially and openly condoned in the Party and Red Army press, who slammed tight the lid on the non-Russian nations and their cultural and national aspirations. Soviet prisons, forced-labor camps, and psychiatric hospitals were filled with non-Russian political prisoners, many of them nationalists and advocates of national rights.

In the period of Mikhail Gorbachev's rule, thousands of independent, informal groups emerged, and as the 1980s drew to a close there were signs of a political awakening of Russian nationalism. Of these groups, some were openly and frequently attacked by the Soviet authorities and state-controlled media. Other groups appeared to have powerful allies at the heights of the Communist establishment. Among the extremist groups, the most sensational was a bizarre, shadowy organization known as Pamyat (Memory). Although it was frequently rocked by factional splits, Pamyat's popularity—its rallies drew thousands of supporters and there were chapters in two dozen Soviet cities—was evidence that in Gorbachev's USSR, the ideology of fascism was alive and well.

Fascism's living embodiment was one Dmitry Vasilyev—leader of Pamyat. A charismatic orator with a flair for the dramatic, Vasilyev was known for taking the stage at public meetings and shedding his extravagant bearded disguises. Located on the third floor of a building on the southern arc of the Sadovoye Koltso, Moscow's Ring Road, Vasilyev's five-room flat had been transformed into a museum whose symbology attested to his political and, in his words, "moral" agenda. At the door, visitors were usually greeted by Vasilyev's son dressed in the Pamyat group's black shirt emblazoned with military insignia from the czarist era. On the wall, amid icons and axes, there hung a poster bearing the Star of David and in it a skull. Above, in large script, was a single word: DANGER. Although it had been produced by the PLO, the poster coincided with Pamyat's anti-Semitic, or as Vasilyev would have it, anti-Zionist, predilections.

A professional photographer, Vasilyev received visitors in an ornate sitting room with vaulted ceilings that had been transformed into a shrine to the spiritual heroes of his movement: Dostoyevsky; Pyotr Stolypin, the czarist interior minister whose aborted agricultural reforms, Pamyat believes, could today save Russian agriculture; Aleksandr Nevsky, the thirteenth-century ruler of Vladimir and victor over the Swedes and Teutonic Knights (Germanic crusaders of the Middle Ages); General Aleksandr Suvorov; and the "Holy" Czar Nicholas II.

In the mid-1980s, Vasilyev was known to have quoted from the program of the CPSU, but by 1989 Pamyat's leader was unremittingly harsh in his assessment of the Party's legacy and its intrusions into family life. "Do you want the Party apparatchik to crawl into bed with you and your wife? Or to tell you that you cannot go to bed because you must attend a commemoration of the Russian revolution?" His voice boomed with rhetorical anger as he spoke of communism's destruction of family and tradition.

He was a strong proponent of a specific idea of unity. "Fascism," he observed, "means unity, unification. There's nothing bad in that." Vasilyev aspired to such unity in national relations as well and lamented the "artificial division" of the Russian, Ukrainian, Polish, Belarusian, Slovak, and Yugoslav peoples, who he believed came from one entity "created by God. We need to return to our original, natural state of unity," Vasilyev liked to argue. The Pamyat leader was an unabashed admirer of Mussolini. "No one can aspire to anything different," he said. "After all, Mussolini spoke of the unity of the nation, the unity of national good." He reserved contempt for Hitler, whose rule wasn't fascist but "national socialist," Vasilyev said, emphasizing the last word. In any event, he told us, "No Christian nation can bring forth a concept of racism. Only one religion has a conception of racism, a conception of the chosen people. [This] Zionist idea was imported into the ideology of the Nazis."

By whom, we inquired? "By the Jew Eichmann. He was a Jew, but he killed his own," Vasilyev charged, his voice filled with passion and grief. "You see," he says, "Eichmann was fulfilling the instructions of *The Protocols of the Elders of Zion*." It didn't take long for Vasilyev's oration, an exceptionally dramatic performance of rhetorical largo and sotto voce, to turn to the hidden source of all that he feels ails Russia and the world: Zionist Jews and their servants, the Freemasons. While there were the frequent references to Jewish control of the world economy and to the internationalization of the "Zionist idea," he bristled at charges that he is an anti-Semite. "I am not the one who is warring with the Semitic tribes. Are the Hebrews the only Semitic tribe? It is they who are killing other Semitic tribes. But does anyone dare call them anti-Semitic? . . . There is no problem of anti-Semitism in the Soviet Union today. It is an invention designed to cover up the brutal ethnocide of the Slavic peoples."

Vasilyev still likes to boast of Pamyat's international plans: "We have to

unite all honest people throughout the world. Patriotic forces have to coalesce. We have to create a single all-European Pamyat front, where we can
gather all patriots. I am a great admirer of [France's Jean-Marie] Le Pen. . . .
I am trying to bring this idea into fruition."

Pamyat on its own would not become a great threat. But because it
offered the public simple answers and simple solutions it found support in
the unorganized segments of society embittered by their sense of powerlessness. Moreover, Pamyat was only one of hundreds of virulently xenophobic
hate groups that emerged in the years of glasnost and perestroika and are
now active in newly independent Russia. Some of these odious groups also
had strong support within the Soviet cultural establishment.

Antidemocratic and xenophobic views were frequently found in the
writings of some of the USSR's most popular and best-selling writers. There
were several central characteristics of Russian nationalism in the era of
glasnost: a nostalgia for the village, which led to calls for increased resources
to support rural life; a nostalgia for the prerevolutionary past and its concomitant concern for the restoration of important monuments; and a hostility toward modernization and all things Western, ranging from rock and roll
to imported technologies. In many of these backward-looking traits were
interests clearly inimical to Gorbachev's reform agenda, for linked to this
Russian nationalism was the idea that democracy in the Western sense was
alien to Russian tradition. In the view of many ultranationalists, democracy
represented disorder and disorder was a strain in Russian culture that emanated from the Jews and their agents, the Freemasons.

Anti-Semitism and Antidemocracy

The Paris-based Russian novelist and literary critic Andrey Sinyavsky has
spent many years grappling with the question of Russian nationalism and its
anti-Semitic inclinations. In his view, while there are, of course, some Russian liberals and Democrats, "the greatest concentration of Russian nationalists is antidemocratic and conservative."

According to Sinyavsky, "Russian nationalists have come awake. And
they have taken on an openly anti-Semitic and antidemocratic character."
Sinyavsky points with particular concern to the work of one ultraconserva-
tive author, the expatriate mathematician Igor Shafarevich, who argues
"that within the powerful Russian nation there is a smaller nation. The great
nation is Russian, the little nation is Jewish." Sinyavsky says that Shafarevich accuses the Jews of "carrying out destructive activities. Many of

Shafarevich's ideas are similar to those of Nazi ideologue Alfred Rosenberg." Shafarevich's views are crystallized in this excerpt from an essay in which he grapples with the sources of what he terms "Russophobia" and the pressures to transform Russia into a democracy:

> Whose national sentiments, then, are reflected? For anyone acquainted with the reality of our country, the answer is beyond doubt. There is only one nation of whose concerns we hear almost every day. Jewish national emotions shake both our country and the whole world, influencing disarmament talks, trade policy, and international connections of scientists. . . . The 'Jewish Question' has acquired an incomprehensible power over the minds of people, eclipsed the problems of Ukrainians, Estonians, Armenians, and Crimean Tatars, while the 'Russian Question' is not recognized at all.

Jews are, the nationalist Shafarevich asserts, " 'an antipeople' among the people." In Sinyavsky's view, Shafarevich's essay is one sign of a dangerous upsurge in anti-Semitism that has accompanied the Russian national awakening. Shafarevich has found new allies inside Russia and has returned to active political life. In June 1992, he emerged as a leader of the Russian National Assembly.

Running through the various strands of much modern-day Russian nationalist thought is the nihilist notion that Russia is dying and that no one has suffered more than Russians. In one strain of Russian nationalism, this sense of despair is linked to the idea that communism has led to the destruction of Russianness. Another belief attributes Russia's decline to the contemporary loss of discipline. The first strain, dissident and anti-Communist, is linked to such voices as those of former political prisoner Vladimir Osipov and dissident priest Father Dmitry Dudko, whose viewpoint is not dissimilar to Aleksandr Solzhenitsyn's. The second kind of nationalism helped bring together establishment-oriented Russian nationalists, national Bolsheviks, neo-Stalinist opponents of liberalization, and Communist apparatchiki. With the collapse of communism, the differences between these tendencies disappeared, and after the coup there was a narrowing of differences between some anti-Communist nationalists—including such Russian members of parliament as the leader of the Constitutional-Democratic Party, Mikhail Astafyev, and Russian Christian-Democratic Union copresident Viktor Aksyuchits—and such neo-Bolskeviks as Sergey Baburin, leader of the Rossiya (Russia) faction in the parliament. They joined in a coalition aimed at forcing Boris Yeltsin and his government out of office, linked by a shared belief that Russia must reverse the loss of her status and reemerge as the region's hegemonic superpower.

This idea had powerful support within large segments of the USSR's cultural establishment. In the waning years of the USSR, many Russian nationalists, firmly ensconced in the Soviet cultural establishment, believed that to save Russia and her empire, it was necessary to infuse the state system with a new nationalist ideology oriented around the Orthodox church. Leading Russian nationalist writers who were pillars of the literary establishment embraced these national Bolskevik ideas, among them the best-selling novelist Vasily Belov and the popular "village" novelist Valentin Rasputin. A writer of undoubted literary ability, Rasputin is likewise a purveyor of an odious imperialist viewpoint. Just after the Soviet invasion of Afghanistan in 1979, Rasputin wrote: "Is Fate not bringing us closer to the time when we shall once again go forth on the field of Kulikovo to defend the Russian soil and Russian blood?" Kulikovo is where the Russians defeated the Tatars in 1380 and not only has a patriotic connotation for Russian nationalists, but is redolent of the struggle between radically different civilizations, not to say races. In 1989, Rasputin defined his ideology succinctly on the pages of *Izvestiya* as "order in the soul—order in the homeland." Despite such views, Rasputin apparently enjoyed Mikhail Gorbachev's support. In March 1990, he was named to Gorbachev's sixteen-member Presidential Advisory Council, with responsibilities for ecological and cultural issues in the advisory-executive body.

Regrettably, the writers Belov and Rasputin were not isolated extremists. In the late 1980s, among the USSR's best-selling books were a novel by conservative Valentin Pikul (2.9 million copies); Krasnoyarsk writer Viktor Astafyev's *Pechal'ny detektiv* (*The Sad Detective*), a novel that recounts the tragic effects of alcoholism and has helped direct Russian nationalists toward temperance campaigns (2.8 million copies); and the Vologda-based Vasily Belov's harshly anti-Western novel *Vsye vperedi* (*Everything Is Yet to Come*) (2.7 million copies). As John Dunlop of the Hoover Institution observed, Belov's novel portrays a "Western oriented Soviet intelligentsia as being in the clutches of a fearful Jewish-Masonic conspiracy." Belov's best-seller, published in a huge edition by an official organ of the Goskomizdat, the USSR State Committee for Book Publishing, invokes a universe full of evil forces. "Satan is there," Belov's novel asserts. "There exists a powerful, determined, evil and clandestine force whose purpose is the destruction of Russia." The novel's clear message: Isn't it "better to die in a nuclear war than to live according to Satan's orders?" Not surprisingly, the best-selling Belov has defended Pamyat.

As for Belov's highly popular colleague Valentin Pikul, he is best known for an earlier novel, *At the Last Boundary*, in which the mad monk Rasputin is depicted as fronting a worldwide Zionist plot and being blamed for all the calamities that befell Holy Russia. Two other Russian nationalist writers were published in enormous editions during the Gorbachev years: Yury Bondarev, famous for his sharp criticism of perestroika at a Communist Party conference in 1988 and noted for his apologias for Stalinism in the 1970s; and Pyotr Proskurin, who headed the archconservative RSFSR Cultural Fund.

Most of these reactionary writers' views were disseminated through a series of mass-circulation journals and periodicals, including the monthlies *Nash Sovremennik* whose editor, Sergey Vikulov, was a defender of Pamyat; and *Moskva*. Additional mass enclaves of the pro-Stalinist national Bolsheviks and Russian nationalists included the youth journal *Molodaya Gvardiya (The Young Guard)*, whose deputy editor, Vyacheslav Gorbachev, wrote the afterword to Belov's xenophobic and anti-Semitic best-seller; and the daily newspapers *Sovyetskaya Rossiya* and *Krasnaya Zvezda*, both of which strongly supported the August 1991 coup.

In October 1988, the liberal weekly magazine *Ogonyok* pointed to the dominance of a small clique of writers who derived vast material advantage from relationships dating to the Brezhnev era. Among those singled out were such national Bolsheviks as Yury Bondarev, whose novel *The Hot Snow* was released in thirty-eight separate editions with a combined print run of more than 8 million; and Anatoly Ivanov, editor of *Molodaya Gvardiya*, one of whose novels had appeared in twenty-one separate editions. What troubled *Ogonyok* was not simply that a small clique of writers dominated literary life under glasnost, but that these favored conservative writers' mega-editions were crowding other, more worthy writers out of the limited Soviet marketplace. Wouldn't it be better, *Ogonyok* provocatively suggested, to publish fewer editions of Bondarev and his cronies, while issuing at last the long-awaited and long-suppressed writings of Pasternak, Mandelshtam, Zoschenko, and Akhmatova?

Coincidental with the publication of these editions, activists from the USSR's many Democratic organizations bitterly complained that the USSR's paper shortage had made it impossible for the independent mass media to enjoy true freedom of speech. A self-described "civil war" broke out over the publishing practices not only of the central publishing houses, but also of an entire range of well-financed, lesser-known, specialized publishing enterprises that were firmly in the hands of the Russian nationalists, neo-Stalinists, and conservatives. Among this category of publishers were a number of specialized libraries that republished numerous titles by a narrow group of conservative Russian writers while keeping the print runs of non-Russian writers who wrote in their native languages at artificially low levels. Thus, despite years of glasnost, extreme Russian nationalists and neo-Stalinists controlled written popular culture, even at the level of the state publishing enterprise.

Russian writers frequently expressed extremist and racist views. At a January 1989 meeting of the Russian Writers' Union, one of the speakers advocated the creation of reservations to house the indigenous non-Russian peoples of the Russian republic. So extreme and embarrassing did the views of the Russian Writers' Union become, that after the coup Russia had two writers' organizations, one democratically inclined and the other embodying the virulent views of what had been Russia's Soviet era cultural establishment.

The high visibility of such cultural figures contributed to the shaping of public consciousness and was a breeding ground for ideas that persist today as a powerful current in the post-Soviet Russian state. In essence, the ideas of national Bolshevism constituted an ideology that inversely paralleled the reformist ideas advanced by Gorbachev.

In the last years of the USSR, there was a palpable link between Russian chauvinism and opposition to political liberalization and economic reform. Throughout the Soviet Union, dozens of unofficial Russian chauvinist organizations were established, sharing a common approach and a common agenda: a return to strict discipline and the restoration of rigorous censorship. They called for the use of force to maintain the integrity of the empire and were deeply opposed to Gorbachev's economic reforms.

"There is a common interest for a strong central state and for a strong army among these nationalists. In this regard, their interests coincide with those of the Party bureaucracy and with the military elite that is fearful of losing its vast resources," Andrey Sinyavsky observed one year before the collapse of the Soviet Union.

Russian chauvinist groups sprang up in the urban centers of Moscow, Saint Petersburg, Ekaterinburg, the Volga region, the Urals, Siberia, and in several of the non-Russian republics with a heavy Russian presence—Belarus, Ukraine, Moldova, and Kazakhstan. They carried high-minded names like Otechestvo (Fatherland), another name for the faction of parliament known as Rossiya which believed that "the Russian people [are the only ones] capable of maintaining the integrity of the huge, multinational state—as has been proved by a millennial history." Otechestvo, whose meetings were attended by Red Army generals and leading figures from the Russian Orthodox church, called for a strengthening of "military-patriotic education" and favored uncompromising economic self-sufficiency. The group's chairman at the time, a prominent Moscow art historian, used the Otechestvo's founding convention to praise Romanian dictator Nicolae Ceausescu's headlong drive toward economic self-sufficiency, without making reference to the immense sacrifices exacted from Romanians.

Perhaps the most infamous expression of reactionary Russian nationalist sentiments came from a once obscure Russian school teacher from Saint Petersburg, Nina Andreeva, who in a letter published in March 1988 in the Central Committee daily *Sovyetskaya Rossiya* became the first conservative voice to directly attack the Gorbachev reforms, and has since become a tribune for the voices of reaction. In a July 1989 letter published in a rightist Communist Youth League monthly Andreeva, who had conspicuously visited and signed the guest book of a private museum to Stalin, forthrightly defended the Soviet tyrant and charged that attacks on Stalin were but a prelude to attacks on Lenin and Leninism itself. She denounced the emergence of mass national movements in the non-Russian republics, charging that they heightened ethnic tensions and advocated secession. Andreeva's letter, which went on to claim that antisocialist forces were creating a counterrevolutionary situation, was a cri de coeur of extremist antireform forces. Andreeva has since become general secretary of the All-Union Bolsheviks' Communist Party of the Russian Federation.

Another nationalist group, formed in the waning days of the Soviet Union was the Union for the Spiritual Revival of the Fatherland, an organization headed by the fanatic Mikhail Antonov, who played a prominent role in polemics concerning Gorbachev's economic reforms. Writing in the journal *Moskva*, a publication of the Russian Writers' Union, Antonov savagely attacked such economists as Leonid Abalkin (Gorbachev's deputy prime minister), Abel Aganbegyan, and Nikolay Shmelev—all leading proponents of liberal economic reforms, and denounced a plan calling for the creation in the USSR of free economic zones, asserting: "[It] offends me, a Russian and a Soviet citizen, offends my patriotic sentiments. We are not an underdeveloped country but a vast industrial power." His attack underscored the unity between tradition-oriented nationalists and the opponents of perestroika within the Party apparat. Antonov became famous for his attack on what he called "economic-mathematical" approaches to reform, advocating that only a program based on religious values and on Russian tradition could rescue Russia from the abyss. Antonov is not new to political extremism. In the 1960s, he was part of a tiny Russian fascist group that regarded the world as dominated by a struggle between order (represented by the Teutonic-Slavic forces in such movements as nazism and Stalinism) and chaos (represented by the Jews). The group called for the deindustrialization of the USSR and for a return to the peasant commune, the obshchina. Although Antonov's Union for Spiritual Revival included extremists and anti-Semites among its supporters, it appears to have avoided the extreme formulations of the more celebrated and notorious chauvinist groups, representing instead a more nuanced, sophisticated approach that sought to rally leading figures of the Soviet establishment whose reputations and positions could not afford a direct association with the even more extreme Pamyat.

Symbols of Unity?

The theme of unity with Russia was omnipresent throughout the non-Russian reaches of the Soviet Union, enshrined in an endless landscape of architectural monuments to the "indissoluble unity of the Russian and non-Russian peoples." Along the Georgian military highway leading out of Tbilisi stood a rusting convoluted mass of steel intended to symbolize the bonds of friendship and cooperation between Georgians and Russians, while in Kiev the Ukrainian capital's sprawling Park of the Pioneers is disfigured by a monstrous steel sculpture of two linked steel arcs depicting what was described as the "reunification of the Ukrainian and Russian nations." War memorials echo the theme of unity. In a park in Alma Ata, in the shadow of China's Tien Shan Mountains, one such memorial bears these words: In Front of Us the Enemy, Behind Us Is Russia, Not One Step Backward. Kazakhstan, native Kazakhs will remind you, is not Russia. The statue makes no sense. It is an appeal to a crude Russian nationalism that seems intrusive and oblivious to indigenous sensibilities.

In the period of growing national assertiveness by formerly hidden nations, these symbols and ornaments were not only anachronistic but offensive to the native population in the non-Russian republics, making them feel like intruders, strangers in their own land. This was especially true in the major cities of most of the non-Russian republics, where Russian culture predominated. Yet such a state of affairs was perfectly sensible to most Russians, observed the writer Andrey Fadin, who held that "the Russian psyche is not ready to be relegated to minority status. Russians have never felt themselves to be a minority anywhere they have gone and they have been unwilling to subordinate themselves to other cultures. They have felt themselves, everywhere, to be the vanguard of a great nation." The symbolism of the sculptures celebrating the inextinguishable Russian presence was an external reflection of their psyche. As Fadin noted: "The Russians have always felt the central power behind their backs, standing behind them."

After the collapse of the USSR, the 25 million Russians living in the non-Russian states found themselves on foreign soil amid the growing assertiveness of the newly independent indigenous peoples, a condition that contributed to heightened anxiety. The Russians had rarely been forced to confront the essence of their colonial relationship with their neighbors. This reaction, of course, was not uniform. Some Russians in the non-Russian republics actively participated in the work of the indigenous popular fronts. Not a few had emigrated from Russia and even developed a sense of loyalty to their new non-Russian homelands, and some worked hand in hand with nationalist movements.

Nevertheless, the collapse of the USSR meant for many Russians a wide-ranging identity crisis. By striking at the heart of a centuries-old imperial state, the disintegrative process in the former USSR left Russians grappling with who they were. In response to anxieties felt by some Russians, new political groups emerged—often with the help of former Communist Party activists—in the Baltic States and in Moldova. Russians there took to organizing what were referred to as interfronts or intermovements whose initial aims were to resist coercive efforts to learn the languages of the national republics to which they had migrated and to act as a counterweight to non-Russian separatists.

As the republics moved forward to assert their sovereignty and later their independence, these movements became the core of an increasingly bitter resistance. In Moldova, for example, such forces proclaimed the Dniester region a Dniester Moldavian Republic, created their own militia and paramilitary forces, and engaged in pitch battles with the Moldovan forces throughout much of 1992. The intermovements and interfronts also considerably complicated the efforts of the Lithuanians, Latvians, and Estonians to restore their native languages to preeminent status, to create new rules for the terms of citizenship, and to build full-fledged independent states. In the case of Estonia and Latvia, where the Estonians and Latvians barely constituted a majority, pro-Russian movements awakened local fears and contributed to prejudices that exacerbated the issue of who was and was not eligible for citizenship. The movements that throughout the course of the Baltic struggle for independence had organized effective political strikes and challenged democratically elected Baltic governments, now poisoned inter-ethnic relations.

When he saw the force of Russian nationalism emerge as a potent factor in Soviet life, Gorbachev occasionally played the Russian card, supporting a highly publicized state commemoration of the Millennium of Christianity in 1988 (an event attended by then Soviet President Andrey Gromyko and Raisa Gorbachev) and endorsing high-profile media coverage of the Communist authorities' rapprochement with the pliant Russian Orthodox church. Gorbachev also began to give impromptu speeches in which he waxed poetic about the Russian character and referred to Russia as "the last haven, the last reservoir of spirituality," encouraging the growth of nationalist trends. He also went out of his way to maintain cordial relations with Russian nationalists in the literary community, taking with him the anti-Semitic and anti-Western novelist Vasily Belov on a trip to Finland in 1989 and the anti-Asian writer Valentin Rasputin on a trip to China.

It is very likely that in these steps Gorbachev sought to undercut his longtime conservative rival Yegor Ligachev, the voice of the disgruntled Party bureaucracy, who was also making public gestures toward Russian nationalists. In July 1988, Ligachev paid a highly publicized visit to an exhibition of the paintings of the Russian nationalist Ilya Glazunov, known for his epic paintings of heroic figures from Russia's past and for his portraits of Brezhnev and Andropov. In 1989, Glazunov had given an interview to *Ogonyok* in which he railed at the reemergence of the avant-garde, openly calling it the "Abram-garde" in an odious anti-Semitic aside.

While Gorbachev was hardly a Russian nationalist, it is quite likely that he as well as his right-wing opponents within the Politburo were fighting for the "hearts and minds" of this potent national force. An editorial in *Pravda* in 1989, on the occasion of the Day of the Union, underscored this. After paying obligatory lip service to the worth of all the USSR's national cultures, the editorial rhapsodized on the necessity of safeguarding Russian bilingualism, leaving unstated the obligation of Russians who live in non-Russian republics to learn a second language indigenous to that republic.

Amid communism's grave ideological and economic crisis, the strong appeal of traditional Russian nationalism that beckoned as an inviting and dangerous source of instant legitimacy was also a potential agent of instability, as attempts by Soviet authorities to play the Russian card contributed to mounting resentment and assertiveness among the non-Russians. Russian nationalism was not only a sharp and dangerous weapon; in a multinational Soviet state in which Russians were a bare majority, it was a double-edged sword.

But even before the emergence of the political forces linked to Boris Yeltsin there were signs of a countervailing anti-imperialist trend among Russians. The Interregional Group of Deputies, which included in its ranks Dr. Andrey Sakharov, was an alliance of Russian and non-Russian Democrats that pressed the case of republican sovereignty. In the fall of 1989, a small Russian Anticolonial Society was formed by Russians in Saint Petersburg. Activists from the pro-Yeltsin Democratic Russia movement began to hold joint conferences and to coordinate actions with proindependence forces from Ukraine, the Baltic States, Armenia, and Georgia.

Yeltsin's narrow victory in balloting for the chairmanship of the Russian parliament was another hopeful sign of the beginnings of a Russian retreat from the empire. In late February 1990, for example, a public opinion poll conducted primarily in Russian cities by the Soviet Academy of Sciences Institute of Sociology indicated that 52.4 percent of those polled supported the right of union republics to secede, another 14 percent partially endorsed this right, and only 7 percent were clearly opposed. Yeltsin played to these sentiments, emphasizing his desire to promote the interests of the Russian Federation first. In seeking to defuse Russian concerns about the fate of the 25 million Russians living outside the Russian republic, he ran on a platform that called for a "law of return" that would give to all ethnic Russians citizenship in the Russian republic and in turn protect their material interests, assuring them of a home and a job in the event they left a non-Russian republic.

In July 1990 Oleg Rumyantsev, a leader of Russia's Social-Democratic Party, outlined the strategy of the Yeltsin forces while on a visit to Washington, D.C. Rumyantsev had recently been named by Yeltsin as secretary of the Constitutional Commission of the Russian parliament and charged with organizing the work of writing Russia's new constitution. Rumyantsev noted that the new document would assert the Russian republic's state sovereignty. "There will never again be an election for a new USSR parliament. Nor will we ever see the election of a Soviet president," Rumyantsev predicted. Russia would instead seek to work out the future terms of a confederation, or more likely, a commonwealth through multilateral treaties with other sovereign republics. "Boris Yeltsin and other republic leaders will not allow Gorbachev to rush through a new treaty of the union that negates the independence and sovereignty we have proclaimed," the young Russian politician argued.

Responding to growing signs of a Russian turn inward, Yeltsin indicated his support for the emergence of "an independent Russian republic" that "as an independent state would sign agreements with other republics, also as independent states," suggesting that it would then be up to each sovereign republic to decide whether it should be part of a federation, or a confederation, or be fully independent.

As the 1990s began and the signs of the Soviet Union's disintegration multiplied, Russians were pulled in two irreconcilable directions and in danger of becoming a nation divided and polarized over its role in history. On one side were Yeltsin and other proponents of a turn inward, away from domination of other nations. On the other were the dangerous forces of anti-Semitism, anti-Western xenophobia, and hostility to democratization, and their proponents within segments of the military and the Communist Party apparat.

While the downfall of the Soviet Union had been driven by pressure from the non-Russian states, the instrument that accelerated the process was the coup of August 19–21, 1991. The main battleground of the coup was Russia; and it was in Russia that the coup collapsed, its failure deriving in large measure from the loyalty that Yeltsin and his government had earned from most Russians—including those who served in the military, the militia, and the security services—because of his efforts to shape a new Russian state.

The Genesis of Statehood

Unlike the process of state formation in such republics as Lithuania, Latvia, Estonia, Armenia, Georgia, and Ukraine, the genesis of the Russian state occurred without great fanfare, almost invisibly. Though Yeltsin pressed for sovereignty, he never did so by explicitly calling for an end to a union of republics, but instead advanced the idea of a sovereign Russian state within a loose confederation of states.

There was no question that Yeltsin was slowly and deliberately constructing a full-fledged state with all its institutions and attributes. His parliament declared Russia's state sovereignty and the precedence of Russian laws in the summer of 1990, began drafting a constitution for the Russian Federation, and devised a national anthem. Yeltsin began to travel overseas, asserting himself as a world leader of a sovereign state, and pressed for a specifically Russian press and mass media. But the process of state-building continued to meet with immense obstacles. For one, Gorbachev's central government still controlled the vast majority of economic levers. And even Yeltsin did not yet dare to suggest that Russia should take control of its own military.

In June 1991 Yeltsin was democratically elected Russia's president, capturing 57 percent of the vote. His closest opponent, Gorbachev's former Prime Minister and Party hopeful Nikolay Ryzhkov, received 18 percent. The balance of the votes went to candidates who represented the highly conflicted nature of Russian public opinion: the crackpot neo-Fascist Vladimir Zhirinovsky, sometimes referred to as "the Russian Mussolini"; reformist Vadim Bakatin, who many suspected had been encouraged to run by Gorbachev in a bid to split the Democratic vote; Armen Tuleyev, a populist Communist appratchik from the Kuzbas coal-mining region who ran to split the pro-Yeltsin vote among miners; and Lieutenant-General Albert Makashov, a right-wing proponent of iron discipline. The results in the six-man contest meant that Yeltsin had at last earned a mandate to press for Russian statehood. Until then he had merely been chairman of the parliament of a Union republic, and one who held a bare and volatile majority at that. Now he was the first democratically elected president in Russia's checkered history.

Yeltsin delighted in emphasizing that he had won the presidential election with broad support from the officers' corps and rank-and-file enlisted men. "This support came despite the fact that there was an explicit order given from the top to vote for Ryzhkov," he observed. "The fact that I got a majority of the vote in the military districts, means that officers did not exert pressure on recruits," Yeltsin observed. "This means that officers and non-commissioned officers supported me." With a mandate in his hands, Yeltsin began pressing his advantage in earnest in the fall of 1991. He and other leaders of the republics negotiated the broad outlines of a new Union treaty with Gorbachev that Yeltsin asserted would give full control of all issues except defense, transportation, and communications to the republics. But because Russia inherited the bulk of the military of the former Soviet Union and because the military elite was steeped in an ideology aimed at preserving the multinational Russian-led state, Yeltsin was careful not to take the lead in pressing for the dissolution of the Union, a stand that could well have eroded the strong backing he had earned among younger officers. By playing the anti-imperial game skillfully and carefully, Yeltsin earned the trust of Marshal Yevgeny Shaposhnikov and other military leaders, using Ukraine's intransigence after the failed August coup to convince the military establishment that the best hope of preserving some semblance of a unified military command was to create a loosely linked community of independent states. Yeltsin's ethnic affairs adviser Galina Starovoitova made clear the essence of Russia's choice: "After the August putsch Russia voluntarily rejected the role of Big Brother and voluntarily relinquished its former imperialist policy. . . ."

While Yeltsin and the Democratic movement that supported him have repudiated the empire and cast their lots with nursing a free Russian nation-state back to health, many Russians have yet to make the psychological break with the empire. A Times-Mirror public opinion poll conducted after the coup found the Russian citizenry split, with half expressing their identity as Russians and half as Soviet citizens. Among Yeltsin supporters, more than two-thirds rejected the Soviet label and identified themselves as Russians. In Andrey Fadin's view: "For two hundred years Russia has sought to be a great power. And because this goal has been attained by virtue of the blood and sweat of the masses it has entered into popular political consciousness. To the extent we can distance ourselves from this imperial tradition, we can become a normal nation."

Yet, while Ukrainians, Georgians, Armenians, Lithuanians, Latvians, and Estonians have clearly spoken for their own national independence and restored their sense of national identity, the Russian nation remains deeply divided over the question of its former empire. A large segment of the Russian citizenry is loath to part with its self-image as the elder brother, and for them the loss of Ukraine, Belarus, Georgia, Armenia, and the Central Asian states, some of which have been under Russian patrimony from one to three centuries, will be felt for years to come. Russia's Yeltsin-led rejection of its imperial burden is likely to be no less wrenching to generations steeped in a sentimental notion of its civilizing mission than it was to the postwar French, particularly because the size and proportion of the Russian population living on foreign soil is far greater than those of France. And while 2 million ethnic Russians have left the Central Asian republics to return to European Russia in the last decade, some 25 million Russians live outside Yeltsin's Russian Federation in what are now newly independent states, representing a potential *pied noir* whose problems will challenge his anti-imperial line in the years ahead.

In the months after the December 1991 dissolution of the USSR, significant political movements began playing to this newly created Russian diaspora and to the residual imperial consciousness among many Russians. Powerful forces that sought to restore the patrimony of a central state above that of the new states of Russia, Ukraine, Belarus, Armenia, and the Central Asian republics, were to be found in virtually all segments of the post-Soviet Russian political spectrum. The first clear signs of their self-confidence surfaced at the April 1992 session of the Russian Congress of People's Deputies.

Because the parliament had been elected in March 1990, well before political parties were able to function freely and when the Communist Party still controlled the government and the mass media, Democrats represented a distinct minority of deputies. In the past, the Communist majority had gone along with Yeltsin because of his broad public support. But now, half a year into the Yeltsin economic reforms, with prices for basic commodities up four-, five-, and sixfold, industrial production plummeting, and with Yeltsin's popularity in steep decline, the anti-Yeltsin forces felt free to attack the Russian president and his government.

The Congress opened amid cabinet reshufflings and dismissals of several leading Democrats from key positions, yet despite these tactical maneuvers intended to assuage hard-liners, the Russian government barely survived a first-day vote of confidence. The entire Congress revolved around the reforms undertaken by then First Deputy Prime Minister Yegor Gaidar in the economic sphere and by Foreign Minister Andrey Kozyrev in foreign policy. Delegate after delegate launched into direct attack on the Yeltsin team's foreign and domestic policies, some seeking to invoke a mood of crisis by emphasizing threats against ethnic Russians in the newly independent states, others speaking of the coming disintegration of Russia itself, and still others denouncing the formation of the Commonwealth of Independent States and urging the restoration of the Union.

On April 7, President Yeltsin sought to take the steam out of this hard-line attack and delivered a ringing defense of his economic reforms, conceding that some corrections would be made in government policy, yet remaining unapologetic about Russia's relations with its neighbors. Russia would remain a "great power," said Yeltsin, but it would be great by virtue of its economic capacities. "We are parting with the remnants of ideologized conceptions and messianic ideas," he declared.

In the end, only a hastily fashioned compromise with the republic's military-industrial complex averted the defeat of the Yeltsin government, a compromise that gave several representatives of large state enterprises and the business community leading posts in the Russian government. While Yeltsin retained significant prerogatives and maintained intact his presidential powers, the ferocity of the attack on the Yeltsin team made it clear that hard-liners believed they had broad support.

The Currents of Challenge

By the middle of 1992 Russian politics had crystallized into three major political currents that differed on a wide range of issues, particularly on Russia's repudiation of its former imperial path and embrace of radical economic reform. The first of these currents was represented by an alliance of Great Russia nationalists and neo-Bolsheviks who sought to restore Russia as a great and powerful state. Grouped together in the Russian Popular Assembly, this coalition included the Russian Unity parliamentary bloc, the Russian Christian-Democratic Union, and the People's Freedom Constitutional-Democratic Party. Leading spokespersons for the popular assembly included former anti-Communist dissidents Mikhail Astafyev and Viktor Aksyuchits and neo-Bolsheviks Sergey Baburin and Nikolay Pavlov. When in mid-June 1992 President Yeltsin signed a far-reaching nuclear arms agreement, Pavlov warned that if attempts were made to implement the radical arms cuts, terrorist brigades would be set up to prevent "a wholesale surrender to the West."

Another hard-line umbrella group in this current (whose name resembled that of the Russian Popular Assembly) was the Russian National Assembly, founded in June 1992 by an organizing committee that included former KGB Major-General Aleksandr Sterligov, mathematician Igor Shafarevich, Lieutenant-General Albert Makashov, and television producer Aleksandr Nevzorov. The political culture of this movement was accurately reflected in a July 3, 1992, interview with the Interfax news agency by the national assembly's cochairman Sterligov, who asserted that "Russian nationalism is being provoked by the Jews, [who] are always trying to push out the Russians [by] seeking dominating positions." Novelist Valentin Rasputin, another cochairman, also reflected the ethos of the coalition by asserting that it should "declare the decisive right to defend a united and indivisible Russia and to support the tens of millions of Russians who . . . suddenly ended up outside Russia."

The national assembly's congress, addressed by leaders of the Russian Unity parliamentary bloc, charged that the Yeltsin government had "betrayed the people [and] sold out the Fatherland" and called for the removal of the "pseudodemocrats" from power, creating "worker patrols," and establishing "Russian and Slavic communities" as a prelude to the restoration of a unified state.

On the fringes of these chauvinist groups was a broad range of neo-Stalinist organizations, whose members often included former deputies from the disbanded USSR Supreme Soviet, that sought to provoke public confrontations through mass protests and general strikes that frequently involved violence. One such protest, led by the Workers' Russia movement, brought thousands of violent demonstrators to the Ostankino television center to protest the putative "tendentiousness" in news reporting. When police dispersed the demonstrators, right-wing newspapers printed inflammatory headlines suggesting protestors had been killed by the authorities. The headlines were pure lies.

If the Great Russia alliance of nationalists and neo-Bolsheviks represented the politics of those whom the failed coup had left far from the levers of power, a second current in Russian political life was represented by those who retained immense material and political resources. Their coalition, known as the Civic Union, brought together powerful forces from the military-industrial sector, Russia's major political parties, and several large parliamentary blocs.

The Civic Union was established as a coalition of the 100,000-strong Free Russia People's Party, headed by the country's Vice President Aleksandr Rutskoy; the 60,000-strong Democratic Party of Russia, headed by Nikolay Travkin; and the Change–New Policy parliamentary bloc, created in 1990 by young left-center deputies in Russia's parliament who initially backed Yeltsin, but after the August 1991 coup strongly supported efforts to maintain the integrity of the Soviet Union. Perhaps the most significant partner in the coalition was the Rebirth Party, the political wing of the Russian Union of Industrialists and Entrepreneurs representing managers of large state enterprises, including those from the military-industrial complex. The driving force behind the Rebirth Party was founder Arkady Volsky, who many suggested hoped to become Russia's Prime Minister. In the summer of 1992, the Civic Union described itself as part of the "constructive opposition" to the policies of the Russian government. It criticized Yegor Gaidar's "shock therapy" economic approach and opposed the Russian government's efforts to reduce the budget deficit at the expense of subsidies to large state enterprises.

In July 1992, the Civic Union entered into a cooperative agreement with the Federation of Independent Trade Unions, the sucessor organization to the old official state trade unions, both of whom shared a belief in maintaining a strong government role in the economy and appeared to oppose rapid privatization.

The power of the military-industrial sector was formidable, as Russia had inherited the bulk of the USSR's former military-industrial complex. According to Interfax, Russia's defense economy employed 6.5 million workers in 1992. Under the Soviet system, the defense complex had been given the right to produce for the civilian sector in an effort to mask the actual extent of Soviet military expenditures. This meant that 78 percent of the defense complex's output was for civilian purposes. The military-industrial complex produced 100 percent of television sets, cameras, and sewing machines, 83 percent of medical equipment, and 67 percent of washing machines—a significant portion of Russia's economic output. As the assertiveness of the Civic Union suggested, promoting economic change in this sector as well as in Russia's gigantic state enterprises would prove a delicate and complex political maneuver.

On the question of post-Soviet relations, the Civic Union made it clear that although it did not favor Russian hegemony over other republics, as did the Great Russia nationalists, the Union did support the revival of a unified federal or confederal state on the basis of the Commonwealth of Independent States. Nikolay Travkin and Aleksandr Rutskoy both believed that the destruction of the USSR had dangerous and undesirable consequences, while Arkady Volsky expressed the strong sentiments among managers of leading state enterprises that Soviet collapse had severed links between factories. He, too, supported building a new confederal "Union of Independent States." High-ranking government officials in Ukraine charged that in pursuit of such an aim, Volsky and his Russian Union of Industrialists and Entrepreneurs had helped subsidize the separatist Crimean Republican Movement and had backed similar secessionist currents in the coal-mining Donbass region.

The third current in Russian political life represented the movements that strongly supported Boris Yeltsin, his Acting Prime Minister Yegor Gaidar, Foreign Minister Andrey Kozyrev, and Secretary of State Gennady Burbulis. These movements included the coalition Democratic Choice, formed by Democratic Russia, the Democratic Reform Movement, the Republican Party, and the Russian League of Businessmen. Another pro-Yeltsin group, called New Russia, constituted a coalition that included the Social-Democratic Party, the People's Party, the Rural Workers' Party, and the Social-Liberal Union. Most of these movements opposed the conservative Russian Supreme Soviet's efforts to weaken Yeltsin's authority. Democratic Choice and Democratic Russia were so unhappy with parliament's anti-Yeltsin stance that in the summer of 1992 they collected a million signatures to force a referendum on new parliamentary elections.

The pro-Yeltsin forces, however, had suffered significant defections since the Russian President had launched his course of radical economic reform, fundamental democratic change, and a move away from the empire. The evolution in the views of one prominent Democrat, Sergey Stankevich, reflects the deep-seated political passions that have torn at the very heart of Russian politics.

We first met Stankevich in February 1989, when he was a newly elected deputy in the USSR Congress of People's Deputies. In his cramped office in a dingy Academy of Sciences building, Stankevich made it clear that he was no proponent of Russian nationalist ideas: "I am a representative of the Moscow Popular Front. We are a group that deemphasizes the national question in favor of economic change and democratic reform." In the next two years, Stankevich, who joined the Communist Party because of his admiration for Mikhail Gorbachev, became a leading spokesman for democratic reform. An ethnic Ukrainian who had been thoroughly assimilated into Russian life and politics, Stankevich was increasingly drawn to the Russian national idea.

As the elected deputy chairman of the Moscow City Council, Stankevich became disenchanted with President Gorbachev's turn to the right in the winter of 1990. By the summer of 1991, Stankevich perceived that a Gorbachev-Yeltsin bloc was possible and he entered into the Russian president's inner circle of advisers. With the collapse of the putsch, Stankevich still held out some hope for a renewal of a union of sovereign states. Yet by early October 1991, he had become sharply critical of the Soviet president: "Gorbachev and the central authorities are playing a destructive role. The existence of central government structures is creating confusion here in Russia. Managers and administrators are uncertain about which regulations, laws, and decrees to obey. The center has not been cooperative. Its main role is to sow confusion. The existence of this dualism of the center and the republic is paralyzing reform. These questions will soon have to be resolved." Stankevich believed that power would have to be ceded to Russia and other republics. He also regretted, but appeared reconciled to, the secession of Ukraine: "Losing Ukraine would be like losing one's arm; painful, but bearable."

Yet soon after the disintegration of the unified state, Stankevich changed his views in the direction of an assertive Russian patriotism, arguing that Russia should build a strong and powerful state to protect ethnic Russians wherever they might live and to project its economic and political strength. In March 1992, he wrote an influential essay, declaring that Russia's destiny was not to be a European but a Eurasian nation; that Russia should orient itself to taking a leading role in the second tier of nations, including those that were part of the developing world; that it was wrong for Russia to attempt to link its destiny with that of the United States, Germany, and the industrialized democracies; and above all, that Russia should take a firm stance in relations with the new post-Soviet states. Although he was then a part of Yeltsin's advisory team, Stankevich appeared to have thrown in his political lot with Russia's outspoken Vice President Aleksandr Rutskoy.

Amid growing strength among hard-line nationalist tendencies, key Yeltsin adviser Sergey Shakhray warned in mid-June 1992 that he was "almost certain" hard-liners would attempt to force Yeltsin from power. The man he predicted could replace Yeltsin as part of a "national-patriotic-Fascist leadership" was Rutskoy. Shakhray's invocation of the Russian vice president was hardly surprising, for Rutskoy had emerged as the clearest voice for an assertive Russia.

Yeltsin had chosen Rutskoy, a decorated Afghan war veteran, as his 1991 running mate in a bid to shore up support from the military. During the putsch, a gun-toting Rutskoy had bravely stood with Yeltsin in the besieged Russian parliament building. Yet soon after the August events, he emerged as a consistent critic of the Russian president's policies, his disenchantment solidifying when he was rebuffed in his effort to be named Russia's prime minister, a post Yeltsin held until the summer of 1992 when he turned the post over to economic reformer Yegor Gaidar. In November 1991, Rutskoy accused the radical reformist Russian government of being a group of "young boys in pink shorts, red shirts, and yellow boots." In December 1991 he asserted that he was opposed to the dissolution of the Soviet Union. Rutskoy even went so far as to suggest that Yeltsin's health problems should make him surrender the prime ministerial portfolio.

In a February 14, 1992, interview with the British ITN television news, Rutskoy asserted that he would like to become Russia's president and denounced the Russian government, suggesting that it be put on trial for ruining Russia and destroying Russian statehood. Throughout 1992, Rutskoy made clear his opposition to Yeltsin policy in a series of high-profile visits to trouble spots in other republics, where he stirred up tension and challenged Yeltsin's anti-imperial line by making territorial claims against newly independent states. While in the Crimea in January 1992, he demanded that the peninsula be reclaimed from Ukraine, declaring on what was Ukrainian soil that the entire Black Sea Fleet was Russian. Later he upped the ante by quipping that there was no need to transfer a portion of the fleet to Russian territory inasmuch as Crimea had "always [been] Russian and will always be Russian."

At the April 1992 session of the Russian Congress of People's Deputies following a visit to Moldova, he delivered a dramatic report of a "bloody conflict" waged by "numerous terrorist groups," crossing over the line of propriety by declaring: "This congress must initiate the protection of Russian citizens and serve as an example to the parliaments of other states of the Commonwealth of Independent States." Of course, with the exception of the Russian 14th Army, the victims in the fighting in the Dniester region had almost exclusively been citizens of independent Moldova, whose Russian population was a minority and whose borders were shared only with Ukraine, not with Russia.

Rutskoy's alienation from the Yeltsin team and his profound disagreement with its policies led him into an alliance with the military-industrial complex, where he joined with the managers of state enterprises in bitterly denouncing privatization efforts in that sector. Asserting his opposition to Russia's "blind rush into the market," he called for a strong central state that would fight corruption and impose labor discipline. Defending the idea of a Great Russia, he called for the restoration of "historical borders" as part of an effort to build a "unified and indivisible Russia." Rutskoy gathered around him a group of associates that included Iona Andronov, who had distinguished himself over the years for his strongly anti-American journalism. According to Russian Democratic leaders, Rutskoy was assisted in crafting his speeches by such reactionaries as the editor of the chauvinist weekly *Den'*, Aleksandr Prokhanov, and former KGB Major-General Aleksandr Sterligov of the extremist Russian National Assembly, who had served as an adviser to Rutskoy before the two had a political parting of ways. Rutskoy's outspokenness did not escape the attention of Yeltsin, who relieved Rutskoy of his responsibilities in supervising defense conversion and appointed him to oversee Russian agriculture, a traditionally difficult and usually thankless task.

Yet there was no denying that Rutskoy's tough talk did win admirers. Public opinion samplings suggested that among Russian citizens he was second only to Yeltsin in popularity. In a poll of soldiers taken in April 1992 by the Center for Military-Sociological, Psychological, and Legal Research, Rutskoy outpaced Yeltsin in popularity by a margin of 48 to 38 percent. Rutskoy's nationalist views also found support within the Russian Fascist movement. In February 1992, Dmitry Vasilyev said that the Russian vice president "will win the hearts of many people. . . . Here's where our interests are linked: Great Russia." Rutskoy, said Vasilyev, is "a true Russian officer. I'd nominate him head commander."

Attacking Yeltsin from another front was his erstwhile colleague, parliamentary speaker, Ruslan Khasbulatov. A man of limited ability but overarching ambition, Khasbulatov began to turn against the Russian president under the slogan of defending the rights and prerogatives of parliament, clamping down on the pro-Yeltsin daily newspaper *Izvestiya* and claiming it as the property of parliament. Supported by the large bloc of right-wing nationalists and neo-Bolsheviks in the Supreme Soviet, Khasbulatov denounced Yeltsin's efforts to consolidate executive power as self-aggrandizement.

Stankevich's, Rutskoy's, and Khasbulatov's conduct should not be surprising. The decolonization of Russia and the establishment of a democratic state with a vibrant private sector involved wrenching changes. This triple revolution of democratic change, economic reform, and withdrawal from the empire also involved trampling on the entrenched interests of many formerly powerful officials.

In April 1992, Yeltsin succeeded in negotiating a new Federation Treaty with most of its internal republics, yet potential conflicts remained in three regions: Tatarstan, Chechnya, and Tuva. Russian politics was likely to be convulsed by a sharp debate about what to do with these internal quasi-states, and even if compromises were eventually found, Yeltsin's enemies were sure to argue fervently that he was promoting the disintegration and dismemberment of the Russian state.

In the summer of 1992, amid growing stridency on the part of extreme nationalists, Foreign Minister Andrey Kozyrev warned that "the threat of an antidemocratic coup exists. The party of war and the party of neobolshevism is rearing its head." But in August 1992, convinced that the opposition to his course was divided and that the military was firmly under his control, Yeltsin dismissed fears of a coup against Russia's new democratic state. Yet the struggle for the hearts and minds of the Russian people was by no means over. The growing appeal of renewing a union of states and the sustained interest in restoring a hegemonic Russia to superpower status continued to pose a dangerous challenge.

Despite opposition by many in the parliament, the Russian president possessed a number of important advantages in his stewardship of the new Russian state. He had the support of substantial segments of the Russian press, including three mass-circulation newspapers—the dailies *Komsomolskaya Pravda* and *Izvestiya*, as well as the weekly *Argumenty i Fakty*, Russia's highest circulation periodical. Democratic values also were supported by such influential periodicals as the *Moscow News* and the daily *Nezavisimaya Gazeta*. Each of these periodicals promoted democratic values, pluralism, and tolerance for the rights of the new post-Soviet states.

Yeltsin also had the advantage of strong presidential rule consolidated in the days following the putsch through the institution of presidential representatives entrusted with wide-ranging powers at the local level. In cases where the local executive authorities and parliament had been implicated in supporting the coup or blocking reforms, these presidential representatives could exercise local executive power, thereby projecting Yeltsin's authority into regions where Democratic groups were weak and badly organized.

Russia's struggle between democratic reformers, representatives of the old order's nomenklatura, and extremists favoring an iron hand and a return to dictatorship came to a head on December 1, 1992, when the Congress of People's Deputies reconvened.

President Yeltsin had sought to stave off a frontal attack by the anti-reform forces by entering into a compromise with the Civic Union. The Russian President had once before given in to the pressure of the Civic Union's influential industrialists and managers, who favored slowing down on economic reform and restoring strong ties with now independent republics.

But pressure from opponents of rapid economic reform and hard-liners opposed to accommodating the increasingly sovereign republics proved intense. In the months before the congress, Yeltsin already had slowed down the withdrawal of Russian troops from the Baltic states and adopted a more aggressive stance in defense of the rights of ethnic Russians in other republics. He had restored Viktor Gerashchenko, the former head of the USSR State bank to the leadership of the Russian banking establishment, setting back the Gaidar government's effort to bring Russia's budget into balance and ushering in a new wave of racing inflation. He also had surrendered his First Deputy Foreign Minister, Fyodor Shelov-Kovedyayev, who had been associated with a policy of cooperation with the republics of the former USSR.

Even as he made these concessions, the Russian president refused to sacrifice the main lines of his policy—movement toward fundamental economic reform and privatization and a move away from the restoration of Russian domination over neighboring republics.

But as the December 1992 Congress of People's Deputies approached, Yeltsin made it clear he was willing to sacrifice a further crop of the dwindling number of democratic reformers still in his inner circle and government team. First to go was Galina Starovoytova, Russia's most popular woman politician, who had served as the President's ethnic affairs adviser. Next to go were Deputy Prime Minister Mikhail Poltoranin, who had been responsible for strengthening the pro-democratic press. Also sacrificed was the head of the inter-republic Ostankino television channel, Yegor Yakovlev, who had angered hard-liners by blocking their access to the airwaves and hiring young democrats to produce lively documentary and news programs. Another casualty was Social Affairs Minister and democratic activist Ella Panfilova. Also let go was Yeltsin's most trusted aide, Gennady Burbulis, who was forced to surrender the post of State Secretary.

Yeltsin hoped these substantial compromises made on the eve of the Congress would be enough to save his Acting Prime Minister Yegor Gaidar and his anti-imperial Foreign Minister Andrey Kozyrev. He certainly had been led to understand that this would be the case by the parliament's erratic and unreliable speaker, Ruslan Khasbulatov. But Khasbulatov's inconsistencies coupled with a powerful voting block representing hardline neo-Stalinists, ultra-nationalists, and segments of the nomenklatura-laden Civic Union denied Gaidar election as Prime Minister and threatened to remove Kozyrev from the leadership of the Ministry of Foreign Affairs.

The Congress also adopted a number of resolutions designed to undermine Russia's cooperative foreign policy. The deputies expressed their unhappiness with Russia's support of UN-backed sanctions against Yugoslavia. They, likewise, adopted a resolution reasserting claims over the Crimea, an action that was sure to heighten tensions with Russia's biggest neighbor—Ukraine. Such actions made it clear that the majority in the Russian Congress sought to launch Russia on an anti-Western as well as pro-imperial course.

His gambit having failed, President Yeltsin plunged headlong into confrontation. He addressed democratic supporters in the company of dismissed aide Burbulis and called for the creation of a new political party to back his democratic course. On December 10, he had met with autoworkers at an auto assembly plant on the outskirts of Moscow, in a bid to build support for his offensive against an intransigent parliament. Hurriedly, he called for a referendum to determine who ought to remain in power—the president or the parliament. The Congress in turn amended Russia's Constitution to prevent such a popular vote.

By December 12, centrists from the Civic Union and democrats from Democratic Russia and the Radical Democrats factions in parliament backed a compromise fashioned by Vitaly Zorkin, head of Russia's consitutional court. The compromise meant that on April 11, 1993, Russian voters would likely be asked to chose between two constitutions—one which favored a Yeltsin-dominated Presidential republic and the second, which would give paramount power to a parliament dominated by hard-liners and more moderate opponents of sweeping reform.

Despite the compromise, Yeltsin was badly wounded by the altercation with Parliament. He had removed a large number of democrats from the government without saving his prime minister.

As significantly, with Russia's future course to be decided in April 1993, there was a distinct danger that all policies would take on a provisional nature and reform would be stalled. The future of Russia, including the very nature of Russia's relations with her former non-Russian dependencies was yet to be determined. Clearly, the path away from empire and toward democracy and market reform seemed more than ever linked to the personal fortune of the charismatic Yeltsin and his capacity—in a climate of steep economic decline and social dislocation—to energize the people and mobilize public opinion against the forces and sentiments of the old order.

As Lev Ponomaryov, the parliamentarian who served as co-Chairman of the pro-Yeltsin Democratic Russia movement told the *Washington Post*, "It would be a mistake to think that the battle has been decided. It has merely been postponed."

The success of a smaller, kinder, and gentler Russia committed to cooperation with the democratic West was linked not only to Yeltsin's success in effecting a redefinition of Russian identity, but also to his success in radically reforming the Russian economy. And despite the difficulties of Russia's passage to a market economy, in late 1992 Yeltsin still remained Russia's most popular political figure.

For this great nation—the key player in Eastern Europe and Central Asia for most of this century—the loss of its dependencies was bound to have been destabilizing. Before the fall of the Soviet Union, Russian politics had been primarily a matter of where one stood on the questions of democratic change and radical economic reform. The dividing line that had once been between Democrats, anti-Communists, and non-Communists on one side and Communists on the other now had to factor in the nature of Russia's relations with her neighbors. The dividing line now was over the question of the empire. Obviously, a hegemonic, imperialistic Russia would in the end also be undemocratic, militaristic, and anti-Western. The stakes were high in Yeltsin's historic effort to wrest Russia from her historic path.

Chapter Eight

The New States: Prospect and Policy

National honor is national treasure of the highest order.

JAMES MONROE

The collapse of the Soviets—the end of Communist rule and the simultaneous disintegration of the Soviet empire—gave birth to fifteen new states in Central Asia, radically altering the geopolitical landscape in Eastern Europe and Eurasia and changing the balance of power that persisted in Europe throughout the postwar era.

Ethnic and territorial disputes have cost thousands of lives and created tens of thousands of refugees from Nagorny Karabakh, the Dniester region of Moldova, Ossetia on the border of Russia and Georgia, and other areas. Despite these violent conflicts, the radical realignment of an empire that had remained virtually intact since the late eighteenth century, has come with relatively little turmoil. It is the first collapse of an empire to have occurred without the accompaniment of a major war.

Still, the rapid collapse of the Soviet Union has left a number of unresolved and highly contentious issues that will continue to vex the leaders of the new states for years to come. Yury Shcherbak, who in mid-1992 was Ukrainian environmental minister, put the predicament of the post-Soviet states this way: "We are all like prisoners escaping from the same prison; we've made our escape but we're bound together by a single chain." This formerly enforced unity is leading the newly independent states to define the nature of their newfound independence, to break the single chain.

As part of this process of liberation, the new states have yet to define, solidify, and stabilize relations among themselves, due to the condition of highly fluid governance. Most of the leaders of the new states stand on shaky ground, and the continuing economic crises that confront their societies are certain to inject even more uncertainty into their political futures. Many of the leaders are holdovers from the old Communist political establishment, while others are novices in political life. Almost all face strong internal opposition and a tense social setting as they embark on the process of creating new states. In such a context, the appeal to the powerful force of nationalism and national dignity remains a card that can be played properly or recklessly, as a constructive sentiment for consolidating statehood and spurring nation-building, or as a divisive means of stirring up age-old ethnic enmities. The post-Soviet political scene is complicated by yet another factor. Despite the evaporation of the Marxist-Leninist ideology that was the basis of their own precarious legitimacy, former Communist elites cling to power by taking up the banner of nation-building and national independence.

Amid economic dislocations, struggles for power, and old elites eager to preserve privilege by any means, simmering ethnic tensions and unresolved interstate issues can prove dangerously destabilizing and incendiary, particularly in the settlement of borders between the newly liberated states. Removing this Sword of Damocles would clearly be in the interests of democratization, but unfortunately peace and security are threatened by the cavalier attitude taken by some of the new states.

Imperial Backlash

The first signal of danger in the border issue came just weeks after the collapse of the Soviet Union, when in December 1991 Boris Yeltsin's then press secretary Pavel Voshchanov provoked a crisis in Ukrainian-Russian relations by suggesting that Russia's borders with Ukraine, and presumably other states, would be reexamined inasmuch as these states had left the Soviet Union. Voshchanov's comment appeared to have violated 1990 and 1991 bilateral Ukrainian-Russian agreements that had confirmed the immutability of the two republics' borders. The Russian government spokesman set into motion a wave of Ukrainian protests that strained Ukrainian-Russian state relations and resulted in dispatching to Kiev a hastily arranged high-level Russian delegation that managed to reduce tensions.

Nevertheless, there were other voices in the Russian government and parliament that continued to stir up the border question. In early 1992 Sergey Baburin and other leaders of the large Rossiya faction in parliament joined in challenging the current borders of Russia's neighbors, asserting that such borders had been "arbitrarily set up by administrative and bureaucratic methods" and arguing in support of "the right of any area outside the Russian Federation to adopt decisions on joining Russia." Others in the Russian political establishment sought to extend the borders of Russia to resemble those of what they referred to as "historic Russia," seeking in essence to revive a pan-Slavic state that would link Russia, Belarus, and Ukraine. Many leading figures in Russian life appeared to support the views of the Russian writer Aleksandr Solzhenitsyn, who argued for the preservation of a unified Slavic state. And Russian Vice President Aleksandr Rutskoy contributed to an atmosphere of dangerous uncertainty when he asserted in an address to the crew of the Black Sea Fleet flagship *Moskva* in Sevastopol on April 4, 1992, that "although there are now sovereign republics on the territory of the former USSR, you can't draw borders between them; you can't put up rows of barbed wire between peoples or sever economic ties between enterprises."

Especially troubling was the growing chorus of important Russian leaders who refused to accept the disintegration of the old Soviet Union and sought its eventual restoration by means of gradually strengthening the powers of the Commonwealth of Independent States. As early as December 14, 1991, Rutskoy had signaled his opposition to the disintegration of the Soviet Union when he denounced "undesirable opposition to the Soviet President" Mikhail Gorbachev and said there were reasons to "doubt the viability of the hastily concluded agreement" that launched the new Commonwealth.

Important voices within the Russian political establishment challenged President Yeltsin's views and argued, with Rutskoy, for the restoration of the old USSR. Among these was Nikolay Travkin, leader of the Democratic party of Russia, who believed that the collapse of the USSR was "regrettable" and was convinced that some form of reintegration of the newly independent states was desirable. Interviewed in July 1992, Travkin asserted: "No one is happy as a result of the collapse of the Soviet Union. Even in Ukraine and the Baltics people are not happy. The only ones who are happy are the fifteen new presidents of the republics who are now received with great ceremony by the U.S. President. But even these leaders have understood that you need to create a true center . . . and they have understood that you need organs not only to coordinate but to control. This already is an indication that—not tomorrow, not fully, and not all of them—the new states are on the road toward some form of confederation, some form of union. This process is objective."

Russian state counselor Sergey Stankevich put it this way: "Strictly speaking, Russia did not withdraw from the union. Russia was and remains a consistent supporter of the closest union among the republics. Strengthening union relations is one of the most important priorities among the national interests of the Russian state." Another voice for the restoration of some form of union among the now sovereign republics was the energetic and clever leader of the hard line national Bolshevik Rossiya faction in parliament, Sergey Baburin, who held that "only a federation can stop all the wars being waged on the territory of the former USSR today. We have to move away from the nation-state structure inherited by Bolshevism. A single federated state is inevitable. The only question is the means and methods of achieving it."

In addition to these diverse voices looking to restore a unified state or seeking Russian hegemony among the countries of the former Soviet empire, those arguing that the Russian Federation would in the end have to reshape its borders included high-ranking members of Boris Yeltsin's team—his ambassador to the United States, Vladimir Lukin, among them. On January 12, 1992, Lukin, then chairman of the Russian parliament's Committee on International Affairs and Foreign Economic Relations, sent a confidential letter to the speaker of the Russian Supreme Council, Ruslan Khasbulatov, in which he recommended a hard-line strategy for Russia to pursue in its relations with Ukraine. As part of that policy, Lukin suggested that President Yeltsin issue a "decree . . . transferring all former USSR Armed Forces to Russian jurisdiction." Lukin urged a similar step with regard to the Black Sea Fleet, adding that such control be taken not only on the territory of Crimea, but also on the Ukrainian mainland, in the port of Mikolayiv.

Lukin conceded that while such actions might initially provoke negative reactions in the West, in the end the West would accept the Russian position. More important, said Lukin, such tough actions would play well in Russia, where nationalist sentiments were on the rise. "Reaction to our actions within Russia is much more important. A soft position will inevitably play into the hands of right-wing Russian nationalists," Lukin warned, "but a firm position will bring forth a broad wave of support for the Russian leadership, and thus will give us more time and opportunities in implementing economic reform." By adopting a hard line and directly challenging Ukrainian interests, Lukin argued, "the Ukrainian leadership will be faced with the dilemma of either consenting to transfer the fleet and bases to Russia, or having Ukraine's jurisdiction over Crimea questioned."

An astute politician, Lukin was prepared to compromise principle for the sake of consolidating support for the Yeltsin government. His policy recommendations—which were rejected by Yeltsin—could well be a harbinger of Russia's future conduct vis-à-vis neighboring states. One thing can certainly be said about Russian politics: In the months after Lukin wrote his letter, the nationalist right had grown significantly stronger. The April 1992 session of the Russian Congress of People's Deputies witnessed the emergence of three nearly co-equal factions: the Democrats who consistently supported Boris Yeltsin; a self-styled "constructive opposition" of centrist deputies who supported Yeltsin's presidency while seeking to block or reverse some of his economic reforms, and who urged a tougher policy line against Russia's neighboring states; and a new alliance of Russian nationalists and national Bolsheviks, who angrily opposed the move away from the empire. With 1993 promising further economic decline and grave social dislocations, the appeal of the Russian nationalist and national Bolshevik right could be expected to grow further.

Perhaps the best-known voice arguing for a return to a federated system was Mikhail Gorbachev, who undertook highly publicized fund-raising trips to the United States and Japan, where he built support for his political foundation, which Yeltsin forces viewed as a meddlesome and dangerous institution around which a Yeltsin opposition might coalesce. At home, Gorbachev became an increasingly active critic of the disintegration of the Soviet Union and a consistent tribune for those seeking the revival of some sort of union state. In countless public appearances and press interviews, Gorbachev consistently argued that the dissolution of the Soviet Union had been a fatal mistake that required rectification, a mistake that had led to a spate of ethnic wars and border disputes and was a harbinger of even greater bloodshed. Gorbachev neglected to note that in the Soviet period such disputes as the Armenian-Azerbaijani conflict over Nagorny Karabakh, and ethnic tensions between Uzbeks and Kazakhs, Georgians and Ossetians, Georgians and Abkhazians, and Tajiks and Russians were as severe, if not more violent, than anything that followed in the first year after the collapse of the USSR.

Appearing on a program broadcast to all the Commonwealth countries on June 28, 1992, Gorbachev criticized the Commonwealth for its inability to develop conflict resolution mechanisms. With regard to the Commonwealth itself, Gorbachev asserted that "nothing is moving and it never will, because behind the declarations and agreements there has to be the practical and routine work, there have to be specific structures and mechanisms." It was necessary, Gorbachev argued, to go beyond bilateral ties between republics. Such ties "are no substitute. The Commonwealth cannot use them to replace the institutions of cooperation that were in the USSR. You see, the Commonwealth has to function as a viable organism and serve the common and realistic interest."

The growing chorus of prominent Russian voices urging a revision of existing borders or seeking the resurrection of a union state prompted former Soviet Foreign Minister Eduard Shevardnadze to propose a five-year moratorium on the changing of borders in the post-Soviet states. Shevardnadze, who in 1992 was serving as president of the State Council of Georgia, clearly recognized the need for more breathing room to enable new states to implement necessary economic changes, regularize their interstate relations, and bring stability to a region that had seen tumultuous if generally peaceful change.

As of late 1992, the views of Russian hard-liners and proimperialists were clearly not shared by Boris Yeltsin and his inner circle. Indeed, the policies pursued by Yeltsin, his Acting Prime Minister Yegor Gaidar, Yeltsin's most trusted adviser Secretary of State Gennady Burbulis, Foreign Minister Andrey Kozyrev, and Ethnic Relations Adviser Galina Starovoytova were firmly on the side of recognition of neighboring states and acceptance of borders in their current configurations. In part, their policy stemmed from an understanding that to question established borders would open a Pandora's Box of claims and counterclaims and make Russia itself vulnerable to separatist movements in such Muslim regions as Tatarstan and Chechnya, while also fueling strong sentiments for autonomy in the Russian Far East and in Siberia.

The borders that were established in the Soviet period frequently did not take ethnic factors into account. In some cases, there was no precise demarcation of where one republic began and another ended. Andrey Kozyrev, whom Yeltsin named in 1990 to serve as Russia's foreign minister, focused on the border issue in a June 7, 1992, interview in the *Moscow News*:

> Yes, we've inherited poorly defined borders. In fact no one tried to define them. Yes, decisions were made by the Politburo, by Khrushchev . . . but what follows from this? Do we start a tussle to snatch back those pieces of land? From whom? Ukraine? Kazakhstan? This would be nearly the same as distributing arms to peoples repressed by Stalin and calling on them to destroy those who live on their territory today. If we go for each other's throats today, heads will be bitten off. All the more so as nowhere in the world are there ethnically or historically substantiated borders.

Kozyrev went on to make clear his opposition to revising borders: "Of course, we can return former Russian lands. Only count me out."

Kozyrev's views were fully consonant with his president's. In a February 19, 1992, interview on Russian television Yeltsin went out of his way to indicate Russia's anti-imperial course, admitting that many in Moscow still operated from the standpoint of "old unionist ideas" from the period when all states "marched in single file." Nevertheless, while Yeltsin rejected the course of action recommended by hard-liners and proponents of a revived union, a number of them occupied prominent positions within the government and parliament of Russia. And parliamentarian Lukin, a strong proponent of hard-line policies, was dispatched to Washington to play a key role in interpreting Russian positions to the remaining superpower.

While Yeltsin's tenure held out the promise of stability and peaceful relations among the newly independent states, powerful political forces in Russia had emerged in opposition to his democratic, anti-imperial, and pro-Western course. Aleksandr Rutskoy, the man who stood a heartbeat away from the Russian presidency, became a popular tribune for the idea of a Great Russia that is "single and indivisible." Among Rutskoy's ghostwriters were the editor of the reactionary weekly *Den'* Aleksandr Prokhanov and the neo-Fascist writer Yury Bondarev. Another of Rutskoy's circle, former KGB Major-General Aleksandr Sterligov, became ever more vehement in his xenophobic views and eventually parted company with the Russian vice president to launch the Russian Popular Assembly, an alliance of right-wing and Fascist groups that included the crackpot neo-Fascist Vladimir Zhirinovsky.

Another hard-line bloc, a coalition of "patriotic forces," was forged in the spring of 1992, uniting such former Communist hard-liners as Sergey Baburin and such long-standing anti-Communists as Christian Democrat Viktor Aksyuchits and Constitutional Democrat Mikhail Astafyev. This coalition dominated much of the debate at the April 1992 Russian Congress of People's Deputies, at times jeopardizing the Russian economic reform program. Moreover, a growing number of Democratic leaders, like Nikolay Travkin of the Democratic Party of Russia and Saint Petersburg Mayor Anatoly Sobchak, did not back the Yeltsin policy of focusing on shaping the Russian Federation and supported instead the restoration of a federated union state on the basis of the Commonwealth of Independent States.

Travkin's Democratic party helped to create a powerful umbrella group, the Civic Union, with Vice President Rutskoy's Free Russia People's Party, and with the Renewal Union of Arkady Volsky, the former Andropov aide who now headed the Russian Union of Industrialists and Entrepreneurs with directors from Russia's military-industrial complex. The Civic Union made considerable headway in pressing its allies into the Russian government. By mid-1992 these included First Deputy Prime Minister Vladimir Shumeiko, and Deputy Prime Ministers Georgy Khizha, who was responsible for industry, transportation, communications, and military conversion, and Viktor Chernomyrdin, who was responsible for the fuel and nuclear power sectors, and who in December 1992 would be named Russia's Prime Minister.

While Khizha and Shumeiko had not been employed in the structures of the former State Planning Committee nor in the Communist Party apparat, there was evidence that representatives of the old guard were also forcing their way into the upper ranks of Russia's government. Among such worrisome signs was the appointment in July 1992 of Viktor Gerashchenko—under whose tenure as head of the USSR State Bank (Gosbank) tens of millions of dollars of illegal subsidies had been transferred to foreign Communist parties—to the position of head of the Russian Central Bank. Other hard-liners who had made their way into the Russian government were Colonel-General Boris Gromov, the former commander of Soviet forces in Afghanistan and later the first deputy to future coup plotter Boris Pugo at the Soviet Ministry of Internal Affairs, who was named deputy minister of defense, and Nikolay Golushko, the former Ukrainian KGB boss who became Russia's deputy minister of security.

As 1993 began, the self-styled centrist Civic Union—often with the support of the hard-line nationalists—was engaged in a concerted effort to purge the anti-imperialist Westernizers, including Foreign Minister Kozyrev from Yeltsin's inner circle and from the Russian government. The growing self-confidence of this group was evident in the increasingly strident views of Russia's vice president. So aggressive were Rutskoy's comments that they provoked an uncharacteristically sharp condemnation from Eduard Shevardnadze. In response to a statement by Rutskoy that "the Georgian leaders must understand that the acts committed in South Ossetia will not go unpunished," to a Russian-inspired shutoff of gas deliveries to Georgia, and to abusive personal comments, Shevardnadze responded bluntly: "I will not lower myself to answer your insults. . . . In your eyes, Georgia is a small and weak country, while Russia is large and powerful, so powerful that some of its leaders claim they have the right to stop the supply of gas from Turkmenistan to other republics." Shevardnadze asserted that Rutskoy's "speeches and statements in the mass media remind me of some of the aggressive statements made during the Afghan war. . . . You are now . . . calling for blood." Shevardnadze also denounced the suggestion made by Ruslan Khasbulatov, speaker of the Russian parliament, that legislators consider the incorporation of South Ossetia, an ethnically distinct part of Georgia, into Russia.

Throughout 1992, Russian Foreign Minister Kozyrev often had spoken of the growing strength and dangerous views of hard-liners and representatives of the nomenklatura within the structures of the Russian government, warning of the possibility of an anti-Yeltsin putsch led by nationalist forces in a June 8, 1992, interview with *Le Monde* and again in a June 30 interview in *Izvestiya*. And Yeltsin's trusted aide and former Deputy Prime Minister Sergey Shakhray also warned in a June 1992 interview that hard-liners would try to depose Yeltsin and establish a "national-patriotic Fascist dictatorship . . . in the fall or winter of [1992]."

The Yeltsin Policy

Despite these looming storm clouds, in the critical year after the failed August putsch Boris Yeltsin and his government were consistent in their pursuit of a policy of cooperation and restraint in interrepublic relations. Significantly, President Yeltsin made clear that a major component of Russia's democratic and Western-oriented foreign policy was a turn away from the empire and the use of force. In an April 7, 1992, address to the Congress of People's Deputies, he declared:

> We are parting with the remnants of ideologized thought and messianic ideas to which the interests of the people and the state were sacrificed. Work to strengthen Russia's international position . . . by no means amounts to an attempt to usurp the role of a superpower that once claimed to decide the world's destiny. Russia is rightfully a great power by virtue of her history, her place in the world, and her material and spiritual potential.

Russia, said Yeltsin, would pursue a "radical change" that saw a "relative decline in the role played by military power."

Foreign Minister Kozyrev and his First Deputy Minister Fyodor Shelov-Kovedyaev, understood that the adoption of the hard-line stance advocated by Rutskoy and Yeltsin's political counselor, Sergey Stankevich, would raise fears about renewed Russian hegemony and the reemergence of Russian imperial ambitions. Such fears, in turn, would block any opportunity to develop a climate of cooperation among the new post-Soviet states, both through the Commonwealth and through bilateral treaties with other former Soviet republics. "The road our opponents propose—namely . . . to an imperial state, a state threatening others, including our CIS neighbors . . . is a dead end, a road leading nowhere, an antipatriotic road," Kozyrev noted on August 2, 1992. On the other hand, said Kozyrev, a policy of Russian restraint made it possible for the post-Soviet states to realize that "we do not intend to dictate and we do not intend to become a new center" and thus pass from a period of "complete dispersal to cooperation on extremely sensitive issues."

At a July 6, 1992, meeting in Moscow, Commonwealth leaders showed signs that Yeltsin's exercise in self-restraint was bearing important political fruit. Steps were taken by the heads of state to set up joint peacekeeping forces that would be introduced onto the territory of any state only with its consent. Moreover, after a prolonged period of disintegration and the collapse of relations between the former Soviet republics, most of the Commonwealth leaders made clear that they recognized the need for some permanent structures that would, above all, coordinate commerce and trade between the new states. In Moscow they agreed to create a Commonwealth Economic Court that would be empowered to examine reputed violations of treaties and agreements.

Nevertheless, even as progress was being made there were differences about the scope of such a new body. Ukrainian President Leonid Kravchuk made it clear that his support was for an economic coordination structure that would have a very narrow ambit: "We are not taking any categorical position . . . that we will not participate in an economic court, a coordinating, monitoring structure, which will not be above states." However, Kravchuk noted, the important thing was to ensure that the Commonwealth of Independent States "is not a state nor a state structure nor a subject of international law."

Despite Kravchuk's skeptical insistence that the Commonwealth confine itself to very narrowly circumscribed duties, Ukrainian-Russian state relations were taking a turn for the better. At a Yeltsin-Kravchuk summit in June 1992 in the Crimean seacoast resort of Dagomys, the two presidents sought to bring stability to interstate relations. In the months after the creation of the Commonwealth of Independent States, Ukrainian-Russian relations had grown increasingly tense regarding the disposition of the Black Sea Fleet and the growing conflict over Crimea. Presidents Yeltsin and Kravchuk had both taken unilateral steps to seize control of the fleet and then had both quickly retreated in the hope of compromise. Amid growing conflicts in the Dniester region of Moldova, in Nagorny Karabakh, and in Southern Ossetia that were claiming hundreds of lives every month, Yeltsin and Kravchuk both recognized that relations between the post-Soviet states were in danger of becoming dangerously chaotic. They also recognized that if Russia and Ukraine—which accounted for nearly 70 percent of the population of the former USSR and an even higher proportion of its industrial potential— could reach stability in their relations, then they could also maintain it.

It was this realization that found these two men, who were by no means great admirers of each other, in the comfortable seacoast resort of Dagomys. There they agreed to a formula of trade based on mutual payments for goods and services on the basis of price relationships that reflected world prices; settled on a system of long-term credits at favorable rates for the repayment of debts; agreed on a process through which Ukraine would introduce its own currency, the hryvnya, without destabilizing the ruble; and agreed to the transfer by Russia to Ukraine of a portion of the former USSR's property abroad, including buildings used by consulates and embassies. They also agreed to move quickly to a settlement of the division of the Black Sea Fleet.

By August 1992, the two sides' positions on the fleet were narrowing, with Russia proposing to transfer 40 percent of the fleet to Ukraine. On August 4, Presidents Yeltsin and Kravchuk met again and announced their agreement to share joint command over the Black Sea Fleet for a period of three years, thus wresting control of the fleet from the command of Commonwealth forces. Sailors and support personnel for the fleet were to be drawn in equal measure from new recruits and draftees from both countries, and all personnel were to swear allegiance to one or the other republic. By defusing the potentially explosive Black Sea dispute, the two leaders had injected a note of optimism into Ukrainian-Russian relations after a period of protracted tension and disagreement.

Moreover, President Yeltsin affirmed that the relationship between Russia and Ukraine was central to Russian foreign policy and emphasized that Russia did not have claims over any Ukrainian territory, including the Crimea. And despite a resolution of the Russian parliament that had declared illegal the 1954 transfer of Crimea from Russia to Ukraine, Yeltsin and Kravchuk restated the validity of earlier treaties confirming the immutability of the two states' borders.

Contentious Issues

Yet despite the apparent rapprochement between Ukraine and Russia and signs of increasing cooperation within the Commonwealth of Independent States, there were a number of unresolved issues that could potentially disrupt the anti-imperial course taken by Yeltsin and his government team, among the most significant of which was the need to protect the rights of ethnic minorities in the new states. Obviously, the establishment of stable, prosperous democracies based on rule of law offered the best hope of reaching that goal.

Yet for Russia, the problem of the rights of the more than 25 million ethnic Russians living outside its borders could not be swept under the rug. In Kazakhstan Russians made up 38 percent of the population, in Latvia 33 percent, in Estonia 30, in Kyrgyzstan 26, in Ukraine 21, and in Moldova and Turkmenistan 13 percent. Some Russian leaders—most notably Vice President Rutskoy—appeared to support the extension of the full protection of the Russian state to these citizens, including unilateral military interventions. Colonel-General Pavel Grachev, who was named Russian Minister of Defense in July 1992, took up a similar line of argument, indicating that Russia would use any means, including force, to protect Russians whose lives might be in jeopardy. Such a stance was extremely dangerous, for it promised to entangle republics in a never-ending cycle of conflicts and potential wars. Such an intrusive attitude on the part of any state would place some citizens under permanent suspicion as being a fifth column, thus preventing their full integration into the states in which they lived.

Given the record of colonial dominance by Russians and the role played by Russified Slavs in the old Soviet empire, the knotty problem of citizenship can best be resolved through multilateral international organizations in which Russia does not play the dominant role. Yet it will prove impossible to escape from this issue, due to pent up frustrations in many of the former outposts of the old Soviet empire. And there are plenty of unscrupulous political movements ready to play on the resentments of indigenous peoples in a bid to build popularity through scapegoating and settling putative scores. President Yeltsin sought to strike a balance between the necessary defense of the rights of Russians and direct interference in the affairs of newly sovereign states when he noted: "We must, of course, rise out in defense of the rights of Russians. But we must do so through political means only."

Another fundamental issue of contention that leaders of the new states faced in the first year after the collapse of the USSR was what to do with the Soviet armed forces. Even before the establishment of the Commonwealth of Independent States, several republics had begun to take steps to create their own armies and national guards. By the spring of 1992, largely as a result of the determined policy of the Ukrainian government to create its own military, the formerly monolithic Soviet military had begun to fragment rapidly. Ukraine was joined first by Moldova, Azerbaijan, and Belarus, and then in May 1992 by Russia in establishing their own armed forces.

This trend toward national armies led to the rapid dissolution of what many had expected would be the powerful combined forces of the Commonwealth of Independent States. Amid the disintegration of a unified army, Commonwealth states agreed that their forces would fulfill certain agreed common strategic tasks, including stewardship over nuclear weapons and nuclear forces on the territories of Russia, Ukraine, Belarus, and Kazakhstan. As the Commonwealth armed forces receded to a narrow supervisory role, Russia began to take control of large segments of the former Soviet armed forces outside its borders, including the former Red Army forces in Eastern Europe and the Baltic States, and also established control over substantial forces deployed in Moldova, Azerbaijan, Armenia, Georgia, and Central Asia. The carving up of the Soviet armed forces was a strong indicator that the disintegration of the USSR was irreversible.

One highly contentious issue had been the disposition of the Black Sea Fleet. Vyacheslav Chornovil, the Democrat and longtime political prisoner who was one of the leaders of Ukraine's Democratic nationalist movement, the Rukh, noted that because of long-standing treaties limiting the mobility of the ships of the Black Sea Fleet, including restricted access to the Mediterranean, the dispute was not central to Ukrainian or Russian security interests, but was the consequence of efforts by two leaders—Presidents Yeltsin and Kravchuk—to play to domestic public opinion. Both Kravchuk and Yeltsin argued Chornovil, needed a dispute over a matter of national honor to divert public attention from economic failures at home.

Whether one accepts Chornovil's analysis or not, it was clear that in large measure control over the Black Sea Fleet was as much a matter of finances as it was of defense and national security. Ukraine's and Russia's leaders were aware that some of the three hundred ships of the fleet could be sold to other countries for hard currency, and so while Ukraine and the Commonwealth, and later Ukraine and Russia, disputed jurisdiction over the Black Sea Fleet, several of the fleet's ships were sold to India for millions of desperately needed dollars.

Even the nuclear weapons that were to be dismantled represented a financial asset in the eyes of republican leaders. One reason Ukraine's leaders were reluctant to transfer all tactical nuclear weapons quickly and expeditiously to Russia was that they considered them a source of enriched nuclear fuel for Ukraine's numerous nuclear power plants. Aware that this fuel could also be sold in a less-enriched form to other countries for as much as $1 billion, Ukrainian leaders insisted in early 1992 that nuclear weapons be dismantled on Ukrainian territory. In the end, Western pressure convinced them to go ahead with the transfer of all tactical nuclear weapons from their territory—a process that was completed by May 1992. But with a substantial reserve of strategic nuclear weapons that are not to be completely removed until 1999, the issue promises to remain a point of contention in the years ahead.

Russian officials asserted that Ukraine had inherited much of the best equipment and the most highly trained forces in the former Soviet arsenal. As Russia's Defense Minister Grachev pointed out in a June 2, 1992, interview with *Izvestiya*, "Following Ukraine's instantaneous privatization of three . . . military districts, we found ourselves in an extremely difficult situation. Let me cite just one detail: We [Russia] have been left with less than one-half of the military transport aviation which was used to move men and equipment." Ukraine, he noted, holds two such divisions, Belarus one, and for "all intents and purposes, Russia actually has only two military transport regiments."

Colonel-General Boris Pyankov was more succinct when he affirmed in a March 7, 1992, interview in the military daily *Krasnaya Zvezda* that Ukraine wound up with much of the most advanced weaponry and technology of the Soviet arsenal. And Andrey Kortunov, director of U.S. foreign policy studies at Russia's USA and Canada Institute, noted in a paper written in the spring of 1992 for the Heritage Foundation: "If the 1990 Paris Treaty on conventional force reductions in Europe is implemented, Ukraine theoretically could keep far more military equipment on its territory than Russia could keep west of the Urals. In fact, the military balance between Russia and Ukraine now surprisingly favors Ukraine. The three Ukrainian military districts contain the best-trained and best-equipped elite troops of the former Soviet army, while almost all divisions now stationed in Russia are second echelon and manned to only fifty percent to sixty percent of their combat capacity." Kortunov went on to echo a recent theme of Russian government officials: "So in a hypothetical conflict, as one of the senior officers of the Moscow General Staff put it, the military forces now in Ukraine could 'easily defeat the whole of Russia just in a matter of days.'"

Whether or not Kortunov's and the Russian military's claims were accurate, they did point to the fact that the fragmentation of the former Red Army had created an entirely new geomilitary setting in Eastern Europe and Central Eurasia, and that the related question of dividing the assets of the former Soviet Union will prove a difficult and contentious undertaking certain to fuel disputes among the leaders of the new states. In August 1992, the issue resurfaced when Ukraine said that it was prepared to sell part of its fleet of advanced long-range bombers at a price of $15 million each.

The broader question of property was equally contentious, particularly the fate of the USSR's vast array of embassies, consulates, residences, and other offices. Most of these properties were expected to be divided among the republics, but one year after the August coup they remained under the jurisdiction of Russia. Recognizing that some measure of equity was needed, President Yeltsin observed in a press interview published on June 15, 1992: "Russia did not proclaim itself the legal heir to the USSR. It would not be right for Russia alone to assume the right of inheritance, because the Union was a federation of states."

In the field of commerce, numerous complex questions also emerged, including how to divide the USSR's hard currency assets, its gold and diamond reserves, and its international debt obligations; how to share now in such jointly financed enterprises as the Baikonur space center in Kazakhstan, which could only survive if the new post-Soviet states pooled their resources; how to equitably distribute the assets of Aeroflot, once the USSR's and now Russia's airline; and how to divide and coordinate what had been a unified railroad system. The non-Russian states were also concerned about the Russian-dominated television and radio networks that had once served the former Soviet Union and were now divided in two: one part serving as the basis of Russian state television and targeted to the Russian Federation, and the second part becoming the Ostankino television company. While run by a Russian-dominated management, Ostankino was intended to serve as a television network broadcasting to all Commonwealth countries. Yet within weeks of its creation, it had been criticized for an alleged pro-Russian bias by a number of non-Russian government and political leaders, many of whom refused to finance Ostankino and demanded that its assets be divided among the independent states.

As the new states moved to take possession of the former USSR assets on their territory, the fact that some of these resources had been jointly financed by the revenues of all the republics made contentious the issue of who owned what. While such issues of ownership will without question be resolved in the future, how they are resolved matters. The more heated the disagreements between the new states become, the more profound and lasting will be the mistrust between them. The failure to settle these issues can poison relations in the years ahead.

Questions of who owns what are transitional. There are, however, several far-reaching factors that stand in the way of a lasting climate of trust between the post-Soviet states. Relations between the new states are also likely to be colored not only by attitudes shaped during the period of imperial and colonial rule, as fears of renewed Russian hegemony have led many of the new states to be extremely wary of lasting relationships with their powerful neighbor, but also by the fact that political and economic change is coming at a radically different pace in many of the republics, creating a disequilibrium in democratic development and economic reform that is likely to impede cooperation.

The states of the former USSR divide along two fault lines, one representing differences concerning the introduction of fundamental democratic and economic reforms, the second representing disparate attitudes about how political, military, and economic relations between the post-Soviet states ought to look.

Democracies and Dictatorships

Along the fault line of democracy and reform as 1992 drew to a close, there were three types of states. In the first type the Communist establishment had been utterly routed and supplanted largely by democratically elected leaders; in the second, old and new coexisted in an uneasy alliance; and in the third, the old guard now wore nationalist colors but still held firm control.

Lithuania, Latvia, Estonia, Azerbaijan, and Armenia fell into the first category. In each of these states powerful, nationwide mass-based popular fronts had been organized by 1988. In the Baltic States the old Communist elite was entirely supplanted and most government and private institutions were in the hands of a mixture of national Democrats and highly skilled members of the former nomenklatura, who were qualified professionals comfortable in the brave new post-Communist order. Anti-Communist Democrats initially gained complete control of government life in Lithuania, only to lose a November 1992 election to former Lithuanian Communists, who had broken with Moscow in 1990. Reform Communists turned Democrats together with long-standing anti-Communists and non-Communists ruled in Estonia and Latvia. The major complicating factors facing these states were the resolution of simmering interethnic problems and the presence in the Baltic region of more than one hundred thousand former Red Army troops under Russia's jurisdiction.

In Azerbaijan, a non-Communist former political prisoner served as the democratically elected president and headed a government that was secular in orientation and deeply interested in settling the bloody conflict over Nagorny Karabakh. Abulfaz Elchibey, elected in June 1992, was outspoken in support of democratic, secular tendencies among the Turkic peoples of Central Asia. Just days after he was elected president with 59.4 percent of the vote, he asserted that "democracy is not well developed in Central Asia today; the old command system is suppressing individual rights. But these regimes will not last long—one year at most." Elchibey showed that he was likely to pursue an active policy of supporting anti-Communist movements in Central Asia and went on to denounce Uzbek President Islam Karimov for "repressing all the progressive people in Uzbekistan." Elchibey asserted that "the Tashkent treaty on the CIS military alliance will not save the totalitarian regimes. The people's movement is gaining strength there. What we are seeing today is the awakening of all the Turkic peoples of the former Soviet Union."

In Armenia, the government and parliament were led by non-Communists and former opposition activists from the Armenian National Movement. Rival political parties were allowed to function openly and, despite some complaints, the press was free.

In the second category were Russia, Kyrgyzstan, Ukraine, Tajikistan, Georgia, Belarus, and Moldova, where Democrats and former apparatchiki coexisted in an uneasy coalition. Yeltsin's Russia occupies something of a middle ground between states in which non-Communists ruled and those where Democratic forces shared power with segments of the old ruling nomenklatura. While Boris Yeltsin has demonstrated his democratic leanings, some observers believe he will remain under intense pressure from the military-industrial complex, which along with the directors of large industrial establishments strengthened their role in ruling circles in the summer of 1992 with the introduction of their representatives into the upper echelon of the Russian government. In the Russia of mid-1992, the parliament had a nondemocratic majority that had been elected in March 1990, in the period before democratic political parties were allowed to function legally and openly. This meant that the parliament would be at loggerheads with Yeltsin's reform agenda. Matters came to a head during the December 1992 Congress of People's Deputies, when President Yeltsin sought to resolve the political deadlock by turning to a public referendum on the Parliament and Presidency.

Kyrgyzstan was led by a non-Communist academic, Askar Akaev. Confronted with the acute problem of finding a new cadre to fill top posts in the central government and in local administrations, Akaev relied on many longtime apparatchiki to run his small, impoverished republic. In Kyrgyzstan, the free press and mass media frequently criticized government leaders.

In the summer of 1992, Ukraine, which had elected a former Communist Party ideology secretary as president, had a government in which the old guard apparatchiki constituted the majority. While the press was relatively open, television continued to be tightly under the control of the old apparat, headed by a Communist Party functionary who participated in the August 1991 coup. As in Russia, the parliamentary majority of Communist holdovers were fearful of showing their true colors. By July 1992, Ukrainian

Democrats had concluded that fundamental reforms were being impeded, and the leading Democratic groups—the Rukh popular front and the New Ukraine centrist bloc—demanded the resignation of the government and called for the holding of new nationwide, parliamentary elections. Such pressures, as well as transport and miners strikes in September 1992, helped bring about the collapse in October 1992 of an anti-reform Prime Minister and his replacement by a coalition government that included many prominent democrats.

In Tajikistan and Georgia, Democrats, oppositionists, and the old nomenklatura shared power. Tajikistan's shaky coalition government, which was under military attack in December 1992, had emerged as a result of mass public protests in the capital city, Dushanbe, while Georgia's was put in place in the aftermath of a violent struggle between the elected but increasingly dictatorial President Zviad Gamsakhurdia and an alliance consisting of his former allies and opponents from the reform wing of the party establishment, who succeeded in deposing Gamsakhurdia.

Two other states in which government was shared between non-Communist nationalists and the Party apparat were Belarus and Moldova. In the summer of 1992, the Belarusian government remained a redoubt of the old nomenklatura. And while parliamentary chairman Stanislav Shushkevich was a non-Communist formerly linked to Belarus's Democratic circles, once in power he distanced himself from such Democratic groups as the Belarusian popular front. A referendum that was likely to lead to new parliamentary elections was believed by the country's Democrats to be the best hope for opening Belarus to fundamental political change.

In Moldova, a bitter and exceedingly violent conflict raged between Moldavian authorities and the renegade government of the self-proclaimed Dniester Moldavian Republic established by old guard apparatchiki speaking in behalf of ethnic Russians and Ukrainians. Moldova's government was mainly made up of former Communists, while the opposition Christian Democratic Popular Front was wedded to a policy of immediate reunification with Romania—something that is rejected by both the republic's Slavic minority and its many ethnic Romanians.

In the third category of states in which the Communist old guard wears nationalist colors but is still firmly in control were Kazakhstan, Uzbekistan, and Turkmenistan. Although President Nursultan Nazarbaev's reputation for enlightened leadership had been warmly greeted by Western leaders, Kazakhstan's opposition groups had little opportunity to address the public via the state-controlled media. And while protests were not violently suppressed, in the summer of 1992 Kazakh authorities halted the publication of eleven alternative publications in Alma Ata through strong-arm administrative measures. According to reports by the Russian Federation news agency ITAR-TASS the authorities explained that their action was taken "due to the poor sanitary conditions in the workplaces." President Nazarbaev had shown no inclination of broadening his government to include Democratic parties and movements and relied primarily on the old Communist establishment in his attempts to hold power in an ethnically diverse state where Kazakhs barely outnumber Russians.

In Uzbekistan, where democratic opposition was substantial, the Communist leadership's repression was intense. In mid-1992 Dr. Abdurakhim Pulatov, chairman of the Birlik Popular Movement, was hospitalized following an assassination attempt. While he was recovering from severe head wounds, Uzbek police entered his hospital and ordered the doctors to expel their patient. Forced into hiding, Pulatov surfaced in Moscow and flew from there to Baku, where he received protection from Azerbaijan's democratically elected anti-Communist president. The Tashkent headquarters of Birlik was destroyed and former presidential candidate Mukhammad Salikh went into hiding, announcing that his Erk Democratic Party had become an underground opposition in the face of severe political and physical repression and intimidation.

Under the iron fist of President Islam Karimov, Uzbekistan's press and television were as strictly controlled as before the coup. An election held in December 1991, in which the Birlik Popular Movement was banned from participating, yielded an 86 percent vote in support of former Communist boss Karimov, amid a Soviet-style voter turnout of 95 percent. Immediately after the questionable election, President Karimov introduced a highly centralized government system that retained members of the old Communist nomenklatura in key government posts, now as members of the renamed but unreformed People's Democratic Party. Karimov also proclaimed his faith in the so-called Chinese path of development and moved to concentrate power in his own hands by relegating his tightly controlled parliament to a clearly subordinate role. By the end of the summer of 1992, Uzbekistan's parliament had not met for well over half a year. And a court moved to ban the Birlik movement.

In Turkmenistan, the ruling ex-Communist President Saparmurat Niyazov retained his unquestioned power in what had emerged as a tightly controlled one-party state. There was no significant organized opposition movement in the resource-rich republic. Meanwhile, Niyazov had taken to making himself a cult figure. Sessions of Turkmenistan's new Mejlis parliament that in Soviet years had been held under the red banner of Soviet power and an image of Lenin were addressed by Niyazov under a gigantic portrait of himself. Government offices large and small contained color photos of the man now lionized in the controlled media as the "founder of independent Turkmenistan." Of all the former Soviet republics, Turkmenistan had shown the fewest signs of independent political life and had the strongest basis for a stable autocratic regime. Its state budget has a considerable surplus fattened by exports like natural gas and cotton, significant hard currency earners.

While the early months of independence had suggested that the newly independent state would reconstitute themselves within a new entity, the Commonwealth of Independent States, with time it became clear that Ukraine, Moldova, and Azerbaijan viewed the idea of a strong Commonwealth as incompatible with their aim of achieving complete state sovereignty. And while the contours of the post-Soviet order are not yet fully defined, it is clear that the Commonwealth is not likely to evolve into a cohesive confederal structure to which all the new states delegate a significant portion of their powers. Because views vary widely among the post-Soviet states concerning the Commonwealth's proper functions, the structure is more likely to be assymetrical. While several states are ready to cooperate more closely on a confederated, multilateral basis, others are willing to participate in only a very limited range of activities. Ukraine, for example, has declared its intention to end participation in any military alliance as soon as the last nuclear weapon leaves its territory. Azerbaijan has gone even further, declaring its unwillingness to remain a part of the Commonwealth except in the very limited role of an observer.

Commonwealth and Independence

One year after the coup, the politically diverse new states were defining their relations with each other. The states most intransigently hostile to any reintegration into either a loose commonwealth or a confederation were Lithuania, Latvia, Estonia, and Azerbaijan, while Ukraine and Moldova demonstrated a high degree of skepticism about anything but the loosest of multilateral structures. For economic reasons, resource-rich Turkmenistan was also skeptical of ceding too much authority. Georgia, which had refused to join the Commonwealth under its erratic and later deposed President Zviad Gamsakhurdia, appeared under Eduard Shevardnadze initially to be interested in membership as long as this meant no surrender of its sovereign rights. But as tensions with Russia over Ossetia grew, Georgia's enthusiasm for participating in the Commonwealth waned.

Occupying an as yet unclear position was Tajikistan, where a sharp political and armed struggle between traditionalist Muslims and Democrats on the one side and the old Communist team headed by President Rakhmon Nabiev on the other remained unresolved, thus leaving undefined Tajikistan's relationship to the Commonwealth.

The greatest enthusiasts for a Commonwealth were Russia, Belarus, and Kazakhstan. According to the Russian daily *Rabochaya Tribuna,* Kazakh President Nursultan Nazarbaev said that his country was eager to propose a closer union of states than the Commonwealth, and that Russia, Belarus, Uzbekistan, Kyrgyzstan, Tajikistan, and Armenia were also ready to join. Nazarbaev's support for a close-knit alliance of post-Soviet states derived from his own republic's specific ethnic context. A union that linked half-Slavic, half-Turkic Kazakhstan could inhibit the separatist urge in the country's predominantly Russian north and dampen the impact of Muslim and nationalist Kazakh currents in the predominantly Turkic south.

Yet some analysts believed that Nazarbaev's long-term political survival was untenable, that eventually Kazakhstan, an enormous state with a territory as large as all of Western Europe, would split into two, with the Slavic north joining Russia and an Islamic and Turkic south entering a confederation of Turkic states.

Driven by a fear that their impoverished economies would be better off if they were linked politically and economically to the more industrially developed European republics, Uzbekistan and Kyrgyzstan were also proponents of a strong Commonwealth. Both states also thought that participation in a cohesive Commonwealth would alleviate the fears of their well-educated Slavic citizens, who were creating great economic displacements by abandoning the Central Asian states and migrating to Russia. Armenia also sought a close alliance with Russia as a means of protecting itself from two much larger Muslim neighbors, Azerbaijan and Turkey.

For Russia, the establishment of a strong alliance with other republics was motivated by Yeltsin's desire to secure a means of protecting the rights of the millions of Russians who now were minorities in other states. By achieving a strong confederation, the Russian president would also be better equipped to defuse the criticism of those who blamed him for the collapse of the USSR.

Belarus went much farther than other Commonwealth states in concluding an extensive alliance with Russia. The alliance, confirmed by Belarusian Prime Minister Vyacheslav Kebich and Russian Acting Prime Minister Yegor Gaidar on July 20, 1992, provided for a unified credit and financial system and a unified ruble zone between the republics. The alliance was cemented by a treaty regulating the coordination of activities in the military sphere, as well as by an agreement on the strategic forces that remained temporarily on Belarusian territory. The two states also agreed to a coordinated budget, tax, and credit policy that would be implemented through an interrepublic economic coordination council. In part, the alliance was based on Belarus's high degree of integration with Russia's economy. As much as 70 percent of Belarus's enterprises were said to manufacture products for the Russian market. Gaidar felt that the agreement signed between the two states would also be supported by Kazakhstan and Kyrgyzstan, and noted that the agreement could be integrated into a broader Commonwealth structure. Having given up the hope of a uniformly strong structure, Russia appeared to be intent on developing a smaller confederation of more closely associated states within a larger and more amorphous Commonwealth.

Despite the inclinations of Kazakhstan's, Kyrgyzstan's, and Uzbekistan's leaders to participate in a strong Commonwealth, there was evidence of a countervailing orientation in the region. The populations of the Central Asian states were increasingly falling under the sway of pan-Turkism, which rather than Islamic fundamentalism was on the rise in the region.

One sign of the sentiment toward growing integration was a so-called working conference of presidents of the Central Asian states, held in Bishkek, the capital of Kyrgyzstan. The avowed aim of the April 1992 conference was an assessment of the viability of a single "Turkic-Asiatic economic and political space." While the meeting did not result in the creation of a formal economic and political structure, the Central Asian leaders made it clear that they were embarking on a path of greater regional cooperation. And although they confirmed their interest in strengthening the Commonwealth, their actions were a clear indication that they were moving in a direction that could eventually weaken the Commonwealth's prerogatives.

Uzbek President Islam Karimov intimated the growing theme of Turkic interests when he asserted on April 23, 1992, that "both in czarist times and during the years of Soviet power our region was perceived as a raw material appendage of the metropolis. Therefore, for all the vast resources of the Central Asian economy, it has not developed normally." The task of the gathering, said Karimov, was to "pool our efforts to create a modern industry here, so as to process raw materials on the spot with the aid of modern technologies." The Central Asian states had gathered, he noted, to demonstrate their "determination to act together for the sake of our great goal."

In part as a result of the intransigence of energy-rich Turkmenistan, the initial effort to create a single investment bank and a unified investment fund for Central Asia was not successful. Nevertheless, Turkmen President Saparmurat Niyazov asserted that "in practice the CIS no longer exists" and made it clear that in the context of an increasingly less viable Commonwealth, Central Asian leaders would seek other forms of political and economic integration.

Irrespective of the future of the Commonwealth of Independent States or of bilateral agreements with Russia, the Central Asian states were being drawn away from Moscow. "We no longer view Moscow as the center through which we relate to the world," said Jenish Kadrakounov, a member of Kyrgzstan's foreign ministry and his country's ambassador to the Conference on Security and Cooperation in Europe in the summer of 1992. "Even in terms of travel it is much more convenient for us to find a window to the West through Istanbul," he noted. "We can understand the language, we feel at home there, and it is much closer than Moscow. Turkey, therefore, is our natural window to the world."

In the post-Soviet world, while geography and self-interest rather than ideology will dominate, the nature of the relations of the post-Soviet states with Russia is likely to be shaped by the sort of Russia that emerges in the years ahead. But the very nature of the new Russian state remains unresolved, for while in the first year of Russia's statehood Boris Yeltsin consistently pushed his country in a democratic, anti-imperial direction, the Russian people are deeply divided on the question of their relations with their neighbors, and Russian political life reveals strong disagreements on the issue of imperial dominance.

Defining Foreign Policy

These divisions are reflected as well in the realm of broader foreign policy. Russia's effort to determine the nature of its relations abroad exposed a conflict between two currents: the Eurasianists, who sought to position Russia as a leader of the developing countries, and the anti-imperial Europeanists or Atlanticists, who sought to work within the consensus shaped by the democratic countries of NATO, the Group of Seven, and the Conference on Security and Cooperation in Europe.

The most comprehensive elucidation of the Eurasianists' case came from Russian State Counselor Sergey Stankevich, who, despite his status as an adviser to President Yeltsin, had emerged as a close associate of Russian Vice

President Aleksandr Rutskoy. In a lengthy article published in March 1992 in the influential daily *Nezavisimaya Gazeta*, Stankevich put forth a comprehensive rationale for a Russian foreign policy that would turn away from an orientation toward the Western democracies, away from the "Atlanticism" that he claimed "gravitates . . . to Europe, to become a part of the world economy in rapid and organized fashion, to become the eighth member of the [Group of] Seven, and to put particular emphasis on Germany and the United States as the two dominants of the Atlantic alliance." Instead of pursuing a pro-Western course, Stankevich argued, Russia should craft a foreign policy that reflects its nature as a "country imbibing West and East, North and South, unique and exclusively capable, perhaps, of the harmonious combination of many different principles, of a historic symphony."

Russia, said Stankevich, ought to seek a new balance between Western and Eastern orientations. As part of such a course, Stankevich noted, it "will most likely be necessary to pay special attention to a strengthening of our positions in the East." Such Eurasian orientation was born of necessity, Stankevich asserted. "The fact is . . . that we are now separated from Europe by a whole chain of independent states." Stankevich further argued that the rapid integration of Russia into economic relations with the United States, Japan, and Europe was "highly problematical." Instead, Russia should pursue the "far broader and qualitatively better opportunities connected with . . . countries of . . . the second echelon." Among these he included Mexico, Brazil, Chile, Greece, India, China, Turkey, and the Southeast Asian countries. By playing a leading role in this second tier of countries Russia could, argued Stankevich, "obtain propitious geopolitical positions in key regions and to rank in time among the world leaders." Interestingly, Stankevich's proposals resembled in some measure the aggressive Third World orientation of Soviet-era foreign policy.

Linking his assertive international stance to more proximate neighbors, Stankevich also proposed that Russia pursue a policy of "diplomatic assertiveness" with regard to the states of the former Soviet Union. As part of this approach, he recommended an emphasis on the "defense of the rights of the populace ethnically connected with Russia [who were] falling victim [to] paranoid ideas of historical or national vengeance" in the non-Russian republics.

If Russia moves along the path advocated by Stankevich, it is likely to become a destabilizing influence in a democratic Europe, and an aggressive global foreign policy would place Russia at odds with the West. Some from the Eurasianist camp have already opposed their government's participation in economic sanctions against Serbia, while others have suggested that Russia should renew its economic and political relations with Iraq. The Eurasianists unanimously opposed Russia's return to Japan of four Kuril islands it had occupied since World War II.

Although the Europeanists continued to control the reins of the Russian foreign ministry, there were signs in the winter of 1992 of growing vigor within the anti-Western camp, as witnessed by democratic leader Stankevich's defection to this camp. His attack on the Yeltsin foreign policy approach had emphasized that Russia's broader foreign policy would inevitably be directly related to the policies Russia pursued with its immediate neighbors. Other signs of a potential shift in Russian foreign policy included mounting demands in the Russian parliament for the resignation of Foreign Minister Kozyrev.

While Russia debated its own foreign policy, other post-Soviet states also sought to define their place in the world. Ukraine and the Baltic States were eager to seek an early integration into the community of European nations and had either severed (in the case of the Baltic States) or drastically reduced (Ukraine) their links to the Commonwealth. Ukraine and the Baltic States likewise appeared eager to draw Belarus away from Russia's sphere of influence by creating a Baltic–Black Sea alliance that could serve as a counterweight to Russian power. Ukraine hoped to benefit from its strong relations with Poland and Hungary by joining the Vysegrad process, through which Poland, Hungary, and the Czech and Slovak republics sought to coordinate their integration into Europe. Ukraine also sought to develop strong links with its Black Sea neighbors and had begun to diversify its sources of energy by entering into long-term agreements with Iran to import oil and natural gas.

Azerbaijan's newly elected President Abulfaz Elchibey defined his state's relations with fundamentalist Islamic states in an interview with the Turkish daily *Hurriyet*. The Azerbaijan Popular Front (Khalq Jibhasi), Elchibey noted, was a secular institution, yet it had already opened forty-five religious shrines. With regard to Azerbaijan's militant neighbor to the south, he asserted: "True religion does not exist in Iran. A wave of fanaticism exists in that country; religion is being exploited in Iran. This is a very dangerous state of affairs." Within days of his election as president, Elchibey made explicit the new orientation of Azerbaijan's foreign policy. In a July 5, 1992, interview on the Ostankino television network, Elchibey asserted: "Our links with Turkey, the United States, Israel, Ukraine, and Russia will become closer and closer, and . . . misunderstanding will gradually recede to the past." The Central Asian republics had rapidly expanded their cultural and commercial relations with Turkey, a relationship that was likely to grow significantly in both Central Asia and the Black Sea region.

A Policy in Disarray

Although by mid-1992 the Bush administration had begun reorienting itself to the new realities of the post-Soviet order, in the decisive early days of shaping the post-Soviet future the United States had been but a passive observer. If anything, the Bush administration had been viewed as an active proponent of Mikhail Gorbachev and the forces of the past. In July 1991, just weeks before the August coup, President Bush had traveled to Kiev, Ukraine, where before a Ukrainian legislature that included a number of former political prisoners elected on a program that advocated Ukrainian independent statehood, the U.S. president endorsed the integrity of the USSR and condemned what he called "suicidal nationalism."

From 1988 until 1991, throughout the period of the accelerating disintegration of the USSR, the United States failed to recognize that Western interests and the interests of democracy were tied to the dismantling of the Soviet superpower. For an administration that prided itself on its foreign policy acumen, the Bush record during the fall of the Soviets was not only dismal but dangerous. In the first hours of the August 1991 coup, when the fate of democracy and reform in the USSR hung in the balance, President Bush did not immediately come forward with a forthright condemnation, suggesting instead that the new junta had stated its commitment to economic reform. Only when it became obvious that the coup was not coalescing and there was growing resistance by Boris Yeltsin and many local leaders did President Bush join the worldwide chorus of condemnation.

In the weeks after the putsch, the Bush administration seemed ill prepared for the fundamental anti-imperial revolution that was emerging. Having misread the gradual erosion of the central USSR government's authority in 1990 and 1991, the United States sided with Mikhail Gorbachev and a fast-collapsing central Soviet government, believing that after a brief period of disorientation the Soviet leader would cobble together a renewed state, albeit with greater powers for the republics.

As part of its pro-Gorbachev tilt, the United States was the forty-fourth nation to recognize the independence of the Baltic States. The United States failed as well to provide leadership in the early days of the emerging Commonwealth of Independent States. As Boris Yeltsin was consolidating his power, President Bush's National Security Adviser Brent Scowcroft insisted on sniping at the Russian president, whom he characterized as unreliable and potentially antidemocratic.

In December 1991 Scowcroft, one of the architects of the Bush administration's pro-Gorbachev, pro-Union tilt, published a mea culpa in which he admitted that U.S. policy toward Ukraine may have been misunderstood. In the weeks that followed, the United States grudgingly became the fifteenth nation to recognize Ukrainian statehood, following the lead of Canada, Poland, Switzerland, Sweden, and Argentina.

This lack of vision persisted long after the Soviet collapse and the emergence of independent states. For months, U.S. policy seemed less interested in developing a necessary package of material aid and technical assistance to sustain democratic transformation than in resolving the question of control over the nuclear arsenal of the former USSR. While nuclear weapons were a legitimate concern, the United States' one-dimensional approach may well have encouraged several of the post-Soviet republics with nuclear capabilities to believe that having an arsenal was the quickest route to being treated seriously by other nations. This one-dimensional approach also meant that the Bush administration was slow to build up a diplomatic presence in the newly independent republics. It was not until a full year after the failed coup that American ambassadors began to establish a presence in most of the new states, and in most cases they were still working with skeleton staffs housed in temporary offices.

As independent Russia moved away from its traditional pattern of imperial rule, some high-level U.S. policymakers continued to be guided by deep suspicions of Boris Yeltsin. U.S. State Department and National Security Council officials failed to recognize Yeltsin's role as an authentic revolutionary who was doing the United States and the West a great service in overseeing the dismantling of a totalitarian superpower. As late as the summer of 1992, high-ranking U.S. officials could not resist sowing doubts about the Russian president's commitment to democratic change and economic reform.

U.S. policy with regard to Central Asia was also slow to develop. The United States appeared unwilling to understand the nature of the regimes that had emerged in the region. After a brief period of inaction, the United States agreed to extend economic aid to all the Central Asian states, irrespective of whether they were led, as in Kyrgyzstan, by a democratically oriented leadership or, as in Uzbekistan, by a holdover Communist regime that brutally suppressed political opponents.

The inertia of the Bush administration's attitude toward the republics translated into delays in developing and funding aid programs in cooperation with Western allies. The Bush administration and State Department blundered when they consented to the wholesale transfer of the USSR's diplomatic properties to Russia, thus angering a number of republics. And when U.S. aid programs did finally take form, they did not explicitly condition aid to respect for basic democratic rights, and tilted unnecessarily to Russia in the proportion of allocated aid. Afterward, the United States' ambivalence over the decolonization of the old Soviet empire persisted in the corridors of the State Department, where the new states were viewed by some policymakers as inherently unstable. But such misunderstandings of the important advantages conferred by imperial collapse were par for the course.

A New Western Policy

To undo this legacy of missteps will require a broad reorientation in U.S. and Western foreign policy, with a heightened degree of sensitivity to the changes that have occurred since the Soviet collapse and with Russia, which represents 50 percent of the population of the former Soviet Union, as a major focal point. Because it is still the predominant military and economic power among the new states, the future of Russia will in large measure affect the future development of the region. The pro-Western, prodemocratic tendencies now at work in Russian politics deserve as much moral, material, and technical assistance as the West can reasonably afford, not only to aid the efforts of these forces to root Russia firmly in Europe, but also to help the Yeltsin government's efforts to reform the state-dominated economy.

The West must also be cognizant of the fact that the Russian experiment with democracy might very well fail. Because Boris Yeltsin is undertaking a triple revolution—of democratic change, market reform, and a move away from the centuries-old Russian-led empire—he has arrayed against him not only a long-standing Russian cultural and political tradition but many powerful political forces as well.

The April and December 1992 sessions of the Congress of People's Deputies in Russia, which nearly derailed the Yeltsin government's reform efforts, revealed the lasting power of conservative and proimperial ideas, with much of the current Russian political establishment undergoing a resurgence of anti-Western sentiments and witnessing the revival of Great Russian nationalism. The economic transformation of Russia, with its vast territorial expanses, cumbersome military-industrial complex, and volatile mix of ethnic Slavs and Asians is likely to prove far more vexing than economic reforms in other relatively homogeneous and compact post-Soviet states. And because tens of millions of Russians live beyond its borders, many of them in the Muslim Central Asian states, Russia is likely to be preoccupied for a long time with its relations in the East. Potential pressures on ethnic Russians are also likely to elicit a flow of emigrants from these regions, further taxing the Russian economy's transition to a free market. Many Russians also have yet to make the psychological break with the empire. Public opinion samplings have shown Russians to be split in their support of Yeltsin and nostalgia for the iron hand—twin trends that could spell trouble for the Yeltsin team should their economic reforms unravel.

The growing opposition to President Yeltsin raises questions about making Russia the only focal point of the West's post-Soviet policies, and requires a second look at bolstering democratic forces and reinforcing the sovereignty and independence of the other republics who have broken free of the old Soviet empire, particularly Ukraine. With its population of 52 million and an armed forces that in mid-1992 numbered over five hundred thousand, making Ukraine the second largest military power in Europe after Russia, this republic's independence is the strongest guarantee of a diminished Great Russian role in the world. Without Ukraine's resources and population, Russia remains an important power, but ceases to be a superpower capable of bullying Central and Eastern Europe or intimidating the nations in Asia and beyond. The permanent loss of Ukraine and other former dependencies could reinforce Russia's turn inward, to looking after the needs of its citizens and defining its legitimate place as a regional power. Such a diminution of Russia's world role would also make it easier for its government to reduce military expenditures in line with its new, more modest mission.

Thus, while everything must be done to shore up support for President Yeltsin and such pro-Yeltsin forces as the Democratic Russia movement and the Republican Party, Ukraine deserves a closer look as a potential anchor of stability in Eastern Europe. Unlike Russia, Ukraine has few of the ethnic, political, and cultural difficulties that will plague Russia's leaders in the years ahead, and none of the wrenching ethnopolitical conflicts represented by the separatist movements in Chechnya and Tatarstan. While Ukraine's population represents different nations (73 percent Ukrainian and 21 percent Russian), their common Slavic roots make for a stable ethnic mix. And with the exception of the Crimea, all of Ukraine's oblasts have a Ukrainian majority.

One year after the coup, mass-based political activism in Ukraine was dominated by pro-Western movements and leaders. Because the most talented Communist officials were frequently taken for service in Moscow, Ukraine's Communist elite was less skilled and has proved less durable than Russia's. By November 1992, moreover, Ukraine was led by a broad-based coalition government, in which democratic reformers occupied a majority of the highest posts.

While civil society was reemerging in Russia, it tended to divide into irreconcilable camps reflecting the traditional fault lines in Russian intellectual life—between prodemocratic Westernizers and proimperialist Slavophiles. In Ukraine on the other hand, most of the structures shared a democratic orientation. Many of the new and numerous language, ecological, cultural, trade union, and political movements were born in the antitotalitarian struggle for statehood. Radical and irredentist Ukrainian nationalist groups were extremely weak even in nationalist western Ukraine. And public opinion samplings in Ukraine revealed less support for the return of an iron hand and more support for democratic rule than did samplings in Russia. Thus, while Russian democracy could well triumph, democracy and a pro-Western orientation are significantly more likely to endure in Ukraine.

In time, a stable and democratic Ukraine, linked to democratic Europe, could act as a stimulus for democratic ideas to the east. A Western-oriented Ukraine with its large Russian population could engage Russia in the West. And if Russia were to fall prey to the revival of obscurantism and imperialism, Ukraine would be for the new democracies of Eastern and Central Europe a welcome buffer state, depriving Russia of its capacity to return to superpower status. Bolstering Ukrainian democracy and assisting Ukrainian statehood materially and technically are therefore in the interests of the democratic community. The moment is ripe for a shift from the U.S. and Western tilt toward Russia and for a policy aimed at building a secure, strong, stable, pro-Western Ukraine.

Shaping the Post-Soviet Order

It is dangerous to attempt to engage in long-term projections about the post-Soviet future, especially in a book such as this, written in a period in which relations between fifteen new states are in the early stages of elaboration and definition. Yet the lines of development outlined herein are among the most probable. Obviously, if the West simply reacts to events—and inevitable crises—as they unfold, it will play only a minor role in shaping developments that will affect the future of not only Europe and Asia, but the world.

The interstate and interethnic conflicts that rage in several of the post-Soviet republics may on the surface seem removed from the immediate interests of the democratic West, but unless order and peace are brought to Eastern Europe and Central Eurasia, all of the West could one day confront dangerous and widening instability. After all, the conflict in the Dniester region of Moldova is a conflagration in the heart of Europe: Moldova's capital Chişinaŭ and Paris are equidistant to Vienna. And were events in Moldova to spin out of control, they would destabilize an entire region, including such nearby states as Romania, Poland, Hungary, and Slovakia. The dispute between Russia and Ukraine over jurisdiction over the Black Sea Fleet and the conflict over the Crimea can also have a destabilizing effect in a region that includes NATO members Turkey and Greece. Similarly, if the conflict between Turkic Azerbaijan and Armenia were to deteriorate into open war, there is a danger that it would draw in Turkey.

How these open or simmering conflicts play themselves out and what role the West plays in diminishing tensions surrounding these post-Soviet trouble spots can have a decisive influence on peace and security throughout Europe. A decisive multilateral Western engagement will not inevitably drag the United States and Europe into endless border and ethnic disputes; it could, however, play an important role in shaping the post-Soviet order. After all, many of the leaders and citizens of the new post-Soviet states look to the West as a source of material aid, technical knowledge, and political inspiration.

But in order for the West and the United States to make a difference will mean reorienting policies away from the Cold War dichotomies and imposing a dual litmus test for support: respect for human rights and democracy, and opposition to the restoration of a union state. Any policy short of this will contribute to constant interstate tensions and could revive dangerous trends within a still-powerful military elite steeped in the imperial ideology of a great unitary multinational state.

In the process of post–World War II decolonization, the United States adopted a position of principle by arguing that it was in the interests of democracy for such European states as Great Britain, Belgium, France, and Portugal to renounce their colonial dependencies in Africa and Asia. This U.S. role also helped push the tide in favor of such democratic leaders as France's Charles de Gaulle, who made a clean break with colonial rule. Similarly, today it is unquestionably in the interests of the United States and other industrial democracies to help see President Yeltsin's anti-Soviet and anti-imperial revolution through to the end.

Yet to advance the process of decolonization will require the industrial democracies to demonstrate moral leadership and, when necessary, to exert pressure against those neoimperialist groups and forces on the post-Soviet political scene that are pressing to restore a central union state structure above that of the newly independent states. Now that the democratic world has recognized the independence of Russia, Ukraine, Kazakhstan, Belarus, and the other former Soviet republics, nongovernmental and state organizations would be wise to reinforce the new status quo. The new nation states require a period of stability in interstate relations if they are to consolidate a democratic and economic transformation. Thus, financial aid ought to be targeted to those states that are both moving toward a democratic market system and engaging in peaceful relations with their neighbors.

While the breakup of the USSR has created a complex and at times dangerous political landscape, the fall of the Soviets has also led to a new environment that is less dangerous and more open to democratic possibilities than the monolithic—if predictable—behemoth of totalitarian rule. The permanent separation of Russia from its former dependencies diminishes the global reach of the former USSR and rids the world of an aggressive and expansionist totalitarian superpower. And if President Yeltsin is given strong support in his effort to build a Russian nation state, we are likely to see the taming of a Russia that menaced Eastern Europe and Asia for several centuries.

The democratic opportunities created as a result of the political, cultural, and economic crises of communism would not have emerged full-blown without the tremendous political force of the many nationalist movements of the once-hidden nations of the Soviet empire, who proved to be an important breeding ground for dynamic new civil societies, giving birth to new political parties, private entrepreneurs, trade unions, environmental groups, and civic associations.

In this period, when it is fashionable to speak of the dangers posed by post-Soviet nationalist movements, and to focus on mounting interethnic and interstate tensions, it is possible to overlook the positive, prodemocratic role played by the reemergence of national pride and patriotism in what had been the USSR. Resurgent patriotism was a basic impulse for the rebirth of civil society, effecting first the unraveling of the Soviet empire and then the fall of the Soviets. If properly directed by leaders of moderate, prodemocratic orientation, patriotism can contribute to the shaping of a liberal, tolerant order in much of what had been a repressive, militaristic regime.

Aid and Assistance

Aid programs ought not to preclude opportunities for promoting and strengthening civil society, but should extend democracy-building initiatives to those post-Soviet states where democratic groups are challenging the old Communist nomenklatura. Material and technical aid should therefore be extended only to those states that respect democratic norms, not to such states as Kazakhstan, Uzbekistan, and Turkmenistan when they suppress democratic opposition. Yet the only step taken in this regard was the U.S. Congress's move to block assistance to Azerbaijan in response to the conflict over Nagorny Karabakh, an action made more in response to pressure from a well-organized Armenian diaspora than as part of a comprehensive and well-thought-out strategy to assist non-Communist democratic governments or movements.

Nongovernmental organizations can offer important support to Democratic groups in the new post-Soviet states. With the collapse of Communist controls in many republics, and with the resultant flowering of independent life, now is precisely the best time for enhanced people-to-people, institution-to-institution contact, cooperation, and material assistance. Exchanges should be matched with training initiatives and open material assistance. Authentically independent groups crave the know-how and are eager to learn about the way institutions function in a democracy. These groups also need broad exposure to the technical experience of their Western counterparts. Western trade unions must reach out to such new trade union movements as the Lithuanian Workers' Union and the Independent Miners' Unions of Russia, Ukraine, Kazakhstan, and Belarus. Western ecological groups can share their expertise with environmentalists from Ukraine's Green World Society, the ecological movement in Armenia, and the antinuclear Nevada movement in Kazakhstan.

Assistance could also be provided to the emerging independent press and to the increasingly independent radio and television networks that have appeared in the Baltic republics, Russia, Ukraine, Armenia, and Azerbaijan. As democratic coalitions take power in various republics, regions, and cities, they discover that the mass media—once the property of the Communist Party—are now the property of the state. The need to create independent media and to privatize state-owned media is now one of the highest priorities of the democratic movements. Thus, assistance can be patterned on the successful support provided by Western nongovernmental institutions to the democratic movements in Poland, the Czech and Slovak republics, and Hungary, which have taken over the reins of government in their renewed democracies.

The nurturing of rudimentary civil society in the new post-Soviet states will ensure that the movement toward a democratic, pluralistic market society will proceed peaceably through negotiations between democratic groups and representative institutions that, if strong and well-established, can help create a climate of stability and civility and protect the rights of ethnic minorities in what are likely to be turbulent and tumultuous transitions to a postcolonial order. Political parties should reach out to the vast array of Christian-Democratic, Social-Democratic, liberal, and conservative political groups that are well developed in the Baltic States and gathering strength in Russia, Ukraine, Belarus, and other republics, thus strengthening the climate of stability. And just as there is a vital role to be played by the West in assisting nascent civil society as it emerges in the fifteen newly independent states, so, too, can democratic groups in Hungary, Poland, Slovakia, and the Czech lands aid the transition to democracy. Activists from Solidarity have already reached out to their Ukrainian, Lithuanian, Belarusian, and other non-Russian neighbors. Their path of resilient, peaceful struggle for democratic change is a model for the peaceful transition to democracy and a free-market economy. The millions of spiritually wounded Russians and non-Russians can also learn much from the experience of Poland's Solidarity, Hungary's Alliance of Free Democrats and Democratic Forum, and the free trade unions and strike committees that have emerged throughout Eastern Europe.

One priority must be to help those organizations building cooperation and dialogue between the various national groups. As Zbigniew Brzezinski has noted in an influential essay titled "Post-Communist Nationalism," published in the winter 1990 issue of *Foreign Affairs*, Communist rule eliminated some of the forces in society most associated with an international outlook, in particular the business class. The restoration of forces that have an ecumenical and transnational democratic outlook is essential to the creation of cooperation between what are certain to be increasingly independent national republics.

A trend of intergroup cooperation emerged well before the collapse of the USSR. At the 1989 founding congress of the Ukrainian nationalist movement, the Rukh, there were delegates representing the republic's Jewish and Russian communities, and fraternal delegates from Baltic, Armenian, Belarusian, and Azerbaijani popular fronts. Cooperation between Democratic national rights advocates was particularly advanced in the Soviet parliament, where the locus of activity was the Interregional Group of Deputies, the liberal faction founded by Dr. Andrey Sakharov. Other trends in group cooperation included a Baltic Council that coordinated activities between Latvia, Lithuania, and Estonia in their march toward independence; a Union of Democratic Forces that acted as a coordinating group for popular fronts and other democratic organizations of Russians and non-Russians; and efforts at dialogue and negotiation between Armenian and Azerbaijani nationalist leaders.

While such trends toward cooperation and integration must be sustained and encouraged, democratic movements in many of the former Soviet states confront an opposite trend: growing fragmentation. In the period before the collapse of the August 1991 coup and the disintegration of the USSR, opposition movements maintained unity by pursuing a common purpose, the defeat of the Communist Party and the winning of state independence. For those movements whose main focus was state independence, the collapse of the Soviet empire meant that the unifying principle of broad-based political coalitions vanished. In some republics, the disappearance of a visible and unified Communist ruling elite has also led to fragmentation of the democratic forces. In most of the new states there has been a proliferation of dozens, in some states hundreds, of parties and microparties. Broad-based national coalitions have in many cases fragmented in the face of group interests or rivalries between powerful political personalities. With parliamentary elections facing many of the newly independent states, such fragmentation may weaken and divide minority governments.

Some democratic leaders argue that the proliferation of parties reflects the undifferentiated social base that was part of a state system in which there were no real owners. Totalitarianism prevented real social interest groups from emerging. The absence of real trade unions, large industrial and commercial interests, a truly independent financial sector, small business, and private landholdings meant that the social basis of modern political parties is absent. In the absence of these well-defined constituencies, party politics is likely to remain chaotic and pose a challenge to highly fragmented and internally divided parliamentary coalitions. The example of Poland's fragmented post-Communist political scene is frequently cited as an example of what awaits emerging democracies in the former USSR. There is also a danger that the old nomenklatura, which has attempted to maintain its control through privatization will reemerge as a major political force. Western involvement with political parties and coalitions can in such a context play a salutary role in helping democratic forces find a new basis for cooperation and coalescence.

In the development of joint ventures and other investments, Western economic investments can promote democratic change if emphasis is placed on cooperating with new entrepreneurs who did not play a leading role in the old Communist order. Western investments can also help diversify the economies of the non-Russian republics that are often remarkably one-dimensional as a result of the high degree of specialization and centralization at work in the Soviet imperial economic system. But if Western commercial interests are to play a constructive role in post-Soviet society, they must be aware of the strong sensitivities of the non-Russian peoples about their native languages, religions, and traditions. Under no circumstances should Western investment in the non-Russian states be used to perpetuate Russification.

While Western attention will inevitably focus largely on resource-rich, industrially advanced countries like Russia and Ukraine, a more active role ought to be pursued in Central Asia. Turkey's government and private sector already appear to be well ahead of Western Europe and the United States. And Turkey is not confining itself to its Turkic brethren, but is strengthening economic and political links with the countries of the Black Sea region. The NATO countries ought to cooperate closely with Turkey's moderate government to promote secular ideas in the Turkic republics of Central Asia, where poverty and frustration could otherwise prove a breeding ground for Iranian-inspired Islamic fundamentalism. Turkish television, which is understood by most of the Turkic-speaking peoples, already has launched an ambitious effort that broadcasts to the Central Asian states for six-to-seven hours per day, while Turkish radio plans to increase programs aimed at Central Asian audiences.

Another important role for the West can be in assisting efforts to prevent interethnic and interstate bloodshed. One instrument for such efforts can be an expanded role for the Conference on Security and Cooperation in Europe (CSCE). The CSCE now encompasses the countries of Europe, the new post-Soviet states, Canada, and the United States. Because of this mix of established industrial democracies and new ones like Poland, Hungary, and the Czech and Slovak republics, the CSCE is likely to be trusted as an honest broker by most post-Soviet states. Already there are encouraging signs that the CSCE can play an important role in resolving post-Soviet interstate and interethnic conflicts, as demonstrated by a request made in July 1992 by Russian President Boris Yeltsin and Ukrainian President Leonid Kravchuk to have the CSCE play the leading role in "improving mechanisms for preventing and settling conflicts in the CSCE region." The two presidents noted a pressing need to develop "anticrisis mechanisms" to deal with the "conflicts flaring up in various parts of Europe today [that] present a real threat to our common security and stability," and called for a unified "Euro-Atlantic" approach.

This statement by the heads of the two largest post-Soviet states represented a significant step in acknowledging the realities of a post-Soviet setting in which most of the newly independent states are deeply distrustful of Russia. And because of the danger of Russian domination over Commonwealth structures, the Commonwealth's peacekeeping forces are likely to be regarded with some suspicion by member states that are most fearful of a renewed Russian hegemony. The Kravchuk-Yeltsin proposal was an important signal that the key post-Soviet republics welcome the involvement of international bodies in conflict resolution within their region.

To take advantage of the democratic possibility offered by the Soviet collapse will require understanding and far greater Western involvement. The emergence of fifteen independent states, each with its own culture, history, traditions, and national interests, will require the training of a new generation of academic experts and policy specialists. The Soviet Union had long been the focal point of U.S. and Western foreign policy. Now, in the aftermath of the USSR's disintegration, this complex region must not be relegated to the back burner.

Developments in Russia, Ukraine, the Caucasus, and Central Asia over the next few years will be decisive to the kind of Europe and world the next century is likely to see. The democratic world's limited but important opportunity to shape some of these developments ought not to be missed.

AFTERWORD

In the fall and winter of 1992 the forces of the old order mounted a concerted effort to replace democrats and insurgents who had ridden a wave of nationalism and anti-Communism to state power in many of the post-Soviet states. Some 15 months after the failed August putsch, many of these forces had reestablished links severed by the banning of the Communist Party and the confiscation of its property. Without access to the property and the organizational structures of the old Communist Party machine, many former apparatchiki had found refuge in local government posts and in a number of other institutions that had escaped the banning of party activity. The most important of these were the old, formerly party- and state-controlled trade union fronts and in segments of the military industrial complex. In some cases, party functionaries had already made considerable fortunes in 1990–91, under the patronage of the Soviet government led by Prime Minister Valentin Pavlov.

Not all of these members of the Communist apparatus had been staunch supporters of the old Soviet order. Many of them had opposed the August 1991 putsch. But while many from the old apparatus had recognized the need for replacing the inefficient, indeed moribund totalitarian model and had fought against the effort of reactionaries to turn back the clock, they had never been enthusiastic about the sundering of the Soviet Union. Throughout 1992, as industrial production plummeted, they began to lose faith in the economic agenda of privatization, price reform, and national sovereignty developed by democrats in Russia and other new nations.

But whether they were reactionaries or moderates, the forces of the old order began mounting a concerted effort to recapture control in a number of the newly independent states, where they had been blocked from the levers of power.

This counter-revolution came in a variety of ways. In Tajikistan, the forces associated with the old regime of Rakhmon Nabiev shot their way into the capital city of Dushanbe, and attempted to restore the old Communist leaders back to power against a coalition of secular reformers and Islamic fundamentalists.

In Lithuania, a two-round election held in October and concluded on November 15, 1992, yielded a clear majority for a party dominated and led by former Communists. While these were reform Communists, who had strongly supported Lithuania's bid for state independence and had even seceded from the old Soviet Communist Party, those elected under the banner of the Democratic Labor Party represented the economic interests of the old Communist order. Included in the new parliament under the DLP list were the leaders of Lithuania's privatized collective and state farms, leading industrialists, and former longtime Communist Party officials. These forces came to power in Lithuania on a wave of social and economic discontent. They capitalized on the economic discontent by promising a broad social safety net to protect workers in a period of transition. They capitalized, as well, on the ruling Sajudis movement's failure to reach an accommodation with Russia, blaming that failure for the severe energy shortages that afflicted the new nation. They built support in the ethnically Lithuanian villages, where anxiety over the dismantling of the old state run farm system was running high. And they derived nearly universal support from the Russian minority, which represented one in five voters.

Whatever the reasons for their triumph, the fact that if in Lithuania— one of the first republics of the old USSR to have made a dash toward freedom—it was possible for the old order to stage a comeback, certainly it would be possible for other new states.

Perhaps, the strongest counter-offensive mounted by the forces of the old order was in Russia. There, such backward looking forces included not so much former Communist Party apparatchiki as the managers and directors of the old statist industrial order and their counterparts from the state-controlled trade unions. This coalition, brought together in the Civic Union, held dominion over vast financial and media resources. Taking advantage of substantial social discontent, and capitalizing on its substantial representation in the Russian parliament, the nomenklatura bloc jeopardized Boris Yeltsin's efforts to nominate a stable pro-reform government team, and provoked what could well be a decisive April 1993 referendum on the nature of Russia's governmental system—a Yeltsin-led, Presidential republic committed to radical political and economic reform or a parliamentary republic in which neo-Stalinists, ultranationalists, and industrial managers would hold sway.

The fateful struggle of Boris Yeltsin and his democratic allies in Russia was yet to be resolved. But its resolution would certainly have an effect on the outcome of the struggle for democracy in a number of other post-Soviet states. Among these was Belarus, where a reactionary government led by

Vyacheslav Kebich continued to ignore democratic due process, and to thwart the reformist and democratic impulses of parliamentary chairman Stanislav Shushkevich.

In Ukraine, where in October 1992 a coalition government that included representatives of the democratic Rukh and New Ukraine movements had come to power, reformist leaders warned of an ominous alliance between the old pro-Stalinist Communist Party and a corrupt criminal commercial class.

Thus, the fate of democrats and the transition to democracy and a market system hung in the balance as 1992 drew to a close. Events in Russia would surely prove central to the success of the democratic revolutions spawned by the struggle of peoples for statehood and independence. But increasingly, the democratic opening represented by Ukraine's and other republics' move toward reform and due process made it clear that, as with the collapse of the USSR in December 1991, not everything necessarily would be decided in Moscow.

Differentiation, and radically different paths of political, economic, and social development represented the likely future of the fifteen post-Soviet states. New nations had risen. And each of these nations was beginning to determine its destiny and develop its identity.

Index